ABOUT NABAT BOOKS

NABAT BOOKS is a series dedicated to reprinting forgotten memoirs by various misfits, outsiders, and rebels. The underlying concept is based on a few simple propositions:

That to be a success under the current definition is highly toxic – wealth, fame and power are a poison cocktail; that this era of triumphal capitalism enshrines the most dismal human tendencies like greed and self-interest as the wellsprings of civilization; that the "winners" version of reality and history is deeply lame and soul-rotting stuff. Given this it follows that the truly interesting and meaningful lives and real adventures are only to be had on the margins of what Kenneth Rexroth called "the social lie". It's with the dropouts, misfits, dissidents, renegades and revolutionaries, against the grain, between the cracks and amongst the enemies of the state that the good stuff can be found. Fortunately there is a mighty subterranean river of testimony from the disaffected, a large cache of hidden history, of public secrets overlooked by the drab conventional wisdom that Nabat books aims to tap into. A little something to set against the crushed hopes, mountains of corpses, and commodification of everything. Actually, we think, it's the best thing western civilization has going for itself.

Memoirs of Vidocq: Master of Crime

François Eugène Vidocq

Books in the Nabat Series

Memoirs of Vidocq: Master of Crime

François Eugène Vidocq

AK Press / Nabat

Edinburgh, London, and Oakland

2003

This edition copyright © 2003 Nabat/AKPress
1st Nabat Edition
Vidocq, Rogue Cop © 2003 Robin Walz

Memoirs of Vidocq: Master of Crime
This edition is a reprint of the 1935 edition translated
and edited by Edwin Gile Rich

ISBN 1 902593 71 5

AK Press	AK Press
674 A 23rd Street	PO Box 12766
Oakland CA	Edinburgh, Scotland
94612-1163 USA	EH8 9YE

A catalogue record for this title is available from the
Library of Congress

Series editor: Bruno Ruhland
If you know of any memoirs by misfits, outsiders,
or subversive types that deserve to be back in print,
please write to Bruno at AK Press in Oakland.

Cover, cover art, book, and series design donated by
fran sendbuehler, mouton-noir – montréal

Prisoners can receive this book by sending $10.00 to
AK Press at the Oakland address noted above.

Table of Contents
Memoirs of Vidocq: Master of Crime

A NOTE TO THE READER

WE FEEL COMPELLED to admit up front that these memoirs are an uneasy fit with the Nabat misfit/outsider concept. From his outlaw beginnings Vidocq ended up as a major insider. The man has been claimed as an inspiration by lawmen from Allan Pinkerton to J. Edgar Hoover and on down. But Vidocq was such an amazing and creative scoundrel, and is such a neglected and seminal figure that we couldn't pass up getting this book back into print. Even more though we think his life is instructive because it rips the mask off the whole sorry fraud of crime and crime-fighting.

First, these memoirs show just how symbiotic the connection and how fuzzy the line is between cops and criminals. In this book a master criminal becomes a master crime fighter, and he hires a bunch of former criminals to staff what would become the first detective bureau. The central technique for fighting crime is paying criminal informers for info. Today law enforcers do their best to gloss over just how utterly central this remains. For anyone who wonders about the boundless ineptitude of our present vast array of police agencies in their inability to catch criminals, the fact is that detecting and intelligence gathering are not really what law enforcement does. Either they use informers or wait for criminals to behave in such dumb ways that they fall into their laps. Crime is really little more than the resentment filled defiance of the most no-hope miserable class of people from the very bottom of the heap in society. Their acts are a doomed-to-land-them-in-jail fuck you back to the norms and rules of society that they (rightly) feel has screwed them. So all that detecting and investigating that takes place on TV shows is hilariously remote from reality. The relationship between cops and criminals is more one of dance partners than adversaries.

There is a way that Vidocq was an even more crucial figure in establishing the vast gulf that lies between the reality of crime and the common perception of it. In the early 1800's, just at the time the middle class was taking center stage, that property was becoming the measure of all things, and that the government was coming to be seen as the legitimate expression of the will of the people, Vidocq offered a new conception of crime and police work that these circumstances required. The police became the protectors of property and the guarantors of order, using science and reason to catch criminals. Vidocq was a pioneer of this in having the idea to gather evidence at crime scenes and keep records of criminals. Vidocq, and even more his pals Balzac,

Victor Hugo, and Alexander Dumas, who all borrowed heavily from his true stories for their fiction, elevated this conception into the mythic realm: it became the forces of order and rationality battling the chaotic and scary forces of darkness. This conception, living on and endlessly transmogrified (but retaining its satisfyingly simple dualism) in countless crime novels, movies and TV shows, has proven to have fantastic resonance. And it has thoroughly infected our notions of crime in the real world.

It has done wonders for making governments seem not just legitimate, but indispensable. Governments like a nice solid amount of crime; like war it is the health of the state. So, little is done to attack the dire poverty that makes people do the desperate and dumb things that we call crime. Instead more cops are hired, more prisons built and more laws passed. The "war on drugs" is where this dynamic becomes mad, turning law enforcement into a racket to divert money to cops and the prison industry.

So our notions of crime need a drastic revision. There are seriously big time criminals: the folks who own and run the government, make the laws, and evade them when necessary. The major league crimes are all committed by dull guys in nice suits, mostly done by trading favors and writing checks, often "campaign contributions." It's all polite and rather abstract, much less immediate than a gun in your face. The wealthy and powerful few commit their crimes in a highly mediated way. It would not make for exciting television or fiction, one of the reasons they can get away with it.

But the net effect is that we have fantastic welfare programs for giant corporations, like the literally hundreds of billions of dollars poured into the US "Defense Department." And the sons and daughters of the lower class are sent off to kill and die for the interests of oil companies and arms merchants. So the vast wealth that capitalism produces is used to rig the system, to make the rich richer, the poor poorer, and to militarize and trash the planet, though it could as easily be used to raise the world's living standards, eliminate the poverty and desperation that cause prisons to fill up, and generally create a world that makes sense. Instead the wealthy few would rather run it as a criminal enterprise. Lately it has become nakedly apparent that the show is being run by a sleazy pack of scammers and scoundrels. Just like Vidocq (but without even a thimbleful of his style and ingenuity) they present themselves as the force of order and reason battling the dark mad forces of badness. For all its pleasing simplicity this spectacle is seeming more than a little threadbare. Interesting times ahead.

"VIDOCQ, ROGUE COP"
ROBIN WALZ

ASIDE FROM A FORTUNE-TELLING MIDWIFE, few would have guessed that Eugène-François Vidocq was born for greatness. From unpromising origins as a two-bit thief, army deserter, grifter, and convict, he rose in fame to become the celebrated chief of the Paris Sûreté police and an internationally renowned private detective. Among his admirers, Vidocq was a brilliant detective, a man of action, master of disguise, expert investigator, and champion of security and order, the kind of detective who "always gets his man." Among his detractors, Vidocq was and always remained a scoundrel and criminal, a con man who emerged from the underworld milieu to become the kind of corrupt detective for whom dissimulation, extortion, and graft are tools of the trade. Yet it is a false distinction, for in Vidocq the criminal and detective are one. He was the world's first anti-hero rogue cop.

Vidocq is the first modern detective in just about every way imaginable. In the early nineteenth century he was first Chief of the Sûreté, a "security force" of police detectives that later developed into the police judiciaire, the official investigative branch of the French judiciary. After resigning from service, he founded the first full-fledged private detective agency in France, so renowned that Allan Pinkerton, founder of the Pinkerton Detectives, called himself the "Vidocq of the West." He is the prototype for fictional detectives as well. To varying degrees, Edgar Allen Poe's Auguste Dupin, Émile Gaboriau's Monsieur Lecoq, and Sir Arthur Conan Doyle's Sherlock Holmes are all heritors of Vidocq. His flamboyant personality inspired nineteenth-century French literary authors, including Honoré de Balzac, Eugène Sue, Alexandre Dumas, Pierre-Alexis Ponson du Terrail, and Victor Hugo. Vidocq was a crime writer in his own right, author of the four-volume Mémoires de Vidocq (abridged and translated for this volume), Les Voleurs, physiologie de leurs moeurs et de leur langage ("Thieves, A Physiology of their Customs and Language"), Les Vrais Mystères de Paris ("The True Mysteries of Paris"), and Les Chauffeurs du Nord ("The Rural Bandits of the North"). Vidocq's legend as a master detective surpasses the man, a legend first penned by his own hand.

"I came into the world on the twenty-third of July, 1775, in a house near where Robespierre had been born sixteen years earlier. It was during the night; rain poured down in torrents; thunder rumbled; as a result a relative, who combined the functions of midwife and sibyl, drew the conclusion that my career would be a stormy one." In self-aggrandizing and melodramatic fashion, Vidocq portrays himself in his memoirs as a heroic man of destiny born of a turbulent age. There is little doubt that he lived through a revolutionary era, although his heroic persona was fashioned over time. In the twilight of the Old Regime of Louis XVI and Queen Marie Antoinette, Eugène-François Vidocq was born into a baker's family in Arras, in the Artois region of northern France. Locally called le Vautrin (the "Wild Boar," the name later adopted by Balzac for his fictional character), Vidocq was a Herculean, improvident, and intemperate youth with a taste for dueling. Before age sixteen, he sought a military career in infantry and light cavalry, fighting alternately on behalf of the French revolutionary army and Austrian counterrevolutionary forces. After an interlude as a deserter, and briefly caught in an ill-fated marriage, at age nineteen Vidocq joined up with the armée roulante, a "roving army" of grifter officers who scammed displaced aristocrats and a chaotic military bureaucracy. Over the next twenty-five years Vidocq was in and out of prison, accused of various petty crimes and a major one of forgery (in the memoir he claims the forgery charge was trumped up, but nonetheless it stuck to him until he received a royal pardon from Restoration monarch Louis XVIII in 1818). Branded and reviled everywhere as a convict, Vidocq was an outlaw. But his fortunes changed once he agreed to become a police spy.

"The names of Baron Pasquier and M. Henry will never be erased from my memory. These two generous men were my liberators. How much I owe them!" During the Napoleonic era, in his mid-thirties and growing weary of criminal life, Vidocq discovered a pair of unlikely benefactors in Paris police prefect Pasquier and commissioner Henry. Initially Vidocq became a spy for the police while still serving sentences within the Bicêtre and La Force prisons. Pasquier and Henry were so impressed by his service that in 1811 they arranged for Vidocq's surreptitious release from prison and they employed him as a detective to ferret out and capture at-large criminals hiding out in Paris. By the following year Vidocq was in charge of the brigade de sûreté, a mobile security force of police detectives who, like him, were former criminals. Over the next fifteen years, the brigade was expanded to twenty-eight agents. Vidocq's most famous exploits as a detective are dramatically recounted in the second and third volumes of his Mémoires (the second half of this edited translation).

In 1827 Vidocq resigned from his position as the Chief de la Sûreté, ostensibly because he disagreed with how the Paris police prefecture was being run. The feeling, it appears, was mutual. While the principle of "it takes a thief to catch a thief" may possess a certain logic, over time the prefecture grew increasingly anxious about a security force whose methods included graft, extortion, and kidnapping. The fact that Vidocq retired after fifteen years of official service with assets approaching half a million francs, substantially in excess of his annual salary of 5,000 francs, added circumstantial weight to suspicions that the Sûreté chief promoted extralegal activities. In the wake of the revolutions that brought "bourgeois monarch" Louis-Philippe to the throne, in 1832 Vidocq was reinstalled as head of the Sûreté. But the appointment was short lived, as in the fall of that year one of his agents was convicted of belonging to the same ring of thieves that supposedly he was investigating, an embarrassing development that forced Vidocq's resignation for a second time. Vidocq had somewhat better success as a paper manufacturer during these years, claiming to have invented a counterfeit-proof type of durable paper and a special formula for indelible ink. But it was success following the publication of his Mémoires that cast Vidocq into the public limelight.

In 1833 Vidocq capitalized on his growing celebrity as a detective through sales of his memoirs by opening his own "private police" business, Le Bureau de renseignements universels dans l'intérêt du commerce. While such "offices of information for businesses" had existed in Paris since the end of the eighteenth century, Vidocq added the dimension of a "private detective" agency. For a small annual subscription, clients were entitled to purchase prepared profiles of known crooks and fraudulent businessmen (files gathered, by in large, during Vidocq's tenure as Sûreté chief). In addition, subscribers could hire Vidocq's private agents to conduct investigations and surveillance into "confidential affairs," not only for commercial interests, but in the realm of private life as well, primarily issues of marriage (ancestry, health, morality, finances) and divorce (adultery). By 1840, Vidocq's private detective agency had become so prosperous that he moved its offices to the Galerie Vivienne, one of the most fashionable glass-covered arcades in Paris. The Prefecture of Police looked askance at the creation of a private "counter-police" and raised doubts about its methods. In 1843, Vidocq was tried and convicted for the illegal detention of persons and fraud (although he subsequently received a royal pardon).

In the aftermath of the Revolutions of 1848, Vidocq performed one last service for the police as a spy. The following year he was placed in the Conciergerie prison, charged with the task of infiltrating an imprisoned circle of revolutionaries (which included socialist leader Auguste Blanqui). Until his death in 1857, he largely rested on his laurels as a famous detective and renowned author of multiple works on criminality. From lowly provincial and criminal origins, Vidocq had gained high society acceptance among Parisian political and literary elites. The man had surpassed himself to become a legendary hero, an inflation that originated in his memoirs.

It is likely that Vidocq was assisted in writing these memoirs. In the original preface to the first volume, Vidocq explains that, due to a broken arm, he had employed the services of a professional writer to assist him. The resulting account, he regrets, lacks literary style and is somewhat given to exaggeration.

Nonetheless and over his reservations, Vidocq assures the reader that the facts contained in the memoir are more or less true (he leaves it for the reader to decide, with promises of a forthcoming second volume). Whatever angle Vidocq was playing on his reading audience, the truth of the Mémoires lies beyond the veracity of the account itself. Meaning is derived less from the accuracy of the chronicle than in the staging of a virtuoso performance in which Vidocq plays at least three heroic roles.

First, Vidocq is the hero of the revolutionary bourgeoisie, champion of a new political order founded upon a propertied and professional middle class. Although the aristocratic privileges and corporate structures of the Old Regime were formally abolished in 1791, France underwent nearly a century of revolutionary insurrections, monarchical restorations, and Napoleonic emperors before establishing a more or less stable parliamentary government during the Third Republic (1871-1940). According to historian Paul Metzner, Vidocq played a virtuoso role in the early and fitful development of that bourgeois social and political order, one that embodied the revolutionary spirit of the age. Just as it was imperative for the bourgeoisie to distance itself as a class from its own ignoble origins, Vidocq moved directly from criminal incarceration into the security force that protects the middle class from underworld riff-raff.

As for the values of the French Revolution itself, Vidocq's commitments were uneven. Fiercely individualistic and energetically opportunistic, and having spent nearly a third of his life as an imprisoned or hounded convict, Liberty was dear to him. Fraternity was a more mixed bag. Choosing one's associates became a political gamble, and Vidocq forsook traditional loyalties of village, kith, and especially the subculture of thieves, for the social expediencies of life as a police spy and detective, performing civic duties for personal profit. As for Equality, there is little in the Mémoires that cries out for the rights of man and the citizen. Vidocq's sense of justice (and injustice) was far more egoistic than principled. Fundamentally distrustful of rule by law, and the official institutions that administer it, Vidocq's conception of social order was essentially one of relentless class struggle, the pitting of an anxious bourgeoisie against an anarchic mob of criminals, the indigent, and the laboring poor. Success in such a war of all against all required, above all, individual fortitude, cunning, and enterprise. For Balzac, who knew Vidocq personally and penned his personality traits into the character of Vautrin, the chameleon – whether criminal or police spy – does not change his rogue skin, only his color. Vidocq's class loyalty was opportunistic. The bourgeoisie, who hired his detective services and purchased his books, buttered his bread far more richly than the criminal or laboring classes.

Vidocq plays a second leading role as a Romantic hero. Vidocq's Paris in the early nineteenth century was a far cry from the "City of Light" of the

Impressionists with its colorful crowds, spacious boulevards, open-air parks, gas lighting, and the Folies Bergères. Rather, his was a claustrophobic Paris, a labyrinth of dark streets, twisted alleyways, dead-end courtyards, and dilapidated buildings, an urban miasma breeding squalor and human misery, poverty, vice, and cholera. The Mémoires share a literary terrain with Romantic social novels that infuse a spirit of moral uplift into such environmental degradation. Impoverished workers forced into lives of crime by stealing bread in order to feed their families, prostitutes with hearts of gold who succor honest gentlemen and virtuous maidens, and orphaned street urchins with sharp wits and ready quips, this is the stuff of Eugène Sue's Les Mystères de Paris and Victor Hugo's Les Misérables. It is the milieu of the "dangerous classes" from which Vidocq emerged and plied his trade as detective.

In its broad structure, the Mémoires chart Vidocq's circuitous journey from the loss of innocence to redemption through wisdom gained by experience. As melodrama, it is the tale of a basically decent person from a working-class background who is cast by circumstance into a life of crime and degradation but, through a philanthropic intervention, is made respectable in the image of bourgeois values. Hugo, who knew Vidocq personally, based both the opposing protagonists in Les Misérables, Jean Valjean and Inspector Javert, on Vidocq. It is noteworthy, though, that he divided Vidocq into two characters, the convict turned benefactor in Valjean and the dedicated functionary as relentless detective in Javert, for it suggests limits to thinking about Vidocq as a Romantic hero. Once Vidocq had passed his own Valjean phase, in effect he became Javert (although lacking the scruples of Hugo's police detective). The inability of Vidocq to embody both aspects of humanist and law enforcer, heart and rational mind, may be attributed to the political fact that, unlike Sue and Hugo, he does not appear to have been a liberal Republican committed to social improvement through legal and civic reform. On the contrary, Vidocq's redemption was due to the arbitrary institutions of discretionary police authority, royal pardons, and marketplace opportunism, and his own role as benefactor, employing ex-convicts on his police squad and in his paper factory, was paternalistic.

Yet it is his third role, the detective as anti-hero, that renders Vidocq the most provocative and sensational of heroes. For at bottom, criminal and detective are at one in the same person. As French philosopher and sociologist Roger Caillois noted more than half a century ago, the most effective crime and detective stories create a powerful phantasmagoria of anarchy versus order, the revolutionary impulses of crime equal to the force of conservatism and order to try and constrain them. This is evident throughout Vidocq's memoirs and in the various roles his character plays in them. In a historical sense, the Mémoires are a continuation of a long premodern tradition of popular crime and adventure stories. Since the advent of the printing press, itinerant peddlers throughout France sold bibliothèque bleue chapbooks (pamphlet-length stories cheaply printed on pulp-quality paper, folded into uncut pages, and wrapped in plain blue-grey grocery paper) that featured the exploits of rogues, highwaymen, thieves, Gypsies, and robust murderers. In addition, there were chapbooks of argot dictionaries, guides to criminal slang and character types, a tradition also continued by Vidocq in the fourth volume of the Mémoires and in Les Voleurs (the latter being a primary source for contemporary French slang dictionaries as well).

What Vidocq added to the equation was the suspect notion of the detective as a modern hero. The corrupt detective and the shady private investigator were entirely new types, supplementing inherited associations of the police with spies, informers, and blackmailers. Since Vidocq was all of these things, he is an ur-figure whose aspects fracture into a kaleidoscope of early detective types. In the Anglo-American tradition, Poe's Dupin requires the detective to think like a criminal, but stops short of being one himself. Conan Doyle's Holmes demonstrates the superiority of the hyper-rational amateur sleuth over the official investigative procedures of the police, yet there is no doubt that his counterpart, Professor Moriarity, remains a criminal nemesis. Within France, Gaboriau's fictional Sûreté detective, Lecoq, adopts new investigative techniques, but refrains from employing crooks and conducting illegal seizures in the name of upholding the law. Throughout the nineteenth century the actual Sûreté sought to distance itself from the "Vidocq syndrome" that associated its detectives with criminals. Nonetheless, a string of Paris police prefects, Sûreté chiefs, and forensic experts produced their own "true life" memoirs, highlighting their own personal exploits. From Gisquet, Canler, Claude, and Goron in the nineteenth century, to Lepine, Morain, Locard, and Belin in the twentieth, eminent police officials in France publicized their intimate knowledge of the criminal world for personal fame and profit.

For in France, more strongly than in England or America, there is a celebrated popular heritage that fuses the criminal and detective into the same anti-hero. It was the "elegant criminal," poet-assassin Lacenaire, who proclaimed in the 1830's that only after having read Vidocq's Mémoires did he understand that his vocation as a thief irrevocably and permanently set him in opposition to society. Novels featuring the criminal-avenger Rocambole, serialized in daily newspapers and reissued in numerous book editions, made Ponson du Terrail the most popular author during the Second Empire of Napoleon III. The early decades of the twentieth century witnessed the apogee of the detective-criminal anti-hero in France, in Maurice Leblanc's aristocratic "gentleman-burglar" Arsène Lupin, Gaston Leroux's convict-avenger Chéri-Bibi, and the notorious archvillain Fantômas by Pierre Souvestre and Marcel Allain. This anti-hero tradition remains alive in France today through the continued popularity of noir crime fiction, "hardboiled" American detective fiction and homegrown French polars, not only in novels, but in bandes désin-nées (folio graphic novels) and films as well.

It all began with Vidocq, a complex hero from a revolutionary era. Whether as a convict or police detective, he remained a shrewd con man throughout. He promised a fragile middle-class society security and order while simultaneously playing upon its social anxieties over, and popular fasci-nation with, criminality. Against modern aspirations to realize an organized, predictable, and well-regulated society, Vidocq has bequeathed us a crime and detective counter-discourse of transgression, uncertainty, pleasure, heroism, and individual liberation. His Mémoires possess more than antiquarian value, they perch at a crossroads where history passes into legend.

REFERENCES

Caillois, Roger. *Le Roman policier.* Buenos Aires: Éditions des letters françaises, 1941.

Chartier, Roger. *Figures de la gueseurie.* Series "Bibliothèque bleue." Paris: Montalba, 1982.

Chevalier, Louis. *Laboring Classes and Dangerous Classes in Paris during the First Half of the Nineteenth Century.* Trans. Frank Jellinek. New York: Howard Fertig, 1973.

Kalifa, Dominique. *Naissance de la police privée: Détectives et agences de recherches en France, 1832-1942.* Series "Civilisations et Mentalités." Paris: Plon, 2000.

Metzner, Paul. *Crescendo of the Virtuoso: Spectacle, Skill, and Self-Promotion in Paris during the Age of Revolution.* Berkeley: University of California Press, 1998.

Vidocq, Eugène-François. *Mémoires de Vidocq, chef de la police de Sûreté jusqu'en 1827* and *Les Voleurs, physiologie de leurs moeurs et de leur langage.* Preface, chronology, documents, and bibliography by Francis Lacassin. Series "Bouquins." Paris: Robert Laffont, 1998.

_____. *Memoirs of Vidocq, The Principal Agent of the French Police.* Philadelphia: T. B. Peterson and Bros., 1859.

_____. *Vidocq, The Personal Memoirs of The First Great Detective.* Trans. Edwin Gile Rich. Cambridge, Mass.: The Riverside Press, 1935.

Robin Walz is author of *Pulp Surrealism: Insolent Popular Culture in Early Twentieth-Century Paris* and co-editor of The Fantômas Website http://www.fantomas-lives.com.

I

I BEGIN TO SHOW PROMISE

I WAS BORN at Arras, but as my constant disguise, the mobility of my features, and a singular aptness in make-up have caused some doubt about my age, it will not be superfluous to state that I came into the world on the twenty-third of July, 1775, in a house near where Robespierre had been born sixteen years earlier. It was during the night; rain poured down in torrents; thunder rumbled; as a result a relative, who combined the functions of midwife and sibyl, drew the conclusion that my career would be a stormy one. In those days there were still good people who believed in omens, while in these more enlightened times men rely on the infallibility of fortune-tellers.

However that may be, we may assume that the atmospherics did not rage expressly on my account. While marvels are often most alluring, I am far from thinking that they paid attention to my birth. I had a most robust constitution, material had not been spared in the making, and one might have taken me for a child of two as soon as I was born. I soon gave signs of that athletic figure, that giant frame which since have thrown fright into the hearts of the boldest and most powerful ruffians. My father's house was on the Place d'Armes, the customary meeting-place for all the blackguards of the quarter, and here I early exercised my muscles in thrashing regularly my comrades, and their parents never failed to complain to mine. All they heard at home were stories of injured ears, black eyes, and torn clothes. By the time I was eight I was the terror of all the dogs, cats, and children of the neighbourhood. At thirteen I managed a foil so well that I was not out of place in a fight. When my father saw that I haunted the soldiers of the garrison, he became alarmed, and bade me to prepare for my first communion; two dévots assumed the task of preparing me for this solemn act. God only knows what benefit I got from their lessons! About the same time I started to learn the trade of baker, my father's profession, as I was supposed to succeed him, although I had an elder brother.

My principal task was to carry bread around the city. I took advantage of these errands to pay frequent visits to the armouries. My parents

were not ignorant of it, but so highly did the cooks praise my willing-
ness and promptness that they shut their eyes on many an escapade.
This tolerance lasted until they discovered a shortage in the till, which
was never left locked. My brother, who was exploiting it just as I was,
was caught in the act, and was sent off to a baker at Lille. The next day,
as they had not confided the reason to me, I started as usual to explore
the blessed till, when I found that it was actually shut up. The same day
my father indicated to me that I should make greater speed on my
routes and that I should come back at a fixed time. So it was evident
that hereafter I should have neither money nor freedom.

I deplored this double misfortune and hurried to confide it to one
of my companions named Poyant, an older boy. As the till had a hole
in it through which to pass the money, he first advised me to insert a
feather covered with glue, but this ingenious device only brought out
light pieces of money, so I had a false key made by the constable's son.
So I again borrowed from the till, and we consumed together the product of our larceny in a sort of tavern where we had our meeting-place.
Here we met, lured by the patron, a good number of well-known rascals, and some unfortunate young fellows who used the same expedients that I did to fill their purses. Soon I found myself in the most
abandoned society in the country – Boudou, Delcroix, Hidou,
Franchison, and Basserie, who initiated me into all their villainies. Such
was the honourable society in which I spent my leisure time, until one
day my father surprised me as he had surprised my brother, took the
key away, thrashed me, and took such precautions that there was no use
in thinking of getting any more dividends on the receipts.

My only resource was to levy tithe on the oven. From time to time
I eased out bread, but as I was obliged to sell it for almost nothing to
get rid of it, it hardly brought me enough to indulge in tarts and drink.
Necessity made me active; I had an eye on everything; all was good –
wine, sugar, coffee, and liquors. My mother had never seen her provisions run out so quickly. Perhaps she would not have discovered so
soon where they were going except that two chickens which I had
determined to confiscate for my profit raised their voices to accuse me.
Stuffed in my trousers where my baker's apron hid them, they crowed
and showed their combs; my mother was warned of the theft, and

appeared at the proper place to prevent it. I received a slap, and was sent supperless to bed.

I did not sleep; an evil spirit must have kept me awake. All I know is that I got up fully determined to steal the silver. One thing alone disturbed me; on each piece the name of Vidocq was engraved in large letters. Poyant, to whom I had explained everything, overcame all my difficulties, and the same day at dinner time I made a clean sweep of ten dinner sets and as many coffee spoons. Twenty minutes later all was pawned, and the day after I had only a farthing left out of the one hundred and fifty francs which the stuff had brought.

I had not appeared at home for three days, when one evening I was arrested by two policemen and led to Les Baudets, a house of detention where they shut up lunatics, prisoners awaiting trial, and criminals from the country. They kept me in the jail for ten days, without telling me the reason for my arrest; finally, the jailer told me that I had been locked up at my father's request. This news calmed my uneasiness a trifle, for I realized that a paternal punishment was being inflicted, and I did not believe that they would hold me according to law. The next day my mother came; I obtained her forgiveness, and four days later I was free. I returned to work with the firm intention of leading an irreproachable life in the future. What a vain resolution!

Promptly I went back to my old habits except for prodigality, for I had excellent reasons for not being ostentatious. Up to this time my father had been rather easy-going, but now he showed a vigilance which would have done honour to the commander of the guard. If he had to leave his place at the till, my mother relieved him at once; it was impossible to get near it, although I was always on the watch. Such constancy made me desperate.

Finally, one of my companions at the tavern took pity on me; again it was Poyant, an arrant rascal. I told him my troubles.

'Well,' he said, 'you are dumb to stay tied down, and, besides, it doesn't look well for a boy of your age to be without a sou. I know what I'd do if I were in your place.'

'Well, what would you do?'

'Your family is wealthy; a thousand crowns more or less wouldn't hurt them; the old misers, it would serve them right if you helped yourself.'

'I understand; I must take in one haul what I can't get piecemeal.'

'You're on. Afterwards get out without being seen or recognized.'

'Yes, but what about the police?'

'Shut up! Aren't you their son? Besides, your mother loves you too well for that.'

This consideration of my mother's affection, combined with the recollection of her indulgence after my last escapade, made a powerful effect on my mind. Blindly, I adopted a project which to my audacity looked easy; it only remained to put it into execution. The occasion was not long in coming.

One evening as my mother was alone in the house, my rascal of a Poyant, playing the kind friend, came to warn her that I was on a debauch, that I was fighting everyone, smashing and breaking everything in the house, and that if I was left alone, there would be at least a hundred francs to pay for the damage done.

At the time my mother was seated, knitting. Her stocking fell from her hands; she got up in a hurry and in great alarm ran to the scene of the supposed row, which we had carefully placed at the other end of the city. Her absence could not last long, so we hurried to take advantage of it. A key I had stolen let us into the shop. The till was closed; and this time I was almost glad to meet the obstacle. Now I recalled my mother's affection, not as a means of escaping punishment, but as a beginning of remorse. I wanted to get out, but Poyant held me back, and his devilish eloquence made me blush at what he called my weakness. When he offered me a pair of pliers with which be had taken the precaution to provide himself, I grasped them almost with enthusiasm. The money drawer was forced; it held nearly two thousand francs which we divided between us, and a half-hour later I was alone on the road to Lille. In my agitation as a result of this despatch, at first walked very fast, so when I reached Lens I was tired out and stopped there. An empty coach passed; I took a place, and in less than three hours I reached the capital of French Flanders from where I immediately went to Dunkirk, in a hurry to get away as far as possible to escape pursuit.

I intended to visit the New World. Fate foiled this project; the port of Dunkirk was empty; I reached Calais, so as to embark immediately, but they asked a fare which was more than I had. They gave me hope that at Ostend transportation would be cheaper on account of the competition, so I went there and discovered that the captains were more set on their prices than at Calais. As a result of these disappointments, I was in such an adventurous state of mind that I would have thrown myself into the arms of the first comer. I am not sure why I expected to meet some good fellow who would take me on board free, or at least make a considerable rebate on account of my good appearance and the interest which a young man always inspires. While I was walking along preoccupied with this idea, I was accosted by an individual whose kindly appearance made me believe that my dream was to be realized. The first words he addressed to me were questions; he understood that I was a stranger; he informed me he was a ship-broker, and when I told him the object of my stay in Ostend, he offered me his services.

'Your appearance pleases me; I like an open countenance; you have in your features an air of frankness and mirth which I like. Come, I want to prove it by getting you a passage for nothing.'

I expressed my gratitude.

'No thanks, my friend; when your business is finished, all right; that will be soon, I hope. While you are waiting, you must be tired of this.'

I answered that I didn't find it amusing.

'If you want to come to Blakenberg with me, we will take supper with some good people who are wild about Frenchmen.'

The broker was so polite to me and invited me so heartily to be his guest that it would have been uncivil to refuse, so I accepted. He took me to a house where we were received by some friendly women with all that unconstraint of such old hospitality which sets no limits on gaiety. At midnight, probably – I say probably because we no longer counted the hour – I had a big head and my legs no longer supported me. Things whirled around me and everything swayed, so without realizing that they had undressed me, it seemed to me that I was clad only in a shirt and was on the same eiderdown as one of the nymphs. Perhaps this was the case; all I know is that I slept.

When I woke up, I was very cold. Instead of the broad green curtains which had appeared to me in my dreams, my heavy eyes saw a forest of masts, and I heard the cry of the watch reserved only for seaports. I tried to rise, and my hand touched a pile of ropes on which I was lying. Was I dreaming now or had I dreamed the night before? I felt myself, shook myself, and when I was standing, it was proved that I was not dreaming, and what was worse, that I was not among those privileged beings to whom fortune comes in their sleep. I was half-clad, and aside from two crowns, which I found in one of my trousers' pockets, there was not a bit of money left. So it became only too clear that, as the broker had hoped, my business had been well done. I was in a rage, but what was the use? I could not even point out the place where I had been stripped; I made up my mind, and went back to the inn where some of my traps might still make up for the deficiencies in my toilet. There was no need to tell my host my hard luck.

'Oh, oh!' he said, as soon as he saw me, 'another one! Do you know, young man, that you got off lucky? You still have all your limbs which is sheer good luck for one who goes to such nests; now you know what a dive is. At least there were pretty sirens! You see all the pirates are not on the sea, nor all the sharks on land. I'll bet they haven't left you a penny.'

Proudly I pulled out the two crowns to show the innkeeper.

'That will pay your expenses,' he replied, and presented the bill at once.

I paid and left him, but I did not leave the city. Most decidedly my voyage to America was put off to the Greek calends, and the Old World was my lot; I was reduced to wallowing on the lowest pitches of civilization, and I was the more disturbed about my future as I had no resources for the present. A career as a sailor was open to me, and I decided to sign on, at the risk of breaking my neck thirty times a day, and climb a ship's shrouds for eleven francs a month. I was ready to sign on as a green hand, when my attention was suddenly attracted by the sound of a trumpet.

It was not that of cavalry, but a clown and his showman, who in front of a booth covered with the posters of a travelling menagerie was calling to the public which never hisses their rude horse-play. I arrived in time to see the beginning of the show, and while a fairly large audience testified its glee by shouts of laughter, I had a presentiment that the showman would give me employment. The clown looked to me to be a good fellow, and I wanted him for a protector. As I knew that one good turn deserves another, when he came down from the stage, I dedicated my last penny to him by offering to share a glass of gin. The clown was sensible to this politeness, promised to speak for me, and when our glass was finished, he introduced me to the director.

He was the famous Cotte-Comus who called himself the first physician in the world. In touring the provinces he had combined his talents with those of the naturalist Garnier. These gentlemen were in company with a troupe of acrobats.

As soon as Comus saw me, he asked me what I could do.

'Nothing,' I answered.

'In that case,' he said, 'they'll teach you; they are all blockheads; besides, you don't look stupid. We'll see whether you have a taste for the business; then I'll engage you for two years. The first six months you will be fed and clothed; at the end of that time you will have a sixth of the collection; the next year, if you are intelligent, I'll give you the same as the rest; while you wait, my friend, I shall know how to keep you busy.'

Introduced in this way, I shared his truckle-bed with the obliging clown. We were awakened at daybreak by the majestic voice of the director, who led me to a sort of den. 'Here,' he said to me, showing me the lamps and wooden candlesticks, 'is your job. Clean them all and put them in order, do you understand? After that you'll clean the animals' cages and sweep out the house.'

I went about the job, but I didn't like it. The grease disgusted me, and I wasn't comfortable with the monkeys, which, frightened by an unknown face, made unbelievable efforts to tear out my eyes. However, I yielded to stern necessity. When I had completed my task, I appeared before the director, who declared that I was to attend to the business and that if I continued to work with such zeal, he would make something of me.

I had got up at daybreak and was very hungry; now at ten o'clock there seemed no question of breakfast, although they had agreed to feed and lodge me. I was sinking with distress, when, finally, they brought me a piece of brown bread which was so hard that I could not finish it in spite of my strong teeth and keen appetite, so I threw the greater part of it to the animals. In the evening I had to light up, and as I was not used to it, I did not display all the speed at the job which the brute of a director wanted, so he gave me a beating, which he renewed the next day and every day thereafter.

A month passed and I was in a deplorable state; my clothes were covered with grease and torn by the monkeys; in fact I was in rags; I was eaten alive by vermin, and as a result of the lack of food I had grown so thin that no one would have known me. This state reanimated my bitter regrets for the paternal home, where I had, been well fed, well dressed, and where I had a good bed and did not have to take care of monkeys.

Such were my feelings when one morning Comus told me that, having considered what was best for me, he thought I would make a good tumbler. So he placed me in the hands of Balmate, nicknamed the Little Devil, with orders to train me. My master nearly broke my back at the first trick he wanted me to do, but I had two or three lessons a day. In less than three weeks I could do all sorts of falls. My teacher was delighted at my progress, and took great pleasure in hurrying me on. A hundred times I thought he would dislocate all my limbs. Finally, we came to the difficult part of the art, and it got harder and harder.

Bruised, tired, and disgusted with such dangerous gymnastics, I told M. Comus that most decidedly I did not want to be a tumbler.

'Oh, you don't care for it,' he said, and without making any objection, he beat me with a horsewhip. From that moment Balmate no longer bothered with me, and I went back to my lamps.

Comus had given me up, and it was now Gamier's turn to busy himself in giving me a job. One day when he had beaten me more than usual (for this exercise he shared the pleasure with Comus), Gamier, measuring me from head to foot, contemplated with marked satisfaction the dilapidation of my clothes which exposed my skin.

'I am pleased with you now,' he said; 'you are exactly what I want. Now you are docile, it depends only on yourself to be happy. Beginning today you'll let your nails grow; your hair is already long enough; you are nearly naked; a concoction of walnut leaves will do the rest.'

I did not know what Gamier meant when he called my friend the clown and ordered him to bring the tiger skin and war club. The clown returned with these objects.

'Now,' Gamier went on 'we are going to have a rehearsal. You are a young savage from the South Seas, and what is more, a cannibal; you eat raw flesh; the sight of blood sets you wild; and when you are thirsty, you put pebbles in your mouth which you crunch; you can only make rough, sharp sounds; you open your eyes wide; all your movements are jerks and you proceed only by leaps and bounds. Finally, take the wooden man in Cage No. 1 as your model.

During this lesson there was a dish of round stones at my feet and a rooster exhausted by having his legs tied together. Gamier took him up and offered him to me. 'Bite into that,' he said. I did not want to bite; he insisted, with threats; I rebelled, and at once asked for my dismissal. All the response I got was a dozen blows, but Gamier did not get off scot-free. Irritated by such treatment, I seized a stake and I certainly should have beaten to death monsieur the naturalist if the whole troupe had not fallen on me and thrown me out of the door under a hail of kicks and blows.

Some days before I had met in a wine shop a mountebank and his wife who ran an open-air puppet-show. We had become acquainted, and I was sure that I had won their interest. The husband complained bitterly at being condemned to such a trade, and often compared himself with Daniel in the lions' den. One could see that he was educated and made for something better than a puppetshow. The future theatrical director was very witty, but his wife did not realize it; he was also very ugly, and she fully appreciated that. She was an attractive brunette, with long eyelashes, and a most inflammable heart easily set alight. I was young; she was, too, only sixteen, while her husband was thirty-five. As soon as I found myself without a place, I went in search of the pair; I had an idea that they would give me useful advice. They gave me dinner and congratulated me on being free from the despotic yoke of Gamier, whom they called the mahmout.

'Since you are now your own master,' said the husband, you must come with us and support us; at least when there are three of us, there will be no more intervals, and you'll help us with the, puppets while Elisa takes up the collection. The public will pay attention and won't go out, and the receipts will increase. What do you say, Elisa?'

She answered that he should do as he wanted, but at the same time she gave me a glance which proved to me that the proposal did not bother her and that we should get along marvellously. I accepted this new job with thanks, and at the next performance I was installed at my post. Conditions were infinitely better than at Garnier's. Elisa had discovered that I was not so badly built as I was dressed, and gave me a thousand provocative looks to which I responded. At the end of three days she confessed that I was her one passion, and I was not ungrateful; we were happy and never left each other. In our lodgings we laughed, played, and joked, and the husband took it all as child's play. While we were at work, we were side by side under a narrow cabin made of four canvas strips decorated with the pompous title, 'Theatre of Amusing Varieties.' Elisa was at her husband's right, and I was at Elisa's right; I replaced her when she was not there, but was supervising the spectators who were going out and coming in.

One Sunday the spectacle was in full blast, and there was a crowd around the booth; Polichinello had beaten everyone; our good boss had only to work one of the figures; wanting to put it aside, he asked for the commissaire; we did not hear him. 'The commissaire, the commissaire!' he repeated impatiently, and at the third call he turned around and saw us in a tender embrace. Elisa in her surprise tried to find an excuse. The husband did not listen, but plunged into her eye the hook on which hung the figure he was playing. Blood flowed instantly; the performance was interrupted, and battle was engaged between the married pair. The booth was overturned, and we were discovered to a numerous circle of spectators who greeted this scene with prolonged laughter and applause.

Such a scandal put me on the streets again; I did not know where to lay my head. If I had had a decent outfit, I might have gone into service in some good house, but my appearance was so pitiful that no one wanted me. In this situation I had only one course to pursue: to return to Arras, but how I was to live until I got there was the question. I was a prey to such perplexities when there passed near me a man whom from his appearance I took to be a travelling pedlar. I engaged him in conversation and he told me that he was going to Lille; that he sold powders, opiates, and tonics, and that sometimes he even pulled teeth.

'It's a good trade,' he added, 'but I am getting old, and I need someone to carry the pack. I need a fine fellow like you, with good feet and good eyesight. If you want to, we'll go together.'

'I'm willing,' I answered, and with no further understanding between us, we went on our way.

After we had walked eight hours, night came on, and we could scarcely see our way when we halted before a miserable village inn.

'Here we are,' said the wandering doctor, rapping on the door.

'Who's there?' cried a hoarse voice.

'Father Godard, with his fool,' answered my guide.

The door opened at once, and we found ourselves among some twenty pedlars, tinmen, mountebanks, umbrella pedlars, jugglers, and the like, who laid a cover for my new boss and feasted him. I thought that they would do me no less honour and I was already placing myself at the table when the host tapped me familiarly on the shoulder and asked me if I was Father Godard's fool?

'What do you mean, fool?' I cried, with astonishment.

'Well, clown, then.'

I confess that, in spite of my very recent memories of the menagerie and the 'Theatre of Amusing Varieties,' I felt humiliated by the term. But I had a devilish appetite, and as I thought the end of the interrogation would be supper, and that, after all, my duties near Father Godard were not well defined, I consented to pass as his fool. When I answered, the host led me into the next room, a sort of barn, where a dozen fellows were smoking, drinking, and playing cards. He said they would serve me.

Soon after, a large girl brought in a wooden bowl on which I seized with avidity. A bit of lamb swam in the water the vessel held, with some thin turnips; the whole disappeared in the twinkling of an eye. When the meal was over, I stretched out with the other mountebanks on some bundles of straw which we had to share with a camel, two bears, and a crowd of educated dogs. The neighbourhood of such bed companions was not reassuring; however, I had to accommodate myself, but I could not sleep. The others snored like good ones.

Father Godard paid my expenses, and however bad the lodging and fare were, as each step brought us toward Arras, it was important for me not to separate from him. Finally, we reached Lille and entered on market-day. Father Godard lost no time; he went straight to the Grande Place, and ordered me to place his table, cash-box, phials, and parcels, and then proposed that we start our show. I had lunched well; the proposal revolted me; I had carried the baggage like a dromedary from

Ostend to Lille, and to put on a show was too much, and only ten
leagues from Arras at that!

I sent Father Godard packing, and at once took my way toward my
natal city whose belfry soon appeared in sight. I arrived at the foot of
the ramparts before the gates closed, but I shuddered at the thought of
the reception I should get; for an instant I was tempted to beat a
retreat, but I could stand no more, between my fatigue and hunger; rest
and food were indispensable, I wavered no longer, but ran toward my
paternal roof.

My mother was alone in the shop; I entered and fell at her knees; I
wept and begged her forgiveness. The woman scarcely recognized me, I
had changed so much, but she was tender with me; she was not strong
enough to repel me; it even seemed that she had forgotten all; after she
had attended to all my needs, she put me back in my old room.
Nevertheless, my father had to be told of my return. She did not dare
to bear the brunt of his wrath, so one of her ecclesiastical friends, the
chaplain of a regiment from Anjou stationed at Arras, undertook to
make peace. After he had given vent to fire and flame, my father consented to forgive me. When I learned that he had been persuaded, I
leaped for joy. The chaplain gave me the news and accompanied it with
a moral lecture which was undoubtedly touching, but I did not retain a
word of it, although I do remember that he cited the parable of the
Prodigal Son. That was almost my own story.

My adventures were the talk of the city; everyone wanted to hear
the story from my own lips; but none, except an actress who belonged
to a troupe playing at Arras, were more interested than two dressmakers
who lived in rue des Trois; I made them frequent visits. However, the
comédienne soon had the exclusive privilege of my attentions, and an
intrigue was the result. An impromptu trip to Lille with my conquest,
her husband, and a very pretty maid, who passed as my sister, proved to
my father that I had rapidly forgotten the tribulations of my first campaign.

My absence did not last long; three weeks had hardly elapsed when,
through want of money, the comédienne gave up dragging me along
with her luggage. I returned quietly to Arras, and my father was
astounded at the assurance with which I asked his consent to enlist.
The best thing he could do was to grant it; he realized it, and the next

day I was wearing the uniform of the Bourbon Regiment. My figure, my appearance, and my skill at arms gained me the advantage of being immediately placed in a company of chasseurs. Some old soldiers took exception to this; I sent two to the hospital, where I soon joined them, wounded by one of their comrades. Such a beginning made me a marked man; they took such pleasure in starting such affairs that at the end of six months, Sans Gêne – that was the nickname they had given me – had killed two men and fought fifteen times. As for the rest, I enjoyed all the good luck of garrison life; my guard duty was always mounted at the expense of some good merchants whose daughters clubbed together to gain my leisure. My mother added to this generosity, and my father gave me extra pay, yet I found ways of getting into debt. So I cut a figure, and felt almost none of the weight of discipline.

Once I was condemned to fifteen days in prison for missing three roll-calls. I was undergoing my penalty in a cell dug under one of the bastions when one of my friends and compatriots was shut up with me. He was a soldier in my regiment, accused of committing several robberies, and he had confessed. There was no doubt that the regiment would give him up, and this idea, combined with the fear of dishonouring his family, threw him into despair. I took pity on him, and, as I saw no other remedy in his deplorable situation, I advised him to avoid punishment either by escaping or by suicide. He consented to attempt the first before trying the second, and, with a young man from outside who came to visit me, I hurried to arrange everything for his flight.

At midnight two of the iron bars were broken; we led the prisoner to the ramparts, and I said to him, 'Come, you must jump or be hanged.' He calculated the height; he hesitated, and ended by declaring that he would run the risk of judgment rather than break his legs. He prepared to go back to his cell; but when he least expected it, we threw him over. He shouted; I advised him to be quiet, and then I went back to my underground apartment, where, lying on the straw, I enjoyed the rest the consciousness of having done a good deed procures.

The next day the disappearance of my companion was noticed; I was questioned, but I was rid of the matter by answering that I had seen nothing. Several years later I met the poor fellow; he looked upon me as his liberator. He had been lame since his fall, but had become an honest man.

I could not stay in Arras perpetually; war had just been declared on Austria, and I went with my regiment. Shortly after I was in the rout at Marquain, which ended in the killing of the brave but unfortunate General Dillon at Lille. After this event we were directed to the camp at Maulde, and then to la Lune, where, under the orders of Kellerman, I took part in the engagement of October 20 against the Prussians. The next day I was made a corporal of grenadiers. I had to christen my stripes, and I acquitted myself with such distinction at the canteen that I had a quarrel about something or other with a sergeant-major of the company I had left. I proposed a duel and he accepted, but once on the ground my adversary pretended that the difference in rank would not let him measure swords with me. I wanted to fight with fists; he filed a complaint, and the same evening I was put in the guardhouse with my seconds.

Two days later they warned us that we were to appear before a council of war. It was imperative that we escape, and we did. My comrade in his cap and coat looked like a soldier undergoing punishment, as he marched ahead of me. I still had my bearskin cap, my haversack, and gun, at the end of which was in evidence a large package sealed with wax and bearing this inscription, 'To the Citizen commanding at Vitry-le-Français.' That was our passport, and it took us without bother to Vitry, where a Jew procured us civilian clothes.

At that time the walls of every city were covered with placards urging all Frenchmen to fly to the defence of the country. Under such conditions they enlisted the first-comers. A sergeant-major of the Eleventh Chasseurs accepted us and gave us route papers. So we went at once to Philippeville, our dépôt.

My companion and I had but little money; fortunately good fortune awaited us at Chalons. In the same inn was a soldier from Beaujolais. He invited us to drink; he was a regular Picard, and I talked to him in the patois of that country. Insensibly, with glasses in hand, such great confidence was established between us that he showed us a pocketbook filled with assignats which he pretended to have found somewhere around Chateau l'Abbaye.

'Comrades,' he said to us, 'I can't read, but if you will show me what these papers are worth, I'll give you your share.'

The Picard could not have made a better appeal. As far as volume went, he had the largest share, but he did not suspect that we had awarded ourselves nine tenths of the sum total. This slight help was not unuseful to us in the course of our journey, which ended in the greatest gaiety. When we reached our destination, we still had something left with which to fatten the pot. In a short time we could ride well enough to be sent to the squadron, and we had been there only two days when we took part in the battle of Jemmapes. It was not the first time I had been under fire; I was not afraid, and I even believe that my conduct won the good will of my chiefs. But the captain announced that I had been posted as a deserter and that I should certainly be arrested.

The danger was imminent. That evening I saddled my horse to go over to the Austrians. In a few minutes I reached their advance posts; I asked to enlist, and they incorporated me in the cuirassiers of Kinski. What I feared most was that I should be obliged to sabre the French the next day. I hastened to avoid this necessity. A pretended illness enabled me to get evacuated to Louvain, where, after some days in the hospital, I offered to give the officers of the garrison lessons in fencing. They were delighted by the proposal. As soon as I was furnished with a mask, gloves, and a foil, a match in which I beat two or three pretended German masters was sufficient to give them a high opinion of my skill. I soon had numerous pupils, and I reaped a harvest of florins.

I was very proud of my success, when as a result of a too severe row with a corporal I was sentenced to receive twenty blows of the *schlag*, which, according to custom, was awarded on parade. This performance made me furious. I refused to give lessons; I was ordered to continue, with the option of teaching or of another punishment. I chose teaching, but the thought of the *schlag* was still with me, and I determined to brave anything to get free. Learning that a lieutenant was going to the army corps of General Schroeder, I begged him to take me with him as his servant, he consented in the hope that I would make him a Saint George. He was wrong, for when we were near Quesnois, I gave up politeness and went to Landrecies, where I represented myself as a Belgian who was abandoning the Austrian flag. They proposed that I enter the cavalry, but the fear of being recognized and shot if I ever found myself brigaded with my old regiment made me give the preference to the Fourteenth Light Infantry.

The army of Sambre-et-Meuse was then marching on
Aix-la-Chapelle; the company to which I belonged was ordered to follow the movement. We went. As we entered Rocroi, I saw the chasseurs
of the Eleventh. I thought I was lost when my former captain, whom I
could not avoid, hastened to reassure me. This brave man, who had
been interested in me ever since he had seen me put to flight the hussars of Saxe-Teschen, announced that an amnesty placed me hereafter
free from all pursuit, and that he would see me back under his orders
with pleasure. I showed that I would not be annoyed if that happened,
so he took it on himself to arrange the matter, and, shortly, I was back
in the Eleventh. My comrades received me with pleasure, and I was not
less satisfied to be back with them.

Nothing was lacking to my happiness when love, which always
plays a part, played one of its tricks on me. One should not be surprised that at the age of seventeen I captivated the housekeeper of an
old bachelor. Her name was Manon; she was double my age, but she
loved me. To prove it she was capable of the greatest sacrifices; nothing
was too dear. In her eyes I was the finest of chasseurs, because I was
hers, and, in addition, she wanted me to be the most natty. I already
had a watch, and I was proud to be decorated with precious jewels,
pledges of the sentiment I inspired, when I learned that Manon was to
be tried for household robbery on the accusation of her master.

Manon confessed her crime, but at the same time, in order to be
sure that after her sentence I should not pass to the arms of another, she
named me as her accomplice. She even went so far as to say that I had
urged her on, which was believable. I was implicated in the complaint,
and I should have had trouble in getting out of the scrape if chance had
not led me to discover some letters which proved my innocence.
Manon was confuted and withdrew her statement. I had been under
arrest at Stenay; I was set free, as white as snow.

My captain had never believed me guilty, and was glad to see me
again. But the chasseurs did not forgive me for having been suspected.
As the result of some allusions and words, I had no less than ten duels
in six days. In the end I was badly wounded and sent to the hospital,
where I stayed for more than a month before I recovered. When I came
out, my chiefs, convinced that quarrels would be renewed if I did not
go away for some time, granted me six weeks' leave.

I went to Arras to pass the time, where I was much astonished to find my father in public employment. As a former baker, he had just been given the oversight of the munition factories. He had to prevent the bread being carried off. At a time of famine, such functions, although he performed them gratuitously, were delicate, and without a doubt they would have led him to the guillotine except for the protection of Citizen Souham. The latter commanded a battalion to which I was assigned provisionally.

When my leave had expired, I rejoined at Givet; from there the regiment soon entered the county of Namur. We encamped in the villages on the banks of the Meuse, and, as the Austrians were in sight, not a day passed without shots being exchanged. As a result of a more serious engagement, we were driven back under the guns of Givet. In the retreat I received a shot in my leg which forced me to enter the hospital and then to remain at the dépôt. I was still there when the Germanic Legion, composed in great part of deserters, masters at arms, and the like, passed through. One of the principal officers proposed that I enter this corps, offering me the rank of sergeant-major. 'Once admitted,' he said, 'you will be free from all pursuit.' The certainty of being rid of pursuit and the remembrance of the unpleasantness my intimacy with Manon had produced, decided me. No doubt if I had continued to serve in this corps, where advancement was rapid, I should have become an officer. But my wound reopened with such serious complications that I had to ask for another leave. I obtained it, and six days later I again found myself at the gates of Arras.

II
I Meet Adversity in Life and Love

AS I ENTERED the city I was struck by the air of consternation on all faces. I questioned some people, but they looked at me with distrust and went off without answering. Something extraordinary was happening, but what was it? Passing through the crowd which moved about in the dark, tortuous streets, I soon reached the Place du Marché aux Poissons. The first object that struck my eyes was the guillotine raising its red timbers above a silent multitude. An old man whom they had just finished binding to the fatal plank was the victim. Suddenly I heard a flourish of trumpets. On a stage which dominated the orchestra was seated a man, still young, dressed in a blue and black-striped jacket. This personage, whose pose announced the monk more than the military man, was leaning nonchalantly on a cavalry sabre with an enormous guard representing a liberty cap. A row of pistols ornamented his waist, and his hat was crowned by a tri-colored plume. I recognized Joseph Lebon. At that moment his ignoble face was animated by a frightful smile; he stopped beating time with his left foot; the trumpets ceased; he made a signal, and the old man was placed under the knife. A sort of clerk, half-drunk, appeared beside the 'avenger of the people,' and read in a hoarse voice a bulletin from the army of Rhin-et-Moselle. At each paragraph the orchestra struck a chord, and when the reading was finished, the head of the unfortunate man fell, to the cry, 'Vive la Republique!' repeated by some of the acolytes of the ferocious Lebon.

I cannot describe the impression that this horrible scene made on me. I reached my father's house almost as undone as he whose agony I had seen so horribly prolonged. There I learned that the victim was M. de Mongon, a former commander of the citadel, condemned as an aristocrat. A few days previously they had executed on the same spot M. de Vieux Pont for the crime of owning a parrot in whose jargon they thought they recognized the cry, 'Vive le Roi!' The bird failed to share the lot of its masters, and, it was said, owed its pardon to the solicitation of Citizeness Lebon, who agreed to convert it.

Citizeness Lebon was a former nun at the abbey of Vivier. On this account, as on many others, she was a worthy spouse of the excure of Neuville; thus she exercised a great influence on the members of the commission at Arras, where sat, either as judges or jurors, her brother-in-law and three of her uncles. The ex-nun was as greedy for money as blood. One evening at the theatre she dared to address the audience as follows:

'Oh, you sans-culottes, one would think that they didn't guillotine on your account. The enemies of the country must be denounced. If you know some noble, some rich man, some aristocratic merchant, denounce him, and you shall have his money.'

The baseness of this monster was unequalled even by that of her husband, who gave vent to every excess. Often after his orgies he was to be seen running about the city, shouting obscenities to the young, brandishing his sabre over his head, and firing his pistol in the ears of women and children.

A former potato merchant, with a red cap on his head, his sleeves rolled up to his shoulders, in his hand a long hazel club, ordinarily accompanied the citeness on her walks, and it was not rare to meet them arm in arm. This woman, nicknamed Mother Duchesne, figured as the Goddess of Liberty on more than one solemn democratic occasion. She attended regularly the sessions of the commission, where she prepared the arrests by harangues and denunciations. She had all the inhabitants of one street guillotined; she left it a desert.

I am often asked how in such deplorable circumstances the taste for amusement and pleasure lost none of its intensity. The fact is that Arras continued to offer me the same distractions as previously. The girls were just as complaisant, and I was easily convinced of it, for in a few days I had gained the love of the young and pretty Constance, only child of Corporal Latulipe, sutler of the citadel, and of the four daughters of a notary who had his office at the corner of the rue des Capuchins. I should have been happy if I had gone no farther, but I took a notion to pay homage to a beauty of the rue de Justice, and I met a rival in my path. He was a former regimental musician, and was one of those men who, without boasting of the success they have won, nevertheless let it be understood that they have been refused nothing. I reproached him for a boast of this kind; he took offence; I added provocation, he gave in, and I had already forgotten my complaint when I was told that he was using offensive words on my account. I at once went and asked for an explanation; but it was useless, and he did not consent to fight until I had given him, in the presence of witnesses, the lowest humiliation.

The rendezvous was set for the next morning. I was prompt, but I had hardly arrived when I was surrounded by a crowd of gendarmes and police who summoned me to surrender my sabre and follow them. I obeyed, and the doors of Les Baudets soon closed on me. Its purpose had been changed since the Terrorists marked the population of Arras for mowing. The concierge, Beaupré, his head covered with a red cap and followed by two great black dogs which never left him, led me to a large garret, where he kept guard over the elite of the country. There we were deprived of all communication with the outside world; we were barely permitted to receive food, and then it did not reach us until it had been turned over by Beaupré, who carried his precautions so far as to plunge his horribly filthy hands into the soup to assure himself that no arm or key was to be found there.

The prisoners grumbled, and he answered anyone who complained: 'You're hard to please for the little time you have to live! Who knows but what you are for tomorrow's batch? Wait, what's your name? So and so! I declare, it is tomorrow.'

And these predictions of Beaupré were the better realized in that he designated the individuals to Joseph Lebon, who, after his dinner, consulted him in these words, 'Whom shall we clean up tomorrow?'

Among the gentlemen shut up with us was Comte de Béthune. One morning they came to find him and lead him to the tribunal. Before taking him to the yard, Beaupré said to him, roughly, 'Citizen Béthune, since you're going down there, what you leave here will be mine, will it not?' 'Freely, Monsieur Beaupré,' answered the old man quietly. 'There are no more monsieurs,' answered the miserable jailer with a scowl; 'we are all citizens,' and at the door, he cried, 'Good-bye, Citizen Béthune!' However, M. de Béthune was acquitted. He was brought back to prison as a suspect. His return delighted us; we thought he was saved, but that evening he was summoned again. Joseph Lebon, in whose absence the sentence of acquittal had been rendered, arrived from the country. He was furious that he had been robbed of the blood of so brave a man, and he ordered the members of the commission to meet immediately. M. de Béthune was condemned and was executed by the light of torches.

This event, which Beaupré announced to us with ferocious joy, gave me serious uneasiness. Every day they sent to death men who knew no more than I did the reason for their arrest, and who from their fortune or social position did not seem designed for political passions. Besides, I knew that Beaupré, although very scrupulous about numbers, cared very little for quality, and that often, when he did not at once see the individual who had been named, he sent along the first-comers, so that the service should suffer no delay. At any moment I might find myself in Beaupré's hands, and one can well imagine that such an expectation was not reassuring.

I had been detained six days when a visit of Joseph Lebon was announced. His wife was with him, and among his followers he had the principal Terrorists of the country, among whom I recognized my father's former barber and a well-cleaner, named Delmotte, alias Lantillette. I begged them to say a word in my favour to the representative. They promised, and I augured the more favourably from this step in that they were both in high favour, However, Joseph Lebon went through the rooms, questioning the prisoners with a ferocious look, and pretending to address terrible questions to them. When he came to me, he looked at me steadily, and said, half-sternly, half-jokingly:

'Oh, is that you, François? So you think you're an aristocrat, and say evil of the sans-culottes? You regret your old Bourbon Regiment? Take care, or I'll order you to the guillotine. However, send me your mother.'

I observed that, as I was in close confinement, I could not see her. 'Beaupré,' he said to the jailer, 'let Madame Vidocq come in.' And he went out, leaving me full of hope, for he had obviously treated me with peculiar kindness. Two hours later my mother came; she told me what I did not know: that I had been denounced by the musician whom I had challenged to a duel. The denunciation was in the hands of a furious Jacobin, the Terrorist Chevalier, who, through friendliness for my rival, would certainly have played me foully, if his sister, on the representations of my mother, had not obtained from him a request for my release.

When I came out of prison, I was led with great pomp to the patriotic society, where they made me swear fidelity to the Republic and hatred of tyrants. I swore all they wanted. Of what sacrifices is not one capable to preserve his liberty?

When these formalities had been fulfilled, I was sent back to my depot, where my comrades showed great joy at seeing me again. After what had happened, I should have been failing in gratitude had I not regarded Chevalier as my liberator. I went to thank him, and I expressed to his sister how much I was touched that she should take such an interest in a poor prisoner. This woman was passionate, but her large black eyes did not make up for her plainness. She thought I was in love with her because I was polite, and took literally some compliments I made her. From our first interview she was so mistaken about my feelings that she went so far as to throw her spell over me. The question of our marriage came up; my parents were sounded. They answered that at eighteen I was too young to think of marriage, and the matter languished.

Meanwhile, they were organizing at Arras battalions which had been raised by the draft. As I was known as an excellent instructor, I was summoned, with seven other non-commissioned officers, to drill the second battalion from Pas-de-Calais. In the number was a corporal of grenadiers named César; he was named adjutant and I was promoted to the rank of lieutenant when we reached our camp near Bailleul. César had been a fencing master in his regiment, and my prowess with the officers of Kinski's cuirassiers will be recalled. We decided that in addition to theory we would teach fencing to the officers of the battalion; they were delighted with the arrangement. Our lessons brought in some money, but far from sufficient for our needs, or, if one prefers, for our whims. Provisions were especially lacking. What doubled our regrets and our appetites was that the mayor, with whom we lodged, kept an excellent table. We tried in every way to ingratiate ourselves in the house, but an old housekeeper, Sixca, always got ahead of us and spoiled our plans for eating. We were desperate and famished.

In the end César found a way to break the insuperable charm which kept us away from the ordinary fare of the municipal officer. At his instigation the drum-major came one morning and beat the reveille under the windows of the mayor's house. One can imagine the uproar.

We took it for granted that our intervention would be invoked to stop this racket. César promised to do all in his power so that the noise would not occur again. Then he hastened to advise the drum-major to drill his pupils behind the house. The old housekeeper gave up; she invited the perfidious César and me rather graciously, but that was not enough. The drums continued their concert until their respectable chief was admitted to the municipal banquet as well as we. After that there were no more drums, except when detachments passed through, and everyone lived in peace, except me whom the old housekeeper threatened with her dreadful favours.

We had been encamped here for three months when the division was ordered to proceed to Stinward. The Austrians had made a demonstration on Poperingue, and the second battalion from Pas-de-Calais was placed in the first line. The night after our arrival the enemy surprised our advance posts, and entered the village of La Belle, which we occupied. We hurriedly formed in line of battle. In this manœuvre in the night our young recruits displayed that intelligence and activity peculiar to the French. Toward six o'clock in the morning, a squadron of hussars appeared on our left, and charged as sharpshooters without being able to break through. A column of infantry followed and charged with the bayonet, but it was only after a heavy engagement that we were forced by superior numbers to withdraw on Stinward where our headquarters were.

When I arrived, I received the congratulations of General Vandamme, and a hospital billet for Saint-Omer, for I had been struck in the leg by two sword thrusts in fighting an Austrian hussar. My wounds were not very serious, for at the end of two months I was able to rejoin the battalion.

Here I saw that strange corps called 'The Army of the Revolution.' The men with their pikes and red bonnets took with them everywhere the guillotine. They said that the Convention had found no better means to assure the fidelity of the officers of the fourteen armies in the field than to place before their eyes the instrument of punishment reserved for traitors. All I can say is that this lugubrious instrument scared to death the population of the country through which it passed. And it did not please the soldiers any more.

We had frequent quarrels with the sans-culottes, who were called Gards de Corps de la Guillotine. For my part I attracted the attention of one of their leaders, who decided that it was wrong for me to wear gold epaulettes when the regulations only prescribed woollen. My fine equipment would certainly have done me a bad turn, and I should have paid dearly for my infraction of the sumptuary law if I had not found means to escape to Cassel. There I was joined by my corps which was disbanded, as were all raised by draft. The officers became privates, and with this rank I was sent to the Twenty-Eighth Battalion of Volunteers which was destined to drive the Austrians from Valenciennes and Condé.

The battalion was in camp at Fresnes. One day there arrived at the farm where I lodged the entire family of the owner of a barge, composed of husband, wife, and two children. One of the latter was a girl of eighteen who would have attracted notice anywhere. The Austrians had taken possession of their barge which was loaded with grain. That was their entire fortune, and the poor people, with only the clothes which covered them, had no other recourse than to take refuge with my host, their relative. This occurrence, their evil plight, and perhaps the beauty of the young girl, whom they called Delphine, touched me.

Scouting about I saw the boat which the enemy were unloading, as they needed supplies. I proposed to a dozen of my comrades that we relieve the Austrians of their capture. They accepted, the colonel gave his consent, and one rainy night we got near the barge without being observed by the sentinel whom we sent to the fishes with five thrusts of the bayonet. The owner's wife had insisted on going with us; she rushed at once for a bag of florins which she had hidden in the grain, and begged me to take charge of it. Then we cast off the lines to let the barge drift to a place where we had an entrenchment, but just as we got into the current, we were surprised by the 'Wer da?' of a sentinel we had not seen in the reeds where he had taken cover.

At the noise of a shot with which he accompanied his second challenge, the near-by post ran to arms, and in an instant the bank was covered with soldiers who rained bullets on the barge. We had to abandon her. My comrades and I jumped into a sort of skiff which we had brought, and the woman did the same. But the owner, whom we had forgotten in the tumult, perhaps held back by a ray of hope, fell into the power of the Austrians, who did not spare him blows with fist or butt of the musket.

This attempt cost us three men, and I had two fingers broken by a shot. Delphine was prodigal in her assiduous care for me. Her mother at once went to Ghent, where she knew that her husband would be sent as a prisoner of war, and we went to Lille, where I spent my convalescence. Delphine had a part of the money we had found in the grain, and we led a joyous life.

The question of our marrying arose, and the matter went so far that one morning I started for Arras to get the necessary papers and the consent of my parents. Delphine had obtained the consent of hers, who were still in Ghent. A league from Lille, I discovered that I had forgotten my hospital billet which it was indispensable that I produce at the municipality of Arras, so I retraced my steps.

When I reached the hotel, I went up to the room we occupied and knocked. No one answered; however, it was impossible that Delphine had gone out so early, for it was hardly six o'clock. I knocked again; Delphine came to open, stretching her arms and rubbing her eyes as if she had awakened suddenly. To test her I proposed that she accompany me to Arras so that I could present her to my parents, and she quietly accepted. My suspicions began to fade away; however, something told me that she was deceiving me. Finally, I noticed that she often cast her eyes on a certain wardrobe. I pretended that I wanted to open it, but my chaste fiancee opposed it, giving one of those pretexts which women always have at their disposal. But I insisted, and ended by opening the wardrobe, where I found hidden in a pile of dirty linen the doctor who had attended me during my convalescence. He was old, ugly, dirty.

My first feeling was one of humiliation at having such a rival; perhaps I should have been more furious if I had found a fine fellow; I leave the decision to the numerous amateurs who have found themselves in such a case. As for me, I wanted to start in by annihilating my lucky, Æsculapius, but, as rarely happens to me, on reflection I held back. We were at a seat of war; they could quibble about my permit and give me a bad time. After all, Delphine was not my wife, and I had no rights over her. All the same I put her through the door with heavy kicks in the latter end, after which I threw out of the window her

clothes and some money to take her to Ghent. I allotted the rest of the
money to myself, as I thought I had earned it, since I had directed the
superb expedition which had retaken it from the Austrians. I have forgotten to say that I left the doctor to effect his retreat in peace.

Rid of my perfidious Delphine, I continued to stay at Lille,
although my leave had expired; one could hide there nearly as easily as
in Paris, and my sojourn would not have been troubled except for
another adventure. I spare details, but it is sufficient to say that I was
arrested dressed in women's clothes as I was fleeing from the wrath of a
jealous husband. I was taken to the Place, where at first I obstinately
refused to explain myself. If I spoke I should give away the person who
had been kind to me, or reveal that I was a deserter.

Some hours in jail, however, changed my resolutions. I had one of
the higher officials called to take my declaration, and I explained
frankly to him my position; he appeared to take some interest. The
general in command of the division wanted to hear the story from my
own mouth; it nearly made him burst with laughter twenty times. He
then ordered me set at liberty, and delivered an order to me to rejoin
the Twenty-Eighth Battalion in Brabant. But instead of following his
directions, I went to Arras, thoroughly decided that I would re-enter
the service only as the last extremity.

My first visit was to the patriot Chevalier. His influence with
Joseph Lebon made me hope that through his intermission I could
obtain an extension of my leave. In fact, it was granted, and again I
found myself introduced into the family of my protector. His sister,
whose good intentions in my regard we already know, doubled her
allurements. On the other hand, the constant sight of her insensibly
made me conscious of her lack of attractiveness. In brief, things came to
the point that I was not astonished to have her declare one day that she
was going to have a child. She did not speak of marriage; she did not
even utter the word; but I saw only too well that that was the road to
take unless I wanted to expose myself to her brother's vengeance, who
without fail would denounce me as a suspect, as an aristocrat, and
above all, as a deserter. My parents were impressed by all these consider-
ations, and in the hope of keeping me near them, they gave their consent to the marriage, which the Chevalier family pressed keenly.

At last it was arranged, and at the age of eighteen I found myself a husband. I even believed that I was nearly the father of a family, but only a few days had gone by before my wife confessed that she had pretended to be with child only to bring me under the marital yoke. One can easily imagine the satisfaction such a confidence gave me. The same reasons which had forced me to contract the marriage, however, compelled me to be silent, so I accepted things as they were and raged inwardly.

In addition, our marriage began under evil auspices. A shop which my wife had started was going badly. I thought the reason was her frequent absences, for she spent all day with her brother. I made these observations, and to pay me back, I was ordered to rejoin at Tournai. I might have complained of this expeditious manner of getting rid of a bothersome husband, but for my part I was so tired of the Chevalier yoke that I resumed with a sort of joy the uniform I had taken so much pleasure in leaving.

At Tournai a former officer of the Bourbon Regiment attached me to his office in charge of the details of administration and particularly in all that concerned the uniforms. Soon the affairs of the division necessitated the sending of a trustworthy man to Arras. I went by post, and I reached the city at eleven in the evening. As I was carrying orders, I made them open the gates, and, from a feeling which I cannot explain, I rushed to my wife's house. I knocked a long time, but no one came to answer. A neighbour finally opened the side door for me, and I rapidly mounted to my wife's room. As I came to it, I heard the noise of a falling sabre, and then the window was opened and a man jumped into the street. It is needless to say that they had recognized my voice. I hastily went downstairs, and I soon met my Lovelace, in whom I recognized an adjutant of the Seventeenth Horse Hussars, on six months' furlough at Arras. He was half-naked; I took him back to the conjugal domicile; he completed his toilet, and we separated only after agreeing to fight the next day.

This scene had aroused the quarter. Most of the neighbours had run to the windows and had seen me seize the culprit, and he had admitted the fact before them. So there was no lack of witnesses to summon and obtain a divorce, and that was what I intended to do. But my chaste wife's family at once started a campaign to stop my proceedings, or at least to render them worthless. The next day, before I could join the major, I was arrested by the gendarmes who already talked of shutting me up in Les Baudets. Fortunately for me I had acquired some confidence, and I felt very strongly that my position was nothing to worry about. I asked to be taken to Joseph Lebon; they could not refuse. I appeared before the representative of the people, whom I found surrounded by an enormous mass of letters and papers.

'So it's you,' he said to me, 'who come here without permission to mistreat your wife again.'

I at once saw what the answer was; I showed my orders, and I invoked the testimony of all my wife's neighbours, and that of the major himself, who could not contradict. Finally, I explained my case so clearly that Joseph Lebon was forced to agree that the wrongs were not on my side. Out of regard for his friend Chevalier, however, he pledged me not to stay in Arras any longer, and as I feared that the wind might change, as it had so often, I promised to defer as promptly as possible to this advice. When my mission was completed, I took leave of everyone, and the next day at daybreak I was on the road to Tournai.

III
MY COLOURS ARE FALSE

I DID NOT FIND the adjutant-general at Tournai; he had gone to Brussels. I arranged matters to go and join him, and the next day I took the diligence for that destination. At first glance I recognized among the travellers three individuals whom I had known at Lille, who passed entire days in pubs and lived in a suspicious manner. To my great astonishment they were wearing the uniforms of different corps; one had the epaulettes of a lieutenant-colonel, and the others of captain and lieutenant. Where could they have got them, I wondered to myself, for I knew they had never served. I was lost in conjectures.

On their part they at first appeared a little confused at the meeting, but they soon recovered and showed a friendly surprise at finding me a private. When I explained how the disbanding of the drafts had made me lose my rank, the 'lieutenant-colonel' promised me his protection, which I accepted, although I did not know what to think of the protector. What I did see clearly was that he was in funds, that he paid for all the meals, where he showed an ardent republicanism, although letting it be understood that he belonged to an old family.

I was no more fortunate at Brussels than at Tournai; the adjutant-general seemed to fly before me, and had just gone to Liége. I went there, counting that this time my journey would not be useless. I arrived; my man had started to Paris the evening before to appear before the bar of the Convention. His absence should not be more than a fortnight; I waited, but no one appeared. I decided to go back to Brussels, where I hoped more easily to discover means to get out of my embarrassing circumstances. To speak frankly I must admit that I was not to be excessively difficult on the choice of means. My education had hardly been such as to make me a man of the greatest scruples, and the detestable society in the garrisons which I had frequented since childhood would have corrupted the most fortunate nature.

So it was without great violence to my delicacy that I was installed at Brussels with a woman of my acquaintance, who had been kept by

General Van der Nott and then had nearly fallen on the public domain. An idler, like all who are thrown into such a precarious existence, I passed whole days and a part of the nights at the Café Turc or the Café de la Monnaie, where by preference gathered the knights of industry and professional gamblers. These people spent money, played a steep game, and, as they had no known resources, I could not understand how they could lead such a life. A young man with whom I was acquainted, and whom I questioned on the subject, appeared to be struck with my inexperience. I had all the difficulty in the world to persuade him that I was as green as I said I was.

'Those men you see there every day,' he finally said, are sharpers; those who make only one appearance are the dupes, who never reappear once they have lost their money.'

Furnished with these instructions, I noted a host of things which had previously escaped my notice. I saw unbelievable tricks of sleight-of-hand, and what proved that I still had some good left in me was that I was often tempted to warn the unfortunate fellow whom they stripped. What happened proved that the players had suspected it.

One evening there was a game at the Café Turc; the dupe lost a hundred and fifty louis, and left, asking for his revenge the next day. I had scarcely put foot outside than the winner approached me, and said, in the simplest fashion, 'Really, monsieur, we have played in luck; you did not do badly to back my game. I won ten games; at the four crowns that you staked, that makes ten louis. Here they are.' I observed that he was mistaken, that I had taken no interest in the game. His only answer was to put the ten louis in my hands and turn his back.

'Take them,' said the young man who had initiated me into the mysteries of the gambling-house and who was beside me. 'Take them and follow me.' Mechanically I did as he said, and when we were in the street, my mentor added: 'They've seen that you follow the deal, and they're afraid that you'll take a fancy to show up the secret. As there is no way to intimidate you, as they know you have a good arm and a wicked hand, they've decided to give you a part of the cake. So you needn't worry about your living; the two cafés will be sufficient, as you can draw four to six crowns a day as I do.'

In spite of my complaisant conscience, I wanted to answer and make some comments.

'You're not a child,' said my honourable friend; 'there's no question of robbery. They only correct fortune rather well, and, believe me, that's the way it's done in the salon as well as in the tavern. There they cheat – that's the accepted word – and the banker, who in the morning in his banking house commits a crime in figuring interest, traps you very calmly that evening at play.'

What could I answer to such formidable arguments? Nothing! The only thing left for me was to take the money, which I did.

These slight dividends, with a hundred crowns which my mother sent me, put me in condition to cut some figure and show my gratefulness to that trailie, whose devotion did not find me altogether insensitive. Our affairs, therefore, were in a good way, when one evening I was arrested at the Théâtre du Parc by several police agents who summoned me to show my papers. That would have been dangerous, so I answered that I had none. They conducted me to Les Madelonettes, and at the examination the next day, I saw that they did not know me, but took me for somebody else. I then declared that my name was Rousseau; that I was born in Lille, and, I added, that I had come to Brussels for pleasure and thought that I did not need papers. In the end I asked to be taken back to Lille at my own expense by two gendarmes. They granted my request, and, by means of some crowns, my escort consented that poor Émilie should accompany me.

It was all right to be sent out of Brussels, but it was still more important not to reach Lille, where I should inevitably be recognized as a deserter. I must escape at any price. That was Émilie's opinion too, and I communicated the project of executing my plans when we arrived at Tournai. I told the gendarmes that, before separating from them the next day when we reached Lille, where I was to be set at liberty immediately, I wanted to pay my adieux by a good supper. They were already charmed by my liberal manners and my gaiety, and they accepted willingly.

That evening, while they slept on the table drunk with beer and rum, thinking that I was in the same state, I descended from the second-floor window by means of sheets. Émilie followed me, and we were soon in the crossroads which they would never dream of searching. So we reached the Faubourg Notre Dame at Lille, where I dressed in a greatcoat of the uniform of the mounted chasseurs, but I took the

precaution to put over my left eye a plaster of black taffeta which made
me unrecognizable. However, I did not judge it prudent to stay long in
a city so near my birthplace, and we went to Ghent. There, through a
romantic coincidence, Émilie discovered her father, who decided to
receive her back in the family. It is true that she consented to leave me
only on the express condition that I should rejoin her as soon as the
business I had in Brussels was finished.

The business I had in Brussels was to begin again to exploit the
Café Turc and the Café de la Monnaie. But to present myself in that
city, I had to have papers which would prove that I was Rousseau, born
in Lille, as I had stated at the examination which preceded my escape.
A captain of Belgian riflemen in the French service, named Labbre, for
fifteen louis, took it upon himself to furnish me the necessary papers.
At the end of three weeks he brought me in fact a birth certificate, a
passport, and a certificate of discharge in the name of Rousseau, all
made with such perfection as I have never seen with any forger. Armed
with these papers, I actually reappeared in Brussels, where the comman-
dant, a former comrade of Labbre's, undertook to arrange my affair.

Tranquil on this score, I hurried to the Café Turc. The first persons
I saw in the room were the false officers with whom, as may be recalled,
I had already travelled. They received me marvellously, and suspecting
from my story of my adventures that my position was hardly the most
brilliant, they proposed that I take the rank of lieutenant of horse chasseurs, doubtless because they saw I wore the greatcoat of that arm. Such
an advantageous promotion was not to be refused. They took my
description there and then, and, as I observed to the committee that
Rousseau was a borrowed name, the worthy lieutenant-colonel told me
to take the name which suited me best. It was impossible to show
greater good will. I decided to retain the name of Rousseau, under
which they delivered to me not a brevet but a route card of a lieutenant
in the Sixth Chasseurs, travelling with his horse, and entitled to lodging
and provisions.

So I found myself incorporated in that rolling army, composed of
officers without commissions or troops, who with their false papers
imposed on the commissioners of war the more easily as at this time
there was little order in the military administration. What is certain is
that during a turn we took in the Low Countries, we got rations every-

where, without the slightest notice being taken. The rolling army was then composed of not less than two thousand adventurers who lived like fishes in water. What was more curious was that advancement was as rapid as circumstances permitted; promotions which always brought lucrative results since they increased the rations. In this manner I was promoted captain of hussars, and one of my companions became a major; but what confounded me most was the promotion of Auffray, our lieutenant-colonel, to the rank of brigadier-general. It is true that, while the importance of the rank and the sort of respectability demanded made the fraud the more difficult to sustain, the audacity of such a combination removed suspicion.

When we returned to Brussels, we had billets for lodgings delivered to us, and I was sent to a rich widow, Baroness d'I—. I was received – as were all Frenchmen at this time in Brussels – with open arms. A pretty chamber was placed at my entire disposal, and my hostess, enchanted by my reserve, warned me that if her hours were convenient, my cover would always be laid. It was impossible to resist such obliging offers. I was overwhelmed with thanks and the same day I had to appear at dinner, where the guests were three old ladies, not including the baroness, who was hardly more than fifty. Everyone was delighted by the engaging manners of the captain of hussars. At Paris I should have been considered slightly *gauche* in such company, but in Brussels I was perfect for a young man whose precocious entrance into the service had injured his education. Doubtless the baroness made some reflections of this kind, for she showed me a slight solicitude which made me think.

As I was sometimes absent to dine with 'my general,' whose invitations, I said, I could not refuse, she insisted that I present him to her friends. In the first place, I did not care to introduce my associates to the baroness; she saw everyone, and we might meet at her house someone who would disclose our little speculations. But the baroness insisted, and I gave in, only I expressed a desire that the general should be received in a small gathering, as he wished to preserve some sort of incognito. So he came. The baroness had placed him near her, and she gave him such a distinguished reception and talked with him so long that I was piqued. To break up this téte-à-téte, I had the idea of asking the general to sing us something with a piano accompaniment. I was well aware that he was unable to read a note, but I counted on the customary earnestness of the company to keep him busy at least for a few moments. My strategy only half-succeeded. The lieutenant-colonel who was in the party offered to replace him. In fact, I saw him seat himself before the piano and sing some bits with sufficient taste to gain applause, while I would have rather seen him at the devil.

At last this eternal evening ended, and everyone withdrew. I was turning over in my mind projects of vengeance against my rival who was going to rob me, I will not say of love, but of the obliging solicitude of the baroness. Preoccupied with this idea, as soon as I was up, I went to see the general, who was rather surprised to see me so early.

'Do you know,' he said, without giving me time to start the conversation, 'do you know, my friend, that the baroness is...'

'Who's talking about the baroness?' I interrupted abruptly. 'There's no question of what she is or isn't.'

'So much the worse,' he replied; 'if you won't talk of her, I have nothing to hear.'

He continued to intrigue me in this way for some time, but he ended by telling me that his interview with the baroness had been concerned solely with me, and that he had advanced matters so far that he believed she was ready – to marry me.

At first I thought my poor comrade had lost his mind. It was most incredible that one of the "wealthiest women of title in the United Provinces would marry an adventurer of whom she knew neither the family, the fortune, nor antecedents. Besides, should I engage in a scheme which sooner or later would be discovered and ruin me? In addition, I was well and truly married at Arras. These objections and several others suggested a sort of remorse at the idea of deceiving an excellent woman who heaped kindly acts upon me, but this did not stop the speaker for a moment.

'All that you say is fine, and I altogether agree with you. If I were to follow my natural *penchant* for virtue, I lack only ten thousand livres a year. But I don't see any reason to be so scrupulous here. What does the baroness want? A husband, and a husband who pleases her. Don't you intend to have every regard for her and to treat her as someone who is useful to us, and of whom we have never had to complain? You talk of the inequality of fortune; the baroness does not consider that. You lack only one thing, and that is a title. Well, I'll give you one. You might well look at me with open eyes; listen, and don't make me repeat.

'You must know some nobleman of your country about your own age. So you are a nobleman; your parents are *emigres*; they are now in Hamburg. You have returned to France to buy back, through a third party, your paternal home, in order to take at leisure the plate and a thousand double louis hidden under the floor in the salon. At the beginning of the Terror, the presence of some intruders, the haste of departure, a decree of arrest against your father did not permit you to delay a moment, and prevented your taking this deposit.

'When you returned to this country, disguised as a tanner, you were denounced by the very man who was to second you in this enterprise. A writ was issued against you; you were pursued by the republican authorities, and you were about to lose your head on the scaffold when I found you on the main road, half-dead from care and want. An old friend of the family, I obtained for you a commission as an officer in the hussars, under the name of Rousseau, while you are waiting until you can rejoin your noble parents in Hamburg. The baroness already knows all this. Yes, all – except your name, which I have not told her, formally, from discretion, but in reality because I don't know the one for you to take. That is a confidence which I reserve for you to make yourself.

'So the affair is arranged; you are a gentleman; there is nothing to retract. Don't talk of that wife of yours; you were divorced at Arras under the name of Vidocq, and you will marry at Brussels under the name of Count B—. Now, listen; until now our affairs have gone rather well, but all that may change at any moment. We have already found that some of the commissioners of war are curious; we may meet some less docile who will cut off our rations and send us to serve in the "Little Navy" at Toulon. You understand – that's enough. The most fortunate thing that can happen to you now is to take up with your old regiment and run the risk of being shot as a deserter. While if you marry, you are assured of a fine existence, and you will be in a position to be useful to your friends. Since we are talking of that, let's make our little arrangements. Your wife has one hundred thousand crowns income a year; we are three; you will give to each of us a pension of a thousand crowns payable in advance, and I will finger thirty thousand francs as the reward of making a count out of a baker's son.'

After this long harangue in which the general skillfully presented all the difficulties of my position, it ended in my resistance breaking down, although, to tell the truth, it was not very obstinate. I consented to everything. I went back to the baroness's house and as Count B— fell at her feet. The scene was played to an end, and, although one would scarcely believe it, I entered so well into the spirit of my role that I succeeded for a moment in deceiving myself, which, it is said, often happens to liars. The baroness was charmed by the sallies and sentimental words with which the situation inspired me. The general was triumphant at my success, and everyone was delighted. Here and there I let escape some expression redolent of the canteen, but the general had taken care to warn the baroness that the political troubles had caused my education to be neglected seriously, and she was content with the explanation.

We sat down to the table, and the dinner went off marvellously. At dessert the baroness whispered to me: 'I know, my dear, that your fortune is in the hands of the Jacobins. However, your parents in Hamburg must be embarrassed; do me the pleasure of sending them a draft which my banker will give you tomorrow.'

I began to thank her, but she interrupted me, and left the table to pass to the salon. I took the opportunity to tell the general what had happened.

'Well, you booby,' he said, 'do you think you can tell me anything? Wasn't it I who whispered to the baroness that your parents might need money? For the time being those parents are you. Our funds are going down, and to dare some coup to procure more would be to risk in gaiety of heart our main affair. I will take care of the negotiation of the draft. At the same time, I hinted to the baroness that you needed some money to make a good show at the marriage, and it is arranged that from now until the ceremony you will have five hundred florins a month.'

In fact, I found this sum on my writing-desk the next day, as well as a coral toilet set and some jewels.

However, the birth certificate of Count B— (I had taken that name) did not arrive. The general wanted it, but he counted on fabricating the other documents. The blindness of the baroness may seem inconceivable to persons who are not in a position to know the extent of the credulity of dupes and the audacity of sharpers. She consented to marry me under the name of Rousseau. I had all the papers necessary for that. Only my father's consent was lacking, and nothing was easier than to procure that through Labbre whom we had under our thumbs. Although the baroness would have consented to marry me under a name she knew was not my own, it would have been repugnant to her to be in some way an accomplice to a forgery for which the only excuse was the need of saving my head.

While we were taking measures to get out of this embarrassment, we learned that the numbers of the rolling army had become so considerable in the conquered districts that the government had opened its eyes at last and had given the strictest orders for the repression of this abuse. We removed our uniforms in the belief that in this way we should have nothing to fear, but the inquiries became so active that the general had to leave the city abruptly and go to Namur. I explained this sudden departure to the baroness by saying that the general was uneasy at my serving under a false name. This incident disturbed her exceedingly on my account, and I could only quiet her by going to Breda, where she insisted on accompanying me.

My word must be accepted when I say that I was touched by such devotion. The voice of remorse, to which one is not entirely deaf at the age of nineteen, made me think; I saw the abyss into which I was going to drag an excellent woman who had shown herself so generous in my regard. I saw that she would soon repulse in horror the deserter, vagabond, bigamist, and forger, and this idea determined me to confess everything. Apart from those who had led me into this intrigue and who had just been arrested at Namur, my resolution grew the stronger.

One evening, just as supper was over, I decided to break the ice. Without going into details about my adventures, I told the baroness that circumstances which it was impossible for me to explain had driven me to appear at Brussels under the two names under which she had known me and which were not mine. I added that events compelled me to leave the Low Countries without being able to contract a union which would have made me happy, but that I should preserve forever the memory of the goodness which she had shown to me.

I talked a long time, and, carried away by my emotion, I talked with a warmth and an ease at which I have never ceased to be astonished when I think of it. It almost seemed as though I were afraid to listen to the reply of the baroness. Rigid, her cheeks pale, her eyes staring like a sleep-walker's, she listened without interruption. Then, looking at me with fright, she arose abruptly, and ran to shut herself in her room. I never saw her again.

Informed by my confession and by some words which without doubt escaped me in the emotion of the moment, she recognized the perils which threatened her, and in her just distrust she perhaps suspected me of being more guilty than I really was. It may be that she believed me some great criminal, even a murderer. On the other hand, if the complication of the disguises made her apprehensions the more lively, the spontaneous confession I had just made should have quieted her uneasiness. Probably the last idea dominated, for the next day, when I awoke, my host gave me a cash-box containing fifteen thousand francs in gold, which the baroness had given him for me before her departure at one o'clock in the morning. I learned this with pleasure, for her presence weighed upon me. Nothing held me at Breda; I packed, and some hours later I was on the road to Amsterdam.

My stay in Amsterdam was very short; I was anxious to see Paris. After I had cashed two drafts which were part of the money the baroness had left me, I started, and the second of March, 1796, I entered the capital where one day my name was to be of some report. Taking lodgings in the rue de l'Échelle, I busied myself at first in changing my ducats into French money and selling a heap of jewels and fancy things which were useless to me, as I intended to settle in some near-by city and enter some calling. I was not to realize my project.

One evening one of those gentlemen who are always around hotels to make the acquaintance of travellers proposed to take me to a gambling-house. Through lack of something to do I let him take me, trusting to my experience at the cafés in Brussels. I soon saw that the crooks in Brussels were only apprentices in comparison with the adepts with whom I was playing. Two sessions relieved me of a hundred louis, and I had enough of that.

But it was written that the baroness's money and I should soon part company. The agent of Destiny was a very pretty woman whom I met in a place where I ate. Rosine – that was her name – at first showed an exemplary indifference. I had been her lover for a month and it had cost me only some dinners, plays, carriages, laces, gloves, ribbons, flowers, and the like, things which cost nothing in Paris – if one does not pay for them.

More and more fascinated by Rosine, I never left her for a moment. One morning when I was at breakfast with her, I saw that she was worried. I questioned her, and she resisted my inquiries, but in the end she confessed that she was bothered by some bagatelles she owed her dressmaker and upholsterer. I eagerly offered my services, but she refused with remarkable magnanimity. I could not even obtain the addresses of the two creditors.

Most good people would have let the matter rest there, but like a real paladin I did not rest a moment until Divine, the maid, had given me the precious addresses. From rue Vivienne, where Rosine lived under the name of Madame de Saint-Michel, I hastened to the upholsterer, rue de Cléry. I announced the object of my visit, and I was at once overwhelmed with attentions, as is usual in such circumstances. I was given the account, which, to my consternation, amounted to twelve hundred francs. However, I had gone too far to withdraw; I paid. At the dressmaker's there was the same scene, and the same dénouement, at about a hundred francs.

That was enough to cool the most intrepid, but the final words had not been spoken. Some days after I had paid the creditors, I was brought to purchase jewels for two thousand francs, and parties of the same sort went on in the same style. I saw with confusion that my money was going, but I feared at that moment to verify my cash and postponed it from day to day. I got to it at last, and found that in two months I had dissipated the modest sum of fourteen thousand francs. This discovery led me seriously to reflect.

Rosine at once sensed my preoccupation. She guessed my finances were low; in this regard women have a feeling which rarely deceives them. Without exactly showing me coldness, she did use more reserve, and as I manifested my astonishment, she answered that she was bothered by 'special matters.' The trap was set, but I had been punished too well by my intervention in her affairs to mix in them again. I took refuge in an affected air and urged her to be patient. She became only the more sullen. Some days went by in this sulkiness; finally, the bomb burst.

As the result of an insignificant discussion, she told me, in a most impertinent tone, 'that she did not like to be crossed, and that those who didn't arrange matters so that she wasn't could stay at home.' This was plain speaking, and I was weak enough to pretend not to understand. New gifts brought me some days of tenderness, but I was not deceived. Then, in the knowledge of all ways in which she could use my blind infatuation, Rosine soon returned to the attack to get me to take up a bill of exchange of two thousand francs, which, if she did not pay, the penalty would be arrest. The idea of Rosine in prison was unbearable, and I was again going to sacrifice myself when chance brought a letter into my hands which opened my eyes.

The letter was from Rosine's 'dear friend' in Versailles, where he was confined. This interesting person asked 'when the booby would be sucked dry,' so that he could reappear on the scene. I had intercepted this agreeable message in the hands of the porter. I went to the house of the perfidious Rosine, but she had gone out. Furious and humiliated at the same time, I could not contain myself. I was in the bedroom, and with a kick I upset a table covered with porcelain and a cheval glass broke into bits. Divine, the maid, who had not lost me from sight, fell at my knees and begged me to interrupt an expedition which might cost me dear. I looked at her; I hesitated, and an element of common sense made me see that she might be right. I pressed her with questions. This poor girl, whom I had always found gentle and good, explained her mistress's whole conduct.

When Rosine met me, she had been without anyone for two months. In the belief that I was well off in view of the way I spent my money, she conceived the project of profiting by the circumstance. Her lover, whose letter I had surprised, had consented to go and live at Versailles until my money was finished. The bill of exchange which I had so generously paid was in her lover's name, and the bills of the dressmaker and upholsterer were also false.

As I was cursing my foolishness, I was astonished that the honest person who had fleeced me so well did not return. Divine told me that it was probable that the porter had warned her that I had the letter, and that she would not come back soon. This conjecture proved true. When she learned of the catastrophe which prevented her plucking the last feather from the bird, Rosine had gone to Versailles in a cab; we know whom she was going to join. The scraps she had left in the apartment were not worth the two months' rent which she owed, and the owner forced me to pay for the porcelain and the cheval glass on which I had wreaked my fury.

Such heavy blows had lessened my already depleted finances in no mean manner. Fourteen hundred francs was all that were left out of the baroness's ducats. I held in horror the capital which had been so fatal to me, and I resolved to regain Lille, where, as I knew the place, I should at least find resources which I had vainly sought in Paris.

IV
I ENCOUNTER THIEVES AND FORGERS

AS A PLACE in the war zone and as a frontier city, Lille offered great advantages to all like myself who were nearly certain to discover useful acquaintances either among the troops in the garrison or among that class of men who, with one foot in France and one in Belgium, really had no domicile in either country. I counted on all this to get me out of trouble, and my hopes were not deceived.

In the Thirteenth Chasseurs I met several officers of the Tenth, and among others a Lieutenant Villedieu, whom we shall meet again. All of these people had known me in the regiment under one of the names which one usually took for the war, as was the custom of the times. So they were not surprised to see me under the name of Rousseau. I passed days with them either in the cafés or in the fencing schools, but it was not very lucrative, and I saw myself on the point of being absolutely without money. Meanwhile, an habitué of the café, called Rentier on account of the regular life he led, who had several times offered me slight courtesies, of which he was very sparing with most people, spoke to me with interest of my affairs and proposed that I travel with him.

Travelling was fine, but in what state was the question. I was too old to hire out as a clown or chambermaid to monkeys and bears, and no one would probably have proposed it. However, it was well to know what to expect. I modestly questioned my new protector on the duties I should have to perform while I was with him.

'I'm a travelling doctor,' he said, 'and I treat secret diseases by an infallible recipe. I also undertake the cure of animals; and, very recently, I have healed the horses of the Thirteenth Squadron of Chasseurs which the regimental veterinary had given up.'

'Well,' I said to myself, 'another quack!'

But there was no drawing back. We arranged to start the next morning and to meet at five o'clock at the gate on the road to Paris.

I was prompt at the rendezvous. My man was, too. When he saw the box a porter was carrying, he told me that it was useless to take it, as he expected to be gone only three days, and that we were to travel on foot. Upon this observation I sent my things back to the inn, and we began to walk rather fast, as my guide told me that we had five leagues to make before noon. In fact, we arrived at that hour at an isolated farm, where he was received with open arms under the name of Caron, although I had always heard him called Christian.

After the exchange of some words, the master of the house went into a room and came back with some bags of crowns of six francs which he spread on the table. My employer took them and examined them one after another with an attention which I thought affected; then he put fifty aside and counted out a like sum to the farmer in different monies, plus a premium of six crowns. I did not understand this operation; besides, the negotiations were carried out in a Flemish patois which I only slightly comprehended. So I was exceedingly astonished when we left the farm, where Christian announced that he would soon return, to have him give me three crowns and tell me that I ought to have some part of the profits. I was not too sure where the profits lay and I made some comments to that effect. 'That's my secret,' he answered, with an air of mystery. 'Later you shall know, if I am pleased with you.' As I remarked that he was sure of my discretion since I knew nothing, unless he changed the crowns against other money, he told me that that was precisely what it was necessary to keep dark for fear of competition. I took that as he told it, and also the money without being too sure how things would turn out.

For four days we made similar excursions to different farms, and each evening I had two or three crowns. Christian, whom they called Caron, was well known in this part of Brabant, but only as a doctor, because, although he everywhere continued his changing operations, he never talked about anything except the illnesses of men or beasts. More and more I found that he had a reputation of raising spells cast on cattle.

A proposition he made me as we entered the village of Wervique should have initiated me into the secrets of his magic.

'Can I count on you?' he asked me, stopping suddenly.

'Without a doubt,' I answered; 'but still I must know what the question is.'

'Look and listen!'

Then he took out of a sort of game-bag four square parcels, like those wrapped up by a chemist, and which appeared to contain some specific.

'You see those four farms,' he said, 'situated some way apart. You are to go there, and get in by the rear, being careful that no one sees you. You will reach the stable or the barn, and throw into the mangers the powder from each package. Above all, take care that you aren't seen. I will attend to the rest.'

I made some objections: they might surprise me as I scaled the enclosure, or arrest me, or ask embarrassing questions. I flatly refused in spite of the prospect of crowns; all Christian's eloquence failed in the face of my resolution. I even told him that I would leave him that instant unless he told me his real trade and the mystery of the money-changing, which appeared to me terribly suspicious. This declaration seemed to embarrass him, and, as we shall soon see, he tried to get out of it by making me a half-confidence.

'My country,' he said, in reply to my last question, 'I have none. My mother who was hanged last year in Temes-war, belonged to a band of Bohemians who frequented the frontiers of Hungary when I was born in a village in the Carpathians. I call them Bohemians so that you will understand, for that is not our name; among ourselves our name is Romamichels, in an argot which we are forbidden to teach to anyone who is not one of us. It is equally forbidden to travel alone, so we are seen in troops of fifteen or twenty. We have exploited France for a long time in raising spells and curses; but today the trade is ruined. The peasant has become too sharp; we have been thrown back on Flanders where they are less strong-minded, and the diversity of the money allows us a good game to practice our trade... As for myself, I was detached from the band three months ago at Brussels for special business, but I have finished all that, and I shall rejoin the troop at Malines ... You are to see whether you want to accompany me. You can be useful to us, but no more childishness.'

Half-embarrassed to know what to believe, and half-curious to push the adventure to the end, I consented to follow Christian, although I was not too sure how I could be useful to him.

The third day we reached Malines; he had announced that we should return to Brussels from there. After we had crossed the city, we stopped in the Faubourg de Louvain, in front of a house of most deplorable aspect. The blackened walls were ploughed with deep cracks, and numerous bundles of straw replaced the broken glass in the windows. It was midnight; I had time to make my observations by the moonlight because we passed nearly half an hour in the front before one of the most horrible old women I have ever met came to open.

We were then introduced into a large hall, where thirty persons of both sexes were smoking and drinking in confusion, all mixed in together in sinister or licentious attitudes. Under their blue turbans, tattooed with red embroidery, the men wore coats of dark blue covered with silver buttons, like the Andalusian muleteers; all the women's garments were in striking colours; the faces were cruel, yet they were having a party. The monotonous sound of a drum, mingled with the barking of two dogs tied to the legs of a table, accompanied bizarre songs, which one might have taken for a funeral hymn. The tobacco and wood smoke which filled this cave hardly permitted one to see in the middle of the room a woman, her head covered by a scarlet turban, executing a savage dance and taking the most lascivious postures.

At our appearance the entertainment was interrupted. The men shook hands with Christian, and the women embraced him; then all eyes turned on me, to my embarrassment. I had heard a lot of stories of the Bohemians which did not reassure me. They might take umbrage at my scruples and despatch me, without anyone knowing what had happened since no one knew that I was in this retreat. My uneasiness became so lively that it struck Christian, who thought he would reassure me by telling me that we were with the 'Duchess' and that we were perfectly safe. Besides, my appetite decided me to take a part in the banquet. The pitcher of gin was filled and emptied so frequently that I felt the need of gaining my bed.

At the first word of this I said to Christian, he led me into a neighbouring room, where some of the Bohemians were already asleep in the fresh straw. I made no objection, but I could not help asking my employer why he, whom I had always seen take good lodgings, should choose such a bad sleeping-place. He answered that in all cities where there was a house of the Romamichels, they had to lodge there under the penalty of being considered false and punished as such by the tribal council. The women and children also shared this military couch, and the way they went to sleep at once announced that it was familiar to them.

At daybreak everyone was up and making a general toilet. Except for their pronounced features, their hair as black as jet, their oily and copper-coloured skin, I should hardly have recognized my companions of the evening before. The men, dressed as rich Dutch horse-traders, had leather money-bags around their waists. The women were covered with gold and silver jewellery and were in the costume of Zeeland peasants. Even the children whom I had seen dressed in rags were now properly clothed, and took on a new aspect.

Soon all left the house and took different directions so as not to reach the market-place together; a crowd from the neighbouring country was beginning to gather there. Seeing that I was thinking of following him, Christian told me that he did not need me that day and that I could go where I liked until evening when we should meet at the Duchess's. He then placed some crowns in my hand and disappeared.

As in our conversation in the evening he had told me that I was not obliged to lodge with the troop, I began by taking a bed in an inn. Then, not knowing how to kill time, I went to the fair. I had hardly made four rounds when I met face to face a former officer whom I had known at Brussels, named Malgaret, playing some suspicious games in the Café Turc. After the first compliments, he questioned me about the reasons for my stay in Malines. I told him a yarn; he made up another on the reasons for his journey, and we were both satisfied in the belief that we had fooled the other.

After some refreshments we went back to the fair, and in every place where there was a crowd I recognized some of the pensioners of the Duchess. As I had told my companion that I knew no one in Malines, I turned my head so that they could not recognize me. Besides, I did not care to confess that I had such acquaintances, but I was engaged with a fellow too wily not to be on the trail.

'There,' he said, looking at me meaningly, 'there are some folks who look at you most attentively. Do they by any chance know you?'

Without turning my head, I answered that I had never seen them, and I did not even know what they were.

'I'm going to tell you what they are,' my companion answered, 'supposing that you don't know. They are thieves!'

'Thieves!' I replied. 'What do you know about it?'

'What you are going to know yourself shortly, if you'll follow me, for I'll lay a large bet that we shall not go far without seeing them "work." Oh, look at that!'

Casting my eyes toward a group in front of a menagerie, in fact I saw distinctly one of the sham horse-traders take the purse of a cattle-breeder, who, a moment after, we saw search through all his pockets with the best faith. The Bohemian then entered a jeweller's shop, where there were already two of the counterfeit Zeelanders, and my companion assured me that he would not come out until he had pilfered some of the jewellery which they displayed before him.

We then left our post of observation to dine together. Toward the end of the meal, seeing that my table companion was disposed to gossip, I pressed him to tell me what the people were whom he had pointed out to me, assuring him that in spite of appearances I knew them only slightly. In the end he decided to tell me, and this is the explanation he gave:

'Some years ago I was in prison in Ghent for six months, as the result of a crooked game, and there I knew the two men of the band whom I have just seen in Malines; we were in the same room. As I passed for a consummate thief, they told me without the slightest distrust all their sleight-of-hand tricks, and they even gave me all possible details on their singular existence. They come from Moldavia, where there are some hundred and fifty thousand of them. Their name changes in every country. They are the Gypsies of England, the Zingari of Italy, the Gitanos of Spain, and the Bohemians of France and Belgium. So they run all over Europe practising the most abject or the most dangerous trades. They clip dogs, tell fortunes, mend crockery, tin, copper, play detestable music at tavern doors, speculate in rabbit skins, and change foreign money.

'They also sell specifics against the diseases of cattle, and to make trade better, they send in advance a confederate who, under the pretext of making purchases, gets into the stables and throws into the mangers drugs which make the animals ill. Then they appear; they are received with open arms, and, as they know the nature of the disease, they neutralize it easily, and the farmer doesn't know how to show his gratitude.

'And that's not all; before they leave the farm, they find out whether the owner hasn't some crowns of such and such a year, or of such and such an imprint, promising to buy them at a premium. The country-man is interested, as are all who only rarely and with difficulty find a chance to make money. The farmer rushes to display his specie, and they always find ways to pilfer a part. It is unbelievable, but they have been seen to pull off the same trick in the same house several times and escape punishment. And what is worse about the business, they profit by all these circumstances and their knowledge of the localities to point out to the bands of robbers the isolated farms where there is money and the ways to get in; it is needless to say that they get their part of the cake.'

Malgaret gave me still more details about the Bohemians, and I determined to leave such a dangerous society at once. He was still talk-ing, from time to time looking out into the street through the window by which we had dined. Suddenly I heard him cry, 'Gad, there's my man from Ghent!' I looked in my turn, and it was Christian, walking very fast and appearing very busy. I could not help exclaiming. Malgaret took advantage of the trouble his revelations had caused me, and had no difficulty in making me recount how I had become con-nected with the Bohemians. Seeing that I was determined to break company with them, he proposed that I accompany him to Courtrai, where he had, he said, some good games on.

After I had withdrawn from the inn the few effects I had brought from the Duchess's place, I started with my new associate. But at Courtrai we did not find the sort of fellows on whom Malgaret counted meeting, and instead of their money it was ours that went. We gave up hope of seeing them appear and went back to Lille. I still had a hun-dred francs. Malgaret played them for me and lost them with what he had left; I have since learned that he had arranged to fleece me with the man who played against him.

In this extremity I had recourse to my acquaintances; some fencing masters to whom I dropped a word about my position gave me a bene-fit match which brought me a hundred crowns. This sum put me out of want for some time, and I began to go about in the public places and to the balls. There I formed a liaison the consequences and results of which decided the fate of my whole life. Nothing was more simple than the beginning of this important episode in my history. At a ball I met a courtesan named Francine with whom I soon found myself on the best of terms. She seemed much attached to me; she was constantly protesting her fidelity, but that did not prevent her sometimes receiving secretly a captain of engineers.

I surprised them one day taking supper tête-à-tête at an eating-house on the Place Riourt. Carried away by rage, I fell on the amazed couple with heavy blows of my fists. Dishevelled as she was, Francine took flight, but her partner stayed, complained of the blows, and I was arrested and taken to prison – the Little Hotel.

While the affair was the subject of inquiry, I received visits from many women of my acquaintance who made it a duty to offer me consolation. Francine heard of this; her jealousy was aroused; she dismissed the disastrous captain; withdrew her complaint which she had made at the same time as he had; begged me to receive her, and I was weak enough to consent. The judges learned of it; they were exasperated, and represented the discomfiture of the captain as a trap concerted between me and Francine. The day of judgment came and I was sentenced to three months in prison.

From the Little Hotel they took me to Saint Peter's Tower, where I obtained a special room which they called the 'Bull's Eye.' Francine kept me company a part of the day, and the remainder of the time I spent with the rest of the prisoners. Among them were two former sergeant-majors, Grouard and Herbaux, the latter the son of a shoemaker at Lille, both condemned for forgery, and a farmhand named Boitel, sentenced to six years' confinement for stealing corn. The last was the father of a numerous family, and he constantly lamented his being taken away, he said, from the exploitation of his little property which he alone could make worth anything.

In spite of the crime of which he was guilty, people took an interest in him, or rather in his children, and several of the inhabitants of the commune had presented in his favour some demands for a commutation of sentence, but without result. The poor fellow was desperate, often repeating that he would give such and such a sum to buy his liberty. Grouard and Herbaux, who were waiting in Saint Peter's Tower for the departure of the chain gang, had the idea of obtaining his pardon by means of a memoir which they drew up in common, or rather they combined in longhand the plan which was so deadly to me.

Soon Grouard complained that he could not work quietly in the midst of the hubbub of the hall which he shared with eighteen or twenty prisoners who sang, chattered, or quarrelled all day. Boitel had rendered me some slight services and he asked me to lend my room to the editors; I consented, although with repugnance, and let them have it four hours a day. They were installed there the next day, and the jailer let them in several times secretly. These comings and goings and the mystery with which they surrounded them would have awakened the suspicions of a man familiar with prison intrigues. But as I was a stranger to all their ways, busy in diverting myself at the canteen with the friends who came to visit me, I concerned myself little with what was done in the Bull's Eye.

At the end of a week, they thanked me for my kindness, and announced that the memoir was finished, and that they had good hopes of obtaining the pardon of the petitioner without sending the papers to Paris, in the expectation that they could arrange for powerful protection from the representatives of the people at Lille. All that did not appear very clear to me, but, I paid no great attention, thinking that it was none of my concern and that I had no reason for uneasiness. However, it took a turn which triumphed over my heedlessness. Forty-eight hours had hardly elapsed after the memoir was finished, when two of Boitel's brothers arrived from the country on purpose to dine with him at the jailer's table. At the end of the meal an orderly came and gave a parcel to the jailer, who opened it and shouted, 'By Jove, good news! It is an order to release Boitel.' At these words they got up in an uproar, embraced, examined the order, congratulated each other, and Boitel, *who had sent out his things that evening*, left the prison immediately, without saying good-bye to any of the prisoners.

Toward ten o'clock the next morning the inspector of prisons came to visit the place; the jailer showed him the order to release Boitel. He only glanced at it and said that the order was a forgery, and refused to let the prisoner go until it had been referred to the authorities. The jailer then announced that Boitel had gone the evening before. The inspector expressed his astonishment that he should have been taken in by an order with signatures he did not know, and ended by discharging him.

He then went away with the order and soon became sure that, independently of the false signatures, it presented omissions and mistakes in wording of such a nature as to strike anyone the least familiar with that sort of papers.

The prison soon knew that the inspector had discharged the jailer for letting Boitel out on a forged order, and I began to suspect the truth. I wanted to force Grouard and Herbaux to tell me the whole story, foreseeing in a confused way that this affair might compromise me. They swore by all their gods that they had drawn up nothing but the memoir, and that they themselves were surprised at such a prompt success. I did not believe a word of it, but as I had no proofs to oppose to what they advanced, I could only await the event.

The next day I was ordered to the clerk's office. In reply to the questions of the examining magistrate, I answered that I knew nothing about the making of the forged order, and that I had only lent my room as the one quiet place in the prison for the preparation of the memoir of justification. I added that all these details could be attested by the jailer, who frequently came into the room during the work, and who seemed to be greatly interested in Boitel. Grouard and Herbaux were also questioned, and then put in solitary confinement; I kept my room. I had hardly got back to it when one of Boitel's comrades came to me and told me the whole intrigue, which until then I had only suspected.

Grouard had heard Boitel constantly repeating that he would be willing to give a hundred crowns to obtain his liberty, and in concert with Herbaux, he devised a means to get him out of prison. The only way they found was to make a forged order. Boitel was taken as he thought, into their confidence, only they told him that there were several persons to win over, and he gave them four hundred francs. It was then that they asked me for the loan of my room, which was indispensable for making the forged order without being seen by the other prisoners. The jailer was then taken into their confidence, judging from his frequent visits and by the circumstances which preceded and followed the escape of Boitel. The order had been brought by a friend of Herbaux, by the name of Stofflet. In addition, it appeared that to induce Boitel to give the four hundred francs, the forgers had persuaded him that they shared with me, although all the service I rendered was the loan of my room.

When I was told of all this, I first wanted to get my informant to make a declaration of these details; but he refused obstinately, saying that he did not want to reveal to justice a secret given him under oath, and, besides, he did not want to be beaten to death sooner or later by the prisoners for having given them away. He even dissuaded me from telling the magistrate, assuring me that I ran not the slightest danger. However, they arrested Boitel in the country; he was brought back to Lille and put in solitary confinement. He named, as having been concerned in his escape, Grouard, Herbaux, Stofflet, and – Vidocq. On this confession we were questioned in turn, and, strengthened by prison advice, I persisted in my first declaration, while I could have got out of the affair instantly by deposing all that I had learned from Boitel's comrade. I was so convinced that no serious charge could be brought against me that I was dumbfounded, when I wanted to get out at the expiration of my three months, to find myself accused in the records as detained for complicity in forging authentic and public writings.

V
I See Much of Prison Cells

I NOW BEGAN to suspect that all this would end badly for me; but a retraction which could not be supported by proofs would be no more dangerous than a silence which it was too late to think of breaking. I was so disturbed by these ideas that I became ill, but Francine nursed me with every care. I was hardly convalescent, when, unable to bear longer the state of uncertainty about the issue of my case, I determined to escape, and escape through the gate, although that may appear rather difficult. Certain observations determined me to choose this way in preference to any other.

The turnkey of Saint Peter's Tower was a forger sentenced to life imprisonment at Brest. When the sentences were revised in accordance with the Code of 1791, he received a commutation to six years in the prisons of Lille, where he made himself useful to the doorkeeper. The latter was persuaded that a man who had passed four years in the hulks was an eagle in surveillance, since he must know all the ways there were to escape, so he promoted him to the duties of turnkey and thought he could not obtain a better. However, it was on the ineptitude of this prodigy of finesse that I counted for success in my project, and it seemed to me that he would be the easier to deceive in that he had the greatest confidence in his own perspicacity. In a word, I planned to pass in front of him in the uniform of an officer who had to visit the Tower of Saint Peter's twice a week, and who served a military prison as well.

I was seeing Francine nearly every day, and she made me the necessary clothes which she brought in her muff. I tried them on; they fitted me marvellously. Some of the prisoners who saw me in this costume assured me that it was impossible for the turnkey not to mistake me for the officer. It is true I was about the same height as the officer whose role I was going to play, and my make-up aged me by twenty-five years. In a few days the officer came to make his ordinary rounds. While one of my friends kept him busy on the pretext of examining his ailments, I hastily disguised myself and presented myself at the gate. The turnkey pulled his cap to me, opened the gate, and there I was in the street. I rushed to Francine's, where I had arranged to go in case of escape, and she soon came to join me.

Here I was almost entirely safe if I could bring myself to stay hidden. But how could I endure slavery nearly as hard as that of Saint Peter's? I had been shut up within four walls for three months, and I had to expend the activity held in check so long. I announced my intention of going out, and as my iron will was an auxiliary of my most bizarre fantasies, I went out. My first excursion succeeded. The next day, as I was crossing the rue Écrémoise, a policeman named Louis, who had seen me during my detention, met me and asked if I was free. He had the reputation of being a bad customer; besides, at a gesture he could summon twenty to help him ... I told him that I was willing to follow him, but I begged him to let me say good-bye to my mistress who was in a house in the rue de l'Hôpital. He consented, and we found Francine there, much surprised to see me in such company. I told her that on reflection I had decided that my escape would do me injury with the judges and that I had concluded to return to Saint Peter's Tower to await the result of the case.

At first Francine did not understand how I could have spent three hundred francs merely to return to prison after three months of it. A signal put her in touch with the facts, and I even found means to tell her to put some ashes in my pocket, while Louis and I drank a glass of rum. Then we took our way to the prison. When my guide and I reached an empty street, I blinded him with my handful of ashes and regained my refuge with all speed.

Louis made a declaration of the facts, and they set on my heels all the police and constables, under a commissioner named Jacquard, who promised to take me if I had not left the city. I was ignorant of none of these dispositions, but instead of showing a little circumspection in my procedure, I affected the most ridiculous bravado. One would have thought that I would have profited by the certain promise of arrest. However, I was pursued vigorously, as we shall see.

One day Jacquard learned that I was going to dine in a house in the rue Notre Dame. He hurried there at once with four policemen. He left them on the ground floor and went up to the room where I was sitting down at table with two women. A recruiting quartermaster was to make the fourth, but he had not arrived. I recognized the commissioner, but he had not the same advantage, as he had never seen me. Besides, my disguise would have foiled all the descriptions in the world. I was not disturbed, but I approached him in the most natural manner, and asked him to go into a closet which had a glass door overlooking the banquet room.

'You are looking for Vidocq?' I then said to him. 'If you will wait ten minutes, I will show him to you. There is his cover, and he can hardly be long. When he comes in, I'll signal to you; but if you are alone, I doubt whether you will succeed in taking him, for he is armed and determined to defend himself.'

'My men are on the stairs,' he said, 'and if he escapes...'

'Take care not to leave them there,' I answered, with pretended earnestness. 'If Vidocq sees them, he will suspect some trap, and then good-bye to the bird.'

'But where shall I leave them?'

'Oh, by Jove, in this closet. But above all, no noise, or all will fail, and I have more interest than you that he should be in the jug.'

My commissioner clapped his men and himself in the closet. The solid door was closed with a double lock. Then, sure of getting away in time, I shouted to my prisoners:

'You're looking for Vidocq. Well, Vidocq put you in the cage. Au revoir!'

And I was gone in a flash, leaving the troop to shout for help, and make unheard-of efforts to get out of the unfortunate closet.

Two other escapades of the same kind succeeded, but I ended by being arrested and taken back to Saint Peter's Tower, where for greater safety they put me in a dark cell with a certain Calendrin, who was undergoing punishment for two attempts to escape. Calendrin had known me during my first stay in prison, and at once made me a party to a new attempt to escape by means of a hole made in a wall of the cells of convicts with whom we were able to communicate. The third night of my new detention, the plan of departure was put into execution. Eight of the convicts who went out first were so fortunate as not to be seen by the officer stationed only a short distance away.

There were seven of us left. We drew straws, as is the custom on such an occasion, to see who should pass the first. Chance favoured me, and I undressed to slip through the opening the more easily, for it was very narrow. But to the great disappointment of everyone, I got stuck in such a way that I could neither go ahead nor draw back. It was in vain that my companions tried to pull me out by my arms; I was caught as though I were in a vice, and the pain of my position became so sharp that, as there was no hope of help from inside, I called the officer to get help from him. He approached with all the precautions of a man who fears a surprise, and, placing a bayonet against my breast, he forbade me to make the slightest movement. At his cries the post ran to arms, the turnkeys hurried with torches, and I was drawn out of my hole, but not without leaving many bits of skin and flesh. Bruised as I was, they immediately put me into the Little Hotel, where I was placed in a dungeon with irons on my hands and feet.

I came out after ten days as a result of my pleas and promises to give up all attempts at escape. I was placed with the other prisoners. Until this time I had lived with men who were far from being irreproachable – crooks, thieves, and counterfeiters; but now I was mixed in with the most consummate rascals. Among them was a compatriot of mine named Desfosseux, a man of singular intelligence and prodigious strength who had been sentenced to hard labor at the age of eighteen, and had escaped from the galleys three times, where he was to be returned with the first chain gang. One should have heard him telling his exploits to the convicts, and calmly saying that some day the guillotine might make his skin and flesh into sausages.

In spite of the secret fear with which this man at first inspired me, I liked to question him about his strange profession, and what led me to mark him out particularly was the hope that he would procure me means of escape. For the same reason I became close with several others who were part of a band of forty or fifty ruffians who ran about the neighbouring country under the orders of the famous Sallambier. Presented by such a distinguished practitioner of crime as my compatriot Desfosseux, I was received with open arms in this circle of bandits, where from morning till night they did nothing but plot new ways of escape. But our guards knew with what sort of men they had to deal, and they watched with such care that they foiled all plans.

The only occasion which assured success offered itself at last, and I grasped it before my companions, sharp as they were, had even thought of it. About eighteen of us had been taken in to be questioned. We were in the judge's anteroom guarded by soldiers and two gendarmes, one of whom laid his hat and coat near me to enter the bar of justice. His companion soon followed, summoned by a bell. I immediately put the hat on my head, wrapped myself in the coat, and, taking one of the convicts by the arm as if I were taking him somewhere, I presented myself at the gate. The corporal of the guard opened the gate, and there we were outside. But what were we to do without money or papers? My comrade escaped into the country. At the risk of being recaptured, I returned to Francine's, who, in the joy of seeing me again, decided to sell the household goods and to fly with me to Belgium. This resolution was carried out. We were about to start when the most unexpected incident, and one which only my inconceivable carelessness could explain, overwhelmed me.

At dark the evening of our departure, I met a woman from Brussels, named Elisa, with whom I had been intimate. She fell on my neck, took me to supper, and, overcoming a weak resistance, kept me with her till the next morning. I pretended to Francine, who had sought me everywhere, that to throw the police off my tracks I had been forced to dash into a house, and I could not get out until daylight. At first she believed me; but chance led her to discover that I had passed the night with a woman, and her boundless jealousy burst into cutting reproaches for my ingratitude. In her excess of rage she swore that she would have me arrested. Having me put in prison was certainly the safest way to assure herself against my infidelities. As Francine was a woman to do what she said she would, I deemed it prudent to leave her until her anger had cooled and it would be safe to reappear in course of time to go with her as we had arranged. However, I needed some of my things, and as I did not want to ask her for them for fear of another explosion, I went alone to the apartment we occupied, to which she had the key. I forced the lock, took what was necessary, and disappeared.

Five days passed; dressed as a peasant, I left the refuge I had chosen in the suburbs; I entered the city and presented myself at the house of a dressmaker who was an intimate friend of Francine's. I counted upon using her mediation to obtain a reconciliation. This woman received me with such an air of embarrassment that, for fear of compromising her, I only asked her to go in search of my mistress.

'Yes,' she said, with a most extraordinary air, and without looking directly at me. She went out. Left by myself, I reflected on this singular reception.

Someone knocked. I opened, thinking to receive Francine in my arms – and there was a crowd of gendarmes and police who fell on me, seized me, and took me before a magistrate who began by asking me where I had been for the past five days. My answer was short; I had never compromised anyone who had received me. The magistrate observed that my obstinacy in refusing to give any explanation might be disastrous, might cost me my head, etc., etc. I only laughed, in the belief that in this phrase he was manœuvring to extract admissions from the prisoner by intimidating him. I persisted in my silence, and they took me back to the Little Hotel.

I had hardly put foot in the courtyard before all eyes were fixed on me. They called to me; they whispered in my ear; I thought that my disguise was the cause of all the commotion, and I paid no attention. They made me mount to a cell where I was alone on the straw, with irons on my feet. At the end of two hours the warder appeared, who, feigning to be sorry for me and to take an interest in me, insinuated that my refusal to declare where I had spent the last five days might injure me in the minds of the judges. I was immovable.

Again two hours went by; the warder reappeared with a turnkey, who removed my irons and made me descend to the office, where two judges awaited me. A new interrogation; the same response. They undressed me from head to foot, and they applied superabundantly blows on my right shoulder which would have killed an ox in order to make the mark reappear in case I had ever been branded. My clothes were taken away, described in the report and deposited in the office, and I went back to my cell clad in a canvas shirt, half-gray, half-black, in tatters, and which might have been used by two generations of prisoners.

All this gave me food for thought. It was obvious that the dressmaker had denounced me, but what was the reason? This woman had no ground of complaint against me; in spite of her fits of passion, Francine would have looked twice before denouncing me; and if I had withdrawn for a few days, it was really less from fear than to avoid irritating her by my presence. Besides, why these repeated interrogations, these mysterious phrases of the warder, and this deposit of my garments? I was lost in a maze of conjectures. While I waited, I was in the strictest confinement, and I stayed there twenty-five mortal days. Then I had to undergo the following questioning, which put me on the track.

'What is your name?'

'Eugène François Vidocq.'

'What is your profession?'

'Soldier.'

'Do you know the girl Francine Longuet?'

'Yes, she is my mistress.'

'Do you know where she is at this moment?'

'She must be with one of her friends, as she has sold her furnishings.'

'What is the name of this friend?'

'Madame Bourgeois.'

'Where does she live?'

'Rue Saint-André, the baker's house.'

'How long had you left this girl Longuet when you were arrested?'

'Five days.'

'Why had you left her?'

'To avoid her anger. She knew I had passed the night with another woman, and in a fit of jealousy, she threatened to have me arrested.'

'Who was the woman with whom you passed the night?'

'A former mistress.'

'What was her name?'

'Elisa – I never knew her other name.'

'Where does she live?'

'In Brussels, where she has, I think, returned.'

'Where are the things which you had at the girl Longuet's?'

'In a place which I will show you, if there is need.'

'Having quarrelled with her, and not wanting to see her, how could you get them back?'

'As a result of our quarrel in the café where she had met me, she threatened at every moment to summon the guard to arrest me. Knowing her quick temper, I went by back streets and gained the house; she had not come back; that is what I counted on, but, as I needed some things, I forced the lock to enter the apartment where I took what was necessary. Just now you asked me where my things were; now I am going to tell you; they are in rue Saint-Sauveur, at the house of a man called Duboc, who will so depose.'

'You are not telling the truth. Before you left Francine *at her home*, you had a lively quarrel. We are assured that you rained blows on her.'

'That is false. I have not seen Francine at her house since the quarrel; consequently I have not mistreated her. She can tell you.'

'Do you recognize this knife?'

'Yes, it is the one I usually use to eat with.'

'Do you see that the blade and handle are covered with blood? Doesn't this sight make any impression on you? You are troubled?'

'Yes,' I answered, in my agitation, 'but what happened to Francine? Tell me, and I will give you all possible explanations.'

'Did nothing special happen when you went to get your things?'

'Absolutely nothing; at least that I can recall.'

'Then you persist in your declaration?'

'Yes.'

'You are imposing upon justice. To give you time to reflect on your position and on the results of your obstinacy, I suspend the interrogation; I will take it up again tomorrow. Officers, watch this man carefully. Go!'

It was late when I returned to my cell; they brought my rations, but the agitation into which the examination had thrown me was so great that I could not eat; it was also impossible for me to sleep, and I passed the night without closing an eye. A crime had been committed, but by whom? By whom? Why did they impute it to me? I had asked myself that question for the thousandth time, without being able to find any reasonable solution, when they came to get me the next day to continue the examination.

After the usual questions, a door opened, and two officers entered supporting a woman. It was Francine – Francine, pale, disfigured, and hardly recognizable When she saw me, she fainted. I wanted to approach her, but the officers held me back. They took her away. I remained alone with the magistrate, who asked me if the presence of that unfortunate woman did not determine me to confess all. I protested my innocence, assuring him that until the present moment I had been ignorant of Francine's illness. They led me back to prison; but the secret was laid bare, and at last I could hope that I should know in all its details the event of which I was so singularly the victim. I questioned the warder; he remained dumb. I wrote to Francine; they warned me that the letters I addressed to her would be stopped at the office. They also told me at the same time that she would not see me.

I was on burning coals; at last I decided to ask for a lawyer, who, after he had read the documents, told me that I was detained for the attack on Francine. The very day I had left her, they had found her bathed in blood, apparently dying, and stabbed with five blows of a knife. My precipitate departure; the removal of my things, which they knew I had transported from one place to another, as if to protect myself against the pursuit of justice, the breaking of the lock of the apartment, the traces of scaling the wall which bore my marks, all tended to mark me as the guilty culprit. My disguise also deposed against me. They thought that I had come disguised to assure myself that she had died without accusing me. One fact, which would have turned to my advantage in any other circumstances, increased the weight of the charges against me. As soon as the doctors allowed her to talk, Francine had declared that she had stabbed herself in despair at seeing herself abandoned by a man for whom she had made every sacrifice. But her attachment for me made her testimony suspect. They were convinced that she held her tongue to save me.

My lawyer had stopped talking for a quarter of an hour; I had listened like a man in a nightmare. At the age of twenty I found myself under the double accusation of forgery and attempted murder, without having participated in either crime! I almost went mad. I ended, however, in doing my best to get together all the facts necessary for my justification. In the examinations which followed those which I have reported, they laid emphasis on the blood which the messenger I had hired to move my things asserted covered my hands. This blood came from a cut I got in breaking the glass to get at the lock, and I could bring two witnesses to support my assertion. My lawyer, to whom I told everything for my defence, assured me that, combined with Francine's declaration, which by itself had no weight, the dismissal of the complaint was certain, which in fact happened a few days later.

Although she was still very weak, Francine came to see me and confirmed all the details the examination had brought to light.

So I was rid of a tremendous weight, without being entirely free
from uneasiness. My repeated escapes had delayed the matter of the forgery in which I was implicated, and nothing indicated an end to it. The
result of the accusation in which I had just triumphed, however, gave
me some hope, and my only thought was of escape when an occasion
offered which I seized almost instinctively. In the room where they had
placed me were two men held in detention; in coming to deliver some
correspondence to the two one morning, the warder neglected to close
the gate. I noticed it, and to descend to the ground floor and examine
everything took but a moment.

Day was just breaking, and the prisoners were all asleep. I met no
one on the stairs, nor was anyone at the gate; I passed through, but a
warder, who was drinking absinthe in the pub opposite, saw me and
started in pursuit, shouting at the top of his lungs, 'Stop! Stop!' He
might well shout, for the streets were deserted, and the hope of liberty
gave me wings. In a few moments I was out of the warder's sight, and I
soon arrived at a house in the quarter of Saint-Sauveur, where I was
sure they would never think of hunting for me. On the other hand, I
had to leave Lille with the greatest speed, for I was too well known
there to be able to remain long in safety.

At nightfall they were on the hunt, and I learned that the gates had
been closed. One could only go out through the wicket, and they had
placed policemen in disguise to observe everyone who appeared. Unable
to go out by the gates, I decided to escape by descending the ramparts.
As I knew the place perfectly, at ten o'clock in the evening I went to the
bastion Notre Dame which I considered the most favourable place for
my project. I made fast to a tree a rope I had bought for the purpose,
and let myself slide down. Soon the weight of my body gave me more
speed than I had calculated on, and the friction so burned my hands
that I had to let go when I was still fifteen feet from the ground. As I
fell, I sprained my right foot so badly that when I attempted to get out
of the moat, I believed that I should never make it. Finally, by tremendous efforts, I reached the pavement.

There I was, swearing eloquently against the moat, the rope, and
the sprain, which did little to get me out of the fix, when a man passed

with one of those barrows which are so common in Flanders. A crown, the only one I had and which I offered him, decided him to load me on the barrow and take me to the neighbouring village. When we reached his house, he placed me on a bed, and hurried to rub my leg with soap and brandy. His wife helped him as best she could, looking with some astonishment at my clothes, which were covered with mud from the moat. They asked for no explanation, but I realized that I had to give one, and to prepare it, I feigned a great need of rest, and asked them to leave me a moment.

Two hours later I called them as if I had just waked, and told them in a few words that, in lifting some contraband tobacco onto the ramparts, I had fallen, and that my comrades, pursued by the customs officers, had had to leave me in the moat. I added that I placed my fate in their hands. These good people, who detested the customs officers as cordially as any inhabitant of any frontier, assured me that they would not betray me for all the world. To sound them out, I asked whether there was not some way I could be carried to my father's house, who lived in the opposite direction. They answered that that would be running a risk, and that it would be better to wait some days until I was in a better state. I consented; to avert all suspicions, it was agreed that I should pass as a relative who was paying a visit. However, no one made the slightest comment.

Resting easy on this score, I began to consider my affairs and the course I should pursue. Obviously I must leave the country and go to Holland. However, to execute this project money was indispensable, and, besides my watch which I offered to my host, I was in command of four francs, ten sous. I could have recourse to Francine, but they could not fail to spy on her, and to address her the slightest message was to lose all. At least I had to wait until the first ardour of the pursuit had cooled down. I waited.

Two weeks passed, and I finally decided to write to Francine; I charged my host with the task of delivering the letter, and told him that this woman served as a go-between with the smugglers, and he should only see her secretly. He fulfilled his mission perfectly, and came back that evening with a hundred and twenty francs in gold. The next day I took leave of my hosts, whose charges were exceedingly modest. Six days later I reached Ostend.

My intention, as on my first voyage to that city, was to go to America or the Indies, but I found only coasters from Denmark or Hamburg, who refused to take me without papers. However, the little money I had brought from Lille was exhausted in the twinkling of an eye, and I was about to find myself again in one of those positions to which one can adjust himself, more or less, but which are none the less disagreeable.

I had often heard of the adventurous and lucrative life of the smugglers on the coast; some of the prisoners had even praised it with enthusiasm, for the trade often becomes a passion, even with individuals who from their fortune or position ought to avoid such a perilous career. As for myself, I confess that I was not attracted by the prospect of passing whole nights at the edge of cliffs, among the rocks, exposed to all the winds, and, in addition, to the shots of the customs officers.

It was with real repugnance that I directed my path to the house of a man named Peters, who had been pointed out to me as one who plied this trade and who could hire me. A seagull with outstretched wings nailed to the door made the domicile easy to recognize. I found the boss in a sort of cellar, which, with the cables, sails, anchors, hammocks, and casks which encumbered it, might have been taken for the between-decks of a ship. He looked at me, through the thick atmosphere of smoke which surrounded him, with a sort of distrust which seemed to me an evil omen. My presentiments were soon realized, for hardly had I offered my services than he fell on me with heavy blows of a club. I certainly could have resisted advantageously, but my astonishment in some way took away all idea of defending myself. Besides, I saw in a court half a dozen sailors and an enormous Newfoundland dog who might have given me a bad time. Thrown out into the street, I sought some explanation of this singular reception, when the idea struck me that Peters might have taken me for a spy and treated me accordingly.

This thought decided me to return to a gin-dealer's in whom I had inspired sufficient confidence so that he might indicate some resource. He began by laughing at my mishap, and ended by communicating a password which should give me free access to Peters. Armed with these instructions, I made my way again to the redoubtable domicile, after I had filled my pockets with stones. In case of a new attack they might serve to protect my retreat.

Fortunately, these munitions proved needless. At the words, 'Beware of the Customs,' I was received in an almost friendly manner, for my quickness and strength made me a precious object in that profession where one is often obliged to transport heavy goods in a hurry. A fellow from Bordelais who formed a part of the troop was told off to mould me and to teach me the tricks of the trade. But I was called to exercise them before my education was far advanced.

I slept at Peters's with twelve or fifteen smugglers, Dutch, Danish, Swedish, Portuguese, and Russian; there were no English and only two Frenchmen. The night after my installation, just as each of us was going to his trucklebed or hammock, Peters suddenly entered the bedroom, which was merely a cellar next to his, and so filled with barrels and bales that we could hardly find room to hang the hammocks. Peters had left off his ordinary costume of a caulker or sail-maker. With a fur cap and a red woollen shirt, fastened by a silver pin, he wore a pair of great fishing boots, which reached to his hips or could be lowered at will to his knees.

'Up, up!' he shouted at the door, striking the ground with the butt of his carbine. 'Clear the decks!!! Clear the decks!!! We will sleep another day. They have signalled the *Écureuil* for the night tide. We must see what she has in her hold – muslin or tobacco. Up, up! Come, my sea-hogs!'

In the twinkling of an eye everyone was up. A box of arms was opened, each one furnished himself with a carbine or a blunderbuss, two pistols, and a cutlass or a boarding hatchet, and we went, after we had drunk several glasses of brandy or arrack. At that moment the troop was made up of only twenty men; but we were joined or awaited at one place or another by separate individuals, so that when we reached the seashore we were forty-seven in number, not counting two women and some peasants from neighbouring villages, who had brought their draft horses and hidden them in a hollow between the rocks.

Night had shut in; the wind veered at every moment, and the sea broke with such strength that I did not understand how any vessel could approach without being dashed ashore. What confirmed this idea was that by the light of the stars I saw a small vessel running along the shore as if she feared to land. Since then it has been explained to me that the only purpose of this manœuvre was to assure that all preparations for landing had been made, and that there was no danger. In fact Peters lighted a dark lantern which he gave to one of us to hold, and extinguished it at once. The *Écureuil* raised a lantern to her topmast which merely shone and disappeared like a firefly in summer. Then we saw her come in with the wind astern and heave to within gunshot of the place where we were.

Our troop then divided into three squads, of which two were placed five hundred yards in advance to hold the customs officers if they took a fancy to appear. The squads were then spaced out, and they had attached to their left arm a string which ran from one man to the next. In case of alarm they would give warning by a slight pull; and each one was ordered to answer the signal by a shot, so a fusillade would extend down the line which could not fail to disturb the officers. The third squad, of which I was a member, remained on the shore to protect the landing and to give help with the cargo.

When all these arrangements were completed, the Newfoundland dog, of which I have spoken, and which was with the company, at a command jumped into the whitecaps and swam vigorously in the direction of the *Écureuil*. An instant after we saw him reappear, holding the end of a cable in his mouth. Peters seized it and began to pull it to him, signalling us to help him. I obeyed the order mechanically. At the end of some fathoms I saw that there were attached to the cable a dozen small casks which floated in to us. I then understood that in this way the vessel avoided getting near the land and running the risks of the breakers.

In an instant the casks, which were wrapped up in a way to make them waterproof, were detached and loaded on horses which were at once evacuated to the interior. A second convoy met with the same success, but at the very moment we received the third, shots announced that the outposts were attacked.

'That's the start of the ball,' said Peters quietly. 'We'll have to see who will dance.' And taking his carbine he joined the advance posts. The firing became heavy; it cost us two men killed and several slightly wounded. From the fire of the customs officers, it was easy to see that

they were our superiors in numbers; but they were frightened and suspected an ambush, so they did not come near us, and we effected our
retreat without their making the slightest attempt to trouble us. At the
start of the fight, the *Écureuil* had raised anchor and gained the open
sea in fear that the firing would attract the government cruiser to that
quarter. They told me that she would probably finish landing her cargo
at another point on the coast, where the shippers had numerous corre-
spondents.

When I got back to Peters's place about daybreak, I threw myself
into a hammock, and came out of it only at the end of forty-eight
hours. The night's labour, the dampness which constantly penetrated
my clothes, while the exercise made me perspire at the same time, all
combined to lay me low. A fever took me. When it was over, I told
Peters that I had decided that the trade was too hard, and that I should
be glad if he would let me go. He took it more quietly than I had
expected, and gave me a hundred francs. I learned later that he had had
me followed for several days to assure himself that I took the road to
Lille, where I had said I was going.

In fact, I did take the road to that city, tormented by a childish
desire to see Francine again and to take her with me to Holland, where
I projected a small establishment. But my imprudence was soon punished. Two gendarmes who were drinking in a pub saw me crossing the
road; and the idea of running after me to see if I had any papers struck
them. They joined me at the turn of a street; the agitation which my
face showed at their appearance decided them to arrest me. They put
me in the local jail. I was already seeking means of escape when I heard
one of the two gendarmes say, 'There's the *correspondance* from Lille. Is
there anyone to go?' In fact, two men from the troop at Lille arrived in
front of the jail and asked if there was any *game*. 'Yes,' answered the
men who had arrested me. 'We have one named Leger [I had taken that
name], whom we found without papers.' They opened the door, and
the sergeant from Lille, who had often seen me at the Little Hotel,
cried, 'Oh, by Jove, it's Vidocq!'

I had to agree. I went, and some hours later, I entered Lille between
my two guards.

VI
ESCAPES ARE IN VAIN

AT THE LITTLE HOTEL I found most of the prisoners whom I had seen set at liberty before my escape. Some of them had had but a short holiday, so to speak. They were either arrested under the prevention of crimes act or for new misdemeanours. One of this number was Calendrin of whom I have spoken before; released on the eleventh, he was back on the fourteenth, accused of burglary and of complicity with the bandits or *chauffeurs,* whose name alone then inspired a general fright. On the reputation which my different escapes had gained me, these people sought me out as a man on whom they could count. For my part I could hardly get away from them. If they were accused of major crimes, they had a powerful interest in keeping our attempts secret, while the poor fellows arrested for a simple misdemeanour might denounce us in fear of finding themselves compromised in our escape; such is the logic of prisons.

However, to escape was not easy. One can gather this from the description of our cells: seven feet square; the walls over six feet thick, lined with planks crossed and bolted with iron; closed by three gratings one after the other, and a double door of wrought iron. With such precautions the jailer might think his boarders were safe, but we put his watchfulness at fault.

I was in one of the cells of the second tier with a man named Duharnel. For six francs, a prisoner, who served as turnkey, furnished us with two saws, a cold chisel, and two levers. We had tin spoons; probably the jailer did not know the use prisoners might make of them. I knew the key to the cells; the same key was used for all on the same row. I made a model out of a large carrot; then I made a mould out of a bit of bread and some potatoes. We needed fire, and we obtained it by making a lamp with a bit of lard and some rags from a cotton cap. Finally, the key was cast in tin; but it did not work, and it was only after several attempts and numerous retouchings that it served.

Thus, masters of the doors, we then had to make a hole in the wall next to the lofts in the Town Hall. A man named Sallambier occupied the last of the cells in the row and he found a way to make a hole by cutting one of the planks. Everything was ready for the escape; it was to take place that very evening, when the jailer came to tell me that my time in the cells had expired and that I was to be placed with the other prisoners.

Never perhaps was a favour received with less enthusiasm than that one. I saw all my preparations lost, and I should have to wait a long time for such a favourable circumstance. However, I had to follow the jailer, who with all his congratulations I sent to the Devil. This *contretemps* affected me so much that all the prisoners noticed it. One of them succeeded in getting the secret of my dismay from me, and made some very just comments on the danger I ran in fleeing with such men as Sallambier and Duhamel, who might not let twenty-four hours pass without committing a murder. At the same time he made me promise to let them go and to wait until another occasion presented itself. I followed his advice and found it good. I even took such precaution that I told Duhamel and Sallambier that they were suspected and that they had not a moment to lose if they would escape. They took the advice literally, and two hours after, they went to rejoin a band of forty-seven *chauffeurs,* twenty-eight of whom were executed during the following month at Bruges.

The escape of Duhamel and Sallambier made a great noise in the prison and even in the city. They considered the circumstances altogether extraordinary; but what was most surprising to the jailer was that I had no part in it. However, it was necessary to repair the damage; workmen arrived, and at the bottom of the stairs to the tower they placed a sentinel with orders to let no one pass, no matter who he was. I was struck by the idea of breaking this order, cleverly, and to get out by the same hole which should have served in my flight.

Francine came to see me every day, and she brought me three lengths of tri-coloured ribbon which I expressly sent her to get. From one bit I made a belt, and I decorated my hat with the rest. Decked out in this way, I passed in front of the sentinel, who took me for an officer of the municipality and presented arms. I climbed the stairs rapidly, reached the opening, and found it guarded by two sentinels, one placed in the loft of the Town Hall and the other in the prison corridor. I told the latter that it was impossible that a man could have passed through that opening; he held to the contrary, and as though I had put the words in his mouth, his comrade added that I could go through with my clothes on. I showed a desire to try, and I slipped through the opening, and there I was in the loft. Pretending that I had hurt myself in the passage, I told the two men that since I was on this side, I was going down to my office at once.

'In that case,' answered the man who was in the loft, 'wait till I open the door'; in fact, he turned the key in the lock. In two jumps I was down the stairs of the Town Hall and in the street, still decorated with my tri-coloured ribbons, which would have got me arrested again if the daylight had not been fading.

I was hardly outside when the jailer, who never lost me from sight, asked, 'Where's Vidocq?' They answered that I was taking a turn in the court. He wanted to assure himself, but he sought in vain, shouting into all corners of the building. I did not answer; an official search had no greater success; none of the prisoners had seen me go out. They were soon assured that I was not in the prison, but how had I got away? Everybody was ignorant of that, even Francine, who assured them most ingenuously that she did not know where I was, for she had brought me the ribbon without knowing the use I intended to make of it. She was held, however, but this measure revealed nothing, and the soldiers who had let me pass were careful not to boast of their prowess.

While they were thus following the pretended authors of my escape, I left the city and reached Courtrai, where the juggler Olivier and the clown Devoye enrolled me in their troupe to play in the pantomime. I saw there several prisoners who had escaped, and their costume, which they never laid aside for the simple reason that they had no other, served marvellously to foil the police. From Courtrai we went to Ghent, and from there we were soon to go to the fair at Enghien. We had been in the latter city five days, and the receipts, of which I had a part, were good. One evening, as I was going on the stage, I was arrested by the police; I had been denounced by the clown, who was furious at seeing me the head employee.

Again they took me back to Lille, where I learned with chagrin that poor Francine had been sentenced to six months' detention as guilty of having helped me in my escape. The turnkey Baptiste, whose only crime had been to take me for a superior officer and in this rank respectfully to let me go out of Saint Peter's Tower, was incarcerated as well for the same misdemeanour. A serious charge was brought against him. The prisoners were delighted at finding an opportunity of taking vengeance, and they asserted that the sum of a hundred crowns had made him take a young man of nineteen for an old soldier of nearly fifty.

I was transferred to the prison of the Department of Douai, where I was locked up as a dangerous man; that is to say, that I was put in a cell immediately with irons on hands and feet. Here I found my compatriot Desfosseux and a young man named Doyennette, sentenced to six years in irons for complicity in a burglary, committed with his father, his mother, and two of his brothers, aged less than fifteen. They had been in the cell for four months, sleeping on straw, eaten by vermin, and living on bread made out of beans and water. I began by having provisions brought, and they were devoured in an instant.

We then talked of our affairs, and my fellow guests announced that for a fortnight they had been digging a hole under the pavement of the cell and it should reach the level of the Scarpe which washed the prison walls. At first I looked upon this enterprise as very difficult. They had to pierce a wall five feet thick without arousing the suspicions of the jailer, whose frequent visits did not permit them to leave in sight the slightest bit of rubbish brought up by the work.

We eluded the first obstacle by throwing through the grated window, which overlooked the Scarpe, every handful of earth or cement which we took out of the mine. Besides, Desfosseux had found a way to unrivet our irons, so that we worked with less fatigue and difficulty. One of us was always in the hole, which was large enough to hold a man. At last we thought we were at the end of our labours, when by probing we met the foundations, which we thought were made of ordinary stones, but which were composed of a layer of the largest sandstone. This circumstance forced us to enlarge our subterranean gallery, and for a week we worked without stopping. In order to hide the absence of the one who was at the task when the rounds were made, we took care to fill his coat and shirt with straw and place the dummy in the attitude of a man asleep.

After fifty-five days and as many nights of stubborn toil, we reached the end at last. We had only to displace one stone and we were at the river-bank. One night we decided to make the attempt. Everything seemed to favour us; the jailer had made his rounds an hour earlier than usual, and a thick fog made us certain that the sentinel would not see us. The stone yielded to our united efforts and fell into the subterranean passage, but at the same time the water poured in as if driven by a millrace. We had calculated badly our distances, and as our hole was some feet beneath the water level, we were flooded in a few minutes. At first, we wanted to dive into the opening, but the speed of the current would not allow this; so we were compelled to call for help or stay in the water all night. At my shouts the jailer and the turnkeys hurried to us, and were struck with astonishment at finding themselves in water up to their knees. Soon everything was discovered, the damage was repaired, and we were locked up in a cell opening on the same corridor.

This catastrophe made me reflect bitterly, but I was soon drawn from my sorrow by the voice of Desfosseux. He told me that we should not despair, but that his example ought to give me courage. It is true that Desfosseux was endowed with a strength of character which nothing could conquer. Throwing himself half-naked on the straw in a cell where he could hardly lie down, burdened with thirty pounds of irons, he sang at the top of his voice, and thought only of means of escape to commit some new crime. The occasion soon offered.

In the same prison as ourselves was the jailer of the Little Hotel of Lille and the turnkey Baptiste, accused of having favoured my escape for pay. When the sentence was delivered, the jailer was acquitted; but they adjourned Baptiste's case, as the tribunal demanded further investigation in which I was to be heard.

Poor Baptiste came to see me and begged me to tell the truth. At first I gave evasive answers, but as Desfosseux told me that the man might be useful to us and should be managed, I promised to do what he wanted. Great protestations of gratitude and offer of services. I took him at his word, and I demanded that he bring me a knife and two large nails which Desfosseux said he needed. I had them an hour later. When Desfosseux learned that I had procured these objects, he cut as many capers as the narrowness of the space and the weight of his irons permitted. Doyennette also showed the greatest joy, and as general gaiety is contagious I felt at ease without knowing why.

When these raptures had quieted down a little, Desfosseux finally told me to look and see whether in the vault of my cell I did not find five stones whiter than the rest. On my reply in the affirmative, he told me to sound the joints with the point of the knife. I then saw that the cement in the joints had been replaced by bits of bread, whitened by some scrapings. Desfosseux told me that the prisoner who had occupied the cell where I was had arranged things in this way to move the stones and escape, when he was transferred to another part of the prison. I then passed the knife to Desfosseux, and he busied himself actively in opening a passage into my cell, when we met the same catastrophe as my predecessor.

The jailer had got wind of something and changed our domicile. All three of us were placed in a cell overlooking the Scarpe, and chained together in such a way that when one moved in the slightest the movement was communicated to the others. This is a frightful punishment if it is prolonged, as it results in a complete deprivation of sleep. At the end of two days Desfosseux saw that we were depressed, and he decided to use a means which he employed only on great occasions and which he was accustomed to reserve for work in preparing for an escape.

Like a great many convicts he always carried in a secret place a case filled with saws. Furnished with these tools, he set to work, and in less than three hours our irons fell, and we threw them out of the window into the river. The jailer came a moment after to see whether we were quiet, and nearly fell over backwards when he discovered us without irons. He asked what we had done, and we answered by jokes. Soon the commissioner of the prison arrived, escorted by a bailiff named Hurtrel. We had to undergo a new examination, and Desfosseux cried, impatiently: 'You ask where the irons are! Well, the worms have eaten them, and they will eat those you put on us again.'

The commissioner saw that we were in possession of that grass which cuts iron, which no botanist has ever discovered, and he made us undress and searched us from head to foot. Then they loaded us with new irons, which were equally cut the following night, for they had not discovered the precious case. This time we took pleasure in throwing them on the ground in the presence of the commissioner and Hurtrel, who did not know what to think. The rumour even spread to the city that there was a sorcerer in the prison who broke irons by touching them. To put an end to these stories and, above all, to avoid drawing the attention of the other prisoners to a way of getting rid of their irons, the public prosecutor ordered us to be locked up and to be guarded with special care, a recommendation which did not prevent our leaving Douai sooner than he expected, or than we ourselves expected.

Twice a week they let us meet our lawyers in a corridor, where the door opened into the tribunal. I found a means of getting an imprint of the lock; Desfosseux made a key; and one fine day, when my lawyer was busy with another client accused of two murders, we all three went out without being seen. Two other doors we met were forced in the twinkling of an eye, and prison was soon behind us. However, I was disturbed by one trouble: our fortune was composed of six francs, and I did not see how we could go far on that treasure. I spoke of this to my companions, who looked at each other with a sinister smile; I insisted, and they told me that the following night they intended to break into a country house in the vicinity, and that they knew the means of exit thoroughly.

That was not for me, any more than the ways of the Bohemians had been. I had been willing to use the experience of Desfosseux to escape, but had no thought of joining in such a crime; however, I avoided any explanation. That evening found us near a village on the road to Cambrai. We had eaten nothing since the prison breakfast, and hunger became importunate; we had to seek food in the village. The appearance of my half-naked companions might arouse suspicions, so it was arranged that I should go for provisions. I presented myself at the village inn, where, after I had taken bread and brandy, I went out by another door than the one by which I had entered, and so went toward a point opposite where I had left the two men whom it was important for me to get rid of. I walked all night, and stopped only at daybreak to sleep some hours in a haystack.

Four days later I was at Compiègne, heading for Paris, where I hoped to find means of existence while I was waiting for my mother to come to my aid. At Louvres I met a detachment of Black Hussars, and I asked the sergeant-major if it was possible for me to enlist; his answer was that they did not recruit. The lieutenant to whom I went next raised the same objection, but, touched by my difficulties, he consented to take me to groom the remounts he was seeking in Paris. I accepted eagerly. A forage cap and an old dolman they gave me allowed me to avoid all questions at the Barrier. I went to lodge in the Military School with the detachment, and then I followed it to its dépôt at Guise.

When we reached that city, I was presented to the colonel, who, although he suspected that I was a deserter, enlisted me under the name of Lannoy, which I took, although I had no papers to prove it. Hidden under this new uniform, I thought I was out of trouble, lost in the ranks of the regiment, and I already began to think of making a career as a soldier when an unfortunate incident brought me again into the abyss.

In returning to quarters one morning, I met a gendarme who had been transferred from Douai to Guise. He had seen me so often and for so long a time that he recognized me at once and called to me. We were in the middle of the city, so it was impossible to think of escaping. I went straight to him, and, assuming great boldness, I made believe that I was delighted to see him again. He responded to my advances, but with a troubled air which seemed a bad augury.

Meanwhile, a hussar from my squadron approached and said, 'Well, Lannoy, have you business with the cops?'

'Lannoy?' said the gendarme, with astonishment.

'Yes, that's my war name.'

'That's what we'll see,' he answered, seizing me by the collar.

I had to follow him to jail. They compared my appearance with the description at the brigade and sent me at once to Douai, by special conveyance.

This last blow did me in completely; and the news which awaited me at Douai did not tend to relieve me. I learned that Grouard, Herbaux, Stofflet, and Boitel had decided by lot that one of them should take the blame for executing the forgery; but as it could not have been done by a single person, they had the idea of accusing me, thus punishing me because I had in a slight way charged them in my last examinations; I learned, besides, that the prisoner who might have deposed in my defence was dead.

If anything could have consoled me, it was to be separated at that time from Desfosseux and Doyennette, who had been arrested four days after our escape, still in possession of the things stolen by breaking and entering the shop at Pont-à-Marcq. I soon saw them, and as they appeared astonished at my abrupt departure, I explained that the arrival

of a gendarme in the inn where I was buying provisions had forced me
to fly haphazard. Once together again we returned to our projects of
escape, which the near approach of our respective sentences made the
more interesting.

One evening we saw a convoy of prisoners arrive, four of whom
were placed in our room in irons. They were the Duhesme brothers,
wealthy farmers from Bailleul, where they had enjoyed the best of repu-
tations until an unforeseen accident had unveiled their conduct. These
four individuals were endowed with prodigious strength and were at the
head of a band of *chauffeurs* who had terrorized the neighbourhood.

None of the members of this band could be discovered. Some
words of a small child of one of the Duhesmes finally blew up the
mine. This child was talking to a neighbour and took it into her head
to say that she had been very scared the night before.

'At what?' asked the neighbour, slightly curious.

'Oh, papa had come in again with some of the black men.'

'What black men?'

'Men with whom papa often goes out at night, and then they come
back in the daytime, and count the money on a counterpane. My
mother uses a lantern for light, and my Aunt Genevieve too, because
my uncles are with the black men. One day I asked my mother what
that meant. She answered, "Be discreet, my girl, your father has a black
hen, which brings him money, but only at night, and so as not to
frighten it, his face must be as black as its feathers. So be careful, for if
you tell a word of what you have seen, the black hen will not come
back any more."'

It is easy to understand that it was not to receive this mysterious
black hen, but to make themselves unrecognizable, that the Duhesmes
daubed their faces with soot. The neighbour thought so too, and told
her suspicions to her husband. He questioned the child in his turn,
and, convinced that the favourites of the black hen were only the *chauffeurs*, he made a declaration to the authorities; then they took such
good measures that the band was arrested, all disguised, just as they
were starting on a new expedition.

The youngest of the Duhesmes had in the sole of his shoe a
knife-blade, which he had found means to hide there on the way from
Bailleul to Douai. Informed that I knew the prison perfectly, he

revealed this fact and asked me if it would be possible to arrange for an escape. I was thinking about it when a justice of the peace, accompanied by two gendarmes, came to make the strictest search in our room and on our persons. No one among us knew the reason; I, however, thought it prudent to hide in my mouth a small file which never left me, but one of the gendarmes saw the movement, and shouted, 'He's just swallowed it.' What? Everyone looked, and we learned that they were searching for the seal which had served to stamp the false order for Boitel's release. Suspected, as we have seen, of having it in my possession, I was transferred to the prison in the Town Hall, and placed in a cell, chained in such a way that my right hand was made fast to my left leg, and the left hand to the right leg. The cell was so damp that in twenty minutes the straw which they had thrown in was as wet as if it had been soaked in water.

I remained in this frightful position for a week, and they decided to put me back in the ordinary prison only when sure that it was impossible that I had got rid of the seal in the ordinary way. When I heard the news, I pretended, as is always the practise in such cases, to be exceedingly weak and hardly able to bear the light. The unwholesomeness of the cell made this appear natural; so the gendarmes fell completely into the trap, and even went so far in their complaisance as to cover my eyes with a handkerchief. We went in a cab.

On the way I lowered the handkerchief, opened the door with that dexterity which has not yet met its equal, and jumped into the street. The gendarmes wanted to follow, but they were embarrassed by their sabres and their great boots. I was already far away before they were out of the carriage.

I left the city at once, and, still decided to take ship, I reached Dunkirk with the money which my mother had sent me. There I made the acquaintance of the supercargo of a Swedish brig who promised to take me on board.

While we were waiting for the moment of departure, my new friend proposed that I accompany him to Saint-Omer, where he was going to deal for a large supply of biscuit. In my sailor's garb I had no fear of being recognized, so I accepted; it was hardly possible for me to refuse a man to whom I was under so many obligations. So I made the voyage, but my turbulent character did not permit me to keep out of a

quarrel in the inn, and I was arrested as a brawler and taken to the
lock-up. There the authorities asked for my papers; I had none, and
from my answers they presumed that I had escaped from some prison,
so the next day they sent me to Douai without my being able to make
my adieux to the supercargo, who must have been astonished by the
adventure.

At Douai I was again placed in the prison of the Town Hall. At first
the jailer had some consideration for me, but his attentions were of
short duration. As a result of a quarrel with the turnkeys in which I
took too active a part, I was put in a dark cell beneath the tower. There
were five prisoners there, and one, a deserter condemned to death,
could only talk of suicide. I told him that there was nothing in that,
and that he would be better engaged in seeking some way of getting out
of this frightful hole, where the rats, running like rabbits in a warren,
ate our bread and bit our faces while we were asleep.

With a bayonet taken from one of the national guards who served
in the prison we began a hole in the wall, in the direction where we
heard a shoemaker tapping boots. In ten days and nights we had
already dug six feet and the noise of the shoemaker drew nearer. On the
morning of the eleventh day, as I was taking out a brick, I saw daylight;
it came from a window looking out on the street and lighted a room
next to our cell where the jailer kept his rabbits.

This discovery gave us new strength. When the evening visit was
over, we removed from the hole all the bricks which were already
detached; in view of the thickness of the wall there were perhaps two
cartloads. We placed them behind the cell door, which opened inward,
so as to form a barricade. Then we went to work with such zeal that
day surprised us when the hole was six feet broad at the opening, and
two feet at the end.

Soon after the jailer arrived with the rations. Finding that the door
resisted, he opened the wicket and saw the pile of bricks. His astonishment was great. However, he summoned us to open; on our refusal, the
guard arrived; then the commissioner of prisons; then the public prosecutor; then the municipal officers with their tri-coloured scarfs. They
parleyed; all this time one of us continued working in the hole, but the
obscurity prevented their seeing it. Perhaps we should have escaped

before they forced the door, but an unforeseen event took away our last hope.

When she came to feed the rabbits, the jailer's wife noticed some mortar which had fallen on the floor. In a prison nothing is immaterial; she examined the wall carefully, and although the last brick had been replaced so as to mask the hole, she recognized the fact that they had been separated. She shouted, the guards came, and with a blow from the butt of the musket they disarranged our edifice of bricks and we were cornered.

From both sides they now shouted to us to clear away the door and surrender, or they would fire. Entrenched behind the material, we answered that the first one who entered would be beaten to death with bricks and irons. Such obstinacy astonished the authorities, and they left us for some hours to calm down.

At noon a municipal officer reappeared at the wicket, which, like the hole, was still guarded, and offered us an amnesty. It was accepted; but we had barely taken down our breastworks when they fell on us with the butts of their guns, the flat of their swords, and the bunch of keys; even the jailer's dog joined the party. He jumped on my back and in an instant I was covered with bites. In this way they dragged us out into the court, where a squad of fifteen men held us in check while they riveted on our irons. When this operation was over, I was thrown into a cell even more frightful than the one I had left, and it was only the next day that the *infirmier* came to dress the bites and bruises with which I was covered.

I had hardly recovered from this shock when the day for my sentence arrived. My repeated escapes and those of Grouard, who had fled at the moment I had been retaken, had postponed it for eight months. The discussion was opened and I saw that I was lost. My fellows accused me with an animosity which was explained by my tardy revelations, although they had been useless to me and had not aggravated their position. Boitel declared that he recalled that I had asked him how much he would give to get out of prison; Herbaux confessed that he had made the forged order, without, however, having put in the signatures, but he added that he had made it on my challenge, and that I had at once taken it away without his attaching the slightest importance to it. On the other hand, the clerks declared that nothing indicated that

I had co-operated materially in the crime; all the charges against me then hung on the unproved allegation that I had furnished that unfortunate seal. However, Boitel, who admitted that he had solicited the forged order, Stoffler, who had brought it to the jailer, and Grouard, who had at least assisted in the whole operation, were acquitted, and Herbaux and I were sentenced – to eight years in irons.

VII
TO THE HULKS AT BREST

WORN OUT by all sorts of bad treatment which I had endured in prison at Douai, harassed by a surveillance which had been doubled since my sentence, I did not appeal, which would have kept me there several months. What confirmed me in this resolution was the news that those under sentence were going to be sent immediately to Bicêtre and combined with a chain gang which was going to the hulks at Brest. It is needless to say that I was counting on escaping on the way. As to the appeal, I was assured that I could present a request for pardon from the convict prison which would have the same effect. However, we stayed at Douai several more months, which caused me bitterly to regret not having proceeded with my efforts for annulment.

At last the order for our transfer arrived, and hard as it may be to believe it in the case of men going to the galleys, it was received with enthusiasm, so weary were we of the vexations of the jailer. However, our new position was rather less than satisfactory. The bailiff Hurtrel, who accompanied us for some reason or other, had made irons of a new model. We each had a ball weighing fifteen pounds on one leg, and we were fastened together two by two with a large iron bracelet. In addition, our surveillance was most active. So it became impossible to think of any escape by way of ingenuity. Only an attack in force could save us. I made the proposition; fourteen of my companions accepted, and it was arranged that the project should be executed on our way through the forest of Compègne. Desfosseux was making the journey, and by means of the saws which he always carried, our irons were cut in three days. A layer of putty prevented our guards seeing the marks of the instruments.

We entered the forest. At the appointed spot the signal was given, the irons fell; we jumped from the wagons, where we were packed together, to gain the underbrush; but the five gendarmes and the eight dragoons who formed our escort charged, sabres in hand. We entrenched ourselves behind the trees, armed with stones which had been piled up to mend the roads, and some arms which we had secured in the first moment of confusion. The soldiers hesitated a moment, but, being well armed and well mounted, they soon had the advantage. At their first round of fire two of us fell dead on the spot, five were badly wounded, and the rest threw themselves on their knees begging for mercy. We had to surrender.

Desfosseux, I, and some others who still held out, were climbing back into the carts, when Hurtrel, who had kept at a respectful distance from the affray, approached one of the poor wretches who doubtless was not hurrying enough, and passed his sabre through his body. Such baseness made us indignant. The convicts who had not yet taken their places in the wagons picked up stones again, and, if it had not been for the dragoons, Hurtrel would have been beaten to death. They shouted that we would be annihilated, and it was so evident that we had to lay down our arms – that is to say, the stones. However, this event put an end to the vexations from Hurtrel, who never approached us without trembling.

At Senlis we were placed in a way prison, one of the worst I have ever known. The jailer combined his duties with those of gamekeeper, and his wife ran the jail. And what a woman! She searched us in our most private parts to assure herself that we had nothing on us which might serve to escape. However, we were sounding the walls when we heard her shout in a hoarse voice, 'Rascals, if I come at you with my strength of an ox, I'll teach you to make music.' We believed what she said, and everybody was quiet.

The second day we reached Paris; we passed the outer boulevards, and at four o'clock in the afternoon we were in sight of Bicêtre.

When we reached the end of the avenue which looks on the road to Fontainebleau, the wagons turned to the right, and passed through a gate over which I read, mechanically, this inscription, 'Home for the Aged.' In the first court a large number of old men dressed in grey were walking up and down; they were the worthy poor. On our passage they crowded near with that stupid curiosity which a monotonous and purely animal life gives. As we entered a second court where the chapel was, I noticed that most of my companions hid their faces with their hands or their handkerchiefs. One might think that perhaps they had some sense of shame; but they were only thinking of being seen as little as possible, in order to escape more easily if an occasion offered itself.

'Here we are,' Desfosseux said to me, as he was sitting beside me.
'You see that square building. That's the prison.' In fact, we had to go
to a door guarded inside by a sentinel. We entered the office, and were
merely registered; our description was postponed until the next day. I
noticed that the jailer looked at Desfosseux and me with a sort of
curiosity, and I concluded that we had been mentioned to him by
Hurtrel, who had gone a quarter of an hour ahead of us since the affair
in the forest of Compiègne.

After we had passed several low double doors and the wicket to the
cells, we were led into a large square court where sixty prisoners were
playing prisoner's base, shouting so that the whole building rang. At
our appearance all stopped and surrounded us, appearing to examine
with surprise the irons with which we were burdened. Moreover, it was
to enter Bicêtre under good auspices to present oneself in such a harness, for they judged the worth of a prisoner – that is to say, his intelligence and audacity for escapes – by the precautions which were taken
to make him safe.

Desfosseux found himself in a place of his acquaintance, and had
no trouble in presenting us as the most distinguished of the
Department of the North. He did more, particularly in praise of me,
and I was surrounded and fêted by the most famous in the prison.
Beaumont, Guillaume père, Mauger, Jossat, Maltaise, Cornu, Blondy,
Trouflat, Richard, one of the accomplices in the murder of the Lyons
courier, never left me.

When we were rid of the irons which we had borne on our journey,
we were taken to the canteen, and for two hours I accepted a thousand
invitations. Then a large man in a forage cap, who they told me was the
inspector of the wards, came for me and led me into a large room called
Fort Mahon, where we were dressed in the garment of the place, which
consisted of a dark grey coat. At the same time the inspector
announced that I was to be the corporal; that is to say, that I should
preside over the distribution of food among my fellow guests. In consequence I had a rather good bed, while the rest slept on field beds.

In four days I was known to all the prisoners, but what gave them
the highest opinion of my courage was that Beaumont, wishing to test
me, sought a groundless quarrel. We fought, and as I was engaged with
an expert in that sort of exercise which is called *savatte,* I was beaten.

However, I took my revenge in a cell, where Beaumont lacked room to use the resources of his art and was beaten in his turn. My first mishap, however, gave me the idea of being initiated into the secrets of the art, and the famous Jean Goupil, the Saint George of *savatte*, who was in Bicêtre, soon counted me among the pupils who did him most honour.

After my sentence I was constantly preoccupied with the idea of avoiding the galleys and gaining a seaport where I might embark, so I contrived, day and night, ways and means of getting out of Bicêtre. In the end I believed that by piercing the flagstones of Fort Mahon we could reach the conduits built under the house, and could reach, by means of a short sap, the insane wards, and once there it would not be difficult to gain the outside. This project was executed in ten days and as many nights. We had to wait, however, until the moon was in the last quarter.

At last, October 13, 1797, at two o'clock in the morning, we descended into the conduit, to the number of thirty-four. By the light of several dark lanterns we soon opened the subterranean passage and entered the insane wards. Now we had to find a ladder, or at least something which would take its place; a rather long pole at last came to hand, and we were about to draw lots to see who would mount first, when the noise of chains broke the silence of the night.

A dog came out of a kennel in a corner of the court; we remained motionless, holding our breath, for it was a decisive moment. After stretching himself as if he only wanted to change his position, the animal put one paw back in his kennel as if he wanted to go in; we believed we were saved. Suddenly, he turned his head toward the place where we were huddled together, and fixed us with his eyes, which seemed like burning coals. A low growl was followed by barks which re-echoed through the whole building. At first Desfosseux wanted to try to wring his neck, but the insolent one was of such a size that the issue of such a fight was doubtful. It appeared more prudent to cower in a large open room which was used in treating the insane, but the dog still continued his concert and his colleagues joined in.

The uproar became so great that the inspector Giroux saw that something extraordinary was happening among the boarders. Knowing his world, he began the rounds of Fort Mahon, and nearly fell over backwards when he found no one. At his shouts, the warder, the turnkeys, and the guards all ran. They soon discovered the way we had taken, and they took the same road to reach the insane wards, where the dog, now unchained, ran straight at us. The guards then entered the room where we were, with fixed bayonets, just as though it was a matter of taking a redoubt. They put us in handcuffs and then took us back, not to Fort Mahon but to the dungeons, but without ill-treating us.

This was the boldest attempt at escape that there had been in the place for a long time, and it caused such confusion among the guards that it was two days before they realized that one convict was missing – Desfosseux. Knowing as I did his cleverness, I believed him far away, when on the morning of the third day, I saw him enter the dungeon, pale, worn out, and bleeding. When the door closed on him, he told me his adventures.

At the moment the guards seized us, he was crouching in a sort of tub which probably served for the baths. When all was quiet, he came out from his retreat, and by means of the pole got across several walls; but he found himself still in the insane wards. However, day was breaking, and he already heard coming and going in the buildings, for nowhere were they so early as in the hospitals. He had to avoid the sight of the employees who would soon be moving about the wards. The wicket of a cell was half-open; he slipped in, and by an excess of precaution tried to burrow in a large heap of straw, but to his astonishment he found crouching there a naked man, his hair dishevelled, his beard bristling, his eyes haggard and bloodshot. The maniac – for he was one – looked wildly at Desfosseux; then he made a swift sign, and as the former stood motionless, threw himself at him as if to tear him to pieces. Some caresses seemed to quiet him; he took Desfosseux by the hand, and made him sit by his side and pulled all the straw under him in the brisk jerky movements of a monkey.

At eight o'clock in the morning a bit of black bread fell through the wicket; he took it, examined it for some time, and ended by throwing it into the slop jar, from which he withdrew it a moment later to devour it. During the day they brought bread, but as the maniac was asleep, Desfosseux took it and ate it, at the risk of being devoured by his terrible companion who might consider it bad to be deprived of his pittance. At dusk the maniac awoke, and talked for some time with extraordinary rapidity. Night came, and his exaltation increased sensibly; he skipped about and twisted himself into horrible shapes, shaking his chains with a sort of pleasure.

In this alarming situation Desfosseux impatiently waited for the idiot to go to sleep so that he could get through the wicket. Toward midnight when he heard no further movement on the part of the idiot, he advanced to it, put his arm through, then his head ... he was seized by the leg; it was the idiot, who with a strong arm threw him back on the straw, placed himself in front of the wicket, where he stayed until day, as immovable as a statue.

The following night, another attempt, and a new obstacle. Desfosseux was getting out of his head and he tried force. A terrible battle ensued, and Desfosseux, struck by the chains, covered with bites and bruises, had to call the warders. At first they took him for one of their patients who had made a mistake, and wanted to put him in a cell, but he succeeded in making them recognize him, and finally gained the favour of being put back with us.

We remained in the dungeon eight days, but though I had become the object of the most active vigilance, I none the less sought to escape, when the day came for the departure of the chain gang.

It was the twentieth of November, 1797. All the morning we bad noticed a more than ordinary movement in the prison. The convicts had not left their cells; the gates opened and closed noisily every minute; the turnkeys went to and fro with a busy air; in the main court they were unloading irons, and the noise reached even our ears. Toward eleven o'clock, two men clad in blue uniforms entered Fort Mahon, where for a week I had been with my companions in the attempt at escape; they were the captain of the chain gang and his lieutenant.

'Well,' said the captain, with a smile, 'are there any return horses [escaped convicts]?' And as he spoke, they crowded around him to pay him court. 'Good day, M. Viez; good day, M. Thierry,' was the cry on all sides. These greetings were even repeated by prisoners who had never seen either Viez or Thierry, but who hoped to gain favour by giving the appearance of acquaintance. It was difficult for the captain not to be moved by this homage; however, he was used to such honours and did not lose his head; he knew his men perfectly. He saw Desfosseux.

'Oh, oh!' he said, 'there's a fellow who can cut his irons, and who has made the trip with us before. I've heard that you just missed being guillotined at Douai, my boy. You did well to miss, for it is better to go back to the hulks than for the executioner to play with your head in the basket. Now, children, be calm, and you shall all have stew.'

The captain had only begun his inspection and he continued to address friendly jokes to all his merchandise, as he called the condemned.

The critical moment arrived; we went down into the Cour de Fers, where the doctor examined us to see whether everyone could stand the fatigue of the journey. We were all declared well, although many of us were in a deplorable state. Each one of the condemned then left off the livery of the house and put on his own garments; those who had none received a smock and trousers, insufficient to keep out cold and dampness. The hats and clothes left to the convicts, if at all neat, are torn in a special way to prevent escape; they tear off the rims of the hats or the collars from the coats. No convict could keep more than six francs; any excess of that sum was given to the captain, who delivered it up on the way as there was need of it.

These preliminaries over, we entered the great court, where we found the guards of the chain gang. Most of them were water-carriers, messengers, or charcoal-burners who practised their professions in between voyages. In the middle of the court was a large wooden box which held the irons that are used successfully in all expeditions of this kind. We were made to approach two by two, graded by height, and attached to a chain six feet long which was at once fastened to a cordon of twenty-six convicts, who from that time on were only able to move as a body. Each one was held to this chain by a sort of triangle called a cravat which opened on one side by turning a bolt, and was closed on the other by a nail riveted in cold. That was the dangerous part of the operation; even the most mutinous and violent characters stayed still then; for at the slightest movement, instead of falling on the anvil, the blows would break the skull, which the hammer grazed at every stroke. Now came a convict armed with long shears, with which he cut the hair and beard, leaving them of unequal length.

The shackling-on of the irons was finished at five in the evening. The guards left, and only the convicts remained in the court. Left to themselves, the men were far from despondent, but gave themselves over to all sort of tumultuous gaiety. Neither ears nor shame were spared. Near me were two men, one an ex-schoolmaster sentenced for rape and an ex-medical officer sentenced for forgery; they talked together mirthlessly. We passed the night on the straw, in a warehouse made out of a church. The guards made frequent rounds to assure that no one was cutting his irons.

At daybreak everyone was astir; the roll was called, the irons inspected; at six o'clock we were placed back to back in long carts, our legs hanging down, covered with frost and shivering with cold. When we reached Saint-Cyr, we had to strip and be searched, which extended to the socks, shoes, shirts, the mouth, ears, nostrils, and more secret places still. They not only sought for files, but for watch springs which would be sufficient to permit a prisoner to cut his irons in less than three hours. The search lasted an hour, and it was really a miracle that half of us did not have our noses or feet frozen.

When it came time to go to bed, we were herded into a cattle shed, where we lay so close together that the body of one served as a pillow for the one next to him; if one got entangled in his chain or in that of his neighbour, blows of a club at once rained on the awkward fellow. As soon as we had lain down on some handfuls of straw which had already served as litter for animals, a whistle blew for absolute silence; it was not to be broken by the slightest complaint, even when to relieve the guard at one end of the stable, the others walked over our bodies.

Supper consisted of a pretended bean soup with bits of spoiled meat. The distribution was made in wooden buckets which held thirty rations, and the cook, armed with a large soup spoon, never failed to repeat to each convict as he presented himself, 'One, two, three, hold out your basin, thief.' The wine was served in the bucket which had served for the soup and meat. Then a guard blew his whistle three times, and shouted:

'Attention, robbers, and answer yes or no. Have you had bread?'
'Yes.'
'Have you had soup?'
'Yes.'
'Meat?'
'Yes.'

'Wine?'

'Yes.'

'Then sleep, or pretend to.'

However, at a table placed at the entrance to the stable, the captain, lieutenant, and sergeant of the guards had a meal a little better than ours, for these men, who profited by every occasion to extort money from the convicts, had a feast and refused themselves nothing. At that moment the stable afforded one of the most hideous spectacles imaginable. On one side, one hundred and fifty men herded in like animals, rolling their wild eyes, and where pain banished sleep; on the other, eight sinister individuals eating ravenously without for a moment taking their eyes off their carbines or their clubs. Small candles attached to the dark walls of the stable threw a reddish light on this scene of desolation; the silence was disturbed only by muffled groans or the rattling of the irons. Not content with striking them right and left, the guards played horrible tricks on the convicts. A man devoured by thirst asked for water. They answered, 'The man who wants water raise his hand.' The unfortunate man obeyed without distrust, and he was at once crushed under blows. Those who had some money were necessarily spared; but that was a small number, for the long stay in the prisons of most of the convicts had exhausted their small resources.

These abuses were not the only ones to be noted in the conduct of the chain gang. In order to save expense of transport, for his own profit, the captain nearly every day made one of the cordons travel on foot. But this group was always made up of the most robust men; that is to say, the most turbulent of the convicts. Unhappy the women they met or the shops discovered on the way. The women were abused in the most brutal manner; the shops were rifled in the twinkling of an eye, as I saw done at Morlaix. A grocery shop had left neither bread, sugar, nor a pound of soap.

One might ask what the guards were doing in the meantime. They gave the appearance of being busy, but they opposed no real obstacle, as they knew that in the end they would profit by the robbery, since the convicts had to turn to them to sell their booty or to exchange it for strong liquors. The same was true of the spoils exacted from the convicts during the journey. They were hardly in irons before their neighbours surrounded them, and stole the little money they had left.

Far from preventing or stopping these robberies, the guards often provoked them, as I saw in the case of an ex-gendarme who had sewed some louis in his trousers. 'That one's fat,' they said, and in three minutes the poor devil found himself stripped. In such cases the victims ordinarily shouted and called on the guards for help, but the latter never failed to arrive when all was over, to fall with heavy blows of the club – on the one who had been robbed. At Rennes the bandits of whom I am speaking went so far in their infamy as to rob a sister of charity who had brought us tobacco and money to a riding school where we were to pass the night.

Our hard voyage lasted twenty-four days. When we arrived at Pont-à-Lezen we were placed in a dépôt of the galleys, where the convicts made a sort of quarantine until they were over their fatigue and it was apparent that they had no contagious diseases. On our arrival we were washed two by two in great tubs filled with warm water; when we came out of our bath, they gave us our clothes. Like the rest I received a red coat, two pairs of trousers, two canvas shorts, two pairs of shoes, and a green cap. Each piece of this trousseau was marked 'G A L,' and the cap bore a metal plaque on which was a number corresponding to that inscribed in the register. When we had our clothes, they riveted an iron to our feet, but without joining us in couples.

The dépôt at Pont-à-Lezen was a sort of lazarette, and the surveillance was not especially rigorous. They even assured me that it was rather easy to get out of its halls and to climb the outer walls. I received this information from one Blondy who had already escaped from Brest. In the hope that I could profit by the news, I had everything ready to seize the occasion. They sometimes gave us bread which weighed eighteen pounds. When we left Morlaix, I had hollowed out one of these loaves and placed in it a shirt, a pair of trousers, and some handkerchiefs; this was a new kind of valise and they did not search it. Lieutenant Thierry had not named me for special surveillance; far from that, for as he knew the reasons for my sentence, he had told the commissioner that with a man as quiet as I was 'they could lead the chain, like a girls' boarding-school.' So I inspired no distrust, and I undertook to execute my project.

First, I had to pierce the wall of the room in which I was confined; a pair of steel scissors which a trusty had left on the foot of my bed when he was riveting leg-irons served to make an opening, while Blondy occupied himself in cutting my irons. When the operation was finished, my comrades made a dummy which they put in my place to deceive the vigilance of the guards, and soon, muffled in the clothes I had hidden, I was in the court of the dépôt. The walls around it were not less than fifteen feet high, and I saw that in order to scale them I needed something in the way of a ladder; a pole took its place, but it was so heavy and so long that it was impossible for me to pass it over the wall to descend on the other side.

After some efforts as vain as difficult, I had to take a risk and jump. This succeeded badly; I hurt my feet so seriously that I hardly had strength enough to drag myself into a neighbouring thicket. I hoped that the pain would die down so that I could go on before daylight, but it became more and more sharp, and my feet swelled so prodigiously that I had to renounce all hope of escape. I dragged myself along as best I could to the gate of the dépôt to give myself up, hoping in this way to lessen the number of lashes which would be mine by rights. A sister whom I asked for and to whom I confessed all began by taking me into a room where my feet were dressed. This excellent woman, moved to pity by my lot, went to the commissioner of the prison to beg for me, and he granted my pardon. At the end of three weeks, when I was completely healed, they took me to Brest.

VIII
I Conceal My Identity

THE CONVICT PRISON at Brest was situated within the precincts of
the port. Piles of rifles and two cannon, levelled at the doors, indicated
to me the entrance to the wards, where I was led after I had been examined by all the guards of the establishment. Convicts, however bold and
hardened they may be, have confessed that it is impossible not to feel a
keen emotion at the first sight of this place of misery. Each ward contained twenty-eight field beds, called 'benches,' on which six hundred
convicts slept in chains; those long rows of red garbs, those shaven heads,
those hollow eyes, those depressed faces, the constant rattle of the irons,
all combined to put the soul in secret terror. But for the convict the
impression was only fleeting; in the feeling that from now on he need not
blush before anyone, he became one with his position. In order not to be
the object of gross raillery, of the odious tricks of his companions, one
had to pretend to share in them, and even exaggerate them; soon, in tone
and gesture the depravity of convention passed into his heart.

The inconveniences and abuses which existed in the convict prison
at Brest made another reason for me to shorten my stay if I could. In
such a case the first thing to do was to assure myself of the discretion of
the comrade with whom I was coupled. Mine was a wine-grower from
near Dijon, about thirty-six years old, sentenced to twenty-four years
for repeated burglary, the sort of idiot whom misery and bad treatment
had brutalized. His mind warped by beatings, he seemed to have
retained only as much intelligence as was necessary to answer with the
agility of an ape or a dog the whistle of the warders. Such a fellow did
not suit my purpose, for to carry out my project I needed a man sufficiently resolute not to recoil at the prospect of the blows which the
guards never failed to administer to convicts even suspected of having
helped or even known of the escape of a prisoner. To get rid of this
Burgundian, I feigned illness; he was coupled to another to work, and
when I was well, I was yoked with a poor devil sentenced to eight years
for stealing chickens from a vicarage.

This fellow at least had some energy left. The first time that we were alone on the bench, he said to me: 'Listen, comrade, you don't seem to me to want to eat the nation's bread too long. Be frank with me, you will lose nothing.' I confessed that I intended to escape at the first opportunity. 'Well,' he said, 'if I had any advice to give you, it would be not to waltz in front of those rhinoceroses of guards until they know your shape; but that's not all you need. Have you any cash?' I answered that I had some money in my purse. Then he told me that he could easily procure clothes from a man sentenced to the double chain, but, to divert suspicion, I ought to buy an outfit as a man who intended to pass his time peacefully. This outfit consisted of two wooden bowls, a small cask for wine, a sort of pad to prevent the irons chafing, and, finally, a small mattress stuffed with oakum.

This was on a Thursday; Saturday evening I had the clothes of a sailor, which I immediately put on under my convict's coat. The next day the section to which I belonged went at the sound of a cannon to work the pumps, a task which was never interrupted. At the gate they examined our manacles and clothes as usual. In the knowledge of this practice, I had stuck over my sailor's clothes, at the breast, a bladder painted skin color. As I intentionally left my coat and shirt open, no guard would think of examining further, and I went out without trouble. When we reached the dock, with my comrade I passed behind a pile of planks; my manacle had been cut the evening before; the solder which hid the marks yielded at the first attempt. Free from the irons, I hastily took off the coat and trousers of a convict. Under my leather cap I put on a wig which I had brought from Bicêtre; then I gave my comrade the slight recompense I had promised him and disappeared by slipping behind some piles of timber.

I passed the gate without any obstacle and found myself in Brest, which was entirely unknown to me. Afraid that any hesitation on my part as to direction would cause me to be noticed, my uneasiness increased. After a thousand twists and turns, I finally reached the only city gate. An old warder named Lachique was always posted there, who was presumed to know a convict by his gestures, his appearance, and his looks. What made his observations easier was that a man who has passed some time in a convict prison always involuntarily drags the leg on which he has drawn the irons. However, I had to pass in front of this redoubtable personage, who smoked solemnly, casting his eagle eye on all who entered or went out. I had been forewarned; I brazened the thing out. When I got in front of Lachique, I placed at his feet a pitcher of buttermilk which I had bought to make my disguise the more complete. Loading my pipe, I asked him for a light. He hastened to give me one with all of the courtesy of which he was capable. After we had blown some puffs of tobacco smoke into each other's face I left him to take the road which lay before me.

I had followed it for three quarters of an hour when I heard three shots from a cannon which they fire to signal the escape of a convict, in order to warn the peasants in the vicinity that they can win a reward of a hundred francs if they seize the fugitive. In fact, I saw many people armed with guns and scythes running about the country, carefully beating the underbrush and even the smallest bits of broom. Some of the labourers even seemed to have brought their arms as a precaution, for I saw several leave their teams with a gun which they took from a furrow. One of these peasants passed very close to me in a crossroad which I had taken when I first heard the cannon shots, but he did not recognize me. In the first place, I was dressed very neatly, and, besides, as I carried my hat under my arm on account of the heat, he could see that my hair was in a queue, which could not belong to a convict.

I continued to get deeper and deeper into the interior of the country, avoiding the villages and isolated houses. At dusk I met two women, whom I asked what road I was on; they answered in a patois of which I did not understand a word. But by showing them some money and making signs that I wanted to eat, they led me to the entrance of the village to a public-house kept by – a keeper, whom I saw under the mantelpiece dressed in all of the insignia of his dignity. For a moment I was upset, but soon collecting myself, I told him that I wanted to speak to the mayor. 'That's me,' said an old peasant in a woollen cap and sabots, sitting at a small table eating buckwheat cakes.

This was a new disappointment, as I had counted on sliding away in the passage between the pub and the town hall. However, I had to get out of it in some way. I said to the functionary in sabots that I had taken the crossroad from Morlaix to Brest and had lost my way. At the same time I asked how far I was from the latter city, expressing a desire to sleep there the same evening. 'You're five leagues from Brest,' he said.

'It's impossible for you to reach it tonight; if you want to sleep here, I'll give you a place in my barn, and tomorrow you can go with the keeper who is going to take back an escaped convict whom we arrested yesterday.'

These last words brought back all my fears, for from the way they were pronounced I saw that the mayor had not taken my story literally. Nevertheless, I accepted his kind offer, but after supper, as we were going to the barn, I cried with all the gestures of a man in despair: 'Oh, my God, I've left my pocketbook at Morlaix, with my papers and eight double louis. I must go back at once – yes, at once; but how can I find the way? If the keeper would go with me; he must know the country? We'll be back tomorrow in time for him to go with the convict.'

This proposition removed all suspicions, for a man who wants to escape does not usually take the company that I asked for; on his part the keeper, looking for a reward, had put on his gaiters at my first words. So we went, and at daybreak were at Morlaix. My companion, whom I plied with drink on the way, was already in fine condition; I finished him off with rum at the first pothouse we met in the place. He stayed at the table to wait for me, or rather under the table, and would have had to wait a long time.

From the first person I met I asked the way to Vannes; it was pointed out in some sort of way, and I went, as the Dutch proverb says, with fear at my heels. Two days passed without trouble. The third day, some leagues from Guemené, at a turn in the road I met two gendarmes who were returning from their opposite number. At the unexpected sight of their yellow trousers and embroidered hats, I made a movement to fly. My two men shouted for me to stop, making a significant gesture to take their carbines from the hooks. They reached me, and I had no papers to show them, but I made up a response by chance. 'My name is Duval, born at Lorient, deserter from the frigate *Cocarde,* now in the roads at Saint-Malo.'

It is needless to say that I had learned this during my sojourn in the hulks, where every day news came from all the ports. 'What!' said the corporal, 'you are August, the son of Père Duval, who lives at Lorient, on the Place, beside the Golden Ball!' I did not contradict; it would be worse to be recognized as an escaped convict. 'My word,' the corporal went on, 'I'm upset to have to arrest you, but now there's no way out. I

must first have you taken to Lorient or Saint-Malo.' I asked him not to
send me to the first of the two cities, as I did not care to be confronted
by my new family, in case they wanted to identify me. However, the
sergeant-major ordered me transferred to Lorient, where they locked me
up in Pontaniau, a house of detention for the navy, and near the new
convict prison which had just been filled with convicts taken from
Brest.

Questioned the next day by the commissioner, I again declared that
I was August Duval, and that I had left my ship, without permission, to
come and see my parents. Then they took me back to jail, where I
found, among other sailors, a young man from Lorient, accused of
assault on a naval lieutenant. After he had talked with me for some
time, he said to me one morning, 'My compatriot, if you'll pay for my
breakfast, I'll tell you something which won't make you sorry.' His air
of mystery, the accent he put on the word compatriot, made me uneasy
and gave me no chance to get out of it. The meal was served, and at the
end he spoke in the following terms.

'Do you trust me? Yes! Well, I'm going to get you out of your
scrape. I don't know who you are, but you certainly are not Duval's son,
because he died two years ago in Saint-Pierre, Martinique.' (I stirred.)
'Yes, he's been dead two years, but no one here knows it, the hospitals
in the colonies are so confused. Now I can give you enough information about the family so that you can pass for him, even in the eyes of
his parents; that will be the easier, as he was very young when he left
home. For greater safety you can pretend a weakness of mind brought
on by your labours at sea and by illness. There's another thing; before
he embarked, August Duval had a design tattooed on his left arm, as
most soldiers and sailors do. I know that design perfectly; it was an altar
with a wreath over it. If you'll get put into my cell for a couple of
weeks, I'll make the same marks on you, so that no one will mistake it.'

My guest appeared frank and open. I explained the interest he took
in my affairs by the desire to trick justice which animates all prisoners;
to put the law off the track, to block its course, or to produce a mistake
is a pleasure of revenge which they are willing to buy at the cost of
some weeks in cells. Now the question was how to get put into the
cells. An expedient was soon discovered. Under the windows of the
ward where we ate was a sentinel. We began by throwing bits of bread

at him, and as he threatened to tell the Jailer, we defied him to complain; whereupon he was relieved. The corporal, who acted important,
entered the office, and a moment later the jailer came to get us without
saying why. We soon discovered, on entering a sort of dungeon which
was very damp but very light. We were hardly inside before my companion began the operation, which succeeded perfectly. It simply consisted of pricking the arm with several needles dipped in red and black
ink. At the end of twelve days the pricks had healed so far that it was
impossible to tell how long they had been made. My companion profited further by this retreat to give me new details on the Duval family,
whom he had known since he was born, and to whom he was, I
believe, related.

This information was of great help when, the sixteenth day of our
detention in the cell, I was taken out to be presented to my father
whom the commissioner had summoned. My comrade had pictured
this man in such a manner that I could not make a mistake. When I
saw him, I fell on his neck, and he recognized me; his wife, who arrived
a moment later, recognized me; a cousin and an uncle also recognized
me. So I was August Duval; it was impossible to doubt it, and even the
commissioner was convinced. But that was not enough to get me set at
liberty. As a deserter from the *Cocarde,* I must be taken to Saint-Malo,
where she had left some men in hospital, and then be tried by a naval
board. To tell the truth, all that scarcely disturbed me, for I was certain
that I should escape on the way. I left at last bathed in the tears of my
parents and stocked with some louis the more, which I added to those I
carried in my hidden case.

As far as Quimper, where I was to be delivered to the *correspondance,* no occasion offered to part company with the gendarmes, who
conducted me, as well as several other individuals – robbers, smugglers,
or deserters. They disposed of us in the city prison. On entering the
room in which I was to pass the night, I saw on the foot of a bed a red
coat, marked on the back with the initials 'G A L,' which I knew only
too well. There slept, wrapped in a poor quilt, a man who, by his green
cap bearing a numbered plaque, I recognized as a convict. Would he
recognize me? Or point me out? I was in mortal terror when the individual, awakened by the noise of the keys and bolts, sat up, and I saw a
young man, named Goupy, who had arrived at Brest at the same time I

had. He had been sentenced to hard labour for life for robbery in the outskirts of Bernai in Normandy. His father served as a guard in the hulks at Brest, where, formerly, he had probably not come for a change of air. Not wanting to have his son constantly under his eyes, he had obtained his transfer to the convict prison at Rochefort; he was on the way to this destination. I told him my story. He promised to keep it secret, and he kept it the more faithfully in that he had nothing to gain by betraying me.

However the *correspondance* did not move, and fifteen days had already passed since my arrival at Quimper, with no question of going. The prolongation of my sojourn gave me the idea of piercing a wall to escape; but recognizing the impossibility of success, I decided to gain the confidence of the jailer, and perhaps furnish myself with an opportunity of executing my project by inspiring him with false security. After I had told him that I had heard the prisoners plotting something, I pointed out the place in the prison where they must have worked. He made the most minute researches, and naturally enough found my hole, which gained me his complete good will. However, I found myself little further ahead, for the general surveillance was made with such a precision that all my combinations were ruined. I then had the idea of getting into the hospital, where I hoped to be more fortunate in executing my projects. All I had to do to get a fever like a horse was to swallow tobacco juice for two days; the doctors gave me a billet at once. When I arrived in the house, I received in exchange for my garments a grey cap and coat.

I intended to spend some time in the hospital in order to learn the exits; but the indisposition caused by the tobacco juice would not last more than three or four days. I must find a recipe to improvise another malady, for, as I knew no one in the wards, it was impossible to procure a new supply of tobacco juice. At Bicêtre I had been initiated into the ways to raise ulcers and sores with which beggars excite the pity of the public. Of all these expedients I adopted the one which consists in making the head swell like a bushel, first, because the doctors infallibly do not understand it, and, secondly, because it is not painful and one can get rid of the marks between one day and the next. Suddenly my head became of prodigious size; loud rumours were heard among the members of the establishment who were not, as it appeared, well skilled, as they did not know what to think; however, I believe I heard the word elephantiasis, or hydropsy of the brain. Whatever it might be, this consultation ended by a prescription, so common in a hospital, of putting me on a rigid diet.

With money I should not have worried about the prescription; but my purse contained only some pieces of gold, and I was afraid that if I had them changed, I should arouse suspicion. However, I decided to try something with a released convict who acted as nurse. This man would have done anything for money, and he soon got me what I wanted. On my expressing a desire to go out into the city for some hours, he told me that if I wore a disguise that would not be impossible, as the walls were only eight feet high. He said that was the way he took, as well as his companions, when he had some scheme on. We agreed that he should furnish me garments and that he should accompany me on my nocturnal excursion, which might end in taking supper with some girls. The only garments, however, he could procure inside the hospital were much too small, and we had to defer the project.

However, one of the sisters of the house passed by my bed. I had noticed in her several times certain worldly dispositions. She was a brunette, highly coloured, and her robust charms set alight the passion of more than one poor wretch among the sawbones and nurses. At the sight of this attractive creature, who must have weighed between one and two hundred, the idea took me to borrow for a moment her claustral trappings. I spoke of this to the nurse as a wild idea; but he took it seriously, and promised to procure for me for the following night a part of the wardrobe of Sister Françoise.

In fact toward two o'clock in the morning I saw him arrive with a package which contained a dress, veil, stockings, and the like, which he had taken from the sister's cell while she was at prayers. All my companions in the ward, nine in number, were sound asleep; however, I passed on to the landing to make my toilet. What gave me the most trouble was my headdress; I had no idea of how to dispose it, but any appearance of disorder in the vestments, always arranged with minute symmetry, would have inevitably betrayed me.

Finally the toilet of Sister Vidocq was finished. We crossed the court and the gardens and reached the place where the walls were easiest to scale. I then gave the nurse fifty francs, which was nearly all I had left. He gave me a hand, and there I was in the deserted streets from which I gained the country guided by my rather vague directions. Although I was rather embarrassed by my skirts, I walked along fast enough so that I had made two leagues by sunrise. I met a peasant who was on his way to Quimper to sell vegetables, and I questioned him on the road I was taking; he gave me to understand that I was on the road to Brest. That was not for me. I made him comprehend that I wanted to go to Rennes, and he showed me a crossroad which joined the main road to that city. I at once dived into it, trembling every moment lest I meet some of the soldiers of the 'Army of England,' which was quartered in the villages between Nantes and Brest. Toward ten o'clock in the morning I reached a small commune. I asked whether there were any soldiers there, showing a real fear that I should get into a wrangle with them which would have led to my discovery. The person of whom I asked this information was a babbling, talkative sacristan, who forced me to come into the presbytery to refresh myself, which with its white walls and green shutters was but two steps away.

The curé, an old man whose face showed his good nature, received me kindly. 'My dear sister,' he said, 'I am going to celebrate mass; when it is over, will you have lunch with us?' I had to go to the church and I was somewhat embarrassed to make the signs and genuflections prescribed for a nun; fortunately the curé's old maidservant was beside me, and I got out of it fairly well by imitating her at every point. When the mass was over, we sat down to the table and questions began. I told these good people that I was going to Rennes to do penance. The curé did not insist, but the sacristan pressed me rather sharply to know why I was punished. I answered, 'Alas, for being curious.' My man was answered, and left that chapter.

However, my position was rather difficult. I did not dare to eat, for fear of showing the appetite of a man; on the other hand, I said more often 'M. le Curé than 'My dear Brother,' so these distractions might have disclosed all if I had not shortened the luncheon. I found a way, however, to get them to indicate the places where the soldiers were quartered, and, furnished with the benedictions of the curé, who promised not to forget me in his prayers, I went on my way, already familiar with my new costume.

I met few people on the way. The wars of the Revolution had depopulated this unhappy country, and I passed through villages where there was not a house standing. At nightfall I reached a hamlet of a few houses, and knocked at the door of a thatched cottage. An old woman opened and took me into a rather large room, but which for dirt would have disputed with the vilest holes in Galicia. The family consisted of father, mother, a young boy, and two girls of fifteen to seventeen. When I entered, they were making some sort of buckwheat cakes; everyone was grouped around the stove, and the faces, lighted as in the pictures of Rembrandt by the sole flames of the hearth, made a picture which a painter would have admired. I had hardly time to pay attention to the effects of the light, as I showed a desire to eat. With all the respect which my costume inspired, they served me the first cakes, which I devoured, without noticing that they were so hot as to burn my palate. Since then I have sat at the most sumptuous tables, where they were prodigal in the most exquisite wines and the most delicate and *recherchés* dishes, but none of them has made me forget the cakes of that Breton peasant.

When supper was over, there was a prayer. Then the father and mother lighted up, and worn out by the agitations and fatigue of the day, I expressed a desire to retire. 'We have no bed to give you,' said the master of the house; 'you will sleep with our two girls.' I observed that, as I was doing penance, I ought to sleep on straw, and added that I would be content with a corner in the stable. 'Oh,' he answered, 'sleeping with Jeanne and Madelon, you will not break your vow, because their bed is made of straw. Besides, you cannot have a place in the stable. A coppersmith and two soldiers on furlough have already asked to pass the night there.'

There was nothing for me to say; only too happy to avoid meeting the soldiers, I gained the boudoir of the two girls. It was a wretched den full of cider apples, cheese, and smoked bacon; in a corner a dozen chickens roosted, and lower down were eight rabbits. The furnishings consisted of a cracked pitcher, a wormeaten stool, and a bit of mirror; the bed, like all those in that country, was simply a coffin-like box, on half-barrels, waiting the hour of bedtime. It was stuffed with straw and was scarcely three feet wide.

Here came a new embarrassment. The young girls undressed freely before me, but I had good reasons to show restraint. Independently of reasons which may be imagined, I had under my feminine garments a man's shirt which would have revealed my sex and *incognito*. In order not to betray myself, I removed some pins slowly, and when I saw that the two sisters were in bed, I overturned, as if inadvertently, the iron lamp which gave us light. I was then able to remove my feminine garments without fear. Climbing in between the canvas sheets I lay in such a way as to avoid all discovery. There, I was motionless, eyes wide open like a hare in a trap, when, a long time before day would break, I heard knocking at the door with blows from the butt of a gun. My first idea, like that of every man who finds himself in a bad way, was that the police had discovered my traces and had come to arrest me; I did not know where to creep. While the blows redoubled, I finally recalled the soldiers sleeping in the stable, and my alarm was dissipated.

'Who's there?' asked the master of the house, waking suddenly.

'Your soldiers of yesterday.'

'Well, what do you want?'

'Fire to light our pipes before we go.'

Our host got up then, sought some fire in the cinders, and opened the door to the soldiers.

One of the two looked at his watch by the light of the lamp, and said, 'It's half-past four. Come on, let's go.'

In fact they went; the host blew out the lamp and went back to bed. As I did not want to dress in front of my companions any more than undress, I got up at once, and re-lighting the lamp, I again put on my coarse dress, and knelt in a corner, pretending to pray while I waited for the family to awake. I had not long to wait. At five o'clock, the mother shouted from bed, 'Jeanne – get up! You must make soup for the sister, as she wants to go early.' Jeanne got up; made soup, which I ate with good appetite, and I left the good people who had received me so well.

After walking all day with zest, that, evening I found myself in a village near Vannes, where I saw that I had been led astray by wrong or badly understood directions. I slept in the village and went through Vannes very early in the morning. It was my intention to reach Rennes, from where I hoped to get to Paris easily, but, as I was going out of Vannes, I had an encounter which decided me to change my plan. On the same road, walking slowly, was a woman followed by a young child, and carrying on her back a box of relics which she showed in the villages while she told her troubles, and selling rings of Saint Hubert or consecrated rosaries. The woman told me that she was going to Nantes by a crossroad. I had so much interest in avoiding the main road that I did not hesitate to follow this new guide. Besides, Nantes offered me more resources, as we shall see.

We reached Nantes after walking eight days, and I left the woman and her relics. She lived in a suburb. The Ile Feydeau was indicated for me. At Bicêtre I had learned from a man named Grenier, called 'the man from Nantes,' that in this quarter was a sort of inn where thieves collected without fear of being disturbed. I knew that on the recommendation of some 'known' names, one was admitted without difficulty, but I only vaguely knew the address, and there was hardly any way of asking. I thought of an expedient which succeeded. I entered several lodging-houses one after another and asked for M. Grenier. At the fourth house where I called, the hostess left two persons with whom she was busy, and led me to a small room, where she said, 'Have you seen Grenier? Is he still ill [in prison]?' 'No,' I answered, 'he is very well [free].' Seeing that I was with the 'mother' of the thieves, I told her without hesitation who I was, and my condition. Without answering, she took me by the arm, opened a door built in the woodwork and made me enter a low room where eight men and two women were playing cards and drinking brandy and liqueurs. 'Here,' said my conductress, presenting me to the company, which was astonished at the appearance of a nun, 'here's a sister who will convert you.' At the same time I pulled off my veil, and three of those present, whom I had seen in the convict prison, recognized me. They were named Berry, Bidaut-Mauger, and the young Goupy whom I had met at Quimper; the others had escaped from the prison at Rochefort. My disguise amused them.

When I awoke the next day, I found on my bed new clothes, linen, everything necessary to complete my toilet. Where had the things come from? I hardly had the leisure to worry about that. The small amount of money I had not spent in the hospital at Quimper, where everything was very dear, had been used on my journey. Without clothes, resources, and acquaintances I at least needed time to write to my mother for help. So I accepted all that was offered me. But one special circumstance shortened my stay in Ile Feydeau. At the end of a week my fellow guests saw that I was perfectly recovered from my fatigue, and one evening they told me that the next day they were going to pull off a trick in a house, Place Graslin, and that they counted on me to go with them. I was to have the post of honour with Mauger on the inside.

That was not for me. I was willing to make use of the circumstances to get me out of trouble and to gain Paris, where, nearer my family, I should not want for resources, but it did not enter into my combinations to enlist in a gang of thieves, because, although I had frequented sharpers and lived on industry, I felt an invincible repugnance at entering on a career of crime of which my precocious experience began to reveal the dangers. On the other hand, a refusal would make me suspect to my new companions, who, in this retreat inaccessible to sight, could put me out of the way quietly, and send me to keep company with the salmon and smelts in the Loire. There was only one decision for me to make, and that was to go as quickly as possible, and I decided to do so.

After I had exchanged my new clothes for a peasant's coat, with which I was given eighteen francs in return, I left Nantes, with a basket of provisions on the end of a stick, which gave me the complete air of a man of the neighbourhood. It is needless to say that I took the crossroads, where, I may say in passing, the gendarmes would be more useful than on the main roads, on which the folk who have something to unravel with justice rarely show themselves.

On leaving Nantes I walked all day and two nights, without stopping at any village, for my provisions allowed me to dispense with that. I was going haphazard – although always determined to gain Paris or the seacoast, in the hope of being taken aboard some ship – when I reached the first habitations of a city which appeared to me to have been recently the scene of a battle. Most of the houses were only a heap of ruins, blackened by fire; all those around the Place had been completely destroyed. Only the church-tower was still standing, and the clock struck the hours only for inhabitants who no longer existed. I was in the Vendée, at Cholet. The master of a miserable pothouse covered with furze, in which I had stopped, suggested a role to me by asking if I came to Cholet for the market the next day. I answered in the affirmative, much astonished at first that the cultivators in the neighbourhood collected in the middle of the ruins and that they still had anything to sell. The host observed that hardly anything was brought to market except cattle from rather distant markets; on the other hand, although nothing had been done to repair the disasters of war, pacification had been nearly completed by General Hoche, and if there were soldiers about in the country, it was only to hold the insurgents in restraint, for they might become formidable.

I was at the market early in the morning, and thinking how I could use the circumstance to my benefit, I approached a cattle-dealer and asked him to listen to me a moment. At first he looked upon me with distrust, probably taking me for a spy, and I hastened to reassure him by saying that it was a purely personal matter. We then went into a shed where they sold brandy. I told him briefly that I had deserted to see my parents who lived in Paris, and I wanted to get a place which would allow me to reach my destination without being arrested. The good man answered that he had no place to give me, but that if I wished to drive a herd of cattle to Sceaux, he would take me with him. Never was a proposition accepted with greater enthusiasm. I entered on my duties at once in the desire to render to my new employer the slightest service that depended on me.

In the afternoon he sent me with a letter to a person in the city, who asked me whether my master had instructed me to receive anything. I answered in the negative. 'That's all right,' the man said – I think he was a notary; 'still you'll take back this bag with three hundred francs.' I faithfully delivered the sum to the cattle-dealer, in whom my correctness seemed to inspire some confidence. We went the next day.

At the end of three days on the road, the boss called to me, 'Louis,' he said, 'do you know how to write?'

'Yes, sir.'

'Count?'

'Yes, sir.'

'Keep account of things?'

'Yes, sir.'

'Oh, well, I need to turn off the road to look at some lean cattle at Saint-Gauburge; you'll drive the cattle to Paris with Jacques and

Saturin; you'll be head-boy.' Then he gave me his instructions and
went.

By this promotion I no longer travelled on foot, which bettered my
position materially; for the drovers who walk are always either stifled by
dust which the cattle raise, or are up to their knees in mud. Moreover, I
was better paid and better fed, but I did not abuse these advantages as I
saw most of the head-boys do who followed the same road. While forage
for the animals was transformed into chickens or joints for themselves, or went to the innkeepers, one could see the poor beasts grow
leaner and leaner.

I drove most faithfully; and when the boss met us at Verneuil, as he
had got ahead of us, he complimented me on the appearance of the
herd. When we reached Sceaux my beasts were worth twenty francs
more a head than the rest, and I had spent ninety francs less on the way
than my confrères. The boss was delighted and gave me forty francs,
and cited me among all the graziers as the Aristides of drovers; in a way
I was put in the order of the day in the Sceaux market. On the other
hand, my colleagues would willingly have beaten me to death. One of
them, known for his strength and skill, tried to disgust me with my
trade by undertaking to be the public vindicator, but what could a
thick rustic do against a pupil of the great Goupie? He succumbed in a
memorable combat with fists. This triumph was the more glorious as
my conduct had been most moderate, and I consented to fight only
when I could not do otherwise. My master was more and more satisfied
with me, and insisted that I stay a year with him as head-boy, promising me a small interest in his trade.

I had received no news from my mother. In this position I should
find the resources I sought in Paris, and, finally, my new costume disguised me so well that I had no fear of the frequent excursions I made
to Paris. In fact, I passed several persons of my acquaintance without
their paying any attention to me. One evening, however, as I was crossing rue Dauphine, to get back to the Barrier d'Enfer, I felt a tap on my
shoulder. My first thought was to flee, without turning around, expecting that whoever is making an arrest counts on that movement to seize
one; but a congestion of traffic barred the way. I awaited what would
happen, and in a glance recognized that I had been panic-stricken.

The man who had so alarmed me was none other than that Villedieu, captain of the Thirteenth Chasseurs, with whom I had been closely connected at Lille. Although he was surprised to see me in an oil cloth hat, a blouse, and leather gaiters, he was very friendly and invited me to supper, telling me that he had extraordinary things to say to me. He was not in uniform, but this did not astonish me, for officers usually wear civilian clothes when they are in Paris. What did strike me was his air of uneasiness and his extreme pallor. As he showed an intention of supping outside the barriers, we took a cab which brought us to Sceaux.

When we reached the Grand Cerf, we asked for a private room. We had hardly been served when Villedieu closed the door with a double lock and put the key in his pocket. Then he said, with tears in his eyes and a bewildered air: 'My friend, I am a lost man – lost. They are searching for me. I must get clothes like yours. And if you will – I have money – much money, we will go to Switzerland together. I know your ingenuity in escapes; you are the only one who can get me out of this.'

Such a beginning was hardly reassuring. Already embarrassed myself, I did not care about getting a new reason for arrest against me by joining myself to a man who, pursued actively, would bring about my discovery. This reasoning, which I made *in petto*, decided me to play close with Villedieu. Moreover, I had no idea what the trouble was. At Lille I had seen him spend more than his pay allowed, but a young and well-turned-out officer has so many means of procuring money that no one paid any attention. I was, therefore, surprised when I heard his story.

In short, it was that he had been tricked by a woman and had been forced to join forces with a band of *chauffeurs* led by the famous Sallambier. At last the two Sallambiers were arrested, and the elder, circumvented by the agents of authority, denounced all his accomplices and indicated how and where they might be arrested. As a result forty-three persons of both sexes were arrested, and at the same time a warrant for Villedieu was issued. Warned by a sergeant-major of the gendarmes, he escaped and reached Paris. Now he asked my assistance.

I was deeply flattered by the confidence Villedieu showed in me, there was no doubt of that, but I found his company very dangerous, so I made up a yarn when he questioned me on my means of existence and especially on my domicile. For the same reason, I was careful not to appear at the rendezvous he gave me for the next day; it would have been exposing myself without being useful. When I left him at eleven o'clock in the evening, I even took the precaution of making several detours before I entered the inn, for fear of being followed by some agents. My master, who was in bed, awoke me early the next day to tell me that we were going immediately to Nogent-le-Rotrou, and then to his properties near that city.

We made the journey in four days. I was received in the family as a hard-working and zealous servant, but none the less I persisted in the intention I had had for some time to go back to my home from which I received neither news nor money. On our return to Paris with cattle, I took leave of my master who let me go with regret. When I left him, I went into a café to wait for a porter who was bringing my things. A paper fell into my hands and the first article I saw was about the arrest of Villedieu. He had been taken only after having brought down two agents charged with his arrest, and he was badly wounded. He was executed two months after in Bruges, the last of seventeen accomplices. He watched their heads fall with a calm which did not desert him for an instant.

This circumstance made me congratulate myself on the stand I had taken. If I had stayed with the cattle-dealer, I should have had to come to Paris at least twice a month; the political police, directed against conspiracies and foreign agents, had taken on a growth and an energy which might be fatal to me, for they watched very minutely all individuals who, called at any moment by their occupations in the departments of the West, might serve as intermediaries between the insurgents and their friends in the capital. So I went in all haste. The third day I was in Arras and entered that evening just as the labourers were coming back from work. I did not go directly to my father's house, but to that of one of my aunts, who warned my parents. They believed me dead, as they had received neither of my last two letters; I never was able to find out how they had gone astray or by whom they had been intercepted. After I had told all my doings at length, I asked for news of the family, which naturally led me to the subject of my wife. I learned that my father had taken her in, but that her debauchery had become so scandalous that they had had to put her out. I did not occupy myself with her; I had something else to think about.

At any moment I might be discovered and arrested at my parents' house, which would get them into trouble. It was urgent for me to find an asylum where the police surveillance was less active than at Arras. We turned our eyes on a village in the neighbourhood, Ambercourt, where an ex-Carmelite, a friend of my father's, lived and who consented to receive me. At this time (1798) the priests still said mass secretly, although there was little hostility to them. Père Lambert, my host, celebrated the divine office in a sort of barn, and as the only one he had to help him was an old man, almost impotent, I offered to fulfil the duties of sacristan. I did so well that one would have said that I had never done anything else in my life. I also seconded Père Lambert in the lessons he gave the children of the neighbourhood. My success in teaching was even so great that it became the talk of the canton.

But this sort of life did not suit me; although, dressed as I was ridiculously in some sort of costume of a lay brother and tolerated by the authorities, I was in no fear of being suspected. On the other hand, my carnal life, which I have always taken into consideration, was very good; my parents sent me beer, birds, and fruit. And I had in my classes some pretty peasant girls. All went well for some time, but in the end I became an object of distrust. I was spied upon, and the spies gained the certainty that I greatly extended my functions and complained to Père Lambert. He in his turn spoke to me about several charges which had been brought against me, but I denied them completely. The complainants were silent, but they redoubled their surveillance, and one night, when I was going to give a lesson to a girl pupil of sixteen, I was seized by four brawny fellows, taken to a hop-yard, my clothes taken off, and I was whipped with bunches of nettles and thistles until the blood came. The pain was so keen that I lost consciousness, and when I recovered my senses, I found myself in the road covered with blisters and blood.

Now what was I to do? If I returned to Père Lambert, I should run new dangers. Night was not far advanced. Although I was in a burning fever, I decided to go to Mareuil, to one of my uncles. I reached there at two o'clock in the morning, worn out with fatigue and covered only by a poor mat which I had discovered. After a little laughter at my mishap, I was rubbed with cream mixed with oil. At the end of a week, I was well and went back to Arras. But it was impossible for me to stay there; the police might be informed at any moment of my stay. So I took the road to Holland, with the intention of settling there. The money I had did not allow me to wait until some opportunity offered to busy myself usefully.

After I had passed through Brussels, where I learned that the Baroness d'I— had settled at London, Antwerp, and Breda, I embarked for Rotterdam. I had been given the address of a tavern where I might lodge. There I met a Frenchman who was very friendly and who invited me to dinner several times. He promised to interest himself in finding me a good place. I answered his kind invitation with distrust, as I knew that all means seemed good to the Dutch Government to recruit its marine. In spite of my reserve, my new friend succeeded in getting me absolutely drunk on a special liqueur. The next day I awoke in the roads aboard a Dutch brig, a war vessel. There was no longer room for doubt; I had fallen through intemperance into the hands of a crimp.

Stretched out near the shrouds, I was reflecting on the singular destiny which multiplied incidents around me, when a man of the crew kicked me and told me to go and get my ship's clothes. I pretended not to understand him. The ship's master then came to give me the order in French. On my observing that I was not a sailor, since I had signed no engagement, he seized a rope as if to strike me. At this gesture I jumped for the knife of a sailor who was eating at the foot of the mainmast, got behind a cannon, and swore to cut open the belly of the first one who advanced. Great uproar among the crew.

At this noise the captain appeared on deck. He was a man of forty, of good appearance, with none of that brusqueness of manner so common with seamen. He listened to my protest kindly, which was all he could do, as he could not change the naval organization of his government.

In Holland at that time in an urgency they seized and threw into the vessels of the line masons, hostlers, or barbers – men of all sorts. So we had on board men who by inclination and habits of life seemed so far removed from naval service that it appeared ridiculous even to think of making them enter it. Of the two hundred who like myself had been pressed, there were not twenty who had ever set foot on a ship. Most of them had been taken by force or when drunk; others had been attracted by the promise of a free passage to Batavia where they could ply their trade. Among the last were two Frenchmen, one a bookkeeper and the other a gardener, both of whom became excellent sailors. To console us, the men of the crew told us that for fear of desertion, we perhaps would be allowed to land in six months.

As far as I was concerned, I had thought of the navy for a long time, and my position would not have been repugnant if I had not been under compulsion and had not the prospect of slavery threatened; add to that the bad treatment on the part of the master, who could not forgive me my first outburst. At the slightest false manœuvre, blows with a rope's end rained on me in such a way that I regretted the clubs of the keepers in the hulks. I was desperate, and twenty times the idea came to me to drop from the tops a halyard block on the head of my persecutor, or throw him overboard when I was on watch some night. I should have put these ideas into execution, if the lieutenant, who had become friendly with me because I taught him to fence, had not eased my position. Moreover, we were to be sent immediately to Helwotsluis, where the *Heindrack,* on which we were to serve as crew, was anchored. On the way we might escape.

The day of transshipment arrived. We embarked to the number of two hundred and seventy recruits on a small smack, sailed by twenty-five sailors and guarded by twenty-five soldiers. The weakness of this detachment confirmed me in the resolution to attempt a surprise, disarm the soldiers, and force the sailors to take us near Antwerp. A hundred and twenty of the recruits entered into the plot. It was arranged that we should surprise the men on watch when the rest of their fellows were at dinner. The plan was carried out with so much success that our men suspected absolutely nothing. The officer who commanded the detachment was seized just as he was going to take tea; however, he met with no ill-treatment. He was persuaded to allow himself to be put in the hold with the soldiers without resistance. The sailors stayed at work; only a man from Dunkirk, one of our men, took the helm.

Night came; I wanted to heave to to avoid falling on some coast guard to which some of our sailors might signal. The man from Dunkirk refused with such obstinacy that it should have inspired my distrust. We sailed on, and at daybreak the smack was under the guns of a fort near Helwotsluis. The Dunkirk man at once announced that he was going ashore to see whether we could land without danger; then I saw that we had been sold, but there was no drawing back. Without a doubt signals had already been given, and at the slightest movement the fort would sink us; we had to wait on events. Soon a boat manned by twenty men put out and boarded the smack. Three officers among them mounted the deck without showing any fear, although it was the stage of a rather lively affair between our comrades and the Dutch sailors who wanted to get the soldiers out of the hold.

The first word of the senior officer was to ask who was the chief of the plot. Everyone was dumb, but I spoke in French and explained that there was no plot; that it was simply a unanimous and spontaneous movement to get out of a slavery which had been imposed upon us. We had in no way ill-treated the commander of the smack; he could testify to that, as could the Dutch sailors, who knew that we should have left the vessel to them after we had landed at Antwerp. I don't know whether my harangue produced any effect, for I was not allowed to finish it, only, as they put us into the hold where we had put the soldiers the evening before, I heard someone say to the pilot 'that more than one would be dancing the next day at the end of a yardarm.'

The smack then steered to Helwotsluis, where she arrived the same day at four o'clock in the afternoon. The *Heindrack* lay at anchor in the roads. The commander of the fort came out in a boat, and an hour after I was taken to him. I found gathered a sort of naval board which questioned me on the details of the insurrection and the part I had taken in it. I sustained, as I had done before the commander of the fort, that as I had signed no act of engagement, I believed I had the right to recover my liberty by all possible means.

They sent me out and summoned a young man from Tournai who had arrested the commander of the smack; they considered us both the leaders of the plot, and it is known that in such circumstances the punishment comes on the guilty. There was nothing for either of us except to be hanged. Fortunately, the young man, whom I had had time to warn, deposed as I had done, sustaining firmly that there had been no suggestion on the part of anyone, the idea of striking the blow having come to all at the same time. We were sure that our comrades would not deny this, for they had shown a lively interest in us, even going so far as to say that, if we were condemned, the vessel on which they were would jump like a caisson; that is to say, they would touch off the powder, free in this way to make a journey in the air. And there were some gay dogs who would do what they said. Whether they feared this threat and the bad example it would set the sailors of the fleet who had been enrolled in the same way, or that the council recognized that we had held ourselves within the legitimate limits of defence in trying to get out of a trap, they promised to solicit our pardon from the admiral on condition that we would keep our comrades under control. We promised all they wanted, for nothing makes the conditions of a transaction so easy as to feel a rope around the neck.

When these preliminaries were over, our comrades were transferred aboard the vessel, and distributed in between decks with the crew which they had come to complete; there was no complaint; there was not the slightest disorder to suppress. It is fair to say that we were not ill-treated as on the brig, where our old friend the master commanded with a rope in hand. In addition, as I gave lessons in fencing to the marines, I was treated with some regard; I was promoted bombardier with twenty-eight florins a month.

Two months went by in this way, but the continual presence of English cruisers did not permit us to leave the roads. I was made for my new position; I did not even think of getting out of it when we learned that the French authorities were seeking their nationals who made part of the Dutch fleet. It was a fine opportunity for any of us who found the service bad, but no one cared to take advantage of it. First, they only wanted us to incorporate us in ships of the French line, a change which offered no advantages; then most of my comrades had, I think, as I had, good reasons not to desire to show their faces to the agents of the metropolis. So everyone kept still; when they sent to the captain to ask for the rolls of his crew, the examination produced no result, for the simple reason that we all bore false names. We thought the storm was over.

However, the search went on; only instead of making inquiries, agents were posted in the ports and taverns charged to examine the men who came on shore on service or leave. It was on one of these excursions that I was arrested. I have preserved for a long time my grati-

tude toward the vessel's cook who honoured me with his personal intimacy since I had found it bad that he gave us tallow instead of butter
and spoiled haddock instead of fresh fish. Taken before the commander
of the place, I declared that I was Dutch; the language was sufficiently
familiar to me to sustain this version. Besides, I asked to be taken
aboard under escort to procure my papers which would prove my citi-
zenship; nothing could have appeared more fair or natural. An officer
was ordered to accompany me, and we went in the boat which had
brought me ashore. When we reached the vessel, I made my man
mount first – we had talked together on friendly terms; when I saw him
hung up in the shrouds, I suddenly pushed off, shouting to the oars-
men to row vigorously, as there was a drink in it. We split the water,
while my officer, still in the shrouds, raged among the crew, who did
not understand him or pretended not to. When I reached land, I ran
and hid in a house of my acquaintance, resolved to leave the vessel, as it
became difficult to appear without being arrested. My flight confirmed
all the suspicions held against me. However, I forestalled the captain,
who tacitly authorized me to do what I thought best for my safety.

A privateer from Dunkirk, the *Barras,* Captain Fromentin, was in
the roads. At this time the authorities rarely visited vessels of this kind,
which in some way had the right of asylum. It was agreeable to me to
go there. I was presented to Fromentin and admitted on my reputation
as master at arms. Four days after, the *Barras* sailed to cruise in the
Sound. It was the beginning of winter, 1799, in which the bad weather
destroyed so many ships on the Baltic coasts. We were hardly on the
high seas when a north wind came up suddenly dead ahead; we rolled
terribly, and I was so ill that I could take nothing for three days except
brandy and water. Half the crew was in the same way, so that a fisher-
man could have taken us without firing a shot.

At last the weather moderated, the wind suddenly changed to the
southwest, and the *Barras,* an excellent sailer, shooting ten knots an
hour, had soon cured everyone. At that moment the watch shouted,
'Ship to port!' The captain seized his glasses and declared that it was an
English coaster under a neutral flag, which the wind had separated
from her convoy. We bore down on him with the wind astern, having
hoisted the French flag. At the second shot, he struck his colours with-

out waiting to be boarded; the crew was placed in the hold and the prize sent to Bergen.

I stayed on board the *Barras* for six months. share of the prizes began to make quite a hoard when we entered the port of Ostend. As we have seen, that has always been fatal to me; what happened this time nearly made me believe in fatalism. We were scarcely inside the dock when a commissioner, gendarmes, and police agents came on board to examine the crew's papers. I have since learned that this measure in some ways came about unexpectedly, as there had been a murder and it was supposed that the murderer might be among us. When my turn for questioning arrived, I declared that my name was August Duval, born at Lorient, and I added that my papers were in Rotterdam at the office of the Dutch marine; they answered nothing, and I thought I was out of it.

When the hundred and three men on board had been questioned, they summoned eight of us, telling us that we were to be taken to the school to give explanations. Not caring for that at all, I slipped away at the turn of the first street, and I had already gained thirty yards on the gendarmes when an old woman who was washing the front of her house threw her broom between my legs; I fell; the gendarmes came up and put the handcuffs on me, without prejudice to a number of blows of the butt of carbines and the flat of the sabre. Bound in this way I was taken to the commissioner, who, after he had heard me, asked if I had not escaped from the hospital at Quimper. I saw that I was caught, since there was as much danger for Duval as for Vidocq. However, I decided for the first name, which offered less unfavourable circumstances than the second, as the road from Ostend to Lorient was longer than that from Ostend to Arras, and might give me greater latitude to escape.

IX
Adepts and Cutthroats

A WEEK WENT BY during which I saw the commissioner only once. Then I was sent with a transport of prisoners, deserters, and others directed to Lille. I had reason to fear that the uncertainty about my identity would end in a city where I had sojourned so often. Warned that we should pass that way, I, therefore, took precautions so that the gendarmes who had conducted me previously would not recognize me. My features hidden under a thick coat of dirt and soot were unnatural from the artificial swelling of my cheeks, nearly as large as those of the angel who in church frescoes sounds the trump of the Last judgment. In this state I entered the military prison where I was to stay some days.

While I was there, to charm away the boredom of seclusion I risked some sessions at the canteen; I hoped that by mingling with the visitors, I might seize some opportunity to escape. My meeting with a sailor whom I had known aboard the *Barras* seemed a favourable augury for the execution of my project. I paid for a meal, and when it was over, I returned to my room. I had been there three hours, dreaming of means to recover my liberty, when the sailor came to invite me to take part in a dinner which his wife had just brought him. So the sailor had a wife; the thought struck me that, to put at fault the vigilance of the jailers, she might procure me garments of her sex or some other disguise. Full of this idea, I went down to the canteen and approached the table. Suddenly there was a cry; a woman fainted; it was my comrade's wife. I wanted to help her – an exclamation escaped me – Heavens, it was Francine! Alarmed by my imprudence, I tried to repress the first movement which had mastered me. Surprised and astonished, the spectators of this scene gathered around me and overwhelmed me with questions. After some minutes of silence, I made up a tale; I had thought I recognized my sister.

This incident had no sequel. The next day we went at daybreak and I was confounded when I saw that the convoy, instead of taking the usual road to Lens, took that to Douai. Why this change of direction? I attributed it to some indiscretion of Francine. I soon learned that it resulted simply from the necessity of evacuating on Arras the crowd of defaulters packed in the prison at Cambrai.

Francine, whom I had suspected so unjustly, was waiting for me at the first halt. In spite of the gendarmes she insisted on embracing me and talking to me; she wept, and I did too. With what bitterness she reproached herself for an infidelity which was the cause of all my misfortunes! Her repentance was sincere; I forgave her heartily and when on the order of the corporal she had to go, she slipped into my hand the sum of two hundred francs in gold.

Finally, we reached Douai; we were at the prison gates and a gendarme rang. Who would open? Dutilleul, the turnkey who, as a result of my attempt to escape, had dressed my wounds for a month. He did not seem to see me. At the office I again found a face of an acquaintance, the bailiff Hurtrel, so drunk that I flattered myself that I was lost from his memory. For three days nothing was said, but on the fourth I was taken before the examining magistrate in the presence of Hurtrel and Dutilleul. They asked me if I was not Vidocq. I held to it that I was August Duval, and that they could assure themselves of it by writing to Lorient, and that in addition the reason for my arrest at Ostend proved it, since I was only accused of desertion from a vessel of the State. My aplomb appeared to impose on the judge; he hesitated; Hurtrel and Dutilleul persisted in saying that they were not mistaken. Soon the public prosecutor, Rausson, came to see me, and equally pretended to recognize me. However, as I was not disconcerted, he was still uncertain, and in order to bring light on the facts, they thought up a stratagem.

One morning it was announced that there was somebody to see me in the office; I went down; my mother had been brought from Arras, and one can imagine with what intention. The poor woman sprang to embrace me. I saw the trap. With no brusqueness I pushed her aside, saying to the judge who was present at the interview that it was unworthy to give this unhappy woman the hope of seeing her son, when, to say the least, they were uncertain of being able to present him to her. However, my mother, put in touch with the situation by a signal from me as I drew back from her, pretended to examine me closely, and ended by declaring that an extraordinary resemblance had deceived her.

Then she withdrew, cursing those who had made her travel so far to be given such false joy.

Judge and turnkeys then fell back into uncertainty when a letter arrived from Lorient which seemed to end it. It mentioned a design on the left arm of the Duval who had escaped from the hospital at Quimper, as a fact which could leave no doubt as to the identity of the individual held at Douai. Another appearance before the magistrate. Hurtrel, already in triumph at his perspicacity, attended the examination. At the first words I saw what the question was, and, rolling up my sleeve above my elbow, I showed them the design which they hardly expected to find there. They verified the exact resemblance with the description sent from Lorient. Everyone fell from the clouds; what further complicated the position was that the authorities at Lorient claimed me as a deserter from the navy.

A fortnight went in this way, without their coming to any definite decision in regard to me; then, worn out by the rigours shown me with the object of obtaining a confession, I wrote to the president of the criminal tribunal to declare to him that I was Vidocq. What had determined me on this step was that I counted on going immediately to Bicêtre, with a transport in which in fact I went. However, it was impossible to escape en route, as I had counted on, our surveillance was so rigorous.

I made my second entrance into Bicêtre the second of April, 1799. 1 again saw there Captain Labbre, who, as may be recalled, had furnished me at Brussels the papers with which I had deceived the Baroness d'I——. He was condemned to sixteen years in irons for complicity in a considerable robbery committed at Ghent. Like the rest of us, he was to go with the first chain gang, whose approaching journey was announced to our considerable discomfort. Captain Viez knew the task he had in hand, and he declared that to prevent any escape he would make us wear handcuffs and a double collar until we reached Toulon. However, our promises made him give up this fine scheme.

When we were put in irons, amid the same scenes as at my first departure, I was placed at the head of the first cordon with one of the most famous thieves in Paris and the Provinces. His name was Jossas, better known as the Marquis de Saint-Amand de Faral, a title he ordinarily used. He was a man of thirty-six, of pleasing figure, and at need displaying the best of manners. His travelling costume was that of a dandy just getting out of bed to go to his boudoir. With light grey trousers, he wore a coat and a cap trimmed with astrakan, and all covered by a wide cloak lined with crimson velvet. His expenses were in keeping with his dress, because, not content with treating himself splendidly at every halt, he always fed three or four of the cordon.

Jossas had no education; but very young he had entered the service of a wealthy colonial, whom he accompanied an his travels, and such were his manners that he was not out of place in any circle. So his comrades, seeing him introduce himself into the most distinguished gatherings, nicknamed him 'Passkey.' He was so thoroughly identified with this role that in prison, put under double chains, among men of the most miserable appearance, he still preserved his airs of grandeur under his convict's coat. Furnished with a magnificent dressing-case, he spent an hour every morning at his toilet, and took special care of his very beautiful hands.

Jossas was one of those thieves who meditate and often prepare for an expedition for an entire year. Operating principally by the aid of false keys, he began by taking an impression of the lock on the outside door. When the key was made, he entered the first room; and if he was stopped by another door, he took a new impression, and a second key was made, and so on, until he reached the end. As he could introduce himself only in the absence of the master of the house, he had to lose considerable time in awaiting the occasion.

He had recourse to the following expedient only in cases where he had given up hope; that is to say, when it was impossible to introduce himself into the house. If he was able to get admitted on some pretext, he soon had taken the impression of all the locks. When the keys had been made, he invited the persons to dinner with him at his house, and while they were at table, accomplices rifled the apartment. He had found means to remove the servants either by asking the masters to bring them to serve, or by having the maids and cooks taken out by their lovers. The porters saw nothing, because the thieves ordinarily only took money or jewellery. If it happened that they found some larger object, they wrapped it in dirty linen, and threw it out of a window to one of their fellows who was there on purpose with a laundry wagon.

It was known that Jossas had committed a host of robberies which all showed a spirit of acute observation and invention, both of which he had to the highest degree. In society, where he passed as a creole from Havana, he often met inhabitants of that city whom he was able to deceive. Several times he brought honourable families to the point of offering the hand of their young ladies. During the course of the negotiations he always found out where the dowry was, and he never failed to make off with it and disappear at the moment of signing the contract.

Of all his tricks the most astonishing was one where a banker at Lyons was the victim. Jossas was introduced on the pretext of discounts and negotiations, and in a short time he was on such terms of intimacy that he had taken the impressions of all the locks, except that of the strong-box, the secret entry to which made all his attempts useless. On one hand the box was sealed in a wall and was lined with iron, so he could not think of breaking into it; besides, the cashier never parted with the key. But such obstacles did not rebuff Jossas. He gained the liking of the cashier and proposed a country party at Collognes. On the day appointed they went in a cab. When they were near Saint-Rambert, they saw on the bank a woman apparently dying, bleeding from the nose and mouth; beside her was a man who seemed in great difficulties to help her. Jossas, pretending great emotion, said that to stop the hemorrhage, it was enough to apply a key to the back of the sufferer. But no one had a key, except the cashier, who at first offered his doorkey; that did not suffice. Then the cashier, frightened by the sight of blood, gave his key to the strong-box, which was applied with much success between the shoulders of the patient. It is obvious that there was a bed of wax there, and that the scene had been staged in advance. Three days later the strong-box was emptied.

As I have said, Jossas was ostentatious and spent money with the facility of a man who makes it easily. He was very charitable, and I could cite many deeds of bizarre generosity. One day he entered an apartment in rue de Hazard which had been pointed out to him as worth rifling. At first the poverty of the apartment struck him, but the owner might be a miser. He continued his search, hunted everywhere, broke everything, and found in a writing-desk only a pile of pawn tickets. He took five louis from his pocket and placed them on the mantel, after writing on the glass, 'Indemnity for broken furniture,' and withdrew, closing the doors carefully for fear that less scrupulous thieves would steal what he had respected.

When Jossas went from Bicêtre with us, it was the third time he had made the journey. After that he escaped twice, was recaptured, and died in prison at Rochefort in 1805.

Aside from a furious drubbing given to two convicts for trying to escape at Beaune, nothing extraordinary happened until we reached Chafflons, where we embarked on a large boat filled with straw, covered with thick canvas. If one tried to take a glimpse of the country or to breathe pure air by raising a corner of the canvas, the convict had blows from a club rained on his back. Although I was exempt from this evil treatment, I was none the less affected by my position. Jossas's gaiety, which never left him, barely succeeded in making me forget for an instant that when I reached the prison, I should be the object of such vigilance that all escape would be impossible. This idea still obsessed me when we reached Lyons.

When he saw I'lle Barbe, Jossas said, 'You'll see something new.' In fact, I saw an elegant carriage, which seemed to be waiting for the boat; as soon as it appeared, a woman put her head out of the door and waved a white handkerchief. 'That's she,' said Jossas, and answered the signal. The boat was made fast to the pier, and this woman got out to mingle with the crowd of curiosity-seekers; I could not see her face, which was covered by a thick black veil. She stayed there from four o'clock in the afternoon until evening. The crowd then dispersed; Jossas was set free and returned with a sausage in which fifty louis were hidden. I learned that Jossas had made the conquest of this woman under the title of Marquis.

Finally, after thirty-seven days of most painful travel, the chain gang entered Toulon. The fifteen wagons reached the port and ranged themselves in front of the ropewalk; they made us get down; an employee received us and led us into the court of the prison. On the way, those who had clothes of any value hurried to take them off to sell or give them to the crowd which assembled on the arrival of a new chain. When the prison clothes were distributed and our handcuffs riveted, we were taken on board a vessel which served as a floating prison. After the trusties had taken our description, the convicts who had escaped were selected and put in double chains. Their escape lengthened their term three years.

As I was in the last class, they sent me to Ward No. 3, where the most suspect convicts were placed. For fear that they would find a chance to escape, they were never put on fatigue. We were always made fast to the bench. Sleeping on bare planks, eaten by vermin, worn out by bad treatment, lacking nourishment and exercise, we offered a deplorable spectacle. I found in Ward No. 3 all the most consummate rascals in the prison. One named Vidal even the convicts themselves held in horror. Arrested at the age of fourteen in a gang of murderers in whose crimes he had taken part, his age alone saved him from the scaffold. He was condemned to twenty-four years in confinement, but he had hardly entered prison when as a result of a quarrel he killed one of his comrades with a knife.

He had been in the prison some years when a convict was condemned to death. At the time there was no executioner in the city; Vidal offered his services, eagerly; they were accepted, and the execution took place, but they had to put Vidal on the bench with the warders, otherwise he would have been beaten to death with blows from the chains. The threats made against him did not prevent his again fulfilling the duties of his odious trade. In addition he took over the whipping of the convicts. Finally, in 1794, when Dugommier took the city, Vidal executed his decrees. He thought he was definitely free; but when the Terror was over, he was taken back to prison, where he was the object of special vigilance.

On the same bench with Vidal was chained a Jew, Deschamps, one of the authors of the famous robbery of the Garde-Meuble. When the convicts listened to the story, they gave it a sinister reception; at the mere enumeration of the diamonds and jewels stolen, their eyes lighted up and their muscles contracted in a convulsive movement. One could judge from the expression of their faces what use they would make of their liberty.

Before he was sentenced for the robbery of the Garde-Meuble, Deschamps had been implicated in an important affair, from which he escaped, though guilty, as he boasted to us, giving details which left no room for doubt. It was the double murder of a jeweller Deslong and his maid, committed with the complicity of the second-hand dealer Fraumont.

DesIong had a rather extensive business. In addition to individual purchases, he did a brokerage business in pearls and diamonds; and as he had the reputation of being an honest man, he was often trusted with valuable objects, either to sell or to get a part by unmounting them. He, also went to sales, and there he made the acquaintance of Fraumont, who attended assiduously, principally to buy vestments and other ornaments pillaged from the churches (1793) which he burned to extract the metal from the lace. From the habit of seeing each other and competing in such operations, a liaison grew up between the two men and they soon became intimate. Deslong hid nothing from Fraumont; he consulted him on all his enterprises, informed him of the value of all the deposits he received, and even went so far as to trust to him the secret of the hiding-place where he placed his most precious valuables.

When he had learned all these details and having free access to Deslong's place, Fraumont conceived the idea of robbing him while he and his wife were at the theatre, where they often went. He needed an accomplice to watch; moreover, it was dangerous for Fraumont to be seen in the house, where everyone knew him, on the day of the deed. At first he had chosen a locksmith, an escaped convict, who had made false keys which would work in Deslong's house, but this man was pursued by the police and had to leave Paris; so Fraumont substituted Deschamps.

On the appointed day, Deslong and his wife went to the theatre. Fraumont hid with a wine merchant to watch for the return of the servant, who ordinarily profited by the absence of her employers to see her lover. Deschamps went into the apartment and quietly opened the door with the false keys. To his astonishment he saw the servant in the vestibule (in fact, her sister who closely resembled her, had left some moments previously). At the appearance of Deschamps, whose face was still more terrifying in his surprise, the girl dropped her work. She was going to shout. Deschamps hurled himself on her, turned her backwards, took her by the throat, and stabbed her five times with a sheath knife which he always carried in his right trousers' pocket. The poor wretch fell covered with blood. While she was dying, the murderer rummaged in all corners of the apartment, but whether the unexpected incident had troubled him, or whether he heard some noise on the staircase, he limited himself to taking some pieces of silverware which were at hand, and went to find his accomplice at the wine merchant's. He told him the adventure. The latter was much affected, not by the maid's death, but by the lack of intelligence and aplomb which Deschamps had shown. He reproached him for not having discovered the hiding-place which he had indicated so well. What heightened his discontent was that he foresaw that, after such a catastrophe, Deslong would be on his guard and that it would be impossible to find a similar occasion.

Deslong indeed changed his lodgings as a result of this event, which terrified him utterly; the few people he received were introduced only with the greatest precautions. Although Fraumont avoided presenting himself, Deslong had not the slightest suspicion of him. How could he have such ideas about a man who, if he had committed the crime, would not have failed to rifle the hiding-place whose secret he knew? Meeting him some days after on the Place Vendôme, he urged him to come and see him, and was more intimate with him than ever. Fraumont went back to his first projects; but having no hope of forcing the new hiding-place, which, moreover, was carefully guarded, he decided to change his plan. Deslong was brought to Deschamps's on the pretext of making a large deal in diamonds, and murdered and robbed of seventeen thousand francs, with which he had furnished himself on the invitation of Fraumont, who struck the first blow himself.

Two days passed. As her husband did not return, and he would not have been gone so long without warning her, and knowing that he had had considerable valuables on him, Madame Deslong did not doubt that something had happened to him. She went to the police; they got their hands on Fraumont and Deschamps, and the revelations of the locksmith, who should have co-operated in the robbery and who was again arrested, would have been fatal to them, but he escaped. This circumstance removed the only witness, so Deschamps and Fraumont were set free.

Condemned afterward to eighteen years in irons for other robberies, Fraumont was sent to the prison at Rochefort. However, he did not consider himself beaten. By means of money he had secured in his expeditions, he subsidized some men to follow the chain gang to facilitate his escape or even to set him free by force if opportunity offered. All was ready for the execution of this project when a prostitute learned of it from some one of those interested and revealed it. Measures were taken in consequence; the escort was warned. When the chain gang left Bicêtre, Fraumont was put in handcuffs which were not taken off until his arrival at Rochefort, where he received special attention; I was assured that he died in prison. As for Deschamps, who soon escaped from Toulon, be was arrested three years later for a robbery at Auteuil, condemned to death and executed at Paris.

X
A Nest of Land Pirates

I HAD NEVER BEEN more unhappy than since my arrival at Toulon. Lost among the vilest rascals, constantly in contact with them, I would rather a hundred times have been reduced to living in a crowd infected with the plague. All my thoughts turned to possibilities of escape. Different plans came to mind; but it was not enough to think of them. To put them into execution it was necessary to await a favourable moment; until then, patience was the only remedy for my ills. Made fast to the same bench with professional robbers who had already escaped several times, I was, as they were, the object of a surveillance difficult to deceive. From their shelters a short way off, the guards could spy on our slightest movement.

Their chief Matthew had the eyes of a lynx, and was so accustomed to the men that at first sight he could tell whether they planned to deceive him. This old fox was nearly sixty, but, with one of those constitutions which seem to defy the years, he was still vigorous. He was one of those men who never wear out. He never spoke without putting his club on the carpet. It was a pleasure for him to tell of the numerous beatings he had given or ordered to be given. Constantly at war with the convicts, there was not a ruse he did not know. His distrust was so great that he often accused men of plotting when they did not even think of it. It is easy to imagine that it was difficult to appease such a Cerberus.

However, I tried to capture his kindness, an enterprise in which no one had succeeded. I soon recognized that I was not lured on by a vain hope; I visibly gained in his estimation. Matthew sometimes spoke to me; it was, the veterans told me, because I had pleased him; there was no untoward incident for which I did not beg forgiveness. I begged him to let me make playthings for children with bits of wood which the convicts who went on fatigue brought me. He granted all I wanted on condition that I would be sensible; I set to work the next day. My comrades made the rough draft and I finished. Matthew found what I had done pretty; when he noticed that I had help in my little work, he could not hide his satisfaction; that had not happened for a long time. 'Well done,' he said, 'that's the way I like to see you amuse yourselves; all of you ought to do the same; that would distract you, and at least the product would let you procure some comforts.'

In a few days the bench was transformed into a workshop, where fourteen men were equally enthusiastic to drive boredom away and to have some money at their disposal; they displayed the greatest activity. But the time came when our manufacture slowed down on account of overproduction; Toulon was blocked with toys of all descriptions; we had to fold our arms. Not knowing what to do, I pretended that my legs were bothering me, so as to get into the hospital. The doctor, to whom I was recommended by Matthew, whose protégé I really was, believed that I could not walk. When one wants to escape, it is well to have such an opinion held of one. Doctor Fernant did not suspect for a moment that I intended to deceive him; he was one of those disciples of Æsculapius who imagined that brusqueness was one of the attributes of his profession; but he was only human and he was very kind to me.

The surgeon-in-chief also liked me; he trusted me with care of his box of dressings; I placed the lint, prepared presses, and in fact was generally useful, and my complaisance won me his regard. There was no one, not even the convict nurse, who was not agreeable to me; however, no one was more difficult than this L'Homme. Although I had been noted as dangerous, M. L'Homme was so delighted at my good conduct and still more by some bottles of wine which I handed him, that he became more visibly human. When I was nearly certain that he did not look on me with distrust, I turned my batteries on him to out-wit his vigilance as well as that of his confrères. I had already procured a wig and black whiskers; in addition I had hidden in my mattress an old pair of boots which a polish made look like new. There was my toilet for head and feet, and I counted on the surgeon for the rest, for he was accustomed to place on my bed his overcoat, hat, stick, and gloves.

One morning when he was busy amputating an arm, I saw that M. L'Homme had followed him to assist in the operation, which was performed at the end of the ward. It was a fine opportunity to disguise myself; I hurried to do so, and under my new costume, I went straight to the exit. I had to pass through a crowd of guards. I took the risk, boldly; none of them paid any attention to me, and I already thought I was out of danger, when I heard shouts. 'Stop, stop! A Convict is escaping!' I was barely twenty steps from the arsenal gate. Without any disconcertment I doubled my speed, and when I reached the post, I said to the guard, pointing out a man who was just entering the city, 'Run along with me; he has escaped from the hospital.' This presence of mind would have perhaps saved me, but as I was going through the gate, I felt someone pull at my wig; I turned around; it was L'Homme. If I resisted, I was dead; I resigned myself to being led back to prison, where I was placed under double chains.

It was clear that I was to be punished; to avoid it, I fell at the commissioner's knees. 'Oh, monsieur,' I said, 'do not beat me; that is all the pardon I ask; I would rather do three years more if you demand it.' The commissioner, although somewhat touched by my prayer, could hardly retain his gravity. At last he answered that he would forgive me on account of the boldness and novelty of the trick. I thanked him, and the moment after I was taken back to the fatal bench to which I was condemned to be fastened for six years. I flattered myself with the hope that I could again take up my manufacture of toys; but Matthew opposed this, and I was, in spite of myself, obliged to remain inactive.

Two months passed with no change in my situation. One night I could not sleep. Suddenly one of those luminous ideas came which only come in the dark. Jossas was awake, and I communicated it to him. Of course it was an attempt to escape; he judged the means I had thought of excellent, marvellous, and he urged me strongly not to neglect it. I did not forget his advice. The commissioner, a good fellow, at last granted my request to be sent on fatigue. I was coupled to a man named Salesse, as evil as a convict could be. The first time that we were alone, he asked me if I intended to escape. I did not think of it, I answered; I was happy enough to be allowed to work.

However, Jossas knew my secret, and he disposed everything for my escape. I had some civilian clothes which I bid under my convict's garments, without my companion even noticing it. A ball with a screw replaced the ball riveted to the irons, and I was ready to go. Three days later, after I had left my companions, I went out on fatigue, and presented myself at the call of the guard. 'Pass, rascal,' said Matthew. There I was in the ropewalk; the place seemed propitious. I told my companion that I had to satisfy a need; he pointed to some piles of wood behind which I could place myself, and he had hardly lost me sight, when, throwing aside my red coat and unscrewing the ball, I fled in the direction of the dock.

The frigate *Muiron* which had brought Bonaparte and staff back from Egypt was being refitted. I went on board and asked for the master carpenter who I knew was in the hospital. The cook to whom I spoke took me for one of the new crew. I applauded his mistake and to confirm him in it I kept up a conversation with him; but was on pins and needles. There were forty pairs of convicts working two yards away. At any moment I might be recognized. At last a small boat left for the city; I jumped in, grasped an oar, and handled it like an old sailor.

We were soon in Toulon. In a hurry to get into the country, I made haste to the gate, but no one could go out unless furnished with a green card provided by the municipality. They refused to let me out, and while I was thinking how I could prove that the order did not apply to me, I heard the three cannon shots which in the distance signaled my escape. I already saw myself in the hands of the guards. In such sad reflections I departed hastily, and in order to meet as few people as possible, I went toward the ramparts. I did not know what to do when I saw a funeral on its way to the cemetery outside the walls. I followed, and, when we reached the cemetery, in my turn I advanced to the edge of the grave, and threw a handful of earth on the coffin; then I separated from the company by taking a winding path. I walked a long time, without getting out of sight of Toulon.

At five in the evening, near the entrance to a pine wood, I suddenly saw a man armed with a gun. As he was well dressed and had a game-bag, my first thought was that he was a hunter; but when I noticed the butt of a pistol outside his coat, I feared that he was one of those Provence men who, at the report of the cannon, never fail to get into the country to track down escaped convicts. If my apprehensions were justified, all flight was useless; so perhaps it would be better to advance than retreat. This I did, and getting near him so that I should be close enough to grapple with him at his first hostile movement, I asked the way to Aix.

'Do you want the crossroad or the main road?' he asked, with meaning.

'It makes no difference,' I answered, hoping by this indifference to avert suspicion.

'In that case, follow this path, and it will take you to the gen-darmes' post; if you do not like to travel alone, you can profit by the *correspondance.*'

At the word gendarmes, I felt myself go pale. The unknown saw the effect it had had on me.

'Come, come,' he said, 'I see that you do not insist on working the main road. Well, if you are not too hurried, I will lead you to the vil-lage of Pourrières, which is only two leagues from Aix.'

He was too well acquainted with the locality for me not to accept his obligingness; I consented to wait. Then, without leaving his place, he pointed to a thicket some distance away where he would soon join me. It was some two hours before he finished his watch. Finally, he came and said, 'Get up!' I arose and followed him, and when I thought we were still in the heart of the woods, I found myself on the edge, fifty yards from a house in front of which the gendarmes were sitting. At the sight of their uniform, I shuddered.

'Well, what's the matter?' asked my guide. 'Are you afraid I'll give you up? If you fear anything, defend yourself with these.'

At the same time he offered me two pistols. I refused them.

'All right!' he answered, and shook hands to show that he was pleased with this proof of my confidence.

Masked by the thickets which bordered the road, we stopped; I did not understand the object of a halt so near the enemy. Our stay was long. Finally, at nightfall, we saw a mail coach arrive from the direction of Toulon; it was escorted by four gendarmes who relieved the men whose neighbourhood had terrified me. The mail went its way; soon it had disappeared. Then my companion took me by the arm and said, briefly, 'Let's go; there's nothing doing today.'

We left at once, changing our direction. After walking about an hour, my guide approached a tree and rubbed his hand up and down the trunk. I recognized that he was counting the notches made by a knife. 'Good!' he exclaimed with a sort of content which I could not explain to myself. After he had drawn a bit of bread from his game-bag and shared it with me, he gave me a drink from his flask. This collation could not have come more apropos, for I needed to recover my strength. In spite of the darkness, we walked so rapidly that I ended by being done in; my feet, deprived of exercise for a long time, were painful, and I was about to declare that it was impossible for me to push on farther when three o'clock struck on a village clock.

'Quietly,' said my guide, getting down to apply his ear to the ground, 'get down, too, and listen. One has always to be on one's guard with this cursed Polish Legion. Did you hear anything?'

I answered that I thought I had heard several men.

'Yes,' he said, 'it's them; don't move, or we are taken.'

He had hardly finished when a patrol reached the bushes where we were hidden.

'Do you see anything?' asked a low voice.

'Nothing, sergeant.'

'God, I should say so; it's as dark as an oven. That madman Roman, may lightning strike him! We'll travel all night in the woods like wolves. Oh, if I ever find him, or any of his men!'

'Who goes there?' cried a soldier suddenly.

'What do you see?' asked the sergeant.

'Nothing, but I heard breathing in that direction' – and truly he pointed to the place where we were.

'Go on, you're dreaming. They've made you so scared of Roman that you always think he's in your cartridge box.'

Two other soldiers pretended that they had heard something.

'Keep still,' replied the sergeant. 'I insist that there's no one here; this will be another time, as usual, that we'll go back to Pourrières without meeting any game; come on, it's time to go.' The patrol seemed ready to go.

'That's a trick,' said my companion to me. 'I am sure that they are going to beat the woods, and come back in a semicircle.'

'Are you afraid?' asked my guide again.

'If I were, this isn't the time for it,' I answered.

'In that case, follow me; here are my pistols. When I fire, fire so that the four shots seem like one. Ready, fire!'

The four shots sounded, and we fled at all speed, without say pursuit. The fear of falling into some ambush had stopped the soldiers; however, we continued our course. When we approached an isolated house, the unknown said to me, 'Now it's daylight, and we're safe.' He then passed through the palings of a garden, and, fumbling around in the trunk of a tree with one hand, he took out a key; it was that of the house, in which we were not slow to install ourselves.

An iron lamp hanging on the mantelpiece lighted up a simple rustic interior. Only I saw in a corner a barrel which seemed to hold powder; higher up, scattered on a plank, were packages of cartridges. Some woman's garments placed on a chair, with one of those broad black hats of Provence, seemed to indicate the presence of a sleeper whose heavy breathing just reached us. While I took a rapid glance around, my guide drew from an old chest a goat's quarter, some onions, oil, a bottle of wine, and invited me to take a meal I badly needed. It appeared that he had some desire to question me, but I ate with such avidity that he had scruples against interrupting me. When I had finished – that is to say, when nothing was left on the table – he led me to a sort of garret, repeating that I was safe there; then he withdrew without my knowing whether he remained in the house, for I was hardly stretched out on the straw when I was conquered by an invincible sleep.

When I awoke, I judged by the height of the sun that it was two hours after midday. A pleasant woman, doubtless the same one whose clothes I had seen, warned by my movements, stuck her head in the door of my garret, and said, 'Don't move; the neighbourhood is full of gendarmes who are rummaging everywhere.'

At dusk I again saw my man of the evening before, who, after some insignificant remarks, asked me directly who I was, whence I came, and where I was going. I was ready for this inevitable questioning, and I answered that I was a deserter from the ship *Ocean*, then in the roads at Toulon; that I was trying to get to Aix, and from there I proposed to go to my home.

'Good,' said my host. 'I see who you are, but who do you think I am?'

'Really, to tell the truth, I took you for a keeper at first; then I thought you were a leader of smugglers; and now I don't know what to think.'

'You'll soon know. In our country we are brave, you see, but we do not like to be forced to be soldiers. So we do not obey the draft when we can do otherwise. The contingent from Pourrières in a body even refused to go. The gendarmes came to seize the refractory men; they resisted; both sides have killed, and all those among the inhabitants who took part in the battle have fled to the woods to escape court-martial. There are sixty of us collected under the orders of Monsieur Roman. If you want to stay with us, I shall be pleased, for last night I saw that you are a good companion, and in my opinion you hardly care to rub against the gendarmes. In addition, we lack nothing, and we run no great danger. The peasants warn us of everything that happens, and furnish us more than we can eat. Come, are you with us?'

I did not believe I ought to reject this proposition, and, without thought of the consequences, I answered that I wanted to be. I then passed two days in the house. The third day I went with my companion, who gave me a carbine and two pistols. After walking several hours through wood-covered mountains, we reached a much larger house than the one we had left; it was Roman's headquarters. I waited for a moment at the door, for it was necessary for my guide to announce me. He soon came back, and took me into a large barn, where I was among some forty individuals, most of whom were grouped around a man whom, from his half-rustic, half-city dress, one might take for a wealthy country proprietor. I was presented to this personage.

'I am charmed to see you,' he said. 'I have been told about your coolness, and I have been forewarned of your worth. If you wish to share our perils, you will find friendliness and freedom here; we do not know you, but with a physique like yours, one always has friends. All our men are honest as well as brave, for we do not consider probity of less worth than courage.'

Such was my reception in this society, to which its chief attributed a political end. What is certain is that after beginning as insurgents who stopped the diligences which carried the State's funds, Roman ended by robbing travellers. The rebels who formed the larger part of the troop at first made such expeditions with no regret, but the habit of vagabondage, inactivity, and especially the difficulty of returning to their families promptly set their resolutions.

The day after my arrival Roman named me to go with six men to the neighbourhood of Saint-Maximin; I did not know the reason. Toward midnight, when we had reached the edge of a small wood which divided the road, we ambushed in a ravine. Our lieutenant ordered profound silence. Soon the noise of a vehicle was heard; it passed in front of us; the lieutenant raised his head, cautiously. 'It is the Nice diligence,' he said, 'but there is nothing doing. There are more dragoons than boxes.' He then ordered the retreat, and we regained the house, where Roman, irritated by our return with empty hands, exclaimed an oath, 'Well, they shall pay tomorrow.'

I had no illusions as to the association of which I was a part. Decidedly I was among highway robbers who terrified whole of Provence. If I were taken, my being an escaped convict would leave me not even the hope of a pardon which might be granted to some of the young with us. When I reflected on my situation, I was to flee; but as I was but recently enrolled in the band, it was probable that they constantly had an eye on me. On the other hand, if I expressed a desire to withdraw, it might arouse distrust. The Roman might take me for a spy and have me shot. Death and infamy threatened me everywhere.

In these perplexities I sounded the man who had introduced me and asked him whether it would be possible to obtain leave from the chief for a few days. He answered dryly that known men might, and then turned his back. I had been with the band eleven days, entirely resolved to escape the honour of their exploits, when one night, sound asleep through an excess of weariness, I was awakened by an extraordinary noise. One of our comrades had been robbed of a well-filled purse, and he was making a hubbub. As I was the last comer, it was natural that suspicion should fall on me. He accused me formally, and all the troop joined in. I protested my innocence in vain; they decided to search me. I was lying down in my clothes; they began to undress me. What was their astonishment on opening my shirt to see – the mark of the galleys.

'A convict!' shouted Roman; 'a convict among us! He must be a spy! Sandbag him or shoot him, whichever is the quicker.'

I heard them load their guns.

'An instant!' the chief ordered. 'First, he must give back the money.'

'Yes,' I said, 'the money will be returned; but it is indispensable that you grant me a private interview.'

They thought I was going to confess; but when I was alone with him, I again asserted that I was not guilty, and I showed him an expedient which would indicate the thief. Roman reappeared holding in his hand as many bits of straw as there were people present. 'Pay attention,' he said to them, 'the longest straw will indicate the thief.' The draw took place, and when it was over, everyone was anxious to bring back his straw. Only one was shorter than the others. A man named Joseph d'Oriolles presented it.

'So it is you?' said the Roman. 'All the straws were the same length; you shortened yours and gave yourself away.'

Joseph was at once searched and the stolen money was found in his belt. My justification was complete. Roman himself made excuses, but at the same time he declared to me that I had ceased to be part of the troop. 'It is a pity,' he added, 'but you can see that having been in the galleys...' He did not finish; he placed fifteen louis in my hand, and made me promise not to speak of what I had seen for twenty-five days. I was discreet.

XI

I AID MY OLD ENEMIES

AFTER THE DANGERS I ran in staying with Roman and his troop, one can imagine what joy I felt in having left them. If I had remained with them, I was certain to arrive promptly on the scaffold. But I was animated by another thought: I wanted to get away from the ways and occasions of crime at whatever cost. I wanted to be free. I did not know how my wish could be realized, but no matter; my part was taken. As it was urgent that I get away as far as possible, I headed toward Lyons, avoiding all the main roads until in the neighbourhood of Orange. Here I met some carters whose loads soon revealed to me that they were going the same way I was. I got into conversation with them, and as they appeared good folk, I did not hesitate to tell them that I was a deserter and that they would do me a great service if, to help me in throwing the gendarmes off my track, they would consent to my having a place with them. This proposition caused them no surprise; it seemed that they had expected that I would seek their shelter. The carters gave me a good reception; the money I let them see added to their interest in my lot. It was arranged that I should pass for the son of one of the leaders of the convoy. In consequence, I was decked out in a blouse, and as I was reputed to be making my first trip, I was decorated with ribbons and flowers, joyous insignia, which brought me the felicitations of everyone in all the inns.

I played the role well enough; but the largesse necessary to sustain it properly bore heavily on my purse, so that when I reached Guillotiere, where I separated from my people, I had only twenty-eight sous left. With such slight resources there was no thought of hotels. After I had wandered for some time in the dark and dirty streets of the second city of France, I noticed a sort of tavern where I thought they might serve me a supper in proportion to the state of my finances. I was not wrong; the supper was mediocre, and soon over. To have an appetite left was one disagreeable feature; not to know where to find a refuge was another. When I wiped my knife, which, however, was not too greasy, I sorrowed at the idea that I was going to be reduced to passing the night under the stars.

At the next table I heard some people speaking the corrupt German which is used in some cantons in the Low Countries and which I understood perfectly. The speakers were a man and a woman already past middle age, whom I recognized as Jews. I had been told that at Lyons these people kept furnished houses, where smugglers were willingly admitted, so I asked them if they could direct me to an inn. I could not have done better; the Jew and his wife kept lodgers. They offered to be my hosts, and I accompanied them to their place. Six beds furnished the quarters in which they put me; none of the rest were occupied, and yet it was ten o'clock. I thought that I should have no one else in the room, and went to sleep with this idea.

When I woke up, words in a familiar argot came to my ears.

'Half-past six struck, and you're still snoring.'

'I should say so. Last night we wanted to rob a goldsmith, but he was on his guard. I've seen the time when I'd have used my poignard and then there'd have been some blood'

'Oh, oh, you're not afraid of going to the guillotine. But when they work that way, they don't get money.'

'I'd rather murder on the open road than break into shops; the gendarmes are always on one's back.'

'And you took nothing? Still there were some snuffboxes, matchsafes, and gold chains. The Jew will get nothing.'

'No, the false key broke in the lock; the man shouted for help and we had to get out.'

'Don't talk so much; there's a man there who can hear.'

The advice was late, but they kept still. I half-opened my eyes to see the faces of my companions, but my bed was the lowest of all, and I could see nothing. I stayed motionless to make them believe I was asleep, but when one of the talkers got up, I recognized a man who had escaped from the prison at Toulon, one Neveu, who had got out some days before I had. His comrade jumped out of bed; it was Cadet-Paul, another one who had escaped. A third, a fourth sat up, and he too was a convict.

I might have thought I was again in Ward No. 3. Finally, I left my cot in my turn. I had hardly put my feet on the floor when a general cry went up, 'It's Vidocq!!!' They crowded around and congratulated me. One of them told me that the whole prison admired my audacity and my success. Nine o'clock struck and they took me to breakfast, where I found the Quinet brothers, Bobbefoi, Rubineau, Metril, and Lemat, all famous names in the Midi. They overwhelmed me with kindness, procured me money, clothes, and even a mistress.

As one may observe, I was in the same situation as at Nantes. I cared no more than in Brittany to practise the trade of my friends, but I expected to receive pecuniary aid from my mother, and I had to live while I waited. I imagined that I should be able to get food for some time without working. I proposed rigorously only to get my subsistence among the thieves. The escaped convicts were discontented at seeing me, sometimes under one pretext, sometimes under another, avoid co-operation in the robberies they committed every day; they denounced me to get rid of an importunate witness and one who might become dangerous. Presumably they thought that I should escape, and they counted on the fact that once I was recognized by the police, having no other refuge than with the gang, I should decide to take sides with them.

I was arrested and taken to prison. On the first words of my examination, I saw that I had been sold. In a fury at this discovery I took a strong decision, which was in some way a start in a career new to me. I wrote to M. Dubois, the commissioner of police, to ask him for a private interview. The same evening, I was taken to his office. After I had explained my position, I proposed to him to put him on the trail of the Quinet brothers, then sought in the case of a murder of the wife of a mason, rue Belle Cordière. In addition I offered to find a way to take all the individuals lodged with the Jew and a carpenter named Caffin. I put my services at the price of leaving Lyons.

M. Dubois must have been more than once a dupe of similar propositions; I saw that he hesitated to trust me.

'You doubt my good faith,' I said. 'Would you still suspect me if I escaped on my way back to prison and gave myself up again as your prisoner?'

'No,' he answered.

'Well, you'll see me again soon if you consent not to have me watched with special care.'

He agreed to my request; I was led out. When we reached the corner of the rue de la Lanterne, I upset the two men who had hold of me by the arms, and regained the Town Hall with all speed. I found M. Dubois there. My prompt appearance surprised him greatly; but sure that he could now count on me, he permitted me to be set at liberty.

The next day I saw the Jew, named Vidal; he told me my friends had gone to lodge in a house which he pointed out to me in the Croix-Rousse. I went there. They knew of my escape, but as they were far from suspecting my relations with the police commissioner and did not suspect that I had guessed from where the blow I had received came, they gave me a friendly reception. In the course of the conversation I accumulated some details on the Quinet brothers and I transmitted them the same night to M. Dubois, who, convinced of my sincerity, put me in touch with the secretary of police. I gave this functionary all necessary information, and I must say that on his part he operated with considerable tact and activity.

Two days before they descended on Vidal on my information, I was again arrested. I was taken back to prison, where the next day arrived Vidal himself, Caffin, Cadet-Paul, Deschamps, and several others whom they had caught in their nets. At first I was without communication with them, for I had judged it proper that I be put in solitary confinement. When I came out of that at the end of some days to be reunited with the other prisoners, I pretended great surprise to find all my people there. No one appeared to have the slightest idea of the role I had played in the arrests. Neveu alone looked at me with a sort of distrust. I asked him the reason. He confessed that from the manner in which he had been searched and questioned, he could not help believing that I had denounced him. I made believe that I was indignant, and for fear that this opinion might become general, I got the prisoners together, told them about Neveu's suspicions, and asked them if they believed me capable of selling my comrades. All answered in the negative, and Neveu had to make excuses.

It was very important for me that these suspicions should be dissipated, for it was certain death for me if they were confirmed. Several examples of such distributive justice which the prisoners had exercised among themselves, had been seen in the prison. A man named Moissel, who was suspected of revealing some matters about a robbery of sacred vessels, had been beaten to death in the court, without his assassin being discovered. More recently another individual, accused of an indiscretion of the same kind, had been found one morning hanged with a rope of straw from the bars of a window. Investigations had met with no success.

Meanwhile, M. Dubois summoned me to his office, where, to avoid all suspicion, they led me with the other prisoners as if there was to be an examination. I entered first. The commissioner told me that there had just arrived in Lyons from Paris several thieves, who were very adroit and so the more dangerous; that, as their papers were in order, they could wait in all security the occasion to pull off a trick, and afterward disappear at once. Their names were then absolutely unknown to me. I told M. Dubois so and added that it was possible that they were false. He wanted me released immediately, so that if I saw these men in one public place, I could assure myself whether I had ever seen them before. But I observed that if I was set at liberty so abruptly, it would not fail to compromise me with the prisoners, in case that I was locked up again for the good of the service. This seemed true, and it was arranged that they would try to think up some way of letting me out on the morrow.

Neveu was among the prisoners who had been taken out for examination at the same time I was, and he followed me into the office. In a few moments I saw him come out in great excitement. I asked him what happened.

'Would you believe that the commissioner asked me if I would find the robbers who have just arrived from Paris? If their arrest depends on me, they will be sure to escape.'

'I didn't think that you were such a blockhead,' I answered. 'I promised to recognize all the crooks and have them arrested.'

'What, you'll be a police spy? Besides, you don't know them!'

'What difference does that make? They'll let me go about the city, and I might find a way to escape, while you'll still be with the jailer.'

Neveu was impressed by this idea. He showed keen regret at having repulsed the offers of the commissioner. As I could not leave him and go out on the search, I urged him strongly to change his decision. He consented, and M. Dubois, whom I had warned, had us taken one evening to the door of the principal theatre where Neveu pointed out all the men. We were then withdrawn, escorted by the police who crowded around us. For the success of my plan and so that I should not be suspected, it was necessary to make an attempt to escape, which would at least confirm the hopes I had given my companion. I told him my project, and, as we passed rue Mercière, we abruptly entered a passage and I pulled the door to behind us. The police ran to the other exit, and we went out peacefully the way we had entered. When the police returned, ashamed of their blunder, we were already far away.

Two days later, Neveu, whom I no longer needed and who could no longer suspect me, was again arrested. As I knew the thieves they wanted, I described them to the police. Unable any longer to be useful to the authorities, I left Lyons for Paris, where, thanks to M. Dubois, I was sure to arrive without trouble.

I left in the diligence on the road to Burgundy. We travelled only in the daytime. At Lucy-le-Bois, where I had slept, as did all the travellers, I was forgotten at the time of departure, and when I woke up the diligence had been gone two hours. I hoped to catch up with it on account of the ruggedness of the road, which is mountainous in those cantons; but as I got near Saint-Brice, I was convinced that it was too far ahead for me to catch up, so I slackened my pace. A man going in the same direction, seeing me covered with perspiration, looked at me attentively, and asked if I came from Lucy-le-Bois. I told him that in fact I did, and the conversation rested there. This man stopped at Saint-Brice, while I pushed on to Auxerre. Worn out with fatigue, I entered an inn, where I dined and hurried to bed.

I had been asleep some hours when I was awakened by a loud noise at the door. There was knocking with heavy blows. I got up half-dressed, my eyes still heavy with sleep, and saw tri-coloured sashes, yellow trousers, and red facings. It was the police commissioner, flanked by a sergeant-major and two gendarmes. At their appearance I could not master my first emotion.

'See how pale he turned,' said one beside me. 'There's no doubt it's he!'

I raised my eyes and recognized the man who had spoken to me at Saint-Brice; but nothing explained the reason for this sudden invasion.

'Proceed systematically,' said the commissioner. 'Five feet, five inches ... all right ... blond hair, eyebrows, and beard, the same ... forehead, ordinary ... grey eyes ... nose prominent ... average mouth ... round chin ... full face ... complexion dark ... rather corpulent.'

'It's he!' exclaimed the sergeant-major, the two gendarmes and the man from Saint-Brice.

'Yes, it's he!' said the commissioner in his turn. 'Blue overcoat ... grey kersey trousers ... white waistcoat ... black tie.' That was about all my costume.

'Well, didn't I say so?' observed one of the men. 'He's one of the robbers.'

The description agreed perfectly with mine. However, I had not robbed; but in my situation, I was none the less disturbed. Perhaps it was only a mistake, perhaps, too ... The audience was restless, carried away by joy.

'Be still,' shouted the commissioner; then he turned a page and went on. 'He will be easily recognized by his pronounced Italian accent. One of the fingers of his right hand has been badly damaged by a shot.'

I spoke before the others did; I showed my right hand; it was in perfect condition. The audience looked at each other; the man from Saint-Brice especially appeared singularly disconcerted; I felt relieved of an enormous weight. The commissioner, whom I questioned in my turn, told me that the preceding night a considerable robbery had been committed at Saint-Brice. One of the men under suspicion of participating in it wore clothes like mine, and was identified by the description. By this chain of circumstances, to this strange freak of chance, was due the disagreeable visit I had received. They made their excuses, which I accepted gracefully, very happy to be rid of them so easily. I got into a rickety old coach which took me to Paris, and from there I steered for Arras.

XII
A PEACE OF MIND SOON LOST

FOR SEVERAL REASONS which can be imagined, I did not go directly to my paternal home; I went to one of my aunts who told me that my father was dead. This sad news was soon confirmed by my mother, who received me with a tenderness in marked contrast with the frightful treatment I had undergone for the past two years. There was nothing she desired so much as to keep me near her, but I had to stay constantly hidden; I resigned myself to it; for three months I never left the house. At the end of that time captivity began to weigh on me. I decided to go out, sometimes under one disguise and sometimes under another. I believed that I had not been recognized, when suddenly the report spread that I was in the city. The entire police went in search to arrest me; at any moment they might visit my mother; but they never found my hiding-place; not that it was large, since it was only ten feet long and six broad. But it was hidden so skillfully that a woman who later bought the house lived there nearly four years without suspicion of the existence of this room, and probably she would have remained in ignorance if I had not shown it to her.

Strong in this retreat, in which I believed it would be difficult to surprise me, I soon took up my excursions again. One day in Mardi Gras, I carried my imprudence so far that I went to a ball, where there were two hundred people. I was dressed as a marquis. A woman recognized me and told her discovery to another woman, who believed that she had grounds of complaint against me, so that in less than a quarter of an hour everyone knew under what dress Vidocq was hidden. The report came to the ears of two sergeants, Delrue and Carpentier, who were policing the ball. The former approached me and told me in a low voice that he wanted to speak to me in private. When we reached the court, Delrue asked my name. I had no trouble to give him one other than my own, and I politely proposed to unmask if he demanded it.

'I do not demand it,' he answered, 'but I should not be displeased to see you.'

'In that case,' I replied, 'be so kind as to untie the strings of my mask; they are tangled.'

In all confidence, Delrue went behind me; and at that moment I upset him with an abrupt backward movement; a blow of the fist sent his assistant rolling on the ground. Without waiting for him to get up, I fled with all speed to the ramparts, counting on scaling them and so escaping to the country. But I had scarcely made a few steps, when, without suspecting it, I found myself in a *cul-de-sac*, which had ceased to be a street since I had left Arras.

While I went astray, the noise of hobnailed boots announced that the two sergeants had pursued me. Soon they arrived sword in hand. I had no arms. I seized the large house-key, as if it were a pistol, and, pretending to aim at them, I forced them to make way. 'Come on, François,' said Carpentier, in a weak voice, 'don't be foolish.' I did not make him speak twice; in a few minutes I was in my redoubt.

This adventure was noised abroad in spite of the efforts the two sergeants made to keep it secret, for it covered them with ridicule. What bothered me was that the authorities redoubled their surveillance to such a point that it became impossible for me to go out. So I stayed walled up for two months which seemed like two centuries. Unable to stand it any longer, I decided to leave Arras. A package of lacework was made up for me, and one fine night I went, furnished with a passport in the name of Blondel, one of my friends, who lent it to me. The description could not pass, but for want of a better I had to put up with it; besides, no objection was made on the way.

I went to Paris, where, while I was busy selling my merchandise, I made some attempts to see whether it would be possible to obtain a revision of my case. I learned that first I must again become a prisoner; but I never could bring myself again to be in contact with the scoundrels whom I appreciated only too well. However, my lacework was sold, but at too little profit for me to think of making that trade a means of existence. A commercial traveller who lodged in the same hotel as I did, to whom I told my position in some words, proposed that I should hire out to a merchant of novelties who went to the fairs. In fact, I got the place, but I kept it only ten months; some disagreements forced me to leave it and return to Arras.

I was not slow to take up the course of my semi-nocturnal excursions. In the house of a young woman to whom I paid some attention there frequently came the daughter of a gendarme. I thought of taking advantage of this circumstance to get advance information of all that was hatched against me. The gendarme's daughter did not know me; but as I was nearly a constant topic of conversation in Arras, it was not extraordinary that she spoke of me, and often in very odd terms.

'Oh!' she said one day, 'they'll catch that rascal in the end. First, there's our lieutenant who wants to get him too much not to take him in the end. I'll bet he'd willingly give a day's pay to get him.'

'If I were in the lieutenant's place, and I wanted to get Vidocq,' I replied, 'it doesn't seem to me that he would escape.'

'Oh, you're like the rest; he is always armed to the teeth. Do you know that they say he fired two pistols at M. Delrue and M. Carpentier. And that's not all; he can change himself into a truss of hay.'

'A truss of hay!' I exclaimed, much surprised at the new faculty accorded me. 'A truss of hay! How?'

'Yes, monsieur. One day my father followed him, and just as he was going to put his hand on his collar, he grasped only a wisp of hay. That's not all talk, the whole brigade saw the hay, which was burned.'

Fortunately, such ideas were not shared by some pretty women in whom I inspired an interest, and if the devil of jealousy had not suddenly taken one of them, the authorities would perhaps not have been busy with me for long. In her spite she was indiscreet, and the police, who were not sure what had become of me, again learned with certainty that I was living in Arras.

One evening as I was coming back from the rue d'Amiens, entirely without distrust and armed only with a stick, I was assailed by seven or eight men. They were the city sergeants in disguise. They seized me by my clothes, and they already believed that they had captured me, when, getting away by a vigorous jerk, I freed the rampart of a bridge and jumped into the river. It was in December; the water was high, the current fast; none of the agents took a fancy to follow me. Besides, they supposed that if they waited for me on the bank, I should not escape; but a drain which I went up disconcerted their foresight, and they were still waiting for me when I was already in my mother's house.

Every day I ran new dangers; and every day the most urgent necessity suggested new expedients for safety. However, at length, I grew tired of a liberty which the need of hiding made illusory. Some nuns had harboured me for some time. I resolved to give up their hospitality and at the same time I dreamed of ways to appear in public without inconvenience. Some thousands of Austrian prisoners were then crowded into the citadel of Arras, from which they went out to work for the citizens or in the surrounding country. The idea struck me that the presence of these foreigners might be useful to me. As I spoke German, I got into conversation with them, and I succeeded in inspiring such confidence in one of them that he confessed to me that he intended to escape. His project was favourable to my views; the prisoner was embarrassed by his Austrian garments; I offered mine in exchange, and by means of some money I gave him, he was only too happy to cede me his papers. From that moment I was an Austrian in the eyes of the Austrians themselves, who, belonging to different corps, did not know each other.

Under this new disguise I became acquainted with a young widow who had a mercer's establishment. She found me intelligent, she wanted me to install myself at her place, and soon we went to all the fairs and markets together. It was evident that I could not help her unless the buyers understood me. So I made up a sort of jargon which became so familiar to me that unconsciously I almost forgot that I knew any other tongue. In other ways the illusion was so complete that after we had lived together four months, the widow did not suspect that the so-called Austrian was one of her childhood friends. However, she treated me so well that it became impossible for me to deceive her for a longer time. One day I risked telling her who I was, and I do not believe that a woman was ever more astonished.

Eleven months went by without anything disturbing my security. People had become accustomed to seeing me in the city. My frequent meetings with the police, who did not even pay attention to me, all seemed to announce a continuance of my well-being, when one day, as we were just sitting down to the table in the rear of the shop, three gendarmes showed themselves through the glass door. I was about to serve the potage; the ladle fell from my hands. But I soon recovered from the stupefaction in which this unexpected incursion had thrown me, and I jumped to the door, bolted it, then jumped through a window and went up to the garret, from which, over the roofs of the neighbouring houses, I precipitately went down a staircase which led to the street. When I reached the door, it was guarded by two gendarmes. Fortunately, they were newcomers who did not know my appearance. 'Go on up,' I said to them; 'the corporal has the man, but he is fighting. Go on up and give him a hand; I'll go and get the guard.' The two gendarmes hurried up and I disappeared.

It was evident that I had been sold to the police; my childhood friend was incapable of such baseness, but she doubtless had been imprudent. Now that they were on the watch for me, should I stay in Arras? I should be condemned to remain in my hiding-place if I did. I could not resign myself to so miserable a life, and I resolved definitely to abandon the city. The mercer insisted on following me; she had some means of transport, and her merchandise was quickly packed up. We went together, and, as always happens in such cases, the police were the last to be informed of the disappearance of a woman whose slightest movement they should have known. According to an old idea, they took it for granted that we should go to Belgium, as if Belgium were the only country of refuge, and while they pursued us in the direction of the old frontier, we advanced quietly toward Normandy by crossroads which my companion had come to know in her mercantile explorations.

We planned to sojourn at Rouen. When we reached that city, I had Blondel's passport which I had procured at Arras. The description it gave of me was so different from my own that it was indispensable that I put it in better order. By means of an ingenious trick, my rehabilitation was soon complete. Furnished with excellent papers, all that was left for me was to go honestly, and I thought about it seriously. In consequence I took a shop, where we did such a good trade that my mother, to whom I had sent news secretly, decided to come and join us. For a year I was really happy. My trade took on some stability; my connections increased; credit was built up, and more than one banking house received with favour paper signed Blondel. At last, after many storms, I thought I had reached port.

But an incident which I could not have foreseen started a new series of vicissitudes. The mercer with whom I lived, this woman who

had given so many strong proofs of devotion and love, was unfaithful to
me. Once I should have given myself to the fury of my anger. Now I
coldly indicated the decree of separation which I was determined on at
once. Prayers, supplications, promises of better conduct, nothing turned
me; I was inexorable. So we shared our merchandise; my associate left,
and I have never heard of her since.

Disgusted with my stay in Rouen by this adventure, which made
some noise, I took up again my trade as itinerant trader. My trips took
in the arrondissements of Mantes, Saint-Germain, and Versailles, and in
a short time I had an excellent clientèle. My profits became considerable enough so that I was able to hire a shop at Versailles with lodgings
where my mother lived while I was travelling. My conduct was free
from reproach; I was generally esteemed in my circles; finally, I thought
I had worn out the fate which constantly threw me into ways of dis-
honour, when, denounced by a comrade of my boyhood, who revenged
himself for some quarrel we had had, I was arrested on my return from
the fair at Mantes. Although I insisted obstinately that I was not
Vidocq, but Blondel, as my passport showed, I was transferred to Saint-
Denis, from where I was to be taken to Douai. By the extraordinary
care which was taken to prevent my escape, I saw that I had been 'recommended'; a glance I got of a paper at the gendarmerie revealed to me
a precaution of a very special kind. This is how I was described:

Special Surveillance
Vidocq (Eugène François), condemned to death as a defaulter.
This man is extremely enterprising and dangerous.

So to keep my guardians on the alert, they represented me as a
great criminal. I went from Saint-Denis in a wagon, bound in such a
way that I could not move; and my escort did not take their eyes off me
as far as Louvres. These dispositions announced the rigours which it
was important that I prevent, and I again found that energy to which
my liberty had been due so many times.

The police had placed me, with other prisoners, in the belfry at
Louvres, which had been made into a prison. I had brought two mat-
tresses, a coverlet and sheets, which, cut up and braided, would serve to
descend to the cemetery; an iron bar was sawed through with the knives

of three deserters who were locked up with us. At two o'clock in the morning I risked myself the first. When I reached the end of the rope, I saw that it did not come within fifteen feet of the ground; I did not hesitate; I dropped. But as in my fall from the ramparts at Lille, I sprained my left foot, and it was almost impossible to walk. However, I tried to get across to the cemetery walls when I heard the light turning of a lock. It was the jailer and his dog, and the nose of one was no better than that of the other. First, the jailer, without seeing me, passed by the ditch where I had crouched, and the mastiff passed without smelling me. When their round was over, they withdrew. I thought that my companions would follow my example, but as no one followed me, I scaled the wall, and there I was in the country. The pain in my foot became sharper and sharper. However, I braved out the suffering; courage gave me strength, and I went fairly rapidly. I had gone barely half a league when suddenly I heard the tocsin. At the first light of day I saw some peasants with their guns spread out in the plain. Probably they did not know what the matter was, but a crippled leg would make me a suspect. Mine was an unknown face; it was obvious that the first who met me would in any event want to assure themselves of my person. Sound, I should have confounded all pursuit, but all I could do was to let myself fall into their hands, and I had not gone two hundred yards before I was apprehended and taken back to the cursed belfry.

The sad result of this attempt did not discourage me. At Bapaume we were put in the citadel, under the watch of a post of conscripts. A single sentinel guarded us; he was under the window, and near enough to the prisoners so that we could converse with him, which is what I did. The soldier I addressed seemed a good fellow; I imagined that it would be easy to corrupt him. I offered him fifty francs to let me escape while he was on watch. At first he refused, but by the tone of his voice and a certain wink of his eye, I thought I saw that he was impatient to get the sum, only he did not dare. In order to make him bolder, I increased the dose and showed him three louis. He answered that he was ready to help us; at the same time he told me that his tour of duty would be between midnight and two o'clock. When our agreement was made, I set to work; the wall was pierced in such a way as to make a passage for us; we only waited for the opportune moment to get out.

Finally midnight struck; the soldier came to tell me that he was there; I gave him the three louis, and I hurried the necessary arrangements.

When all was ready, I called, 'Is it time?'

'Yes. Hurry!' the sentinel answered, after a moment's hesitation.

I thought it singular that he had not answered at once; I thought there was something dubious in this conduct; I listened, and I seemed to hear marching; by the light of the moon I saw the shadows of several men on the slope; there was no doubt; we had been betrayed. However, I might have been too hasty in my judgment. To assure myself, I took some straw, and hastily made up a dummy and dressed it; I held it to the exit which we had made. Instantly a stroke of a sword which would have broken an anvil showed me that I had had a fine escape, and confirmed me more and more in the opinion that conscripts are not to be trusted. The prison was suddenly invaded by the gendarmes. They set up a *proces-verbal*. They questioned us, they wanted to know all. I declared that I had given three louis; the conscript denied it; I persisted in my declaration; he was searched and the money was found in his shoes; he was locked up in a cell.

As to us, they made terrible threats, but as they could not punish us, they contented themselves with doubling the guard. There was no means of escape, at least unless one of those occasions occurred for which I was constantly looking. It came sooner than I hoped. The next day was the day of our departure. We were taken down into the court of the barracks, where confusion reigned. It was caused by the simultaneous appearance of a new transport of convicts and a detachment of conscripts from the Ardennes which was going to the camp at Boulogne. The adjutants disputed the terrain with the gendarmes in forming their squads and calling the roll. While each was counting his men, I slipped furtively into the body of a baggage wagon which was leaving the court. In this way I crossed the city, without a movement and making myself as small as possible, so that I should not be discovered. Once outside the ramparts, all I had to do was to slip out. I grasped the opportunity when the carter, always thirsty like all people of that sort, had entered a pothouse to refresh himself; and while the horses waited on the road, I relieved the vehicle of a weight with which it was not supposed to be loaded. I at once went and hid in a field, and when night fell, I set out.

XIII
GOOD INTENTIONS COME TO NAUGHT

I MADE MY WAY through Picardy toward Boulogne. At this time Napoleon had given up his project of a descent on England; he had gone with his Grand Army to make war on Austria; but he had still left numerous battalions on the shores of the Channel. The uniforms were most varied, and their diversity would be favourable to hide me. However, I thought it would be a bad plan to disguise myself in any other way than by borrowing a uniform. For a moment I thought of really being a soldier. But to enter a regiment papers were necessary, and I had none. So I gave up that project. However, it was dangerous to stay in Boulogne if I could not find a way to creep in somewhere.

One day, when I was more troubled and uneasy than usual, I met a sergeant of naval artillery named Dufailli whom I had seen in Paris. Like myself, he was from Arras, but as he had embarked when almost a child on a warship and had passed most of his life in the colonies, he knew nothing of my misadventures. He only looked upon me as a *bon vivant*, and some rows we had had in a public-house, where I had energetically supported him, gave him a high opinion of my courage.

'So that's you,' he said. 'And what are you doing in Boulogne?'

'What am I doing? I'm trying to find a job in the train of the army.'

'Oh, you're after a job? Don't you know that it is devilish hard to get one today? If you'll follow my advice ... But, listen, we can't talk here; let's go to Garland's.'

He signalled me to follow him, and I obeyed. He led me into a low room where were a Captain Paulet and his men, most of whom were drunk with enthusiasm and wine. As soon as we appeared, there was but one shout, 'There's Dufailli! There's Dufailli!'

'Honour to him!' said Paulet; then he offered him a seat beside him. 'Sit down here, old fellow; they are right when they say Providence is great. M. Boutrois, some glasses, as if it rained wine. Come on, no more trouble,' Paulet went on, pressing Dufailli's hand.

Paulet had not taken his eyes off me. 'It seems to me I know you,' he said; 'you've already swung a marlinspike, my boy.'

I answered that I had been on the privateer *Barras*, but that I had never seen him.

'In that case we'll get acquainted; I don't know, but you look like a good dog. What shoulders and what a build! This spark will make a famous fisher of Englishmen!' As he finished, Paulet put his red cap on me. 'That suits you,' he remarked, in a tone which showed kindness.

I saw at once that the captain would not be sorry to have me in his crew. Dufailli had not yet lost the use of his tongue, and he exhorted me to take advantage of the occasion; that was the good advice he had promised me, and I followed it.

It was arranged that I should make a cruise and that the next day I should be presented to the owner, M. Choisnard, who would advance me some money. I waited impatiently the moment to sail; M. Choisnard's five-franc pieces would not permit me to cut much of a figure, and as long as I was on land, I feared some unpleasant encounter. I sat around for a month with a diligence which astonished me, dividing my time between piquet, broad jokes, and small beer.

At last this state of inaction passed. Paulet wanted to take up the course of his customary exploits. We hunted about, but the nights were not dark enough and the days were too long. All our pitiful captures were miserable vessels carrying coal, and a sloop of little value, on which we found some lord or other, who, in the hope of recovering his appetite, had taken a sail with his cook. We sent him to Verdun to spend his revenue and eat trout.

The quiet season was approaching, and we had almost no booty. The captain was taciturn and gloomy; the mate was desperate, and swore and cursed from morning to night; and from night till morning he was in a towering rage. All the crew would have drunk blood. Our disposition was such that we would have attacked a three-decker. It was midnight; we had sailed from a little bay near Dunkirk, and were headed toward the English coast. Suddenly the moonlight appeared through a rift in the clouds and spread its rays over the waters of the Channel; a short distance away were white sails; a brig of war was ploughing through the glittering waves.

Paulet recognized her. 'Boys,' he shouted, 'she is ours! Everyone down on his face, and I'll answer for it.' In a moment he led us on board. The English defended themselves furiously; a terrible battle began on their deck. The mate who, according to his custom, was first aboard, fell among the dead; Paulet was wounded, but avenged himself and his mate; he beat down all around him; I have never seen such a slaughter. In less than ten minutes, we were masters of the ship, and the tri-coloured flag was hoisted instead of the red. Twelve of our men had succumbed in the action, where both sides displayed an equal desperation.

Among those who had perished was a man named Lebel, who resembled me so strikingly that singular mistakes happened every day. I remembered that my double had papers in regular order. 'By Jove,' I ruminated, 'this is a fine chance. One never knows what will happen; Lebel will be thrown to the fishes; he doesn't need a passport, and his will work for me marvellously.'

The idea seemed excellent; I had only one thing to fear – that Lebel had placed his pocketbook in the owner's office. I was overcome with joy when I felt it on his breast. I took it at once without being seen by anyone, and when they had thrown the sacks into the sea, I felt relieved of a great weight, at the thought that hereafter I was rid of that Vidocq who had played me so many bad turns.

That very evening on my return to Boulogne I learned that, in accordance with the orders of the general-in-chief, all individuals in every corps who had been reported as worthless fellows were to be arrested immediately and embarked on men-of-war. This was a sort of press-gang which they were going to use to purge the army and put an end to the demoralization, which began to be alarming. So there was no way in which I could avoid society except to leave the *Revanche*. Furnished with Lebel's papers, I enlisted in a company of naval gunners, serving on the coast. As Lebel had been a corporal in that army, I obtained the rank at the first vacancy, or in about a fortnight. My regular conduct and a perfect understanding of the manœuvres, which I knew like an artilleryman of the old school, promptly won the kindness of my chiefs. Three months passed, and I deserved only praise; I proposed to continue to deserve it, but a career of adventure does not cease to be one suddenly.

Nothing was more frequent in Boulogne than duels, and the fatal mania had even won over the peaceful Dutchmen of the fleet under the orders of Admiral Wehrwel. Not far from the camp at the foot of a hill was a small wood near which one never passed, no matter at what hour of the day, without seeing along its borders a dozen men engaged in what they called affairs of honour.

One day, from the extremity of the plateau, which was covered by a long line of barracks, I lowered my gaze on the stage of this bloody scene, and I saw at some distance from the little wood two men, one walking after the other, who was beating a retreat through the plain. From the white pantaloons I knew that the champions were Hollanders. I stopped for a moment to watch them. Soon the assailant retreated in his turn. Finally, both being equally afraid, they retreated at the same time, waving their sabres. Then one became bolder, and threw his dirk at his adversary, and they followed him to the edge of a ditch which he could not cross. Then both of them gave up using their sabres, even as projectiles, and went to it with their fists and settled their quarrel in this way.

I was amusing myself with this grotesque duel when I saw, near a farm where we sometimes went to eat, two individuals who were taking off their coats and preparing to take their swords in the presence of their seconds, one a sergeant-major of dragoons, and the other a quartermaster of artillery. They soon crossed weapons. The smaller of the combatants was a sergeant of gunners. He broke away with unparalleled boldness. In the end, after he had travelled in this way some fifty yards, I thought he was going to be run through, when suddenly he disappeared as if the earth had swallowed him. At once I heard a burst of laughter. After this first loud gaiety, the seconds approached, and I saw them stoop over.

Led on by a feeling of curiosity, I went to them, and I arrived very opportunely to help them pull out of a hole, made for a hog trough, the poor fellow whose sudden disappearance had struck me with astonishment. He was almost asphyxiated, and covered with mud from head to foot. The open air gave him back the use of his senses, but he did not dare to breathe and was afraid to open his mouth and eyes, so foul was the liquid into which he had plunged. In this grievous situation the first words that he heard were jokes. I felt outraged by this lack of generosity, and, yielding to my righteous indignation, I darted at the antagonist of the victim one of those glances which among soldiers needs no interpretation.

'That's enough,' he said. 'I'll wait for you without stirring.' I was hardly on guard when on his arm opposite the foil I had picked up, I noticed a tattoo mark which I seemed to recognize; it was the figure of an anchor, the shank encircled by the coils of a serpent. 'I see the tail,' I cried, 'and look out for the head,' and, as I gave this warning, I thrust on my man and touched him on the right breast. 'I am wounded,' he said. 'Is that the first blood?' 'Yes, the first blood,' I answered, and, without waiting, I tore up my shirt to bandage the wound. He had to show his breast. I had guessed where the serpent's head was – it was at the end of his bosom, and that was where I had aimed.

Seeing that I was examining his features one after the other and this mark, my adversary became uneasy. I hastened to reassure him by whispering in his ear, 'I know who you are; but don't be afraid; I am discreet.' ' I know you, too,' he answered, taking me by the hand, 'and I shall be silent.' He was a convict who had escaped from the prison at Toulon. He told me his alias, and that he was a sergeant-major in the Tenth Dragoons, where he surpassed in luxury all the officers of the regiment.

The sergeant-major, whom I had wounded but slightly, proposed to sign a treaty of peace at the Canon d'Or, where there were always fish stews and ducks plucked in advance. He paid for a princely lunch which lasted until supper, for which his adversary paid. When the day was over, we separated, the sergeant-major making me promise to see him again.

As I thought that I had got my foot on the ladder and wanted to be promoted, I took pains to lose as Lebel all the bad habits of Vidocq, and if the necessity of attending the distribution of rations had not taken me to Boulogne at times, I should have accomplished my object. But every time I went into the city, I had to visit the sergeant-major of dragoons, and then a whole day was given up to drunken bouts, and in spite of myself I acted contrary to my projects of reform.

On the strength of a supposed uncle, whose succession he said was assured to him, my former colleague in the prison led a very agreeable life; the credit which he enjoyed as a son of a family was almost unlim-

ited. No wealthy man in Boulogne failed to take to his home a personage of such high distinction. The most ambitious fathers desired nothing so much as to have him for a son-in-law, and he could hardly make
a choice among the young ladies. He lived like a colonel, with his dogs,
horses, servants; he affected the tone and manners of a grand seigneur,
and had to the highest degree the art of throwing dust in the eyes and
pushing himself forward. This reached such a point that the officers
themselves, who are ordinarily so terribly jealous of their prerogatives,
considered it natural that he should eclipse them.

Fessaro was the real name of this sergeant-major whom I had
known in prison as Hippolyte. In a word, he was a shrewd fellow, with
all the tricks to inspire confidence. An inch of land in his own country
would have given him a chance to bring a thousand lawsuits, and
would have been the beginnings of a fortune which he would have
made by ruining his neighbours. But Hippolyte had nothing in the
world, and could not even start a suit, so he had become a sharper, then
a forger, then ... But I anticipate.

Every time I came to the city, Hippolyte paid for my dinner. One
day at dessert he said to me: 'Do you know, I admire the way you live
like a hermit in the country, accept the allotted allowance, and have in
all only twenty-two sous a day. I cannot understand how you can condemn yourself to such privations; I would rather die. But you pull off
some tricks on the sly, and you must have some resources.'

I told him that my pay was sufficient; that I was fed, clothed, and
that I lacked nothing.

'All right,' he replied. 'However, there are some growlers here, and
you must have doubtless heard them talk about the "Army of the
Moon." You must join them; if you want me to, I'll give you a district;
you can exploit the country around Saint-Leonard.'

I knew that the 'Army of the Moon' was an association of criminals,
and that their leaders had so far escaped the investigations of the police.
These bandits had organized murder and robbery within a radius of
more than ten leagues; they belonged to every regiment. At night they
roamed about the camps or lay in wait on the roads, making false
rounds or patrols, and holding up whoever offered hope of the slightest
booty. In view of what I knew, Hippolyte's proposition was well calculated to alarm me. Either he was one of the leaders of the 'Army of the

Moon' or he was a secret agent sent by the police to prepare the disbanding of that army, or perhaps both. My situation was embarrassing. I could not, as at Lyons, get out of it by denouncing the instigator. What good would a denunciation have done me if Hippolyte were an agent? So I restrained myself and rejected his proposition, declaring firmly that I was determined to stay an honest man.

'Didn't you see that I was joking?' he asked. 'And you take it seriously; I only wanted to feel you out. I am delighted to find you with such feelings. That's the way I feel too. I have gone back to the better way, and now the Devil himself could not make me leave it.'

A week after the interview during which Hippolyte had given me an opening which he had withdrawn so promptly, the captain at inspection sentenced me to twenty-four hours in the guardhouse for a spot which he pretended to see on my equipment. I nearly burst my eyes trying to find that cursed spot, but I never did. However that might be, I gave myself up at the guardhouse without a complaint; twenty-four hours are soon over. My sentence was to expire at noon the next day.

At five o'clock in the morning, I heard the trot of horses, and, soon after, the following dialogue. 'Who comes there?'... 'France'... 'What regiment?'... 'Imperial corps of gendarmes.'

At that word gendarmes, I shuddered involuntarily. Suddenly the door opened, and they called Vidocq. Never did this name, falling unexpectedly in the middle of a gang of crooks, astound them more than it did me at that moment. 'Come on, follow us!' shouted the corporal; and to be sure that I should not escape, he took the precaution of fastening me to him. I was at once led to prison, where I found myself in a numerous and a good company.

'Did I not say so?' cried an artilleryman, as he saw me enter. 'The whole camp is coming here! I'll bet my head that it was that scoundrel of a sergeant-major of dragoons who played this trick.'

'Oh, go and find your sergeant-major,' interrupted a second prisoner. 'If he's still walking, he's a long way off now; he skipped last week .... All the same he was a sly dog. In less than three months forty thousand francs in debt in the city. And, besides... !'

'Oh,' said another, 'what's the use of jabbering about cutting off his head! We're in prison, and no matter who put us here.'

He was right. It was altogether useless to roam about in conjectures, and one would be blind not to recognize Hippolyte as the author of our arrest. For my part, I could not be wrong, for he was the only one in Boulogne who knew that I had escaped from prison.

The arrival of six new prisoners, who paid for their welcome with great liberality, was an occasion for rejoicing. I had known most of them as part of Paulet's crew. They were to be locked up for some days as a punishment, because, when they had been left aboard a prize, they had, contrary to the rules of warfare, robbed the English captain. As they had not been compelled to give them back, they brought guineas with them, and spent them with a high hand. We were all satisfied. The jailer, who received at least some drops of this shower of gold, was so pleased by his new guests that he relaxed his surveillance. I was the only one to nourish projects of escape, but precisely that it should not be discovered, I affected to be without a care, that the prison was my real element. Everyone would have presumed that I felt like a fish in the water.

I was only drunk the once. That night at two o'clock in the morning everyone was snoring. I was terribly thirsty and my body was on fire; half-awake, I got up and got a drink, but at daylight I was still ill. A turnkey announced that fatigue duty was to be done. It afforded a chance to get the open air, so I offered to take the place of one of the privateers whose garments I put on. As I crossed the court, I met an officer of my acquaintance, arriving with his coat over his arm. He told me that he had made a row at the theatre and had been sentenced to a month in prison; he had come of his own accord to be locked up. 'In that case,' I said, 'you can begin your duties right now; here's the bucket.' The officer was accommodating, and did not require urging. While he did fatigue duty, I passed swiftly in front of the sentinel who paid no attention to me.

Once out of the château, I took flight toward the country, and stopped only at the bridge at Brique, in a small ravine, while I reflected on ways to foil pursuit. At first, I had an idea of going to Calais, but my unlucky star led me to return to Arras. I reached Bèthune without accident, where I lodged with an old regimental acquaintance. I was well received, but however prudent one may be, there are always unforeseen circumstances. I should have preferred the inn to my friend's hospitality. I had run into danger, for he had recently married, and his wife's brother was one of those rebellious brutes whose soul is insensible to glory and thrills only at peace. It naturally followed that the domicile I had chosen, and even those of all the young man's relatives, were frequently visited by messieurs the gendarmes. These gentlemen invaded the residence of my friend a long time before daylight. With no respect for my sleep, they summoned me to show my papers. For want of a passport which I could show them, I tried to explain; it was waste labour.

The corporal, who had looked at me with special attention, suddenly cried: 'I am not mistaken; it's he! I saw the rogue at Arras; it's Vidocq.'

I had to get up, and a quarter of an hour later I was in prison in Bèthune. I did not stay there long; the day after my arrest, I was on the road to Douai under heavy escort.

XIV
THE VILLAINOUS PAST PREYS UPON ME

I HAD HARDLY put foot in the courtyard when Rausson, the attorney-general, who was irritated at my repeated escapes, appeared at the grating, and shouted, 'Well, so Vidocq's arrived! Is he in irons?'

'Oh, monsieur,' I said, 'what have I done to you that you wish me such hardship? Is it a great crime that I have escaped several times? Have I abused the liberty which I value so highly? When they caught me, was I not busy creating means to lead an honest life? I am less guilty than unfortunate! Have pity on me and on my poor mother, who will die if I am sent back to prison.'

These words and the note of truth with which I uttered them made some impression on M. Rausson. That evening he came back and questioned me for a long time on the way I had lived since I had got out of Toulon, and, as I could support what I said by irrefutable proofs, he began to show some kindness. 'Why don't you draw up an appeal for pardon?' he asked me, 'or at least for a commutation of sentence? I will recommend you to the chief justice.' I thanked the magistrate for what he wanted to do for me, and the same day a lawyer in Douai, M. Thomas, who took a real interest in me, had me sign a petition which he had had the kindness to draw up.

I was expecting an answer, when one morning I was summoned to the office. I thought they were going to give me the minister's decision. Impatient to learn it, I followed the turnkey with the eagerness of a man who hurries for good news. I counted on seeing the attorney-general, but it was my wife whom I saw, with two unknown men. I tried to guess what the object of her visit could be, when, in the most unembarrassed tone, Madame Vidocq said: 'I have come to tell you that our decree of divorce has been granted. As I am going to marry again, this formality is necessary. In addition, the bailiff will read you the decree.'

Except seeing myself set at liberty, nothing more agreeable could have been announced than the dissolution of this marriage; I was forever rid of a person I detested. I do not know whether I was sufficiently master of myself to conceal my joy, but surely my face must have shown it, and if, as I strongly suspected, my successor was present, he could go away convinced that I did not envy him the treasure he was going to possess.

My detention at Douai was terribly prolonged. I was there five months, and nothing came from Paris. The attorney-general showed much interest in me, but adversity made me suspicious, and I began to fear that he had lured me on in vain hope, in order to turn me away from escaping until the departure of the chain gang. Struck by this idea, I again took up my projects of escape with eagerness.

The jailer Wettu looked upon me as pardoned in advance, and he had some regard for me. We even dined together frequently in a small room, the only window of which looked out on the Scarpe. It seemed to me that by means of this opening, which they had neglected to bar, some day or other, at the end of a meal, it would be easy to be impolite. Only, first, it was essential to be assured of a disguise, by which, once out, I could throw off the trackers. I took some friends into my confidence, and they placed at my disposal the dress of an officer in the light artillery, which I promised to use on the first occasion.

One Sunday evening, I was at table with the jailer and the bailiff Hurtrel. The Beaune had made the gentlemen gay; I ordered more bottles.

'Do you know, my jolly dog,' Hurtrel said to me, 'that it would not have been well to put you here seven years ago. A window without bars! Hang it, I wouldn't trust you!'

'Go on, Papa Hurtrel, one would have to be made of cork,' I answered, 'to risk jumping from such a height.'

'That's so,' observed the jailer, and the conversation rested there; but I had decided. Some people soon came in, the jailer sat down to play, and when he was fully occupied with his game, I jumped into the river.

At the noise of my fall, everyone ran to the window, while Wettu shouted to the guard and turnkeys to pursue me. Fortunately for me, dusk hardly allowed them to make out objects, and my hat, which I had intentionally thrown on the river-bank, made them think that I had come out of the river immediately. But meanwhile I continued to swim in the direction of the water-gate, under which I passed with difficulty because I was benumbed with cold and my strength began to be exhausted.

Once outside the city, I gained land. My clothes were wet through and weighed a hundred pounds. Nevertheless, I held to my course and stopped only at the village of Blangy, two leagues from Arras. It was four o'clock in the morning; a baker was heating his oven, and he dried my clothes and furnished me some food. When I had recovered, I went my way and headed toward Duisans, where there lived a widow of a former captain, one of my friends. An express was to bring to her house the uniform which my friends in Douai had procured for me. I no sooner had it than I went to Hersin, where I hid a few days with one of my cousins. Advice which reached me very apropos made me begone. I knew that the police were convinced that I was still in the country and had ordered a beat which was even then on the way to my retreat. Resolved to escape, I did not wait for it.

It was clear that Paris alone offered me a refuge. But to get to Paris it was necessary to go back to Arras, and if I passed through that city I should be recognized without fail. I bethought myself of a way to escape the difficulty.

Prudence suggested that I get into my cousin's covered cart. He had an excellent horse and he was the best man in the world in his knowledge of the crossroads. He agreed, on his reputation as a perfect guide, to make me turn the ramparts of my natal city. That was all that was necessary; my disguise would do the rest.

I was no longer Vidocq, at least if one did not look too closely, so when we arrived at the bridge at Gy, I was not much disturbed to see eight of the gendarmes' horses tied before the door of an inn. I confess that I should have been willing to pass without this encounter, but, as I had made it, only by daring would it cease to be perilous.

'Come on,' I said to my cousin, 'we must show some cheek here. Get down, quickly, quickly, and have them serve you something.'

He got down at once and presented himself at the inn with all the appearance of a sharp fellow who is not afraid of the eyes of the whole brigade.

'Well,' said one of the gendarmes, 'are you driving your cousin Vidocq?'

'Perhaps,' he said, laughing, 'look and see.'

The gendarme, in fact, approached the wagon, but rather from curiosity than suspicion. At sight of my uniform, he raised his hand to his cap respectfully, and said, 'Greetings, Captain,' and soon after he mounted his horse with his comrades.

'Bon voyage!' my cousin shouted to them, cracking his whip. 'If you take him, write to us.'

'Get out!' answered the sergeant-major who commanded the troop, 'we know the place and the word is Hersin; tomorrow at this time he'll be locked up.'

We continued on our way very peacefully. However, I had one fear – military insignia might expose me to some quibbling with disagreeable results. The war with Prussia had begun, and few officers were to be seen in the interior, at least unless they had been brought there by some wound. I decided to wear my arm in a sling. I had been disabled at Jena, and, if I was questioned, I was ready to give not only all the details of that day, which I had read in the bulletins, but all I had been able to collect by hearing a mass of stories, true or false, from witnesses, ocular or otherwise. In sum, I was thoroughly versed on the battle of Jena, and I could talk to every comer with knowledge of the case; no one knew more than I did.

At Beaumont I acquitted myself perfectly in the role, where the weariness of the horse, which had made thirty-five leagues in a day and a half, forced us to halt. I had already made inquiries at the inn when I saw a sergeant-major of gendarmes go straight to an officer of dragoons and invite him to exhibit his papers. I approached the sergeant-major in my turn and asked him the reason for this precaution. 'I asked him for his route orders,' he answered, 'because, when everyone is in the army, France is not the place for any officer in good health.' 'You are right, comrade,' I said, 'service must be done,' and at the same time, so that he would not take a notion to see whether I was in order, I invited him to dinner with me.

During the meal I won his confidence to such an extent that he asked me when I was in Paris to try to get his residence changed. I promised all, and he was content. However it was, the flagons were emptied rapidly, and my guest, in his enthusiasm for my protection, began to talk disconnectedly, a prelude to drunkenness, when a gendarme came to him with a package of despatches. He broke the bands with an uncertain hand, and tried to read, but his dimming eyes made useless all attempts of this kind, so he asked me to supplement him in his functions. I opened a letter, and the first words which struck my eyes were the following: 'Arras Brigade.' I ran it over at a glance. It was the advice of my passage to Beaumont. It added that I must have taken the diligence at the Lion d'Argent. In spite of my agitation, I read the description, changing it as I went along. 'Good, good!' said the most sober and vigilant sergeant-major; 'the coach doesn't pass until tomorrow morning; we'll attend to it.' And he wanted to begin drinking again, but his strength deceived his courage; he had to be carried to bed, to the great scandal of everyone there, who repeated with indignation. 'A sergeant-major! A man of rank! To be in such a state!'

One can well believe that I did not await the awakening of the man of rank. At five o'clock I took my place in the diligence, which took me the same day to Paris without trouble. My mother was still living at Versailles and she joined me. We lived together for some months in the Faubourg Saint-Denis, where we saw no one except a jeweller named Jacquelin whom I had to take into my confidence up to a certain point, because he had known me at Rouen under the name of Blondel.

It was at Jacquelin's that I met a Madame B., who holds first rank in my affections. Madame B., or Annette, was a rather pretty woman, whose husband had deserted her on account of bad circumstances. He had fled to Holland, and there had been no news of him for a long time. So Annette was entirely free. She pleased me; I liked her spirit, her intelligence, her good heart; I dared to tell her so. From the first she looked upon my attentions without much reluctance, and soon we could not live without each other. Annette came to reside with me, and, as I was again taking up my trade of itinerant dealer in novelties, we decided that she should accompany me on my rounds.

The first trip we took together was most fortunate. Only at the moment I was leaving Melun the innkeeper at whose place I had stayed warned me that the commissioner of police had shown some regret that he had not examined my papers, but that what was postponed was not lost, and an my next passage he would pay me a visit. This advice surprised me; I must already have been pointed out as a suspect. If I went on, perhaps I should be compromised. I turned back for Paris, promising not to make another excursion until I had succeeded in making my chances less unfavourable.

I started in the early morning, and I arrived early at the Faubourg Saint-Marceau. As I entered, the news agents were crying this finale, 'which condemns two very-well-known individuals to be put to death today on the Place de Grève.' I listened. It seemed to me that the name Herbaux rang in my ears – the author of the forgery which had caused all my misfortunes. I listened more attentively, and this time the crier, whom I approached, repeated the sentence with variations: 'Here is the decree of the criminal tribunal of the Department of the Seine, which condemns to death the following: Armand Saint-Léger, former sailor, born at Bayonne, and César Herbaux, returned convict, born at Lille, accused and convicted of murder, etc.'

There was no doubt left; the wretch who had ruined me was going to rest his head on the scaffold. Shall I confess it? I felt a feeling of joy, and nevertheless I shuddered. Perhaps one will be astonished at the alacrity with which I hurried to the Palais de Justice to assure myself of the truth. It was not yet noon, and I had all the trouble in the world to reach the gate, near which I took up my position to wait for the fatal moment.

Four o'clock struck at last. The grating opened; a man appeared in the cart; it was Herbaux. His face had a deadly pallor; he showed a firmness which the convulsive movement of his features denied. He pretended to speak to his companion, who had already reached a stage where he could not hear. At the signal of departure, Herbaux, with a face which he forced to look audacious, cast a glance on the crowd; his eyes met mine. He stirred; his colour increased. The cortège passed. I stayed as motionless as the bronze clusters to which I clung, and I should doubtless have been there a long time in this forgetful attitude if an inspector had not ordered me to move on. Twenty minutes after, a cart carrying a red basket, escorted by a gendarme, passed the Pont-au-Change on the trot and headed toward the cemetery for the condemned. Then with sorrowful heart I left and regained my lodgings in sad reflections.

Although the definite execution had no direct influence on me, it dismayed me. I was terrified at being in contact with such brigands destined for the executioner. I blushed in some way for myself. I wanted to lose my memory and create an impenetrable demarcation between the past and the present. I saw myself tracked anew like a wild beast; my persuasion that I should be prevented from becoming an honest man made me despair; I was silent, morose, discouraged. Annette saw it; she wanted to console me; she pressed me with questions; my secret escaped; I have never had occasion to regret it. The activity, zeal, and presence of mind of that woman became most useful. I needed a passport. She got Jacquelin to lend me his, and so that I could use it, he gave me the most complete information about his family and connections. Furnished with these instructions, I took up my travelling, and went through Lower Burgundy. Nearly everywhere I had to show that I was in order. If they had compared the description with the man, it would have been easy to uncover the fraud, but no observation was made anywhere. For more than a year, except for some alarms which aren't worth mentioning, the name of Jacquelin brought me luck.

One day, when I had unpacked at Auxerre, and was walking quietly about the port, I met a man named Paquay, a professional thief whom I had seen at Bicêtre, where he was confined for six years. It would have been agreeable to me if I could have avoided him, but he accosted me so unexpectedly that from the first words he spoke I was convinced that it would not be prudent to try to refuse to know him. He was very curious to know what I was doing, and, as I saw from his conversation that he proposed to go into partnership with me in some robberies, I thought it a good way to get rid of him, to speak of the police of Auxerre, whom I represented as most vigilant and, consequently, most formidable. I thought I saw that I had made some impression. I heightened the picture, so that, finally, after he had listened to me with an uneasy attention, he suddenly exclaimed, 'The devil, it seems that it isn't good here; the coach goes in two hours, and if you want to, we'll take ourselves off.' 'If it's a question of getting away,' I said, 'I'm your man.'

On that I left him, after promising to rejoin him as soon as I had finished some preparations which I had to make. An escaped convict is in a pitiful condition. If he does not want to be denounced or implicated in some crime, he is always reduced to taking the initiative himself; that is to say, he must be the denouncer. I went back to the inn and wrote the following letter to the lieutenant of the gendarmes, who I knew was on the trail of the authors of a robbery recently committed in the diligence office:

> Monsieur:
>
> A person who wants to be unknown to you warns you that one of the authors of the robbery committed in the coach office in your city is going, at six o'clock, by coach to Joigny, where his accomplices probably await him. In order not to miss him, and to arrest him in good time, it would be well that two gendarmes in disguise mount in the coach with him. It is important that he be taken with prudence, and that they do not lose sight of the individual, for he is a most adroit man.

This missive was accompanied by a description so minutely drawn that it was impossible to mistake him. The time for departure arrived. I reached the quays by twists and turns, and from the window of a public-house at which I was posted, I saw Paquay enter the coach. Soon after the two gendarmes embarked. I recognized them by a certain appearance which one can imagine but cannot analyze. At intervals they passed each other a paper on which they cast their eyes. Finally their looks rested on my man, whose costume, contrary to the custom of thieves, was a bad sign. The coach started, and I saw it go with the greater pleasure in that it removed for all time Paquay, his proposals, and even his revelations, if, as I doubted, he thought of making any.

Later, some fears arose in my mind about Paquay. On reflection, it seemed to me that in this circumstance I had acted thoughtlessly. I felt a presentiment of some misfortune, and this presentiment was realized. Paquay was taken to Paris and then brought back to Auxerre for identification. He learned that I was in the city; he had always suspected that I had denounced him, and he took his revenge. He told the jailer all that he knew about me. The latter reported to the authorities, but my reputation for probity was such in Auxerre, where I made sojourns of three months, that, to avoid a troublesome scandal, a magistrate summoned me and warned me of what had happened.

I did not need to confess the truth to him; I had only the strength to say, 'Oh, monsieur, I want to be an honest man!' Without answering, he went out and left me alone. I understood his generous silence.

In a quarter of an hour I was lost from sight, and from my retreat I wrote to Annette and told her about this new catastrophe and advised her to stay at Les Faisan for a fortnight and to tell everyone that I had gone to Rouen to make purchases, and to join me in Paris at the end of that time. In fact, she arrived there the day I had named, and told me that the day after my departure the gendarmes in disguise had visited the shop to arrest me. As they did not find me, they had said that they would get me in the end.

So they were going to continue the search. This was a *contretemps* which deranged all my plans. As I had been described under the name of Jacquelin, I saw that I must abandon it, and again renounce an industry which I had created. What course should I take? That was my sole pre-occupation when by chance I became acquainted with a merchant tailor in the Cour Saint-Martin. He wanted to sell his business. I negotiated with him, in the persuasion that I should be safer nowhere than in the heart of the capital, where it is easy to be lost in the crowd.

In fact, nearly eight months went by without anything coming to disturb the tranquillity which Annette, my mother, and I enjoyed. My establishment prospered; it increased daily. I did not limit myself, as my predecessor had done, to making clothes, but I also traded in cloths. I was, perhaps, in a way to make my fortune when one morning all my troubles began again.

I was in my warehouse. A messenger appeared and told me that I was wanted at an eating-house in the rue Aumaire. I presumed that it was about some deal, and I went to the place indicated. They took me into a small room, and I found there two men who had escaped from the prison at Brest; one was Blondy. 'We've been here ten days,' he said, 'and we haven't a soul. We saw you yesterday in a warehouse; we learned that it's yours, and we were very pleased. I told my friend, "Now we needn't worry, because we know you, and you aren't a man to let your comrades stay in trouble."'

The thought of seeing myself at the mercy of two bandits whom I knew capable of anything – even of selling me to the police – short of ruining themselves, overwhelmed me. I did not omit to express how pleased I was to find myself with them. I added that, as I was not wealthy, I regretted that I could not favour them with more than fifty francs. They seemed satisfied with this sum, and left me, announcing that they intended to go to Châlons-sur-Marne, where they had, they said, 'business.'

I should have been only too happy if they had left Paris forever, but in saying good-bye they promised to come back soon, and I was left in terror of their near return. Were they going to consider me their milch cow and set a price on their discretion? Would they not prove insatiable? Who could answer to me that their demands would not exceed all possibilities? I already saw myself as the banker of these gentlemen and many others, for it was to be presumed, according to the usual custom among thieves, that if I failed to satisfy them, they would hand me on to their acquaintances and so I should ransom myself by new expenditures. I could be on good terms with them only until the first refusal; when they reached that end, they would doubtless play me some bad turn. With such good-for-nothings at my heels, it may be understood that I was not at ease. If my situation was not pleasant, it was made still worse by a fatal encounter.

It may or may not be remembered that my wife, after her divorce, had married a second time. I thought she was in the Department of Pas-de-Calais, busy in making her new husband happy, when one day I found myself face to face with her in the street; it was impossible to avoid her, for she had recognized me. I then spoke to her, and without going back to the past, as the dilapidation of her toilet showed me that she was not among the most fortunate, I gave her some money. Perhaps she imagined that this was an interested generosity; however, there was none at all.

It never occurred to me that the ex-Madame Vidocq would denounce me. To tell the truth, later, in thinking over our old quarrels, I judged that my heart had counselled me in the direction of prudence. So I applauded myself for what I had done, and it appeared to me most proper that this woman in her distress could count on me for some help; if I were in prison or away from Paris, I could no longer relieve her misery. That was a consideration for me which should determine her to keep silent, or at least I believed so. We shall see whether I was wrong.

The support of my ex-wife was a charge to which I resigned myself, but the burden was heavier than I knew. A fortnight had passed since our interview, when one morning I was asked to go to rue de

L'Échiquier. I went, and at the back of the court in a ground-floor apartment, rather neat but poorly furnished, I saw not only my wife, but more, her nieces and their father, the Terrorist Chevalier, who had just been released from a six months' sentence for stealing silverware. A glance was enough to convince me that a whole family was on my hands. All of them were absolutely destitute; I detested them; I cursed them; yet there was nothing better for me to do than tender my hand. I bled myself for them. If I reduced them to despair, I should be lost, and rather than go back in the power of the prison guards, I was resolved to sacrifice my last sou.

At this time it seemed as if the entire world was leagued against me. At every moment I had to unloosen my purse strings, and for whom? For beings who in the thought that my liberality was obligatory were ready to betray me as soon as I no longer seemed to them an assured resource. When I returned from my former wife's apartment, I again had proof of the misery attached to the condition of an escaped convict: Annette and my mother were in tears. During my absence two drunken men had asked for me, and on the response that I was not there, they had answered by invectives and threats which left me no doubt as to the perfidy of their intentions. From the description Annette gave me of the two individuals, it was easy for me to recognize Blondy and his comrade Duluc. I had no trouble in guessing their names; moreover, they had given an address with a formal injunction to bring them forty francs; they were the only ones capable of intimating such an order. I was obedient, very obedient; only, when I paid my contribution to these two scoundrels, I could not help observing that they had acted very inconsiderately.

'See the fine trick you've pulled,' I said; 'they knew nothing at the house, and you've told all. The establishment is in my wife's name, and perhaps she'll want to put me out, and then I'll have to scratch the pavements.'

'You'll come and rob with us,' answered the two brigands.

I tried to show them that it was infinitely better to work for a living than always to be in fear of the police, who, sooner or later, would catch the malefactors in their nets. I added that one crime often led to another, and that he who thought he was running the risk of the pillory was heading straight for the guillotine. The conclusion of my discourse was that they would be wise to renounce the perilous career they had embraced.

'Not bad!' Blondy exclaimed, when I had ended my harangue. 'Not bad! While we are waiting, could you point out some charmer we could strip? You see, we are like Harlequin; we need money more than advice.' And they left laughing in my face.

I called them back to protest my devotion, and begged them not to come to the house again.

'If that's all,' said Duluc, 'we'll refrain.'

'Oh, yes,' said Blondy, 'we'll refrain, since that displeases madame.'

The latter did not refrain long. On the second day, at nightfall, he came to my warehouse and asked to see me in private. I took him up to my room. 'We are alone?' he asked, taking in the place at a glance. When he thought he was sure that there were no witnesses, he pulled out of his pocket eleven silver covers and two gold watches which he placed on the table.

'Four hundred francs the lot; it's not dear for those gold watches and silverware. Come on, count out the cash.'

'Four hundred francs!' I answered, deeply troubled by such an abrupt demand. 'I haven't them.'

'No matter, sell them.'

'But if they ask questions?'

'Arrange that; I need the dust; or if you'd like it better, I'll send you some buyers from the Préfecture. Do you understand what that means? Cash, and not so much ceremony.'

I understood only too well. I already saw myself denounced; deprived of the condition I had made for myself and taken back to the convict prison. The four hundred francs were counted out.

XV
A Fugitive Once More

HERE I WAS a receiver – a fence. In spite of myself I was a criminal; but after all I was, since I had lent my hands to crime; one cannot conceive of a hell like that in which I lived. I was constantly troubled. Remorse and fear assailed me at the same time; night, day, at every moment, I was on the alert. I did not sleep; I had no appetite; my business no longer occupied me; all was odious. All? No; Annette and my mother were near. But it was a question whether it was not necessary to abandon them. Sometimes I shudder at the remembrance of my apprehensions. My home was transformed into an abominable den; sometimes it was invaded by the police, and the search brought to light the proofs of a crime which would bring down on me the prosecution of the law. Harassed by the Chevalier family who ate me up; tormented by Blondy, who did not cease to get money out of me; terrified by all that was horrible and incurable in my position, ashamed at being tyrannized over by the vilest creatures on earth, irritated at being unable to break that moral chain which bound me irrevocably to the opprobrium of mankind, I felt driven to despair, and for a week I revolved in my mind the most sinister projects.

Blondy, that execrable Blondy, was the one against whom all my rage turned. I would have strangled him with good heart, and nevertheless I still received him and managed him. Carried away and violent as I was, such patience was a miracle; Annette ordered it. How many sincere wishes I made that in one of the frequent excursions on which Blondy went, some good gendarme would get his hand on his collar. I flattered myself that that was a near event, but every time that an absence a little longer than usual made me presume that at last I was rid of the rascal, he reappeared, and with him my cares returned.

One day I saw him arrive with Duluc and an ex-law clerk, named Saint-Germain, whom I had known at Rouen, where, like so many others, he enjoyed provisionally the reputation of an honest man. Saint-Germain, to whom I was the trader Blondel, was astonished by the meeting, but two words from Blondy were enough to give him the key to my story – I was a thorough scoundrel. Confidence gave place to astonishment, and Saint-Germain, who at first sight had scowled, cheered up. Blondy told me that all three were going to the outskirts of Senlis, and asked for the loan of my carriage which I used to go to fairs. Happy at getting rid of these good-for-nothing wastrels at this price, I hastened to give them a letter to the person who took care of it.

They were given the carriage with the harness. They started, and I was without news of them for ten days. Saint-Germain brought it. He entered my place one morning. He seemed frightened and appeared to be worn out with fatigue.

'Well,' he said, 'the comrades are arrested.'

'Arrested!' I exclaimed, in a transport of joy which I could not contain; but I regained my presence of mind at once and asked for details, pretending that I was astounded.

Saint-Germain told me very briefly that Blondy and Duluc had been arrested merely for travelling without papers. I did not believe what he said; and I did not doubt that they had pulled off some stroke. What confirmed me in my suspicions was that when I proposed to send them money, Saint-Germain answered that they had what they needed. When they left Paris they had had fifty francs among the three of them. Certainly with such a small sum, it would have been difficult to save; how did it come about that they were not still destitute? My first thought was that they had committed some considerable robbery, about which they did not care to take me into their confidence. I soon discovered that it was a much graver matter.

Two days after Saint-Germain's return, I took a fancy to go and see my carriage which he had brought back. I first noticed that the veneer had been changed. On getting inside, I saw on the blue-and-white lining some red spots which had been newly washed. And when I opened the box, I found it full of blood, as if a corpse had been placed in it. All was clear, the truth was more frightful than my conjectures. I did not hesitate. Perhaps more interested than those who had committed the murder in getting rid of the traces, the following night I took the carriage to the banks of the Seine, in an isolated place, and set fire to the straw and wood with which I had stuffed it. I withdrew only after it had been reduced to ashes.

The next day I told Saint-Germain what I had noticed without mentioning that I had burned my carriage, and he finally confessed that they had hidden in it the corpse of a Carter whom Blondy had murdered, until they had found an opportunity to throw it into a pit. This man, one of the most audacious scoundrels I have ever met, spoke of this deed as though he were talking of the most innocent action; with a laugh on his lips and a most detached tone, he related even the slightest circumstances. He horrified me; I listened to him in a sort of stupefaction. When I heard him declare that he needed the impression of the locks of an apartment whose tenant I knew, my terror was at its height. I tried to protest.

'What's that to me?' he answered. 'Business is business. Since you know him, that's another reason. You know the goods; lead me there and we'll share them. Come on,' he added, 'no shuffling out of it; I want the impression.'

I pretended to go back to my eloquence.

'What scruples are you showing!' he said. 'Shut up! You make me sick! All is said, and we'll go halves.'

Good God, what a partnership! I was hardly able to take joy in Blondy's fall. Blondy might yield me certain consideration; Saint-Germain never; and he was more imperious in his demands. Exposed to seeing myself compromised at any moment, I determined to make overtures to M. Henry, chief of the division of safety in the Préfecture of Police. I went to see him, and, after I had unveiled my situation, I declared that if he was willing to tolerate my sojourn in Paris, I would give him precious information on a great number of escaped convicts whose retreats and projects I knew.

M. Henry received me with some kindness; but after he had reflected a moment on what I had said, he answered that he could make no engagement with me.

'That ought not to prevent your making the revelations,' he said. 'We'll then judge how meritorious they are, and perhaps...'

'Oh, monsieur, no perhaps; I should risk my life! You don't know of what the persons I want to describe are capable. If I should be taken back to prison, after a judicial inquiry had established that I had had relations with the police, I am a dead man.'

'In that case, we will not talk of it.' And he let me go without asking my name.

I was broken-hearted at the failure of my attempt. Saint-Germain could not fail to come back; he would summon me to keep my word; I did not know what to do. Should I warn the person we had agreed to rob together? If it had been possible to get out of accompanying Saint-Germain, it would have been less dangerous to follow such a course. But I had promised to assist, and there was no way under any pretext in which I could get away from my promise. I waited for him as one awaits the decree of death. One week, two weeks, three weeks passed in such perplexities. At the end of that time I began to breathe freely; after two months I became altogether tranquil; I believed that like his two comrades he had been arrested somewhere. I still remember that Annette burned at least a dozen candles to 'their intention.' 'My God!' she sometimes cried, 'grant that they shall stay where they are!' The torment had lasted a long time; the moments of calm were short; they preceded the catastrophe which would decide my life.

The third of May, 1809, at daybreak, I was awakened by blows on the door of my shop. I went down to see what the matter was, and I was going to open when I heard a colloquy in a low voice: 'He's a vigorous man, take precautions!'

More than doubtful about the reasons for this early visit, I went up to my chamber in all haste. Annette, informed of what was happening, opened the window, and, while she held the agents in conversation, I slipped out in my shirt by an exit on the landing and rapidly mounted to the upper floors. On the fourth floor I saw a door half-open and went in; I looked and listened; I was alone. In an alcove was a bed hidden by crimson damask curtains; forced by the circumstances and sure that the staircase was already guarded, I threw myself under the mattress; but I had hardly crouched down when someone entered. He spoke; I recognized the voice; it was a young man named Fossé, whose father slept in the next room.

Just then the commissioner and his men, after going through the house from top to bottom, reached the fourth floor landing. He searched the room at the back, and then came into the one where I was. 'And this bed?' he said, raising the strip of crimson damask, while at my feet I felt one of the corners of the mattress move. He let it drop nonchalantly. 'There's no more Vidocq here than on the palm of my hand. Come on, he must have made himself invisible,' the commissioner continued, 'we'll have to give up.' The enormous relief these words gave me may be imagined.

Finally, the whole gang of searchers withdrew, the wife going with them with all sorts of politeness. But she soon came back two steps at a time, all out of breath. I was still in a funk. Then the whole family went out, and I remained under lock and key, reflecting on the perfidious insinuations of the police, who deprived me of the assistance of my neighbours by representing me as an infamous scoundrel – as they had.

I was shut in for two hours; there was no noise in the street, or in the house; the crowd had dispersed. I began to be reassured when I heard a key in the lock, and a moment later the family entered. Without hesitation I threw off the mattress, abruptly discarded the strip of damask, and showed myself to the astonished family. It is easy to imagine the surprise of these good people. While they looked at me, speechless, I began to tell them as briefly as possible how I had got in and how I had hidden under the mattress. The husband and wife were astonished that I had not stifled in my hiding-place. They were sorry for me, and with a cordiality which is not rare among the common people, they offered me refreshments which were most necessary after so hard a morning.

After the reception the family had given me, it was improbable that I should have to repent of showing myself to them; however, I was not fully reassured. They were not well off; and it was possible that this first impression of kindness and compassion, which even the most perverse feel, would give place to a hope of obtaining some reward from the police by giving me up. And then suppose that they were not always in earnest, was I free from the results of some indiscretion? Fossé guessed at the secret of my uneasiness, which he succeeded in dissipating by protestations of sincerity which could not be denied.

He took charge of watching out for my safety. He began by making a reconnaissance, as a result of which he informed me that the police, persuaded that I had not left the quarter, were permanently established in the house and the adjacent streets; he also told me that they were going to visit the tenants again. From all these reports, I concluded that it was urgent to move off, for it was believable that this time they would search the lodgings to the bottom.

The Fossé family, like most of the workers of Paris, were accustomed to take supper at a wine merchant's in the neighbourhood, carrying their food with them. It was arranged that I should wait for that time to go out with them. Until night, then, I had time to take measures; I busied myself in getting news to Annette; Fossé arranged the message. It would have been most imprudent to get in direct communication with her. This was how it was done: Fossé went to the rue de Grammont, where he bought a patty, in which he slipped this note:

> I am safe. Be on your guard; trust no one. Don't be taken in by promises which they have neither the intention nor the power to keep. Confine yourself to these four words – *I do not know.* Play stupid, which is the best way to prove that you have sense. I cannot give you a rendezvous, but when you go out, always take rue Saint-Martin and the boulevards. Above all, don't turn around; I'll answer for everything.

This patty was entrusted to a messenger and addressed to Madame Vidocq. It fell, as I had foreseen, into the hands of the police, who allowed it to be delivered after they had read the note. So I had achieved two ends at the same time: I had tricked them by persuading them that I was no longer in the quarter, and had reassured Annette by letting her know that I was out of danger. My expedient had succeeded. Made bolder by this first success, I was a little calmer to make my preparations for my retreat. Some money which I had taken by chance from my table served to procure trousers, shoes, and a blouse; a blue cotton cap completed my disguise. When the time came for supper, I went out of the room with all the family, carrying on my head a large platter of mutton stew; its appetizing odours explained well enough the purpose of our excursion. However, my heart beat none the less when I met face to face an agent on the second-floor landing whom I had first seen hiding in a corner.

'Blow out your candle,' he shouted abruptly to Fossé.

'Why?' asked the latter, who had taken the light so as not to arouse suspicions.

'Come on, not so many reasons,' replied the police spy, and he blew it out himself.

I would have willingly embraced him. In the alley we fell on several of his colleagues who were more polite and who lined up to free us a passage. At last we were outside. When we had turned the corner, Fossé took the platter, and we separated. In order not to attract attention, I walked very slowly as far as the rue des Fontaines. Once there, I did not amuse myself, as the Germans say, in counting the buttons on my coat, but I went in the direction of the Temple. Walking rapidly, I reached the rue de Bondy, when it occurred to me to decide where I was going.

It was not sufficient to have escaped the first search; the later one might be more vigorous. At this critical juncture I resolved to use for my safety the individuals whom I considered my denouncers. They were the Chevaliers, whom I had seen the evening before. In their conversation they had let drop some words which were only explained afterward. Convinced that I need no longer have any consideration for them, I resolved to take vengeance on them and at the same time force them to disgorge as much as I could.

It is not far from the boulevard to the rue de l'Échiquier, and I fell like a bomb on the Chevalier domicile. Their surprise at seeing me at liberty confirmed all my suspicions. At first Chevalier thought up a pretext to go out, but closing the door with a double turn and putting the key in my pocket, I seized a table knife and told my brother-in-law that if he made a sound, it was all over with him and his relations. This threat produced its effect. I was with people who knew me and who deserved to feel the violence of my despair. The women were more dead than alive, and Chevalier, petrified and as motionless as the stone urn on which he leaned, asked me in a low voice what I wanted of him. 'You'll find out,' I answered.

I started by demanding a complete suit of clothes which I had furnished him the month before; in addition, I made him give me a shirt, boots, and a hat. I had paid for all these things, and he was making restitution. Chevalier did so, sulkily. I thought I read in his eyes that he was meditating some project; perhaps he had a way to let the neighbours know about the embarrassment my presence caused him; prudence demanded that I assure my retreat in case of a midnight search. A window which looked out on the garden was closed by two iron shutters; I ordered Chevalier to raise one, and, as in spite of my instructions he did it extremely awkwardly, I did the work myself. I did not notice that the knife which had inspired him with such fear had passed from my hands to his. When the operation was completed, I retook my weapon. 'Now,' I said to him, and also to the terrified women, 'you can go to bed.' I was hardly in a condition to sleep. I threw myself on a chair and passed a most uneasy night.

At daybreak I made Chevalier get up, and asked him if he had any money. On his reply that he had only a little, I told him to give me four sets of silverware, which he owed to my liberality, to take his permit of residence, and follow me. I did not exactly need him, but it was dangerous to leave him in his lodgings, for he could have aroused the police and put them on my track before I could take my measures. Chevalier obeyed. I feared the women the less, as I took a precious hostage with me. Although they did not altogether share the feelings of the latter, I contented myself with locking them in. By the streets of the capital which are deserted even in the middle of the day, we reached the Champs-Élysées. It was four o'clock in the morning and we met no one. I carried the silver; I was careful not to leave it to my companion for I might want to disappear without inconvenience if he rebelled or raised a row. Fortunately, he was docile; besides, I had the terrible knife, and Chevalier, who did not reason, was persuaded that at the slightest movement he made, I would plunge it in his heart. This salutary terror, which he felt the more keenly in that he was not without reproach, answered for him.

We walked a long time to the neighbourhood of Chaillot. Chevalier, who did not see how this would end, walked along beside me mechanically; he was prostrated almost to the point of idiocy. At eight o'clock I put him in a cab and took him to the Bois de Boulogne, where in my presence he pawned the four sets of silver, on which they lent him a hundred francs. I took possession of this sum; and, satisfied at having recovered so apropos in a lump what he had extorted piecemeal, I got back into the cab with him and rode to the Place de la Concorde.

I got out there, but I gave him this advice, 'Remember to be most circumspect. If I am arrested, no matter who is the cause of my arrest, look out!' I suggested to the driver that he go at top speed to rue de l'Echiquier, No. 23; and to be sure that he went in that direction, I watched him for a moment. Then in another cab I went to an old-clothes dealer who gave me a labourer's garments in exchange for mine. In this new costume I made my way to the Esplanade des Invalides, to find out whether it was possible to buy a uniform of that establishment. A man with a wooden leg, whom I questioned without affectation, directed me to a second-hand dealer, rue Dominique, where I would find a complete outfit.

This dealer was, as it appeared, something of a talker. 'I'm not curious,' he said (that is the usual prelude to all indiscreet questions), 'you have all your limbs, no doubt this uniform is not for you.'

'On the contrary,' I answered, and, as he showed some astonishment, I added that I was going to play a part in a comedy.

'In what play?'

'In *l'Amour filial.*'

When the bargain was completed, I went at once to Passy, where at a lodging-house whose owner was on my side, I effected my metamorphosis. It took me only five minutes to make me the most crippled of cripples. My arm, drawn into the hollow of my breast and held there by a strap and my belt, had entirely disappeared; some ribbons, introduced into the upper part of the sleeve, the end of which was attached to my coat, looked marvellously like a stump; a pomade which I used to tint my hair and beard finished making me unrecognizable. In this disguise I was so sure of disconcerting observers that that very evening I dared to show myself in the quartier Saint-Martin. I learned that the police not only still occupied my lodgings, but that they were making an inventory of the merchandise and furniture. From the number of agents I saw coming and going, I was easily convinced that the search continued with redoubled activity, which was rare at that time when administrative vigilance was not too zealous unless it was a question of political arrests.

Alarmed by such a display, anyone else would have judged it prudent to get away from Paris without delay, at least for some time. It would have been expedient to let the storm pass, but I could not decide to abandon Annette in the midst of the tribulations which her attachment for me had brought down upon her. She had to suffer much on this occasion. Locked up at the Prefecture, she was in solitary confinement for twenty-five days, and she was only let out under the threat to send her to Saint-Lazare if she persisted in refusing to indicate the place of my retreat. With a dagger at her breast, Annette would not speak. One can judge of my chagrin at knowing that she was in such a deplorable situation. I was unable to deliver her; if it had depended on me, I should have flown to her assistance. A friend to whom I had lent some hundreds of francs paid them; I made him keep part of that sum for her. Full of the hope that her detention would soon end, for after all they could reproach her with nothing except having lived with an escaped convict, I made preparations to leave Paris, determined that if she was not set free before my departure, I would let her know later where I had gone.

I was lodging in rue Tiquetonne, with a leather-dresser named Bouhin, who agreed for a compensation to get a passport and turn it over to me. His description and mine were exactly alike; he was blond, with blue eyes, florid complexion, and, by a singular chance, his right upper lip was marked by a slight scar. Only his height was less than mine; to grow and reach my height before he presented himself for measurement, he had only to put two or three packs of cards in his shoes. In fact, Bouhin had recourse to this expedient, and, although I had the strange faculty of lessening my height four or five inches in case of necessity, the passport he sold me exempted me from this reduction. Provided with this paper, I was congratulating myself on a resemblance which guaranteed my liberty, when Bouhin (I had been in his house a week) entrusted me with a secret which made me shudder. He was a counterfeiter, and, to give me a sample of his skill he cast in front of me eight five-franc pieces which his wife passed the same day. One may imagine how alarmed I was by Bouhin's confidence.

First, I drew the conclusion that in all likelihood at any moment his passport would be a bad recommendation in the eyes of the gendarmes; because in his trade Bouhin sooner or later would be under arrest. Consequently, the money I had given him was rashly risked, and there was no advantage in being taken for him. That was not all. In view of the suspicion which, in the eyes of the judges and the public, is insepa-rable from an escaped convict, it was presumable that if Bouhin was taken as a counterfeiter, I should be considered his accomplice. I saw myself succumbing under a mass of such presumptions and appearances. Perhaps my lawyer, ashamed of undertaking my defence, would think himself reduced to imploring the clemency of the judges. I heard my death sentence pronounced.

My apprehensions were redoubled when I learned that Bouhin had an associate, a doctor named Terrier, who came to the house frequently. It seemed to me that at the mere sight of his face all the police in the world should be at his heels. Without knowing who he was, I should have thought that, by following him, it would be impossible not to reach the source of some crime. In a word, he was a bad sign for every place that saw him enter. In the persuasion that his visits would bring harm to the house, I asked Bouhin to give up such a doubtful industry as that he practised. My best arguments went for nothing. All I obtained as the result of my appeals was that, to avoid a search which would certainly deliver me to the police, he would suspend his manufacture and uttering of money so long as I stayed with him. This did not prevent my surprising him two days later again at work on his great scheme. This time I judged it seemly to appeal to his collaborator. But I was told not to meddle in their affairs.

By the turn the discussion took, I saw that it was superfluous to continue it, and that I should act wisely to be on my guard and to leave Paris as soon as possible. It was a Tuesday. I wanted to go the next day, but warned that Annette would be set at liberty at the end of the week, I proposed to defer my departure until she came out. However, on Friday, at three o'clock in the morning, I heard someone knock lightly on the street door; the character of the knock, the time, the circumstances, all gave me the feeling that I was to be arrested. Without saying anything to Bouhin, I went out on the landing, went up the stairs, and, when I reached the top of the staircase, climbed out on the roof and crouched behind a chimney.

My presentiments had not deceived me. In an instant the house was full of police, who searched everywhere. Surprised not to find me, and doubtless warned by my clothes, which I had left near the bed, that I had escaped in my shirt and could not be far away, they drew the conclusions that I had not taken any of the usual ways. Lacking cavaliers to send in pursuit, they ordered up the tilers, who explored the roof, and I was found and taken, the nature of the terrain not permitting me to attempt a resistance which would have ended in a most perilous leap. Except for some cuffs which I received from the police, my arrest showed nothing remarkable. I was taken to the Prefecture, where I was questioned by M. Henry. He recalled perfectly the step I had taken some months previously and promised to do all he could to make my position easier. However, I was transferred to La Force and then to Bicêtre, to await the next departure of the chain gang.

XVI
My Début With The Police

I BEGAN TO BE DISGUSTED with my escapes and the sort of liberty they procured; I did not want to return to the prison, but I preferred Toulon to Paris if the latter was to continue to receive such creatures as Blondy, Duluc, and Saint-Germain. I was in this mood among a goodly number of these pillars of the galleys, whom I knew only too well, when some of them proposed that I help them to attempt to take to our heels through the Cour des Bons Pauvres. Once I should have smiled at this project. I did not reject it, but I criticized it like a man who had studied localities, and in such a way as to preserve that preponderance which my real successes and those which they attributed to me had won. With such scoundrels it is always an advantage to be considered the most thorough rascal and the most ingenious one; this was my well-established reputation. Everywhere that there were four prisoners together, at least three had heard of me. At Brest, Toulon, Rochefort, Antwerp, in fact everywhere, I was considered the most crafty and intrepid of thieves. The worst convicts sought my friendship, because they thought there was still something they could learn from me; and the neophytes accepted my words as instructions from which they might profit.

At Bicêtre I held a real court. The convicts crowded about me and surrounded me, and made me offers of services of which it would be difficult to give an idea. But now all the prison glory was odious to me. The more I read into the souls of the criminals, the more they showed themselves to me, the more sympathy I felt for society which nourished such a breed in its bosom. Decided that whatever might happen I would take the side of honest men, I wrote to M. Henry again to offer my services, without any other condition than that I should not be sent back to the convict prison, but should end my term in some jail or other.

My letter indicated with so much precision the sort of information that I could give that M. Henry was impressed. A single consideration made him hesitate – this was the example of several persons who had been arrested or sentenced, had agreed to lead the police in their searches, and had given only insignificant advice or had been themselves taken in the very act. To this so powerful consideration I opposed the reason for my sentence, the regularity of my conduct every time I had been free, the firmness of my efforts to earn an honest living, and, finally, I showed my books, my accounts, and I invoked the testimony of all persons with whom I had done business, and especially that of my creditors who had the greatest confidence in me.

The facts I alleged militated powerfully in my favour. M. Henry submitted my request to the Prefect of Police, M. Pasquier, who decided to grant it. After a sojourn of two months at Bicêtre, I was transferred to La Force, and, to avoid my being suspected, they spread rumours among the prisoners that I had been implicated in a very bad affair and that my examination was to be begun. This caution combined with my reputation put me in good odour. Not a prisoner dared call in question the crime imputed to me. Since I had shown so much audacity and perseverance in escaping a sentence of eight years in irons, my conscience must be burdened with some capital crime, capable, if I was found guilty, of leading me to the scaffold. They whispered and even said aloud in talking about me, 'He's a murderer,' and as in that place a murderer ordinarily inspires great confidence, I was careful not to refute an error so useful to my projects.

The engagement I had undertaken was not so easy as one might think. To tell the truth, I had known a crowd of criminals, but constantly decimated by excesses of all kinds, by justice, by the frightful régime in the prisons and jails, by want, this hideous generation had passed with inconceivable rapidity. A new generation held the stage, and I was even ignorant of the names of the individuals who composed it; I was not even acquainted with the notables. A multitude of thieves were then exploiting the capital, and it would have been impossible for me to furnish the slightest indication about the leaders among them; only my old renown could put me in the way of getting intelligence about the staff of these Bedouins of our civilization. But it served, I will not say more than, but as much as I desired. Not a robber entered La

Force that he did not make haste to seek my company, and he held it necessary for his *amour-propre* to appear to be close to me. I flattered this singular vanity, and in this way I slid insensibly on the way to discoveries. Information came to me in abundance, and I found no obstacles in the way of my acquitting my mission.

To give the measure of the influence I exercised on the minds of the prisoners, it is sufficient to say that at will I inoculated them with my opinions, my likes and dislikes; they thought as I did and swore by me. At the same time I was a powerful protector and a guaranty of immunity. The first prisoner whose bondsman I became was a young man who was accused of serving the police as a secret agent. It was pretended that he had been in the pay of Inspector-General Veyrat, and it was added that, going to report to his chief, he had stolen a basket of silver. To rob an inspector was not bad, but to go to report! Such, however, was the enormous crime imputed to Coco-Lacour, my successor. Threatened by the whole prison, hunted, rebuffed, maltreated, no longer daring even to put foot in the courts where he would have assuredly been beaten to death, Coco came to solicit my protection. To predispose me in his favour he began by making confidences which I knew how to use.

First, I employed my credit to make peace for him with the other prisoners, who gave up their projects of vengeance; I could not have done him a greater service. As much from gratitude as from a desire to talk, Coco soon left nothing hidden from me. One day he appeared before the examining magistrate. 'My,' he said on his return, 'I was lucky; none of the plaintiffs recognized me. However, I do not consider myself safe. Somewhere there is a devil of a porter whose watch I stole. I was obliged to talk to him for a long time, and my features must be engraved on his memory. If he was called, he could prove that something went wrong at the examination. 'Besides,' he added, all porters are students of faces; it's part of their job.'

This observation was true, but I suggested to Coco that it was improbable that the man would be discovered, and, in fact, would never present himself, as he had neglected to do so thus far. In order to confirm him in this opinion, I talked to him about the carelessness and laziness of certain people who do not like to get about. What I said concerning getting about brought Coco to name the quarter in which the owner of the watch lived; if he had only told me the street and number, I should have had nothing more to desire. However, I refrained from asking for such complete information, as it would have betrayed me; besides, what I had seemed sufficient. I addressed M. Henry, who started a campaign of exploration. The result was what I had foreseen; they unearthed the porter, and Coco, confronted by him, was overpowered by the evidence. The court condemned him to two years in jail.

At this time there existed in Paris a band of escaped convicts who committed robberies daily, without there being any hope of putting an end to their brigandage. Several of them had been arrested and discharged on account of lack of proof; obstinately taking refuge in denials, they had braved justice for a long time. They had to be taken in the act or caught with convincing evidence, and, to surprise their stores, it was necessary to know where they lived, which the police had never been able to discover.

Among these individuals was a man named France, alias Tormel, who when he arrived at La Force had nothing more pressing than to ask me for ten francs; and I was as urgent in sending them to him. On that he came to join me, and, as he was moved by my conduct, he did not hesitate to give me his entire confidence. At the moment of his arrest he had concealed two notes of a thousand francs each from the search by the police, and he turned them over to me, asking me to advance him the money as he needed it. 'You do not know me,' he said, 'but the notes will answer for me; I'll trust you with them, because I know that they are better in your hands than in mine; later we will change them; it would be suspicious to do it today; it's better to wait.' I agreed with France, and, according to his desires, I promised to be his banker; I ran no risk.

Arrested for breaking and entering at an umbrella merchant's, France had been examined several times and he persistently declared that he had no domicile. Nevertheless, the police were informed that he had one, and they were the more interested in discovering it, in that they were nearly certain to find there both burglars' tools and stolen goods. M. Henry let me know that he counted on me to get the information. I manœuvred to that end, and I soon knew that at the moment of his arrest, France occupied, at the corner of rue Montmartre and rue

Notre Dame des Victoires, an apartment let in the name of a fence named Joséphine Bertrand.

This information was positive, but it was difficult to make use of it without compromising me with France, who, as he had opened himself to me alone, could suspect no one else if he was betrayed. I succeeded, however, and he so little suspected that I had abused his secret that he told me all his worries, as the plan I had agreed on with M. Henry was put into execution. In addition, the police so arranged it that they seemed to be guided only by chance. This is how it was done.

The police got in their interests a tenant in the house where France lived. This tenant remarked to the owner that for three weeks he had noticed no movement in the apartment of Mademoiselle Bertrand; this was to give a warning and arouse conjecture. The other tenants remembered an individual who was accustomed to come to the apartment and they were astonished that they no longer met him; they talked about his absence, and the word disappearance was mentioned. Here the commissioner of necessity intervened. Then came the opening of the apartment in the presence of witnesses; next followed the discovery of a great number of things which had been stolen in the quarter; and, finally, they seized the instruments which had been used in effecting the robberies.

Now the question was, what had become of Joséphine Bertrand. The police went to the people whom she had given as references when she had hired the apartment, but they could learn nothing about this woman. They only knew that a girl, Lambert, who had succeeded to the lodging in rue Montmartre, had just been arrested; and as this girl was known to be France's mistress, they concluded that the two individuals had a common haunt. In consequence France was taken to both places and was recognized by the neighbours. He pretended that they were mistaken, but the jury before whom he appeared decided otherwise, and he was sentenced to eight years in irons.

Once France was convicted, the police were easily able to follow the traces of his trusty friends. Two of the principal ones were named Fossard and Legagneur. The police got on their track, but the cowardice and maladroitness of the agents let them escape the search which I directed. The first was the more dangerous in that he excelled in the manufacture of false keys. For fifteen months he had seemed to defy the police, when I learned one day that he lived at a hairdresser's, rue du Temple. It was almost impossible to arrest him outside his house, as he was very skillful in disguising himself and could detect a police officer two hundred yards away. On the other hand, it was better to take him among the tools of his profession and the products of his labour. But such an expedition presented obstacles, When they knocked at his door, Fossard never answered; and it was probable that, in case of surprise, he had managed an exit and facilities to reach the roof.

It appeared to me that the only way to arrest him was to take advantage of his absence to get into his apartment and lie in wait there. M. Henry agreed with me. The locks were picked in the presence of a commissioner, and three agents were placed in a closet next to the alcove. Nearly seventy-two hours went by without anyone appearing. At the end of the third day their provisions were exhausted, and the agents were about to withdraw when they heard a key in the lock – Fossard was coming back. At once two of the agents, obeying the orders they had received, jumped from the closet and hurled themselves on him. But Fossard armed himself with a knife which they had forgotten on the table, and frightened them so that they themselves opened the door which their comrade had closed. After he had put them under lock and key in their turn, Fossard went down stairs tranquilly, leaving the three agents all leisure to frame a report, including everything except the circumstance of the knife, which they were careful not to mention.

Before he was transferred to the Conciergerie, France, who still believed in my devotion, recommended one of his friends to me. His name was Legagneur, an escaped convict, who had been arrested in rue de la Mortellerie, just as he was committing a robbery with false keys. This man was deprived of his resources as a result of the departure of his comrade, and he thought that he would withdraw the money he had on deposit with a fence in rue Saint-Dominique.

Annette came to see me at La Force most assiduously, and sometimes seconded me with much dexterity in my searches. She was charged with this commission with the fence, but, whether from distrust, or a wish to appropriate the deposit, he received the messenger badly, and, as she insisted, he went so far as to threaten her with arrest. Annette returned to announce her failure.

At the news Legagneur wanted to denounce the fence, but this resolution was only the result of his first transport of rage. When he
calmed down, Legagneur thought it better to defer his vengeance, and
above all to make it profitable. 'If I denounce him,' he told me, 'not
only will there be nothing coming back, but he might arrange it so that
they would not catch him in a slip. I'd rather wait until I get out; I'll
know how to make him pay!'

As Legagneur had no hope of anything from the fence, he determined to write to two of his accomplices, Marguerit and Victor
Desbois, who were both famous thieves. Convinced of that old truth
that small gifts make friendship, he sent them some impressions of
locks which he had taken for his own use. Again Legagneur used
Annette as an intermediary. She found the two friends in rue des Deux
Ponts, in a miserable entresol, a sort of hole where they never went out
without previously taking all precautions. They did not live there.
Annette, whom I had advised to do everything she could to find their
domicile, had the good wit not to lose them from sight. She followed
them for two days under different disguises, and, the third day, she
could affirm that they slept in a house which had an exit on some gardens. M. Henry, whom I did not leave in ignorance of this circumstance, prescribed all measures that the nature of the locality demanded,
but the agents were no more adroit or brave than those from whom
Fossard had got away. The two thieves escaped through the gardens.

Legagneur had been taken in his turn to the Conciergerie and was
replaced in my room by the son of a wine merchant at Versailles,
named Robin. He was closely bound to all the sharpers in the capital,
and he gave me, in the form of conversation, the most complete information on their antecedents, their present position and their projects. It
was he who brought to my attention an escaped convict named
Mardargent, who was held only as a deserter. He had been condemned
to twenty-four years in irons; he had lived in the prisons; by means of
notes and recollections, we promptly became acquainted. He believed,
and he was not mistaken, that I should be glad to see my former companions in misfortune; he pointed out to me several among the prisoners. I was so fortunate as to send back to the galleys a good number of
these individuals whom justice in default of sufficient proof would have
again returned to society. Never had more important discoveries been

made than those which marked my début with the police. I was hardly enrolled in its administration, and I had already done much for the safety of the capital and even for that of all France.

My stay at Bicêtre and La Force lasted twenty-two months, and there was not a day during that time that I did not render some important service. I believe I should have been a permanent spy, so far were the prisoners from supposing that there was the slightest connivance between the agents of authority and myself. Even the jailers and warders did not suspect the mission entrusted to me. Adored by the thieves, esteemed by the most determined bandits, I could count on their devotion for all time; they would have let themselves be cut to pieces on my account. What proves it is that at Bicêtre, Mardargent, of whom I have just spoken, fought several times with prisoners who dared to say that I had left La Force only to serve the police. Coco-Lacour and Goreau, held in the same place as incorrigible thieves, took up my defence with no generosity.

M. Henry did not leave the Prefect of Police in ignorance of the numerous discoveries which were due to my sagacity. This functionary, whom he represented to me as a man on whom one could count, finally consented to my imprisonment being ended. Every measure was taken so that it would not be thought that I had regained my liberty. The police came to La Force to get me, and took me away without neglecting any of the rigorous precautions. They put the handcuffs on, and I mounted in the usual vehicle, but it was arranged that I should escape on the way, and in fact I did escape. That same evening all the police were after me. This escape made a great noise, especially at La Force, where my friends celebrated it by rejoicings; they drank my health and wished me bon voyage!

XVII
VICTIMS OF MY CRAFT

THE NAMES OF Baron Pasquier and M. Henry will never be erased from my memory. These two generous men were my liberators. How much I owe to them! They gave me more than the life which I would have sacrificed for them a thousand times, and I think they will believe me when they know how often I exposed it to obtain a word or look of satisfaction from them.

I breathed again, moved about freely, and now that I was a secret agent I had regular duties, in which M. Henry undertook to instruct me. My task was difficult to fulfil. M. Henry guided my first steps; he eased my difficulties, and if in the end I acquired some celebrity in the police, I owed it to his counsels and to the lessons he gave me. Endowed with a cool and reflective disposition, M. Henry possessed to the highest degree that gift of observation which distinguishes guilt under the most innocent appearance. He had a prodigious memory and an astonishing insight; nothing escaped him; added to that, he was an excellent judge of faces. Rarely did a criminal whom he examined leave his office without confessing his crime or giving some clue, unknown to himself, by which to convict him.

As soon as I was installed as a secret agent, I began to pound the pavement in order to become familiar with it and to be able to do my work usefully. These excursions, during the course of which I made a great number of observations, took me twenty days, during which I was only preparing myself to act; I was studying the terrain. One morning I was summoned by the chief of the division. It was about the discovery of a man named Watrin, accused of having made and put in circulation counterfeit money and bank-notes. Watrin had already been arrested by the police inspectors, but as usual they had not known how to keep him. M. Henry gave me all the information he judged proper to put me on his tracks. Unfortunately, this information consisted only of data of his old habits; the places he had frequented were described to me, but it was not believable that he would come to them at once, since in his position prudence prescribed that he flee all places where he was known. So I had left only the hope of reaching him in some indirect way when I learned that he had some of his effects in a furnished house, boulevard Mont Parnasse, where he had lodged. The officials took it for granted that sooner or later he would present himself to demand them or at least that he would have somone else demand them for him. That was my opinion too.

In consequence I directed all my search on that point, and after getting acquainted with the mansion, I lay in wait near-by night and day in order to have an eye on the comings and goings. This supervision had lasted nearly a week. Finally, tired of seeing nothing, I conceived the idea of getting the master of the house in my interests and hiring an apartment, where I established myself with Annette. My presence would not be suspect. I had occupied this post for a fortnight, when one evening towards eleven o'clock I was warned that Watrin had just appeared, accompanied by another individual. I was slightly indisposed and had gone to bed earlier than usual. I got up hurriedly and went down the stairs two at a time, but with all my diligence I could only reach Watrin's companion. I had no right to arrest him, but I foresaw that if I intimidated him, I might be able to obtain some information. I seized him, threatened him, and soon he told me, trembling with fear, that he was a shoemaker and that Watrin lived with him, at rue des Mauvais Garçons Saint-Germain, No. 4.

That was all I needed to know. I had thrown only an overcoat over my shirt, but, without stopping for other garments, I ran to that address and arrived in front of the house just as someone was going out. Persuaded that it was Watrin, I tried to seize him. He escaped me; I dashed after him up the staircase, but, just as I was reaching for him, a kick in my chest sent me down twenty steps. I dashed after him again and with such speed that, to get rid of my pursuit, he was obliged to get into his quarters through a window on the landing. I then knocked on his door and summoned him to open. He refused.

Annette had followed me. I ordered her to go in search of the police, and, while she went to obey, I imitated the noise of a man going downstairs. Watrin was deceived by this feint, and wanted to assure himself that I had really gone. He put his head out of the window.

That was what I wanted, and I at once grabbed him by the hair. He seized me in the same way, and a fight started. Clinging to the dividing wall which separated us, he opposed an obstinate resistance; however, I felt that he was weakening. I gathered my strength for a last jerk; already he had only his feet left in the room; another effort and he was mine. I pulled him out vigorously and he fell into the corridor. To deprive him of the shoemaker's knife with which he was armed and drag him outside was the work of a moment.

Accompanied only by Annette, I led him to the Prefecture, where I received the felicitations of M. Henry, and then those of the Prefect of Police, who gave me a pecuniary reward.

Watrin was a man of rare address; he practised a rude profession, yet he executed forgeries which demanded the greatest delicacy of touch. He was condemned to death, but he was reprieved an hour before he was to be led to punishment. The scaffold had already been erected; it was taken down; the virtuosi had made a useless change of base. The report spread that he was going to make revelations, but, as he had nothing to tell, some days later the sentence was executed.

Watrin was my first capture and it was an important one. The success of my début aroused the jealousy of some of the police; some inveighed against me, but in vain. They did not forgive me for being more skilful than they were; on the contrary, my chiefs had a decided liking for me. I doubled my zeal to deserve their confidence more and more.

About this time a large number of false five-franc pieces had been put in circulation. They showed me several, and on examination it seemed to me that I recognized the work of my denouncer Bouhin and his friend Doctor Terrier. I resolved to get at the truth. In consequence I spied on the movements of these two individuals, and, as I could not follow them closely without being recognized and so arousing their distrust, it was difficult to get the light I needed. However, by force of perseverance, I became certain that I was not mistaken, and the two counterfeiters were arrested in the act of manufacture. Some time after they were condemned to death and executed.

In a city as populous as Paris the number of evil resorts is rather large; and in them all the men of tarnished reputation meet. In order to see them and watch them, I assiduously frequented these places of ill-fame, sometimes under one name and sometimes under another, changing my costume often as a person who needs to escape the eyes of the police. All the thieves whom I saw habitually would have sworn that I was one of them. In the persuasion that I was a fugitive, they would have been quartered to hide me, for not only did they have full confidence in me, but they liked me. As a result they told me about their plans, and, if they did not propose that I co-operate with them, it was for fear of compromising me, in view of my position as an escaped convict. However, all were not so delicate.

I had been at my secret investigations for some months, when by chance I met Saint-Germain, whose visits had so many times filled me with consternation. He was with a man named Boudin whom I had seen as a restaurant keeper in rue des Prouvaires, and whom I knew as one knows a host to whose place one goes from time to time to take a meal and pays for it. Boudin had no trouble in remembering me; he even bordered on a sort of familiarity, to which I pretended not to respond.

'Have I done something to you,' he asked, 'that you don't seem to want to talk to me?'

'No, but I've learned that you have been a police spy.'

'Well, if that's all! Yes, I was a spy, but when you know all, I'm sure you will bear me no ill-will.'

'Certainly,' said Saint-Germain, 'you'll have no ill-will; Boudin is a good fellow, and I'll answer for him as for myself. Things often happen in life which one can't foresee. If Boudin accepted the place you speak of, it was only to save his brother. Besides, you ought to know that if he had bad principles, I should not be his friend.'

I found Saint-Germain's guaranty excellent, and I made no more difficulty about talking to Boudin.

It was natural that Saint-Germain should tell me what had happened since his last disappearance which had given me so much pleasure. After he had complimented me on my escape, he told me that, since I had been arrested, he had recovered his old place, but that he had quickly lost it again, and was now reduced to expedients. I asked him for news of Blondy and Duluc. 'My friend,' he said, 'the two who did in the carter with me have been cut down at Beauvais.' When he announced that those two scoundrels had paid the penalty for their crimes, I had but one regret: that the head of their accomplice had not fallen on the same scaffold.

After we had emptied several bottles of wine, we separated. As he left me, Saint-Germain remarked that I was rather poorly dressed and asked me what I was doing. As I told him that I was doing nothing, he promised to think of me if ever a good occasion presented itself. I observed that as I rarely went out for fear of being arrested, it might be that we should not meet soon. 'You can see me when you want to,' he said. 'I even demand that you come to see me.' When I had promised, he gave me his address, without learning mine.

Saint-Germain was not so formidable a being to me now; I even believed that I should not lose him from sight, for if I was to watch malefactors, no one was more worthy than he of my attention. In the end, I conceived a hope of purging society of such a monster. While I waited, I waged war on the whole herd of crooks who infested the capital. At the moment robberies of all kinds multiplied in a frightful manner; one heard only of railings carried off, doors forced, leads stolen; more than twenty street-lamps were taken one after another, in rue Fontaine-au-Roi, without the thieves who took them down being arrested. For one whole month inspectors had been on watch to surprise them, and the first night they relaxed their vigilance, the street-lamps again disappeared, as if it were a defiance to the police. I accepted the job for myself, and to the great disappointment of the Arguses of the Quai du Nord, in a short time I delivered to justice these impudent thieves, who were all sent to the galleys.

I made new discoveries every day; all those sent to prison went on my indication, Nevertheless, none of them had the slightest idea of accusing me of having them sent to jail. I arranged things so well that nothing transpired either inside or outside; the thieves of my acquaintance considered me the best of comrades; the rest thought themselves fortunate to be able to initiate me into their secret, either for the pleasure of entertaining me or to consult me.

It was especially outside the Barrier that I met this world. One day I was going over the outer boulevards when I was accosted by Saint-Germain; Boudin was still with him. They invited me to dinner; I accepted, and at dessert they did me the honour of proposing that I should make a third in a murder. Two old men were in question; they lived together in the house where Boudin had his habitation in rue des Prouvaires. Shuddering at the confidence which these scoundrels made me, I blessed the invisible power who had urged them toward me. At first I hesitated to enter the plot, but in the end I pretended to give in to their keen and pressing solicitations. It was arranged that we should wait until a favourable moment to put this abominable project into execution.

When this resolution had been taken, I said au revoir to Saint-Germain and his companion, and, resolved to prevent the crime, I hastened to make a report to M. Henry, who sent for me at once in order to obtain the fullest details on the revelation I had just made to him. His intention was to assure himself that I had really been solicited, and that in a badly understood duty I had not had recourse to provocations. I protested that I had in no way taken the initiative, and, as he believed he recognized the truth of this declaration, he announced that he was satisfied, which did not prevent his making a speech on *agents provocateurs* that touched me to the depths of my being.

Although I did not need the lesson, I thanked M. Henry, who advised me to stick to the heels of the two murderers and to neglect nothing to prevent the execution of the deed. According to his instructions, I did not let a single day go by without seeing Saint-Germain and his friend Boudin. As the *coup* they planned was to bring in some money, I concluded that it would not seem extraordinary if I showed a little impatience.

'Well, when is the famous affair?' I asked every time we were together.

'When?' Saint-Germain answered. 'The pear isn't ripe. When the time comes,' he added, pointing to Boudin, 'there's the friend who'll warn you.'

Several meetings had taken place and nothing was decided. I again addressed the usual questions to Saint-Germain.

'Ah, this time,' he said, 'it is for tomorrow. We'll wait for you to talk it over.'

The meeting-place was outside of Paris. I was careful not to fail in attendance, and Saint-Germain was no less prompt.

'Listen,' he said to me. 'We have thought over that affair which cannot be pulled off for the present, but we have another one to propose, and I warn you in advance that you must be frank and answer yes or no. Before we take up the project which brought us here, I owe you a confidence which was made us yesterday. A fellow named Carré, who knew you at La Force, pretends that you got out on condition of serving the police and that you are a secret agent.'

At the words 'secret agent,' I felt almost suffocated; but I soon recovered. It was necessary that nothing should show, as Saint-Germain was watching me and waiting for my explanation. That presence of mind which never deserts me found itself immediately.

'I am not surprised,' I answered, 'that I am represented as a secret agent. I know the source of that story. Perhaps you don't know that I was to be transferred to Bicêtre, and that I escaped on the way. I have stayed in Paris because I could not go anywhere else. One has to live where he has resources. Unfortunately, I have to stay in hiding; I escape the search by disguising myself; but there are always some who recognize me, those, for example, with whom I lived in intimacy. Among the latter are some who would like to have me arrested, either to injure me or through self-interest. Well, to get rid of that desire, every time I have thought them capable of denouncing me, I have told them that I was attached to the police.'

'That's good,' Saint-Germain replied. 'I believe you, and to give you a proof of my confidence in you, I am going to let you know what we are going to do this evening. At the corner of rue d'Enghien and rue Hauteville lives a banker whose house looks out on a rather large garden, which will be a help in our expedition and to our flight. The banker is away today, and his strong-box, in which he keeps a lot of gold and silver, as well as bank-notes, is guarded by only two persons. We have decided to take it this very evening. Until now we are only three to execute the plan, and you must be the fourth. We count on you; if you refuse, you will confirm our opinion that you are a police spy.'

As I did not know the mental reservations of Saint-Germain, I accepted eagerly; Boudin and he seemed pleased with me. I soon saw a third man appear whom I did not know, a cab-driver named Debenne. He was the father of a family and had allowed himself to be drawn in by these wretches. They began to talk of one thing and another; I was already thinking of what steps I could take to arrest them in the act, but to my great astonishment, when the moment came to pay the scot, I heard Saint-Germain address us in these terms:

'My friends, when one risks his neck, he should look closely. Today we are going to play a game which I don't want to lose. That luck may be on our side, I have decided as follows, and I am sure that you will all applaud my measures. At midnight all four of us are to get into the house in question. Boudin and I will look after the interior, and you two will stay in the garden, ready to help us in case of surprise. If this operation succeeds, as I think it will, it ought to give us enough to live quietly for some time. But it is important for our mutual safety that we do not leave each other until the hour of fulfilment.'

This final word, which I pretended not to have heard well, was repeated. This time, I said to myself, I don't know how I shall get out of the business or what means to employ. Saint-Germain was a man of unusual rashness, avid of money, and always ready to shed blood to get it. It was only ten o'clock in the morning, and the time till midnight was long. I hoped that during the time we had to wait, an opportunity would present itself to slip away adroitly and warn the police. Whatever might happen, I agreed to Saint-Germain's proposition and made not the slightest objection to this precaution, which was the best guaranty of everyone's discretion. When he saw that we agreed with him, Saint-Germain, who through his energy and conception was really the leader in the plot, spoke a few words of satisfaction. 'I am pleased,' he told us, 'to see you in such sentiments. For my part, I will do all that I can to deserve to be your friend for a long time!'

It was arranged that we should all go together to his place, rue Saint-Antoine. A cab took us to the door. When we arrived, we went up to his room, where we were to be detained until the moment of departure. Confined within the four walls, face to face with these brigands, I did not know to what saint to dedicate myself. To invent a pretext to go out was impossible; Saint-Germain would have made me out immediately, and at the slightest suspicion, he was capable of blowing out my brains. No matter what happened, I had decided to resign myself to events; there was nothing better to do than to help gracefully in the preparations for the crime. They began immediately. Some pistols were brought to the table to be unloaded and recharged. We examined them; Saint-Germain noticed a pair which did not seem to him to be of further use; he put them to one side.

'While you dismount the batteries,' he said to us, 'I'm going to change these.' And he started to go out.

'One moment,' I said; 'according to our arrangement no one should leave this place unaccompanied.'

'That's true,' he answered. 'I like one to be faithful to his agreements; so come with me.'

'But these gentlemen?'

'We'll shut them up under a double lock.'

We did what he said; I accompanied Saint-Germain. We bought some bullets, powder, and flints; the poor pistols were exchanged for others, and we returned. Then we finished our preparations, which made me shudder; the calmness of Boudin, sharpening two table knives on a stone, was horrible.

However, time passed; it was one o'clock, and no expedient for salvation had presented itself. I yawned, I stretched, I simulated boredom, and, going into the next room, I threw myself on a bed as if to rest. After a few moments I seemed still more tired from this inactivity, and I saw that the rest were not less so.

'If we had something to drink,' Saint-Germain said to me.

'An admirable idea,' I cried, jumping with pleasure. 'Appropriately I have at my house a basket of excellent burgundy if you want to send for it.'

Everyone agreed that nothing could be more to the point. Saint-Germain despatched a porter to Annette whom I advised to come with the provision. We agreed to say nothing in front of her, and while they promised to do honour to my largesse, I threw myself on the bed for a second time, and traced these lines with a pencil: 'Get out of here, disguise yourself, and do not lose track of us, Saint-Germain, Boudin, and me; be careful not to be noticed; take care to pick up anything I let fall, and take it down there.' Although very short, my instructions were sufficient. Annette had received similar advice before, and I was sure that she would understand the full meaning.

Annette was not slow to appear with the basket of wine. Its appearance brought gaiety. Everyone complimented her; I waited to celebrate until she was ready to go, and then, as I embraced her, I slipped her the note.

We dined copiously, after which I offered the opinion that Saint-Germain and I should go alone to reconnoitre the place, and examine it by daylight in order to provide against all accidents. This prudence was natural. Saint-Germain was not astonished; only I proposed to take a cab, while he thought it better to walk. When we reached the place, he pointed out the most favourable spot to scale, and I noted it well enough so that there should be no mistake. When our reconnaissance was completed, Saint-Germain told me that we needed some black crêpe to cover our faces, so we went to the Palais Royal to buy some. While he went into a shop, I made a pretext and closed myself up in a lavatory, where I had time to write all the information which would put the police in a way to prevent the crime.

Saint-Germain had kept me in sight as much as possible and he took me to a taproom, where we drank some bottles of beer. When we were about to re-enter our retreat, I saw that Annette was watching for our return. Sure that she had seen me, near the threshold I let the paper drop, and abandoned myself to fate.

It is impossible for me to convey all the terrors which preyed on me while we were waiting for the moment of the expedition. In spite of the warning I had given, I feared that the measures would be too late, and then, when the crime was consummated, could I alone undertake to arrest Saint-Germain and his accomplices? I recalled that in many circumstances the police had abandoned their agents, and that in others they had been unable to prevent the tribunals confounding them with the guilty. I was in such cruel apprehensions, when Saint-Germain charged me to go with Debenne, whose cab was to be stationed at the street-corner to receive the bags of gold and silver. We went down, and as I went out I saw Annette, who made a signal that she had delivered my message. At the same time Debenne asked me where the rendezvous was. I do not know what good genius then suggested to me, the thought of saving this wretch. I had observed that he was not bad at heart, and it seemed to me that he had rather been pushed toward the abyss by want and perfidious advice than by a fatal propensity for crime. So I assigned him a post at another spot than the one indicated, and rejoined Saint-Germain and Boudin at the corner of the boulevard Saint-Denis.

It was still only ten-thirty. I told them that the cab would only be ready in an hour and that I had given Debenne his orders to be at the corner of rue du Faubourg Poissonnière. He would come at the agreed signal. I made them understand that if he was too near the place where we were to operate, the presence of the cab might arouse suspicions, so I had judged it more proper to keep him at a distance. They approved this precaution.

Eleven o'clock struck; we took a drink in the Faubourg Saint-Denis, and we headed for the banker's house. Boudin and his accomplice walked along smoking their pipes; their tranquillity frightened me. Finally, we were at the foot of the post which was to serve as a ladder. Saint-Germain asked me for my pistols. At that moment I thought he had made me out and wanted to take my life. I gave them to him. I was wrong; he opened the fire-pan, changed the cap, and returned them. After he had done the same to his own and Boudin's, he set the example by climbing the post, and both, without stopping smoking, jumped into the garden. I had to follow. Trembling, I gained the top of the wall. All my apprehensions returned. Had the police had time to set an ambush? Such was the question I asked myself; such were my doubts. Finally, in this terrible uncertainty, I made a resolution – to prevent the crime even if I succumbed in the unequal struggle.

Just then Saint-Germain saw me astride the coping, and, impatient at my slowness, cried, 'Come on, get down.' He had hardly finished these words when suddenly he was assailed by a number of men; he and Boudin made a vigorour resistance. Shots were fired on both sides; bullets whistled, and after a battle of some minutes the two assassins were taken. Several agents were wounded in this action; Saint-Germain and his assistant were too. As a mere spectator of the engagement, I should have met with no grievous accident. However, to play my part to the end, I fell on the field of battle, as if I had been mortally hit. An instant after, they wrapped me in a quilt, and in this way I was carried into a room where Boudin and Saint-Germain were. The latter appeared deeply touched by my death; he shed tears, and they had to use force to prevent his falling on what he believed was only a corpse.

I remember no event in my life which has brought me more joy than the capture of these two scoundrels. I applauded myself for having delivered society from two monsters, at the same time that I felt happy at having kept the cabman Debenne from the fate which was reserved for them.

XVIII
THE NATURE OF MY CRAFT

THE THIEVES AND ROBBERS were frightened for a brief moment by several arrests I made one after another, but they were not slow to reappear in greater numbers and perhaps more audacious than ever. Among them were several escaped convicts, who in the prisons had perfected a most dangerous skill which they had come to Paris to practise. Their presence spread terror. The police resolved to put an end to the excursions of these bandits, and I received an order to plan in advance with the regular police force every time I was about to make a capture. One can see what my task was – I had to go into all the disreputable places in the city and vicinity.

In a few days I managed to know all the dives where I could meet malefactors: the Barrier de la Courtille and those of du Combat and de Menilmontant were where they congregated by preference. Their headquarters were there and the criminals were constantly in force. Woe betide the agent who was found there, no matter what the reason. He would inevitably have been beaten to death. The gendarmes did not even dare to show themselves, so imposing was this assembly of bad lots.

I was less timid, and I did not hesitate to risk myself in this herd of wretches. I associated with them; I fraternized with them; and I soon had the advantage of being considered one of them. It was while I was drinking with these gentlemen that I learned about the crimes they had committed or premeditated. I circumvented them with such skill that they made no difficulty about revealing where their domiciles were or those of the women with whom they lived. I can say that I inspired in them a boundless confidence, and if some of them, more discreet than their confrères, permitted themselves to express the slightest suspicion in my regard, I think they would have been punished that very instant. So I obtained from them all the information I needed. When I gave the signal for an arrest, it was almost certain that the individuals would be taken in the very act, or with the stolen goods, which would justify their sentence.

Not a day passed that I did not make important discoveries. No crime was committed or was about to be committed that I did not learn all the circumstances. I was everywhere; I knew all, and when I called upon the authorities to intervene, my information never proved wrong. M. Henry was astonished by my activity and my omnipresence, while several of the officers of the regular police did not blush to complain. The inspectors were little used to being up several nights in a week and found the service I occasioned them too arduous when it was in some ways permanent; they complained. Some were even so indiscreet, or so cowardly, as to reveal the *incognito* by which I manœuvred so usefully. Their conduct brought them severe reprimands, but they were neither more circumspect nor more devoted.

It was hardly possible for me to live almost constantly among these criminals without their proposing that I join them in their crimes. I never refused, but at the time of the deed, I always invented a pretext not to go to the rendezvous. Thieves in general are so stupid that there was no excuse, no matter how absurd, which I could not get them to accept. I affirm that often it was not even necessary to bother about a ruse to fool them. Once arrested, they saw no more clearly; besides, supposing they were less stupid than they were, measures had been taken so that they would not even think of suspecting me. I have seen them escape at the time of the arrest, and hurry to the place where they knew I should be, to give me the sad news that their comrades had been taken.

When one is in well with thieves, nothing is easier than to find out about the receivers or fences. I uncovered several, and the information I gave was so positive that they never failed to follow their clients to prison. Perhaps it will not be without interest if I tell the means I used to deliver the capital of one of these dangerous men.

The authorities had been on his track for some years, and had not succeeded in taking him in the act. Frequent searches in his domicile had produced no result; there was not the slightest bit of merchandise which would furnish proof against him. Nevertheless, the police were assured that he bought from thieves; and several of the latter, who were far from believing that I was attached to the police, had indicated to me that he was a solid man in whom one could trust. Information about him was not lacking, but it was necessary to seize the stock of stolen goods. M. Henry had set to work to reach this end, but either through the blunders of the agents or the skill of the fence, had always failed.

The authorities wanted to find out whether I should be more fortunate, and I attempted the enterprise. This is how I did it. I posted myself some distance from where the fence lived and watched for him to go out. At last he showed himself, and once he was outside, I followed him some way down the street and suddenly accosted him, calling him by a name not his own. He affirmed that I was in error; I declared in my turn that I recognized him perfectly as an individual who for a long time had been the object of search by the police of Paris and the departments.

'But you are mistaken,' he said. 'My name is So-and-so, and I live at such a place.'

'I don't believe it.'

'Oh, this is too much; do you want me to prove it?'

I consented on condition that he accompany me to the local station. We entered. I invited him to show his papers; he had none. I then asked that he be searched, and they found on him three watches and twenty-five double Napoleons, which I placed in deposit until he could be taken to the commissioner. These objects were wrapped in a handkerchief and I took it. After I had disguised myself as a messenger, I hurried to the receiver's house. His wife was there with some other persons; she did not know me, and I told her that I wanted to talk to her in private. When I was alone with her, I pulled the handkerchief from my pocket and presented it to her as a sign of recognition. She still did not know the reason of my visit, yet her features were disturbed and she was troubled.

'I do not bring you too good news,' I said. 'Your husband has just been arrested; they are holding him and have taken all he had on him. From some words which the police let slip, I am afraid that he has been sold. That's why he wants you at once to get rid of what you well know; if you wish, I'll give you a hand; but I warn you, there is no time to lose.'

The warning was urgent; the sight of the handkerchief and the description of the objects which had been wrapped in it, left no doubt of the truth of the message. The receiver's wife fell headlong into the trap I had laid. She told me to go and get three cabs, and to come back at once. I went out to discharge my commission; but on the way, I gave an order to my agents not to lose the vehicles from sight and to stop them when the signal was given. The cabs were at the door; I entered the lodgings, and the moving was already under way. The house was full of objects of all kinds – clocks, candelabra, Etruscan vases, cloth, muslin, linen, and the like. All this merchandise was taken from a closet the entrance to which was masked by a large clothes-press so well placed that it would have been impossible to detect the fraud. I helped in the loading, and, when it was ended, the wife asked me to follow her. I did as she wished, and, when she was in one of the cabs, ready to start, I raised one of the glasses, and suddenly we were surrounded. The two were taken before a court of assize, where they lost, under the weight of an accusation, in support of which such a formidable mass of irrefutable material existed and which would serve as a witness.

A short time after I forced this fence to yield, a sort of gang was formed in the Faubourg Saint-Germain, which by preference exploited the other quarters of Paris. It was composed of individuals who appeared to be dependent on a chief named Gueuvive, alias Constantin, alias Antin, by abbreviation.

Gueuvive, or Antin, was a former master-at-arms, who, after having led the life of a hired thug in the pay of courtesans of the lowest class, was as a thief undergoing the vicissitudes of a criminal career. He was, I was assured, capable of anything, and if they could not prove that he had committed murder, there was no doubt that he would shed blood in case of necessity. His mistress had been assassinated in the Champs-Élysées, and he was strongly suspected of the crime. However that was, Gueuvive was a most enterprising man; most audacious, and extraordinarily bold; at least his comrades considered him so, and he enjoyed a sort of celebrity among them.

For a long time the police had had an eye on Gueuvive and his accomplices, but they could not reach him; and every day some new attempt against property announced that the gang were not idle. Finally, it was decided to make a serious attempt to make an end to the crimes of these brigands. In consequence I received an order to go after them, and to try to take them, as they say, with their hands in the bag. Emphasis was laid on the latter point, which was of the highest importance. I dressed up in a suitable costume, and that very evening I started my campaign in the Faubourg Saint-Germain by circulating about the dives. At midnight I entered one run by a man named Boucher and took a drink with some prostitutes. While I was with them, I heard, at the next table, the name of Constantin. At first I imagined that he was there, and I questioned one of the girls, cleverly. 'He isn't here,' she told me, 'but he comes every day with some of his friends.'

From the tone in which she spoke I thought I saw that she was in touch with the habits of these gentlemen. I asked her to supper with me in the hope that she would talk. She accepted, and when she was fairly animated by the effects of the spirits, she explained the more openly in that my costume, my gestures, and especially my language confirmed her in the idea that I was a thief. I left her only when she had told me the places Gueuvive frequented.

At noon the next day I went to Boucher's. I found there my girl friend of the evening before; I had hardly entered when she recognized me. 'There you are,' she said; 'if you want to talk to Gueuvive, he is here.' And she pointed to a man between twenty-eight and thirty, neatly dressed. I accosted him by asking for a pipe of tobacco; he looked at me and asked me if I was a soldier. I answered that I had served in the hussars, and soon, glass in hand, we began a conversation on the armies.

While we drank, time passed, and something was said about dinner. Gueuvive told me that he had arranged a party, and I would give him pleasure if I would join them. This was not the time to refuse, and I accepted the invitation without ceremony. We went to the Barrier du Maine, where four of his friends were waiting. On our arrival we went to the table; none of his friends knew me; I was an unknown face to them, so they were circumspect. Nevertheless, some slang words which slipped out at intervals told me that all the members of this amiable party were thieves.

They wanted to know what I did; I made up a story in my manner, and, after I had told it to them, they not only believed that I came from the provinces, but that I was a thief who wanted to get hold of something. I did not explain myself positively in this regard, but by affecting certain mannerisms which revealed the profession, I let them see that I did not know what to do with myself.

Wine was not spared; tongues were loosened so well that before the end of the meal, I knew the home of Gueuvive, that of Joubert, his worthy assistant, as well as the names of several of their comrades. When we separated, I let it be understood that I did not know where I was going to sleep. Joubert offered to take me to his place, and he led me to rue Saint-Jacques, where he occupied a room on the second-floor back, sharing the bed with his mistress Cornevin.

Our interview was long. Before we slept, Joubert overwhelmed me with questions. He insisted on knowing what my means of existence were; he inquired whether I had papers – his curiosity was inexhaustible. In order to satisfy him, I evaded or lied, but always trying to make him think I was a confrère. Finally he said, as if he had made it out, 'Don't pretend; you're a thief!' Seeming to take offence, I answered that he was wrong and that if he meant that as a joke, I should be obliged to leave. Joubert was silent, and nothing more came up until ten o'clock next day when Gueuvive came to awaken us.

It was agreed that we should breakfast at La Glacière. We went. On the way Gueuvive took me one side and said: 'Listen, I see you're a good fellow; I want to do you a service. Don't be so artful; tell me who you are and where you come from.' Some semi-confidences gave him the idea that I might be an escaped convict from Toulon, and he advised me to be discreet with his comrades. 'They are the best fellows in the world, but they talk a lot.'

'Oh, I'm on my guard,' I answered, 'but I don't think I shall grow rusty in Paris; there are too many fly-cops for me to be safe.'

'That's true,' he said, 'but if Vidocq doesn't know you, you have nothing to fear, especially with me, for I can scent the blackguard the way the crows smell powder.'

'Well,' I replied, 'I'm not so smart as that. However, if Vidocq were here, according to the description they've given me, his features are so engraved on my mind that it seems to me I should recognize him at once!'

'Oh, shut up! It's easy to see that you don't know that hypocrite. Imagine, he changes at will; in the morning, for example, he will be dressed as you are; at noon, another way; and in the evening, still another way. No later than yesterday, I met him posing as a general. But his disguise didn't fool me. However, he's better than the rest; I can spot them at a glance; and if my friends were like me he'd have kicked the bucket a long time ago.'

'Bah! All the Parisians say that, and he is still here.'

'You're right,' he said. 'But to prove that I am not like those boobs' if you'll go with me this evening, we'll wait at his door and settle his case.'

I wanted to find out whether in fact he did know where I lived. I promised to second him, and toward dusk it was agreed that each of us should put ten two-sou pieces in a handkerchief, and give some good clouts to Vidocq when he came in or went out.

The handkerchiefs were ready and we started out; Constantin was already in good spirits, and he led to rue Neuve Saint-François, right in front of No. 14, where in fact I lived. I could not conceive how he had learned my address. I must confess that the fact made me uneasy, and, in addition, it seemed strange that he did not know me in the flesh. We watched several hours, and Vidocq, as one can well imagine, did not appear. Constantin was not even bothered by this *contretemps*. 'He's escaped us today,' he said, 'but I swear that I'll meet him, and he'll pay for the guard he made me mount.'

We got back at midnight, and we postponed the party till the next day. It was somewhat exciting to see myself in requisition to co-operate in a trap against myself. Constantin was much pleased by my good will; from that moment he kept nothing from me. He had planned a robbery in rue Cassette, and he proposed that I take part. I promised to participate, but at the same time I declared that I could not and would not go out at night without papers. 'Well,' he said, 'you wait in the room.'

Finally the robbery took place, and, as it was very dark and Constantin and his companions wanted to see clearly to walk, they had the boldness to take down a street-lamp which they carried at the head of the procession. When they came back, they planted this lantern in the middle of the room and began to review their booty. They were in the heights of joy as they contemplated the results of their excursion, but fifty minutes had hardly passed since their return when there was a knock on the door. The thieves in their astonishment looked at each other without answering. It was a surprise I had arranged for them. The knocking was repeated. Then Constantin ordered silence by a sign, and said, in a low voice, 'I'm sure it's the police.' Suddenly I got up and slipped under the bed; the knocking redoubled, and they had to open.

Then a squad of inspectors invaded the room, arrested Constantin and four others, and made a general search. They examined the bed where Joubert's mistress was; they sounded under the couch with a cane, and they did not find me. I expected that.

The commissioner drew up a written report, inventoried the stolen merchandise, and carried it to the Prefecture along with the five thieves.

When the operation was over, I came out from my hiding-place and found myself with Cornevin, who could not get over her astonishment at my good luck, which she did not understand. She wanted me to stay, but I answered, 'What are you thinking of! Suppose the police come back.' I left her, promising to rejoin her at L'Estrapade.

I went home and took a rest, and at the appointed time I was promptly at the rendezvous. Cornevin was waiting for me. I counted on her to obtain the complete list of Joubert's and Constantin's friends. As I was a good fellow with her, she promptly put me in relations with them. In less than a fortnight, thanks to the assistance of an agent whom I launched in the troop, I succeeded in having them arrested with their hands full; they were nineteen in number. They were all condemned to the galleys, and Constantin as well.

Just as the chain gang was leaving, Constantin saw me and became furious. He broke out in invectives against me; but without taking any offence at his gross insults, I approached him and said, coolly, that it was surprising that a man like him who knew Vidocq, and enjoyed the precious faculty of smelling a police spy as far as the crows smell powder, should have allowed himself to be done in this way. Overwhelmed and confused by this crushing reply, he lowered his eyes and was silent.

I was not the only secret agent: a Jew named Gaffré was my associate. He was employed before I was, but his principles were not mine, and we did not agree for long. I saw that his conduct was bad. I warned our chief, who recognized the truth of my report, expelled him, and ordered him to leave Paris. The police also used as spies many of the lowest criminals. M. Henry had long understood the danger of using these two-edged tools, and had dreamed for a long time of getting rid of them. It was with this end in view that he had enrolled me in the police, which he wished to purge of all the men who had a *penchant* for theft.

When I entered the police, all the secret agents of both sexes leagued against me naturally enough; foreseeing that their reign would end, they did all they could to prolong it. I had a reputation of being inflexible and impartial. I did not take with both hands, as they say, and it was natural that they should be my declared enemies. They did not spare attacks to make me succumb, but they were useless efforts – I rode the storm. I was denounced every day, but the voice of my slanderers was powerless. M. Henry had the Prefect's ear, and answered for my actions. He decided that every denunciation against me should be communicated to me immediately, and that I should be permitted to refute it in writing. Soon M. Henry did nothing without consulting me. We passed whole nights in working out combinations for repression, which became so efficacious that in a short time the number of complaints of robbery were considerably diminished.

For about six months I walked alone, with no aids except some prostitutes who were devoted, when an unforeseen circumstance made me independent of the regular police, who up to this time had skillfully taken to themselves the credit for my discoveries.

In 1810, robberies of a new kind, inconceivably bold, suddenly aroused the police to the existence of a band of malefactors of a new sort. Nearly all these robberies had been committed by the aid of ladders and breaking in. Apartments on the first, and even on the second floor had been rifled by these extraordinary thieves who until then had attacked only the wealthiest houses. It was even easy to note that these scoundrels operated in such a manner as to indicate that they had a perfect acquaintance with the locality.

All my efforts to discover these adroit thieves had been without success when a robbery which it seemed impossible to execute was committed in rue Saint-Claude, in a second-floor apartment in the very house of the police commissioner of the quarter. The cord of the lantern suspended over the door of that functionary had served as an aid in scaling the wall. A horse's nose-bag had been left on the scene of the crime, which led to the presumption that the thieves might be cab-drivers, or at least that cabs had helped in the expedition.

M. Henry had me get information on the cabmen, and I discovered that the nose-bag had belonged to a man named Husson who drove cab No. 712. 1 made my report. Husson was arrested, and from him the police got information about two brothers named Delzève. The elder brother was soon in the hands of the police. Questioned by M. Henry he made several revelations which resulted in the arrest of one Métral who had been employed as a floor-polisher in the house of the Empress Joséphine. He was the receiver of the gang, twenty-two in all, who in the end were all condemned to the galleys.

In the course of 1812, I had delivered to justice the principal members of the gang. However, the younger Delzève had not been taken, and he continued to escape the police investigations. On the thirty-first of December, M. Henry said to me: 'I believe that if we manage well, we should arrest Écrevisse [Delzève's surname]. Here it is New Year's and he can't fail to see the laundress who has given him and his brother asylum so often. I have a feeling that he will come there either this evening or tonight, or at any rate in the morning.'

I agreed with M. Henry, and in consequence he ordered me to go with three inspectors and watch near the domicile of the laundress. I received this order with that satisfaction which has constantly been a presage of success. Accompanied by the three inspectors, I went to the indicated place at seven o'clock. It was excessively cold; the ground was covered with snow; winter had never been so severe.

We took our posts. The inspectors shivered, and, unable to bear it longer, proposed that we leave our stations. I was half-frozen too, as all I had for protection was a very light coat of the commissioner's. At first I made some objections, and, although it would have been most agreeable to me to withdraw, it was agreed that we should stay till midnight. The hour fixed for departure had hardly struck when they summoned me to keep my promise. So we abandoned the post which we were ordered to hold till daylight.

We went toward the Palais Royal; a café was still open; we went in to get warm, and, after we had taken a bowl of warm wine, we separated, each of us intending to go to his lodgings. As I went toward mine, I reflected on what I had just done. 'What!' I said to myself, 'it is an unforgivable act of baseness to forget so rapidly your instructions and to impose on your chiefs in this way.' My conduct seemed not only reprehensible, but more than that, I considered that it deserved the severest punishment. I was in despair at having followed the impulse of the inspectors. I decided to repair my fault and to return alone to my assigned post, determined to pass the night there or die on the spot. So I went back and crouched in a corner so that Delzève would not see me in case he took a notion to come.

I had been there an hour and a half; my blood was frozen; I felt my courage weaken; suddenly I had a bright idea. Not far away was a deposit of rubbish and the vapour from it showed it was fermenting. I ran to it, dug a hole which came up to my waist, and got into it; the slight warmth restored my circulation.

At five o'clock in the morning I was still in my retreat, where, except for the odour, I was fairly comfortable. Finally, the door of the house which I was watching opened to let out a woman, who did not shut it. At once, without any noise, I got out of the dump, and a few minutes later I entered the court. I looked, but I saw no light anywhere. I knew that Delzève's associates had a special way of calling him by whistling, as the cabmen do. I imitated it, and the second time, I heard someone say, 'Who's calling?'

'It's Chauffeur [a coachman who had taught Delzève to drive], whistling for Écrevisse.'

'Is it you?' said the same voice [it was Delzève].

'Yes; Chauffeur wants you, come down.'

'I'm coming; wait a minute.'

'It's too cold,' I answered. 'I'll wait in the pub on the corner. Hurry up, do you hear?'

The pub was open; business is early on New Year's. However, I was not tempted to drink. In order to deceive Delzève, I opened the side door and let it slam to without going out. I hid under the staircase in the court. Delzève came down soon after. I saw him and walked straight to him and seized him by the collar. Holding my pistol to his breast, I notified him that he was my prisoner. 'Follow me,' I said, 'and at the slightest movement, I'll break a limb; besides, I'm not alone.'

Dumb with stupefaction Delzève did not answer a word and followed me mechanically. I ordered him to let down his braces; he obeyed. From that moment I was his master; he could neither resist nor flee.

I hurried to take him away. The clock struck six as we entered the rue du Rocher. A cab passed; I signalled it to stop; the state in which the cabman saw me inspired some fear for the cleanliness of his vehicle, but I offered to pay double, and he consented to take us in. So there we were rolling along the pavements of Paris. To be absolutely safe, I bound my companion, who now that he had recovered his senses might want to rebel. I might not have used these means, but relied on my strength, but as I proposed to make him confess, I did not want to fall out with him. When Delzève was in such a state that it was impossible for him to escape, I tried to make him listen to reason. In order to win over, I offered him refreshments and he accepted. The driver got us some wine, and without any fixed destination we continued to ride as we drank.

It was still early. In the persuasion that it would be advantageous to prolong the tête-à-tête, I proposed to Delzève that we take breakfast in a place where we could have a private room. By this time he was thoroughly appeased and seemed to hold no rancour; he did not refuse the invitation, and I took him to the Cadran Bleu. But before we arrived, he had already given me precious information on a good number of his allies, who were still free in Paris, and I was convinced that at table he would unbosom himself completely. I made him understand that the only way to make himself interesting in the eyes of justice was to make revelations, and to fortify his resignation, I let fly arguments of a certain philosophy which I have always used successfully for the consolation of those under arrest. Finally, he was perfectly well disposed, when the cab stopped at the door to the restaurant. I made him enter ahead of me, and as we were ordering, I told him that, as I wanted to be able to eat in peace, I invited him to let me tie him in my own way. I consented to leave him in full use of his arms and a fork – one does not need more liberty at table. He was not offended at the precaution, and this is what I did. With two napkins I bound each leg to the legs of the chair, three or four inches from the floor, which would prevent his getting up without risk of breaking his head.

He breakfasted with good appetite and promised to repeat in the presence of M. Henry all that he had confessed to me. At noon we took coffee; Delzève was slightly drunk, and we took a cab, entirely reconciled and good friends. Ten minutes later we were at the Prefecture.

M. Henry was surrounded by the police who were paying their New Year's calls. I entered and offered this greeting: 'I have the honour to wish you a Happy New Year, accompanied by the famous Delzève.'

'That's what I call a New Year's gift,' said M. Henry when he saw the prisoner. Then, addressing the officers: 'It would be desirable, gentlemen, that each of you had a similar gift to offer the Prefect.' Immediately after, he ordered me to take Delzève to the dépôt, and said to me kindly, 'Vidocq, go and rest; I am pleased with you.'

The arrest of Delzève brought me striking evidence of satisfaction, but at the same time it increased the hatred which the regular police and its agents showed me. joining in chorus with the thieves and evil-minded folk, all the employees who were not happy in the force threw fire and flame against me; to hear them, it was a scandal and an abomination to use my zeal to purge society of the malefactors who troubled its rest. They concluded that if I was the most skilful of agents, I must have been the most skilful of thieves.

M. Henry was struck by the absurdity of their imputations, and answered them with this observation: 'If it is true that Vidocq commits robberies every day, that's one more reason to accuse you of incapacity. He is alone; you numerous; you are told that he steals. How is it that you do not take him in the act? Alone he has been able to take some of your colleagues in the very act, and you, all of you, aren't able to do the like.'

The inspectors would have been embarrassed to answer. They kept still; but it was evident that the enmity they bore me would increase, and the Prefect of Police decided to make me independent. From that moment I was free to act as I judged proper for the good of the service; I took my orders directly from M. Henry, and had to account for my operations to him alone.

XIX
I LODGE WITH THE ENEMY

IT IS RARELY that a convict escapes from prison with the intention of reforming; most often he proposes to gain the capital to practise the fatal skill which he has been able to acquire in the convict prisons, which, as are most of the prisons, are schools where they are perfected in the art of appropriating another's goods. Nearly all the great robbers have become experts only after a more or less long sojourn in the galleys. Such were the famous Victor Dubois and his comrade Mangenet, alias Tambour, who in their different appearances in Paris committed a large number of robberies which people like to recount as a proof of their skill and audacity.

For some years these two men had been in every departure of the chain gang and had always managed to escape. They were again in Paris; the police were informed, and I was ordered to get on their track. Everything pointed to the conclusion that they were acquainted with convicts who were just as dangerous. The police suspected that a piano teacher, whose son Noël was a famous highwayman, gave asylum to the latter.

Madame Noël was a well-educated woman, an excellent musician, and in the middle class, where she gave lessons to the young ladies, she passed for a distinguished artiste. She gave private lessons in the quarter, where the elegance of her manners, the purity of her language, a slight exquisiteness of costume, and certain airs of grandeur which reverses of fortune do not altogether efface, induced one to believe that she might belong to one of those numerous families to whom the Revolution left only hauteur and regrets. To see her and hear her, if one did not know her, Madame Noël was a most interesting woman; and the more so because there was something touching about her existence; it was a mystery; no one knew what had become of her husband.

Some people were sure that she had been widowed very young; others that she had been deserted; they also pretended that she had been the victim of seduction. I don't know *which* of these conjectures was nearest the truth, but what I do know is that Madame Noël was a slight brunette, with a keen eye and impish look, which seemed, however, to go with her appearance of gentleness, and this was confirmed by the friendliness of her smile and by the tones of her voice in which there was much charm. There was something of the angel and the devil in her face, but more of the devil than the angel, for the years had developed the traits which characterize evil thoughts.

Madame Noël was obliging and good, but only to individuals who had some quarrel with justice; she received them as a soldier's mother receives her son's comrades. To be welcome with her it was sufficient to belong to the 'same regiment' as Noël of the Spectacles, and then as much for love of him as taste, perhaps, she loved to do service. So she was regarded as the 'Mother of Thieves'; they came to her house; she provided for all their wants; she carried her complaisance so far that she even sought 'work' for them, and when a passport was indispensable for their safety, she did not rest easy until she had succeeded in procuring it for them. Madame had many friends among her own sex; and ordinarily the passport was taken out in one of their names; it was hardly delivered before a good bath of muriatic acid had removed the writing, and the gentleman's description and his arranged name had replaced the feminine description. Madame Noël usually had in hand a reasonable supply of these washed passports.

All convicts were Madame Noël's children; but she pampered most particularly those who were connected with her son. She showed them a boundless devotion; her house was open to all of them and it was their meeting-place. And there must be some gratitude among such people, for the police were informed that the convicts often came to Mother Noël's merely for the pleasure of seeing her. She was the confidante of all their plans, all their adventures, all their alarms; finally, they trusted her without limit, and they were sure of her fidelity.

Mother Noël had never seen me; my features were entirely unknown to her, although she had often heard my name. So it was not difficult to present myself to her without arousing her fears. But to bring her to the point of indicating the retreat of the men whom it was important to discover was the end I sought, and I presumed that I should not attain it without using considerable ingenuity. First, I resolved to pose as an escaped convict; but it was necessary to borrow the name of a thief whom her son or his comrades might have painted

in glowing colours. A slight resemblance was indispensable in addition.
I sought among the number of convicts of my acquaintance to find
whether one existed who was in relations with Noël of the Spectacles,
and I found none near my own age or whose description was anything
like mine. Finally, by torturing my mind and drawing on my memory, I
remembered a certain Germain, alias Royer, alias Capitaine, who was
friendly with Noël, and who, although he did not resemble me in the
slightest, I proposed to represent.

Germain had escaped from prison several times, as I had, and that
was all we had in common. He was nearly my age; but he was shorter; he
had brown hair, mine was blond; he was thin, I did not lack embonpoint;
his complexion was swarthy, my skin was white and florid; and to that
Germain had a very long nose, snuffed a large quantity of tobacco, and
had a nasal voice.

I had some task to play Germain. The difficulty did not alarm me.
My hair was cut in the prison fashion, and tinted black, as was my
beard, which I allowed to grow for a week. In order to darken my face,
I washed it with a decoction of walnut leaves. To complete the imitation, I put a plaster held on by gum on the outside of my nose; this was
not superfluous, because it contributed to give me Germain's nasal
accent. My legs were also arranged with art; I raised some blisters by
rubbing my feet with a composition, the recipe for which I had learned
at Brest. I indicated the marks of the irons, and when all this toilet was
completed, I assumed the dress which conformed to my condition. I
had neglected nothing to give reality to my metamorphosis, neither the
shoes nor the shirt marked with the terrible letters 'G A L.' My costume was perfect, and I started toward Madame Noël's house, rue
Ticquetonne.

I arrived and knocked; she opened, and at a glance she understood;
she made me come in. I saw that I was alone with her, and I was going
to tell her who I was.

'Oh, my poor boy,' she exclaimed, 'one does not have to ask where
you come from; I'm sure you're hungry?'

'Yes, I am hungry,' I answered, 'for I've had nothing for twenty-four
hours.'

At once, without waiting for an explanation, she went out and
returned with a plate of pork and a bottle of wine which she placed

before me. I did not eat, I devoured; I choked so as to eat the faster; all disappeared, and between mouthfuls I had not said a word.

Mother Noël was delighted at my appetite. When the table was cleared, she gave me a dram. 'Oh, mama,' I said, throwing my arms around her neck to embrace her, 'Noël told me that you were good.' From that I went on to tell her that I had left her son eighteen days before and to give her news of all the convicts in whom she was interested. The details into which I entered were so true and so well known that the idea that I was an impostor could never have entered her head.

'You must have heard of me,' I went on. 'I have had many misfortunes. My name is Germain, alias Capitaine; you must know the name.'

'Yes, yes, my friend,' she said, 'I know you. My son and his friends have told me about your misfortunes; be welcome, my dear Capitaine.' When I believed that I could do so without trouble, I asked her what had become of Victor Dubois and his comrade Mangenet.

'Dubois and Tambour,' she answered, 'oh, my dear, don't talk about them. That rascal of a Vidocq has caused them trouble. Since that Joseph [a former inspector of police] met them twice in the street and told them that if they came into the quarter they would fall under his axe, they have been obliged to evacuate.'

'What, aren't they in Paris any more?' I exclaimed, a little disappointed.

'Oh, they are not far,' Mother Noël answered. 'They have not left the neighbourhood. I even have the pleasure of seeing them from time to time. I hope that they'll make me a visit shortly. I think they would be pleased to see you.'

'Oh, I assure you that they would be no more pleased than I should, and if you write to them, I am sure that they would hurry to send for me.'

'If I knew where they were,' Madame Noël answered, 'I would go myself, and try to find them for your pleasure, but I don't know their retreat. What you'd better do is be patient and wait for them.

'Do you know Vidocq and his two dogs, Lèvesque and Compère?' she asked.

'Oh, yes, unfortunately,' I answered. 'They've arrested me twice.'

'If that's the case, take care; Vidocq often goes about disguised. He dresses up in all sorts of costumes to arrest poor fellows like you.'

I had to be thoroughly well versed to keep up with Mother Noël; there wasn't a prison custom which she did not have at her finger-tips. She not only knew the names of all the thieves whom she had seen, but she was instructed in the least details of the life of most of the others. She related with enthusiasm the stories of the most famous, notably that of her son whom she worshipped as much as she loved him.

'Then you'd be pleased to see your dear son again?' I asked.

'Oh, yes, very pleased.'

'Well, that's a happiness which I believe you'll soon enjoy. Noël has everything ready for his escape. Now he's only waiting for a propitious moment.'

Madame Noël was happy in the hope of embracing her son; she shed tears of tenderness. I confess that I was deeply moved myself; so much so that I gave a moment's consideration whether this time I was not overstepping my duties as a secret agent. But on reflecting about the crimes the Noël family had committed and considering the interests of society, I was firm and inflexible in my resolution to pursue my enterprise to the end.

In the course of our conversation, Mother Noël asked me if I 'had anything in sight' (projecting a robbery), and after offering to find me something in case I had not, she questioned me as to whether I was skilful in making false keys. I answered that I was as good as Fossard. 'If that is so,' she told me, 'I am at ease; you'll soon be fitted out again.' And she added, 'Since you are ingenious, I'll buy you at the ironmonger's a key which you can fit to my lock so that you can come in and go out when you please.'

I showed how much I was touched by her kindness, and, as it was late, I went to bed thinking of a way to get out of this difficulty without running the risk of being assassinated, if by chance the rascals for whom I was searching arrived before I had taken my measures.

I did not sleep and got up as soon as I heard Mother Noël light her fire. She found me an early bird, and told me she was going to get what I needed. She brought me an uncut key, and gave me files and a small vice which I fixed to the foot of the bed. Now that I had tools, I set to work in the presence of my hostess who saw that I knew what I was doing and complimented me on my work. What she admired most was the expeditious manner in which I went at it. In fact, in less than four hours I had made a well-wrought key; I tried it, and it worked nearly perfectly; a few strokes of the file and it was a masterpiece. Now, like the rest, I could come into my lodgings when I pleased.

I was Madame Noël's pensioner. After dinner I told her that I wanted to go out until dusk, in order to make sure that an affair I had in view was now feasible. She approved the idea, but advised me to take care of myself.

'That brigand of a Vidocq,' she said, 'must be feared, and if I were in your place, before I undertook anything, I should wait until my feet were healed.'

'Oh, I won't go far,' I answered, 'and I'll come back soon.'

The assurance that I would come back promptly seemed to allay her uneasiness. 'Well, good luck,' and I went limping out.

So far everything had gone according to my desires; one could not be more in Madame Noël's good graces. But if I stayed in her house, who would answer for it that I should not be beaten to death? Two or three convicts might come at once, recognize me and do me up. Then, good-bye to my ingenuity. So without losing Madame Noël's friendship I must prepare against any such danger. It would be imprudent to let her suspect that I had reasons to avoid the sight of her habitués. Consequently, I tried to arrange matters so that she would bow me out herself; that is to say, would advise me, in my own interests, not to sleep at her house.

I had noticed that Madame Noël was very closely associated with a woman who sold fruit and who lived in the house. I detached one of my assistants to go to this woman and ask her secretly and awkwardly for information about Madame Noël. I dictated the questions, and I was the more certain that the fruiterer would not fail to divulge this step in that I prescribed to my aide to advise her to be discreet.

The event proved that I was not wrong. My agent had no sooner fulfilled his mission than the fruiterer hurried to report what had happened to Madame Noël, who in her turn lost no time in taking me into her confidence. Posted on the doorstep of the officious neighbour, as soon as she saw me she came straight toward me and without preamble invited me to follow her. I turned back, and when we reached the Place des Victoires, she stopped, looked around, and when she saw that no one noticed us, she drew near me and told me what she had learned.

'So,' she said at the end, 'you see, my poor Germain, that it would not be prudent for you to sleep in the house; it would be more prudent for you not to come in the daytime.'

Madame Noël certainly did not suspect that this *contretemps,* which really seemed to affect her, was my work. So as to turn away suspicion more and more, I pretended to be still more sorry than she was. I cursed, accompanied by two or three oaths, that scoundrel of a Vidocq, who never gave us any rest. I stormed against the necessity of finding a place outside of Paris, and I took leave of Mother Noël, who, as she wished me good luck and a prompt return, slipped a thirty-sou piece into my hand.

I knew that Dubois and Mangenet were expected; besides, I was informed that they came and went whether Madame Noël was in or not; it was rather ordinary for this to happen while she went out to give lessons. It was important for me to know all the subscribers. To reach this end, I disguised several of my aides and posted them at the street corner, where they mingled with the commissionnaires in such a way that their presence was not suspected.

When I had taken these precautions, so that I should give every indication of fear, I let several days go by without going to see Madame Noël. Then I went to see her one evening, accompanied by a young man whom I presented as the brother of a woman with whom I had lived, and whom I had met by chance as I was getting ready to leave Paris. He had given me a refuge. The young man was a secret agent; I was careful to tell Mother Noël that he had my entire confidence, and she could consider him as my other self; that, as he was not known to the police spies, I had chosen him as my messenger to her every time I judged it imprudent to show myself. 'Hereafter,' I added, 'he will be our intermediary; he will come every two or three days to get your news and that of our friends.'

'I declare,' said Mother Noël, 'you've had a miss; twenty minutes earlier and you would have seen a woman who knows you well.'

'Who is it?'

'Marguerit's sister.'

'That's so, she's often seen me with her brother.'

'Yes, and when I spoke of you, she described you feature by feature.'

Madame Noël regretted deeply that I had not come before the departure of Marguerit's sister, but doubtless not as much as I congratulated myself on having escaped an interview which would have baffled all my projects. For if this woman knew Germain, she knew Vidocq, too, and it was impossible that she would take one for the other, so great was the difference between them. Then Madame Noël gave me a useful warning by telling me that Marguerit's sister often came to visit her. I promised myself that this girl would never meet me face to face, and to avoid seeing her, every time I came I had my pretended brother-in-law go ahead, who, when she was not there, was ordered to let me know by making a sign at the window. At this signal I hurried in, and my aide-de-camp went to watch in the vicinity to avoid a disagreeable surprise. Not far away were other aides to whom I had given Mother Noël's key, so that they might be ready to succour me in case of danger. At any moment I might fall unexpectedly among some escaped convicts, and if they recognized me, they might fall on me; in that case a broken pane of glass was to indicate that I needed reinforcements to equalize the party.

My measures were all taken; the dénouement was at hand. It was Tuesday; a letter from the men I sought announced their arrival for the following Friday. Friday was to be an unlucky day for them. In the morning I went to a public-house in the neighbourhood, and in order that I should not be seen, supposing that they passed and repassed as was their custom before they entered Mother Noël's domicile, I sent my pretended brother-in-law on ahead. He soon came back to tell me that Marguerit's sister was not there, and that I might present myself in all security.

'You aren't deceiving me?' I observed to this agent, whose voice seemed sensibly changed. As soon as I looked at him, I thought that I noticed that constriction in the muscles of his face which indicate that a person is adjusting himself to lie. Something, I don't know what, seemed to indicate that I was engaged with a traitor. That was the first impression which struck me like a flash. We were in a private room. Without hesitating I took my man by the collar and told him, in the presence of his comrades, that I knew of his perfidy, and if at that very moment he did not confess all, it was all over with him. He was terrified and muttered some words of excuse, and confessed that he had told Mother Noël everything.

If I had not guessed his indiscretion, it might perhaps have cost me my life. The traitor was arrested and, young as he was, as he had two crimes to expiate, he was sent to Bicêtre, then to Oleron, where he ended his career.

One may imagine that the escaped convicts no longer came to rue Ticquetonne, but they were arrested none the less a short time afterward.

Mother Noël never forgave the trick I had played her. To get her revenge, she devised a scheme to make nearly all of her effects disappear in one day. When this removal was accomplished, she went out without closing her door, and shouted that she had been robbed. The neighbours were called as witnesses; a declaration was made to the commissioner, and Mother Noël designated me as the thief, for, as she assured him, I had a key to her room. This accusation was serious; it was immediately sent to the Prefect of Police, and the second day it was communicated to me. My justification was not difficult. The Prefect and M. Henry saw the imposture at once, and investigations they ordered were so well directed that the effects removed by Mother Noël were found. They had the proof that she had accused me falsely, and to give her time to repent, they locked her up for six months in Saint-Lazare.

XX
THE CLUE OF THE YELLOW CURTAINS

WE HAVE SEEN what trouble the faithlessness of an agent caused me. I had known for a long time that the best-guarded secret is one entrusted to no one, but that sad experience convinced me more and more of the necessity of working alone every time that I could. That is the course I pursued on an important occasion.

After they had served several sentences, two escaped convicts, Goreau and Florentin, alias Châtelain, were held at Bicêtre as incorrigible thieves. Wearied of their sojourn in the cells where they might as well have been buried alive, they sent a letter to M. Henry in which they offered to furnish information which would make it possible to take several of their comrades who were daily committing robberies in Paris. One named Fossard, a man sentenced to life imprisonment who had escaped from prison several times, was the one they designated as the most adroit, at the same time representing him as the most dangerous. 'He was,' they wrote, 'unrivalled in boldness, and he should be approached only after precautions had been taken, in view of the fact that he was always armed to the teeth, and was resolved to blow out the brains of the police agent who was daring enough to try to arrest him.'

The chiefs of the administration asked nothing better than to deliver the capital of such a scoundrel. Their first thought was to use me to discover him, but the informers had observed to M. Henry that I was too well known to Fossard and his concubine not to fail in such a delicate operation in case I was entrusted with it. So it was decided to have recourse to the regular police. The information necessary to direct their search was put at their disposal, but, whether they were unlucky or did not care to meet Fossard, 'armed to the teeth,' he continued his exploits. The numerous complaints to which his activity gave rise announced that, in spite of their apparent zeal, these gentlemen, according to their custom, were making much noise but doing little work.

The result was that one day the Prefect, who wanted more work and less noise, summoned them and reproached them, probably rather severely, to judge from the discontent which they were unable to repress on this occasion. They were just coming from this blowing-up when I happened to meet one of them named M. Yvrier. I bowed to him; he came toward me, almost swollen to bursting with rage. When he was near me, he said: 'Oh, there you are, monsieur the doer of great things. You're the cause of our being reprimanded on account of one called Fossard, escaped convict, who, it is pretended, is in Paris. To hear Monsieur the Prefect one would think that the only one in the administration capable of anything is you. If Vidocq, he told us, had been sent in pursuit, there's no doubt that he would have been arrested long ago. Come along, M. Vidocq, make a slight attempt to find him; you who are so adroit, prove that you have as much shrewdness as they say you have.'

M. Yvrier was an old man, and I had need to respect his age, not to retort with temper to his impertinent attack. Although I felt piqued at the tone of bitterness which he took in talking to me, I was not at all angry and contented myself by answering that for the moment I had hardly the leisure to busy myself with Fossard; that I was saving his capture for the first of January to offer him as a New Year's gift, as I had offered the famous Delzève the previous year.

'Go your way,' answered M. Yvrier, irritated by this persiflage, 'the result will show us what you are – a presumptuous man, a trouble-maker.' He left me muttering in his teeth some other qualifications I did not understand.

After this scene, I went to M. Henry's office and told him about it.

'Oh, so they're mad,' he said, laughing. 'So much the better.'

Then he gave me the following information:

'Fossard lives in Paris in a street which leads from the market to the boulevard, that is to say, starting with the rue Comtesse d'Artois to rue Poissonniere, passing through rue Montorgueil and Petit Carreau. It is not known on what floor he lives, but the windows of his apartment may be recognized by yellow silk curtains and others of embroidered muslin. There is living in the same house a small dwarf, a seamstress, a friend of the girl who lives with Fossard.'

As one can see, this information was not so precise as to enable one to go straight to the end. A dwarf and yellow curtains, with other curtains of embroidered muslin, were certainly not easy to find in a space as large as that which I had to explore. Without a doubt such a combination of circumstances would present itself more than once. How many dwarfs, old and young, could be counted in Paris, and who could number the yellow curtains? To sum up, the data were rather vague; however, the problem must be solved. I would try and see whether my lucky genius, as a result of my investigations, would not lead me to put my finger on the exact spot.

I did not know where to start. However, as I foresaw that in my rounds I should meet principally women of the people, that is to say, the gossips, I soon fixed on the sort of disguise suitable to assume. It was obvious that I needed to appear as a very respectable gentleman. Consequently, by means of some artificial wrinkles, a queue, white crêpe, and a large gold-headed cane, a three-cornered hat, buckles, appropriate trousers and coat, I changed myself into one of those good sixty-year-old citizens whom all the old maids consider well preserved. I had the complete appearance and dress of one of those rich men whose ruddy and winsome faces indicate ease and the fancy of making the happiness of some unfortunate woman past middle age. I was certain that all the dwarfs would desire me, and then I had the appearance of such an honest man that it was impossible that they should scruple to receive me.

Disguised in this way, I started to go up and down the streets, nose in the air, noting all the curtains of the colour which had been described to me. I was so occupied with this census that I neither heard nor saw anything around me. If I had been a little less wealthy in appearance, I should have been taken for a metaphysician or perhaps a poet. Twenty times I just missed being crushed under cabs; from all sides I heard cries of 'Look out! Look out' and turned to find myself under a wheel or embracing a horse. Sometimes, too, while I was wiping off the foam that covered my sleeve, a cut of the whip reached my face; or, when the driver was less brutal, there were pretty thoughts of this nature, 'Get out, old dummy!' One even went so far, I remember, as to call me 'old cocked hat.'

This review of yellow curtains was not the affair of a day. I wrote more than a hundred and fifty in my notes. And I could not tell but what the curtains behind which Fossard hid had been sent to the cleaner and replaced by white, green, or red. No matter, if luck was against me, it could also be favourable. So I took courage, and although it was very painful for a sexagenarian to climb and descend a hundred and fifty staircases, that is to say, about seven hundred and fifty flights of stairs, as I felt my legs strong and my breath deep, I undertook the task, sustained by a hope of the same kind as led the Argonauts to voyage in search of the Golden Fleece. I was searching for my dwarf. In my ascents on how many landings did I play the sentinel for entire hours in the persuasion that my lucky star would show her to me! The heroic Don Quixote was never more ardent in the pursuit of his Dulcinea. I knocked at the doors of all the dressmakers; I examined them all one after the other; but there were no dwarfs. They were all ravishing.

I passed several days in this way without meeting the shadow of my aim. It was a devilish trade; I was worn out every evening, and I had to begin again every morning. Still, if I had dared to ask questions, perhaps some charitable soul would have set me on the way, but I was afraid of giving the game away. In the end, worn out by this manœuvre, I tried another means.

I had noticed that dwarfs are generally chatterers and curious; nearly always it is they who make the talk of the quarter, and when they do not, they record it for use as slander; nothing happens that they do not know. Starting with these data, I concluded that under the pretext of getting provisions the unknown who had already caused me so many steps would, no more than any of the rest, neglect to gossip with the milkman, the baker, and fruiterer, mercer, or grocer. In consequence I decided to place myself within reach of the largest possible number of these media of talk. And as there is no dwarf who in her desire for a husband does not make a parade of all her merits as a housekeeper, I was persuaded that as mine would get up early, to see her I had to arrive early on the scene of my observations. I was there at daybreak.

I employed my first session in orienting myself. The question was to what dairy my dwarf would give the preference. Undoubtedly to the one which was nearest, where there was the most talk, and which was most frequented. That at the corner of the rue Thévenot appeared to combine these conditions. Around it were small jars for everyone, and in the middle of a crowded circle, the merchant never stopped serving or talking. The customers formed a queue, but that did not disturb me.

The important thing was that I had recognized a meeting-place, and I promised myself that I would not let it out of my sight.

I was there at my second session, impatiently on the lookout for a female dwarf, but only young girls came. With their graceful figures and slender forms there was not one who was not as straight as an 'I.' I was in despair ... At last my star appeared on the horizon; it was the model, the Venus of dwarfs. It seemed to me that I saw one of those fairies of the Middle Ages, in whom a deformity was one charm the more. This super-natural being approached the milk-seller and talked to her for some time, as I had expected. Then she took the cream, at least that was what she had asked for, and went into the grocer's; then she stopped a moment with the tripe dealer who gave her some lights, probably for her cat. Then, her purchases finished, she went into the side entrance of a house, the ground floor of which was occupied by a cooper. My gaze at once turned to the windows, but I did not see the yellow curtains for which I had sighed. However, remembering the thought which had already come to mind, that curtains, no matter what the shade, have not the immovability of a dwarf, I decided not to withdraw until I had had an interview with the little prodigy whose appearance had pleased me so much. I imagined that in spite of my disappointment about one of the major circumstances which were to be my guides, the interview would furnish me some light.

I decided to go upstairs. When I reached the mezzanine floor, I asked on what floor a small, slightly deformed woman lived.

'Do you want to talk to the dressmaker?' was the reply, laughing in my face.

'Yes, it's the dressmaker, a person with one shoulder slightly prominent.'

They laughed again, and pointed to the third-floor front. Although the neighbours were very obliging, I was on the point of taking offence at their jeering hilarity. They were really impolite; but my tolerance was so great that I willingly forgave them for finding the situation comic. Besides, was I not a good man? So I kept to my role. They had pointed out the door; I knocked, and it was opened. There was my dwarf. After the usual excuses on the importunity of my visit, I asked her to grant me a short audience, adding that I had to talk of an affair of personal interest to me.

'Mademoiselle,' I said, with a sort of solemnity, after she had made me seat myself opposite her, 'you do not know the reason which has brought me to you, but, when you learn, perhaps my course will arouse your interest.'

The dwarf imagined that I was going to make a declaration. The colour mounted to her face, and her gaze became animated, although she forced herself to lower her eyes. I went on:

'Without doubt you will be astonished that at my age one can be as much in love as at twenty.'

'Oh, monsieur, you are still robust,' said my amiable dwarf.

'I am very well,' I answered, 'but that isn't the question. You know that in Paris it is not rare for a man and a woman to live together without being married.'

'What do you take me for, monsieur, to make me such a proposition?' cried the dwarf, without waiting for me to finish. Her mistake made me smile.

'I did not come to make you a proposition,' I replied. 'I only want you to be so kind as to give me certain information about a young lady who, I have been told, lives in this house with a man who passes as her husband.'

'I don't know her,' the dwarf answered dryly.

Then I gave her a rough description of Fossard and his mistress Tonneau.

'Oh, I know him,' she said. 'A man about your figure, nearly as stout as you are, about thirty or thirty-five, a fine gallant; the lady, an attractive brunette, beautiful eyes, fine teeth, superb eyelashes, a slight growth of hair on her upper lip, a turned-up nose, and with all that an appearance of kindness and modesty. They lived here, but they moved a little while ago.'

I begged her to give me their new address, and on her reply that she did not know it, I pleaded with her tearfully to help me to find an unfortunate creature whom I still loved in spite of her perfidy. The dressmaker was touched by my tears; I saw that she was moved, and I became more and more pathetic.

'Oh, her infidelity will kill me! Take pity on a poor husband, I conjure you; do not hide their retreat; I will owe you more than life itself!'

Dwarfs are sympathetic; in addition, a husband is in their eyes so precious a treasure that they cannot understand how a wife can be unfaithful, so my dressmaker was horrified, sympathized with me most sincerely, and protested that she wanted to be useful to me.

'Unfortunately,' she added, 'their moving was done by commissionnaires who are strangers in the quarter. I am completely ignorant where they have gone or what has become of them, but if you would see the owner...'

The good faith of this woman was obvious. I went to see the owner. All he could tell me was that they had paid the rent, and had no references.

Aside from the certainty that I had discovered Fossard's former lodgings, I was hardly further along than before. Nevertheless, I did not want to abandon the game without exhausting all means of inquiry. Ordinarily the commissionnaires of one quarter know those of another; so I questioned those in the rue du Petit Carreau, to whom I represented myself as a deceived husband, and one of them pointed out to me one of his colleagues who had helped in moving my rival's furniture.

I saw the individual indicated and told him my pretended history. He listened to me, but he was a knave and intended to play me up. I pretended not to see it, and to recompense him for having promised to take me next day to the place where Fossard had moved, I gave him two five-franc pieces. They were spent the same day on the girls.

The first interview took place two days after Christmas. We were to see each other again on the twenty-eighth. There was no time to lose if I was to be ready on the first of January. I was prompt at the rendezvous; the commissionnaire, whom I had had followed by my agents, was careful not to be missing. Again some five-franc pieces passed from my purse to his. I also paid for his lunch. Finally, he decided to start, and we arrived near a pretty house, situated at the corner of the rue Duphot and rue Saint-Honoré. 'Here it is,' he said. 'We'll find out in the wine-cellar downstairs whether they're still here.' He wanted me to regale him for the last time. I was not deaf; I went in and we emptied a bottle of Beaune together.

I withdrew in the certainty that at last I had found the refuge of my pretended wife and her seducer. I no longer needed my guide, so I dismissed him, expressing my full gratitude. But to assure myself that he did not take money from both sides, I recommended my agents to watch him closely and, above all, to prevent his coming back to the wine merchant's. To be frank, I had him locked up, a just reprisal. 'My friend,' I said to him, 'I have given the police a five-hundred-franc note to recompense the one who leads me to find my wife. It belongs to you, and I'm going to give you a note so that you can get it.' In fact I gave him a note which he took to M. Henry. 'Take the gentleman to the cash-box,' the latter ordered. The cash-box was the dépôt, where my commissionnaire had time to recover from his joy.

It had not been demonstrated that Fossard's home had been pointed out to me. However, I reported to the authorities what had happened, and I was immediately provided with an order to effect the arrest. Then the rich man changed suddenly into a coal-man, and in this guise, under which neither my mother nor the employees of the Prefecture who saw me most frequently would have made me out, I busied myself in studying the ground on which I had to operate.

Fossard's friends – that is to say, his denouncers – had advised that the agents charged with the arrest should be warned that he always had on him a dagger and pistols; and that a double-barrelled gun was hidden in a cambric handkerchief which he held constantly in his hand. This advice made precautions necessary; besides, from Fossard's known character they were convinced that he would not hesitate at murder to escape a condemnation worse than death. I wanted to operate so that I should not be a victim, and it seemed that a way considerably to diminish the danger was to have an understanding in advance with the wine merchant who was Fossard's landlord.

This wine merchant was a good man, but the police have such a bad reputation that it is not always easy to induce honest folk to lend their assistance. I decided to assure myself of his co-operation by binding him to me in his own interests. I had already had some sessions with him in both my disguises, and I had had the leisure to become acquainted with the locality and to get in touch with the personnel of the shop. I went back in my ordinary clothes, and told the good man that I wanted to speak to him in private. He entered a room with me, and I spoke to him nearly as follows:

'I am ordered to warn you on the part of the police that you are to be robbed. The thief who has prepared this coup and will perhaps execute it himself lodges in your house. The woman who lives with him sometimes comes in and places herself near your wife in the bar. While she has been talking to her, she has managed to procure the impression of the key which opens the door through which they can enter. All has been foreseen; the spring on the alarm bell will be cut with scissors, while the door will be ajar. Once inside, they will rapidly go up to your chamber. If they have the slightest fear of your waking up, as you are engaged with a most consummate rascal, I don't need to explain the rest.'

'They'll do us in!' said the terrified wine merchant, and he at once called his wife to give her the news.

'Well, my dear, we must distrust everyone! So that Madame Hazard wants to cut our throats? They'll come to butcher us this very night?'

'No, no, sleep in peace,' I answered. 'It's not for tonight. The receipts aren't good enough; they'll wait. But if you're discreet, and will consent to help me, we'll put everything in good order.'

Madame Hazard was the girl Tonneau; she had taken this name, the only one under which Fossard was known in the house. I engaged the wine merchant and his wife, who were terrified by my confidence, to receive their tenants, whose projects I had revealed, with the same kindliness as usual. It need not be asked whether they were disposed to serve me. It was arranged between us that I should hide in a small room at the foot of the staircase so that I could watch Fossard pass in and out, and, in addition, arrange for an occasion to seize him.

The twenty-ninth of December I was at my post early. It was excessively cold; my watch was long, and the more uncomfortable in that we were without a fire; motionless, and my eye riveted to a hole made in the shutters, I was hardly at my ease. At last, toward three o'clock, a man went out. I followed; it was Fossard. Until then I had had some doubts. Certain of his identity, I wanted to execute my writ immediately, but the agent with me pretended that he had seen the terrible pistol. I hastened my step to verify the fact. I passed Fossard, and retracing my steps I regretted to see that the agent was not mistaken. To attempt the arrest was to expose myself, and perhaps uselessly. I then decided to postpone the party, and recalling that a fortnight previously I had flattered myself that I would hand over Fossard only on the first of

January, I was almost pleased by the delay. Until then I must not relax my vigilance.

At eleven o'clock the thirty-first of December, when all my batteries were mounted, Fossard came back; he suspected nothing and went up the stairs humming. Twenty minutes after, the disappearance of his light indicated that he was in bed. The propitious moment had come. The commissioner and the gendarmes whom I had warned were waiting at the nearest post, and I summoned them. They entered without making a noise, and we at once began to deliberate on the means of taking Fossard without running the risk of being killed or wounded. They were persuaded that at the least surprise this brigand would defend himself with determination.

My first thought was not to act before daylight. I was informed that Fossard's companion came down very early to get milk; we could then seize the woman, take her key, and suddenly enter her lover's room. But what would happen if, contrary to custom, he came down first? This thought led me to think of another expedient.

The wine merchant's wife, to whom, as I had learned, Madame Hazard was kindly disposed, had one of her nephews with her. He was a boy of ten, rather intelligent for his age, and most precocious in his desire for money in that he was a Norman. I promised him a reward on condition that, in the pretence that his aunt was ill, he would ask Madame Hazard to give him some cologne. I practised the little man in assuming the piteous tones fitting to such a circumstance, and when I was satisfied with him, I distributed the roles. The dénouement was near. I made everyone take off his shoes and I took off my own so that we should not be heard in going upstairs. The little man was in his shirt; he rang; there was no answer; he rang again. 'Who is it?' someone asked. 'It's me, Madame Hazard; Louis; my aunt's ill and begs you to give her a little cologne; she's dying. I have a light.'

The door opened; but hardly had the girl Tonneau presented herself than two strong gendarmes seized her and placed a towel over her mouth to prevent her crying out. At the same instant, more rapid than the lion which leaps upon its prey, I sprang on Fossard. Stunned by the event, already bound and tied in his bed, he was my prisoner before he had time to make a single gesture or proffer a single word. His astonishment was so great that it was nearly an hour before he could utter a word. When a light was brought and he saw my blackened face and my clothes of a coalman, he showed such an increase of terror that I thought he believed the Devil had him. When he came to himself, he thought of his arms, his pistols and dagger, which were on a table; his gaze turned in that direction; he gave a start, but that was all. Deprived of his power to do injury, he was docile and content to fret.

A search was made in the domicile of this brigand reputed to be so fearful, and a quantity of diamonds and jewels and the sum of eight to ten thousand francs were discovered. While the search was going on, Fossard had recovered his spirits and confided to me that he still had hidden ten thousand-franc notes. 'Take them,' he said, 'we'll share them, or rather you'll keep what you want.' In fact, I took the notes as he desired.

We got into a cab and were soon at M. Henry's office, where the objects found at Fossard's were deposited. They were again inventoried; when the last article was reached, 'There's nothing left to us but to close the *procès-verbal,*' said the commissioner who had accompanied me for the sake of the regularity of the expedition. 'One moment,' I cried, 'here are ten thousand francs which the prisoner handed to me.' And I exhibited the sum, to the great regret of Fossard, who gave me one of those looks which mean, 'That's a trick I'll never forgive.'

At the time of Fossard's arrest the Sûreté was already in existence, and after 1812, the date at which it was created, I was no longer a secret agent. The name Vidocq had become popular. The first expedition which brought me into evidence was directed against the principal meeting-places in La Courtille. One day M. Henry had expressed the intention of making a sweep at Denoyes' – that is to say, in the resort most frequented by bullies and evil characters of all sorts. M. Yvrier observed that it would take a battalion to execute that measure. I exclaimed at once, 'Why not the Grand Army? If they'll give me eight men, I'll answer for the success.' We have seen that M. Yvrier was naturally very irritable; he turned red, and pretended that I was only chattering.

However that might be, I maintained my proposition and I was given the order to act. The crusade which I was going to undertake was directed against thieves, escaped convicts, and a goodly number of deserters from the colonial battalions. Having provided an ample supply of handcuffs, I went with two aides and eight gendarmes. When we reached Denoyes' I entered the hall followed by two gendarmes. I invited the musicians to be silent; they obeyed; but soon there was a murmur, succeeded by repeated cries, 'To the door! To the door!' There was no time to lose; it was necessary to impose on the shouters before they proceeded to deeds. I immediately exhibited my writ, and in the name of the law summoned everyone, the women excepted, to go out. There was some difficulty about complying with this injunction, but in a few minutes even the most mutinous resigned themselves and started to evacuate. Then I posted myself in the passage and, when I recognized one or several of the individuals wanted, I marked a cross on the back with white chalk. That was a sign to designate them to the gendarmes who were waiting outside and who arrested and bound them as soon as they went out. They seized at the exit thirty-two of these rascals.

The boldness of this surprise attack made a noise among the people who frequented the barriers; in a short time it was established among all the crooks and evil rascals that there was in the world a man named Vidocq. The boldest among them promised to kill me at the first meeting. Some attempted the adventure; but they were repulsed with loss, and the checks which they received made me so terrible by reputation that at length it reflected on all the individuals in my brigade.

The formation of the brigade followed closely after the expedition to La Courtille. At first I had four agents; then six; then ten; then twelve. In 1817 1 had no more; however, with this handful of men, between the first of January and the thirty-first of December, I effected seven hundred and seventy-two arrests and thirty-nine searches where stolen objects were seized. From the moment that the thieves knew that I was to be called to the functions of principal agent of the Sûreté, they thought themselves lost.

XXI
I AVOID SNARES

WHEN I ENTERED the police service, I was well aware how dangerous was the calling I was embracing. However, I did not despair of
escaping the dangers of the profession. All the misadventures I witnessed were so many experiences the more from which I drew up rules
for my conduct, so that my lot should be less precarious than that of
my predecessors.

I have spoken of Gaffré, under whose orders I was in some sense
placed when I entered the service. Gaffré was then the only secret agent
on a salary. I had no sooner joined up than the notion took him to get
rid of me. I pretended that I was unaware of his intention, and, if he
proposed to ruin me, on my side I meditated ways to foil his projects. I
was engaged with a strong party, for Gaffré was cunning. When I knew
him, he was called the dean of thieves. He had begun at the age of
eight, and at eighteen he had been whipped and branded in the Place
du Vieux Marché, Rouen. His mother was the mistress of the famous
Flambard, chief of police in that city. At first she tried to save him, but
although she was one of the most beautiful Jewesses of her time, the
magistrates granted nothing to her charms; Gaffré was too guilty. He
was banished. However, he did not leave France, and when the
Revolution broke out, he was not slow to resume the course of his
exploits with a band of *chauffeurs* or brigands among whom he figured
under the name of Caille.

As is the case with most thieves, Gaffré had perfected his education
in prison. There he became universal; that is to say, there was no sort of
graft in which he was not a past-master. So, contrary to custom, he
adopted no speciality; he was essentially the man of the occasion; everything served his turn, from murder to picking pockets. This general
aptitude and variety of means had enabled him to amass a small hoard.
He could have lived without 'working,' but people of Gaffré's caste are
industrious. Although he was rather well remunerated by the police, he
added to his appointments the produce of some illicit bits of good luck,
which did not prevent his being considerably esteemed in his quarter,

where, with his acolyte Francfort, he had been named captain in the National Guard.

Gaffré was afraid that I would supplant him, but the old fox was not sufficiently skilful to hide his apprehensions from me; I watched him, and I was not slow to discover that he was manœuvring to get me into a trap. I appeared to be running straight into it, and he was already inwardly enjoying his victory, when, in the wish to play me a trick which I guessed, he was caught in his own net. As a result of this event, he was confined in the dépôt for eight months.

I never let Gaffré know that I suspected his perfidy. He continued to dissimulate his hate for me, so that to all appearances we were the best friends in the world. There were also several thieves who were secret agents with whom I had been associated during my imprisonment. They detested me cordially, and, although we were pleasant to each other, they could flatter themselves that their dislike was requited. Goupil, the Saint George of savatte, was one of those who pursued me with his intimacy; constantly attaching himself to my person, he filled the office of tempter, but he was no more lucky or skilful than Gaffré. They all tried to get their hooks into me, but thanks to the advice of M. Henry I was invulnerable.

Gaffré had recovered his liberty, but he did not renounce his design of compromising me. He plotted with Manigant and Compère to get me sentenced, but as I was persuaded that as he had failed the first time, he would be sure to return to the charge, I was constantly on the watch.

One day there was a religious ceremony at Saint-Roch which was certain to attract a large crowd. Gaffré announced that he had been ordered to go there with me. 'I'll also take our friends Compère and Manigant,' he told me. 'We are informed that there are many strange thieves in Paris at the moment, and they can point out those they know.' 'Take whom you wish,' I answered, and we went.

When we arrived, there was a considerable crowd; duty demanded that we should not all congregate on one spot. Manigant and Gaffré went forward. Suddenly at the place where they were, I noticed that they squeezed against an old man. Pressed against a pillar, he did not know what to do. In respect for the holy place he did not cry out, but his whole face was contorted, his peruke was in disarray; he lost his foothold; his hat, which he followed with his eyes with remarkable anxiety, bounded from shoulder to shoulder, sometimes getting farther, sometimes nearer, but always rolling. 'Gentlemen, I pray you,' were the only words he pronounced in a pitiful tone; holding his gold-headed cane in one hand, and a snuffbox and a handkerchief in the other, he waved both arms in the air.

I comprehended that they were taking his watch, but what could I do? I was too far from the old man; any advice I could give would be too late; then Gaffré was a witness and an actor in the scene. If he said nothing, he doubtless had reasons for keeping silent. I made the wisest decision; I kept silent in order to see what would happen. In the space of the two hours the service lasted, I had occasion to observe five or six of these artificial crushes in which I always saw Gaffré and Manigant. The latter was one of the most skilful pickpockets in Paris. The small séance in the church of Saint-Roch was not most productive; however, without counting the old man's watch, he took two purses and some other objects of little value.

When the ceremony was over, we went to dinner at an eating-house. The faithful paid the expenses of this repast, and nothing was spared. We drank freely, and at dessert they confided to me what it would have been impossible to hide. First, there was the matter of the purses, in which they found a hundred and seventy-five francs. When the bill was paid, there were a hundred francs left, and they gave me twenty francs as my share, recommending me to be discreet. As money bears no name, I thought there was no inconvenience in accepting it. The guests showed that they were delighted at my having come through, and two flasks of Beaune were emptied to celebrate my initiation. They did not talk about the watch; I said nothing so as not to appear better informed than they wanted me to be, but I was all eyes and ears. I soon acquired the certainty that Gaffré had the watch. Then I pretended to be drunk, and the waiter led me out. As soon as I was alone, I wrote the following note in pencil:

Gaffré and Manigant have just stolen a watch in the church of Saint-Roch; in an hour, at least if they do not change their minds, they will go to the Marché Saint-Jean. Gaffré carries the object.

I went downstairs in all haste, and while Gaffré and his accomplice believed me still on the fifth floor, I was in the street where I sent a messenger to M. Henry. I went back upstairs without loss of time; my absence had not been too long. When I reappeared, I was out of breath and red as a cock. They asked me if I felt better.

'Yes, much,' I babbled, nearly falling on the table. They tried to give me some sugar and water. 'What!' I cried, 'water for me, me water!'

'Yes, take it, it will do you good!'

'You believe so?'

I reached for it, but instead of taking the glass, I upset it and broke it. I then gave myself to some drunken jokes which diverted the spirits of the society. When I supposed that M. Henry had had time to receive my despatch and take his measures, I imperceptibly recovered my composure.

When we withdrew, I saw with pleasure that our itinerary was not changed. In fact, we took the direction of the Marché Saint-Jean, where there was a guardhouse. When I saw from a distance soldiers sitting before the door, I suspected the less that their presence on the public way was the result of my message, in that Inspector Manager was on observation behind them. When we passed, they came to us, took us politely by the arm, and invited us to enter the post. Gaffré could not imagine what that meant; he thought the soldiers had made a mistake. He wanted to argue; they summoned him to obey, and soon after he had to submit to being searched. They began with me and found nothing. Then came Gaffré's turn; he was uncomfortable; finally, the fatal watch came out of his fob; he was slightly disconcerted. But when they were examining him and he heard the commissioner say to his secretary, 'Write, a watch mounted in brilliants,' he grew pale, and looked at me. Had he any suspicion from whom that came? I do not think so; for he was convinced that I was ignorant of the theft of the watch, and, more, he was convinced that even if I did know about it, I could not have squealed, since I had not left him.

On being questioned, Gaffré pretended that he had bought the watch; they were persuaded that he was lying, but, as the person who had been robbed was not present to demand it, it was impossible to condemn him. However, he was held a long time administratively, and after a long stay in Bicêtre, he was sent to Tours. Later he returned to Paris. This scoundrel died in 1822.

At this time the police had so little confidence in their agents that there was no sort of expedient to which they did not have recourse to test them.

One day Goupil was detached on my account and he made me a singular proposition.

'You know François, the tavern-keeper?' he asked me.

'Yes, what of it?'

'If you want to, we'll pull a tooth.'

'And how?'

'Several times he's addressed the Prefecture to obtain permission to stay open a part of the night; they've always refused, and I've given him to understand that it depends on you to get his request granted.'

'You're wrong, for I can do nothing.'

'You can do nothing! That's news! Certainly you can do nothing, but you can always give him the hope that you'll obtain it for him. If you play it well, François is a gentleman who will finance us. He's already warned that you have a drag with the administration; he has a good opinion of you, so without doubt he'll give up at the first request.'

'Do you think he'll let go the money?'

'Do I think so? He'll think as much of six hundred francs as a farthing; we'll grab the stakes and then send him kiting.'

'All right, but if he kicks up a row?'

'Oh, well, send him about his business. Besides, don't worry, I'll take charge of everything.' Goupil took me by the hand, and holding it in his, continued: 'I'll go to François and announce you for this evening. I shall be supposed to have you at the rendezvous at eight o'clock, but you'll only come at eleven, because, so to speak, you've been delayed. At midnight they'll tell us to go; then you'll pretend to be offended, and François will give you the boot. You are a man in the know, the rest goes without saying. Au revoir.'

Goupil at once went toward La Courtille, where he went rather frequently, and I toward the Prefecture of Police, where I told M. Henry about the proposition which had been made me.

'I hope,' said the chief, 'that you'll not lend yourself to this intrigue.'

I protested that I was in no way disposed to, and he showed that he knew that I was of good will, as I had warned him.

'Now,' he said, 'I'm going to give you a proof of my interest in you,' and he got up to take a box which he opened. 'You see it's full; those are the reports against you; there's none lacking; however, I employ you, because I don't believe a word of them.'

These reports were the work of inspectors and the regular police who out of jealousy accused me of thieving constantly.

Gaffré and Goupil had failed in their manœuvres to compromise me, so Corvet in his turn wanted to try and see whether I would not succumb. One morning I wanted to procure some information, so I went to this agent's house. His wife was also attached to the police. I found the married pair in their lodgings. Although I knew them only from having co-operated with them in several unimportant discoveries, they put so much kindness into giving me the information for which I asked, that, as a man who knew how to live with people with whom he had relations, I offered to regale them with a bottle of wine at the nearest wine-shop. Corvet alone accepted, and we went together to install ourselves in a private room.

The wine was excellent; we drank one bottle, then a second, then a third. A private room and three bottles of wine are more than enough to inspire confidence. For about an hour I thought that I saw that Corvet had some overture to make to me. At last, as he was a little above himself, he said, 'Listen, Vidocq,' abruptly placing his glass on the table, 'You're a good fellow, but you're not frank with your friends. We know you "work," but you're double-faced. If it weren't for that, we could do good business.'

At first I seemed not to understand.

'Come,' he said, 'I'm going to talk to you like a brother; after that I don't think you'll play any more tricks. Serving the police is good, that's right; but one doesn't make much. Look, if you want to be discreet, there are two or three jobs I have my eye on. We'll do them together; that won't prevent us from doing our friends afterward.'

'What!' I said. 'Would you abuse the confidence they have in you? That's no good, and I swear that if they knew in the shop, they'd send you to spend two or three years at Bicêtre.'

'Oh, there you go like the rest,' Corvet observed. 'You're too delicate. You, delicate!'

I showed my astonishment at such language, and I added that I was persuaded that he intended to test me, or perhaps set a trap.

'A trap!' he cried. 'A trap, it isn't worth the trouble! I'd rather be sentenced for life; one must be an ass to think that. When I say a thing, I mean it. And to prove that it isn't as you believe, I'm going to tell you that no later than this evening, I'm going to make a haul. I've already prepared all my stuff; the false keys are tried. If you want to come with me, you'll see how I've arranged.'

'I thought as much. Either you've lost your mind, or you want to get around me.'

'Come, do you think I've as little feeling as that? Since I tell you that you needn't put your finger in the pie, what more is necessary? I'll do the job with my wife; it's not the first time I've taken her, but it depends on you whether it will be the last. With two men there are always more resources. This job today doesn't concern you. You'll wait for us on the corner of rue de la Tabletterie, in the café. It's nearly opposite the house where we'll do the snitching, and, as soon as you see us come out, you follow us. We'll go and sell the stuff, and you shall have your part. After that you'll no longer distrust us.'

There was such an appearance of sincerity that I really did not know what to think of Corvet. Did he want an associate or did he want to ruin me? I still had some doubts in this regard, but in either case, it was obvious that Corvet was a knave. By his own confession his wife and he committed robberies. If he spoke the truth, it was my duty to bring him to justice; if, on the contrary, he was lying in the single hope of drawing me into a criminal act to denounce me, it was best to push the intrigue to its dénouement; it was lost time to show the authorities that he wanted to tempt me. I tried to turn Corvet away from his design, but when I saw that he persisted, I pretended to let myself be won over.

'Come,' I said, 'since the matter is decided, I accept your offer.'

He at once embraced me, and the rendezvous was fixed at a wine merchant's at four o'clock. Corvet went home. When he had left me, I wrote to M. Allemain, police commissioner, rue Cimetière Saint-Nicholas, to inform him of the robbery which was to be committed that evening. At the same time I gave him all the instructions necessary to take the culprits in the very act.

At the hour agreed upon, I was at the post. Corvet and his wife did not delay their appearance. I consumed with them the *gallon de rigueur,* and when they had this encouragement, they went their way to their task. A moment later I saw them enter an alley in the rue de la Haumerie. The commissioner had taken his measures so well that they arrested the couple at the moment when, laden with booty, they came out of the room which they had stripped. This interesting pair was sentenced to ten years in irons.

Once I had arrived at the post of Chief of the Sûreté, I no longer had to beware of the traps in which they had so often tried to take me. The time of proofs was over; but it was necessary to be on guard against the base jealousy of some of my subordinates who coveted my place and did everything to supplant me.

Coco-Lacour was notably one of those who took the most trouble to fawn upon me and injure me at the same time. At the time this wheedler turned aside fifty yards and would have upset all the chairs in a church to salute me, I was absolutely sure that there was a snake in the grass. No one was less taken in than I by the slight attentions of a man who bent double when he only needed to bow. But as I was conscious that I did my duty, it did not concern me whether this exaggerated politeness was true or false.

Hardly a day went by that my spies did not warn me that Lacour was the soul of certain secret meetings where there was every sort of talk about me. They said his aim was to bring about my fall; he had formed a party which conspired with him; I was the tyrant who must be brought down. At first the conspirators were content with abuse, and as my fall was constantly in view, for their mutual pleasure they vied with one another in predicting it. Each one shared in advance the heritage of Alexander. From blustering and scandal Lacour and his faithful passed to more realistic drama. At the approach of the assizes, during which Peyois, Leblanc, Berthelet, and Lefebre were to be tried for burglary, they spread the rumour that I was on the verge of a catastrophe and that I really could not get out of it with clean hands.

This prophecy was launched among all the wine merchants in the vicinity of the Palais de Justice and was promptly reported to me. But I was no more disturbed by it than by so many others which had not been realized. Only I thought I noticed that Lacour doubled his facility and slight cares in my regard. He saluted me more respectfully and more affectionately than usual; his eyes avoided meeting mine more and more. At the same time I noticed with three others of my agents, Chrétien, Utinet, and Decostard, a doubling of zeal for service and a complaisance which astonished me. I was instructed that these gentlemen had frequent conferences with Lacour; without the least thought in the world of spying on them in my personal interest, I surprised them whispering and talking about me.

One evening I heard one of them rejoicing that I could not parry the thrust which they were going to aim at me. But what was this thrust? I had no idea, but when Peyois and his fellow accused were tried, the judicial proceedings revealed to me an atrocious machination, tending to establish that I was the instigator of the crime which had brought them to the dock. Peyois pretended that he had addressed himself to me to ask whether I knew a recruiting sergeant who had to furnish a substitute; that I had proposed the robbery to him, and that I had even given him three francs to buy the jimmy with which the burglary had been committed.

Berthelet and Lefèbre confirmed what Peyois had said, and a wine merchant, named Leblanc, who was implicated with them and who appeared to have been the real lender of the funds to acquire the instrument, encouraged them to persevere in a system of defence, which, if it was admitted, would necessarily have the effect of absolving him. The advocates who pleaded this case did not fail to make all possible use of the pretended instigation imputed to me. As they said after the conviction, if they had not decided the jury to render a decision favourable to their clients, at least they had cast terrible suspicions against me in the minds of the judges and the public. Then I thought it urgent to clear myself, and, certain of my innocence, I prayed the Prefect of Police to order an investigation to prove the truth.

Peyois, Berthelet, and Lefèbre had just been sentenced; I imagined that, as they no longer had any interest in maintaining the lie, they would confess that they had slandered me. I presumed further, that in case their conduct had been the result of a suggestion, they would make no difficulties in naming the advisers of the imposture which they had had the audacity to sustain before justice.

The Prefect ordered the enquiry I had solicited, and at the moment I was entrusting the direction of it to M. Fleuriais, police commissioner for that quarter of the city, a first document, on which I had not counted, proved the prelude for my justification. It was a letter from Berthelet to the wine merchant Leblanc, who had been declared not guilty. It read in part:

> If you abandon me, I will make a new revelation
> about the jimmy you furnished, and, what is more, was
> found in your house, which we have hidden from justice,
> and that a chief of police has been cited in this affair,
> although he is innocent, and that they have tried to make
> him a victim.

According to usage this letter, which was to pass secretly, was given to the jailer, who took cognizance of it and at once sent it to the Prefecture of Police. In consequence, Leblanc was unable either to answer it or come to Berthelet's aid; the latter lost patience, and in the execution of his threats, he wrote another letter, to me this time. It said in part:

> I, Berthelet, wish to make known in the presence of
> the authorities the truth and your innocence. I declare
> that I know where the jimmy was bought, from what
> house it came, and the name of the one who furnished it.

M. Fleuriais questioned Berthelet, who declared that the jimmy cost forty-five sous; that it had been bought in the Faubourg du Temple, at a junk-shop, and that Leblanc, informed of the use they were to make of it, had advanced the money to pay for it. He ended his declaration as follows: 'Leblanc, who was tried with us, had pledged me not to charge him, and not to refute Peyois, who was to say that it was M. Vidocq who had given me three francs to buy the jimmy; and he promised to give me a sum of money if I would sustain the same thing; I consented in the fear that if I told the truth, my case would be worse.'

Lefèbre was then brought in, without his having been able to communicate with Berthelet; he confirmed the latter's declaration in what concerned Leblanc. 'If I did not say,' he added, 'that it was he who furnished the money to buy the jimmy, it was because Peyois had induced me to say that it was he, Peyois, who had bought it. As Peyois was compromised in the robbery, he did not want to charge Leblanc, who had done well by him and who might do more as a result.'

One Egly, chief of the employees of the Conciergerie, and Lecomte and Vermont, two prisoners detained in the place, reported several conversations in which Berthelet, Lefèbre, and Peyois had agreed before them that they would inculpate me wrongfully. All three condemned had agreed to say in their testimony that I had constantly influenced them to do wrong. Vermont told further that one day, blaming them for compromising me without a motive, they had answered, 'Bah, we'd compromise the Holy Father to save ourselves; but it turned out badly.'

Peyois, the youngest of the condemned, was less frank in his answers; his friendship for Leblanc led him at first to conceal part of the truth; however, he could not help admitting that I was foreign to the purchase of the jimmy.

Three days after Peyois had been transferred to Bicêtre, he wrote to the chief of the second division of the Prefecture of Police and confessed that he had constantly imposed on justice; he also testified a desire to make sincere revelations. This time the whole truth was to be known. Utinet, Chrétien, Decostard, and Coco-Lacour, who had come to the hearing to depose in the judgment of the imposture, were suddenly unveiled; it became evident that Chrétien had used every effort in the intrigue which was to bring about my expulsion from the police.

A declaration which the mayor of Gentilly received brought to light the entire infamy of this machination, of which Lacour, Chrétien, Decostard, and Utinet had promised the complete success. They had sent Peyois to me, when he had come on the pretext of asking whether I could indicate a recruiting officer who needed a substitute; again, it was they who had engaged Berthelet to present himself at my office to advise me of certain robberies which might be committed. They had also set up a scaffolding of probability as a result of my relations with thieves before they were arrested; under the weight of this structure they planned to overpower me.

According to all appearances, it was not impossible that they had sometimes closed their eyes on the expeditions of Peyois and his fellows on the condition that, if they were taken in the very act, they would adopt a system of defence in conformity with their interests. There existed no trace of a transaction of this kind, but it must have occurred, and the procedure of my agents, either during the examination or since the sentence of the culprits, left not the slightest doubt in this regard. When Peyois was arrested, Utinet and Chrétien at once went to La Force and had an interview with him in which they persuaded him that it was only by accusing me that he could give his case a favourable turn; that if he did not want to be condemned, he had only to call them as witnesses as to what they had agreed in advance; that they would sustain his assertion, and depose in the same sense as he; that they would even say that they had seen him give me the sum of three francs.

The two agents did not limit themselves to this advice; to be certain that in any event Peyois would not retract, they told him that they had at their service a powerful protector whose influence would save him from any sort of sentence, and who, if by chance a sentence was inevitable, would still have a sufficiently long arm to break the condemnation.

When the hearings opened, Utinet, Chrétien, Lacour, and Decostard hurried to attest the facts which Peyois imputed to me. However, this young man, to whom they had promised impunity, was astonished by the verdict. They apprehended that, at last enlightened on his position, he would repent of his deception and would uncover their perfidy; therefore, they hastened to reanimate his hopes, and not only did they demand that he lodge an appeal, but they offered to engage a defender at their expense and also to pay all the expenses of the appeal. Peyois's mother was equally importuned by the intriguers; they made her the same offers of services and the same promises. Lacour, Decostard, and Chrétien took her to a wine merchant's, and there, in the presence of a bottle of wine and the woman Leblanc, they exerted all their influence to demonstrate to Peyois's mother that if she seconded them and her son was submissive to their opinion, it would be easy to save him. 'Don't worry,' said Chrétien, 'we'll do everything necessary.'

Such was the information the enquiry produced. It became evident to the magistrates that the incident of the jimmy furnished by Vidocq was an invention of my agents.

XXII
MY RENOWN INCREASES

I SHOULD HAVE WISHED to spare the reader an account of matters which are only of interest to my reputation, but before I go further, I desire to show that it is not always well to put faith in the idle stories my enemies have given out against me. What did not the detectives, the thieves, and the crooks think up? All, none less than the others, wanted to see me evicted from the police.

'So-and-so is locked up,' a thief told his woman when he came back to his shelter in the morning or evening.

'It's not possible!'

'Oh, my God, it's as I tell you.'

'Who did it?'

'Do you need to ask? That scoundrel of a Vidocq.'

Two promoters – they are numerous in Paris – would meet.

'Have you heard the news? Poor Harrisson is in La Force.'

'You're joking.'

'I wish I were; he was busy treating for some merchandise on which I'd have had a commission. Oh, well, my dear fellow, the devil was in it; he was arrested on taking delivery.'

'By whom?'

'By Vidocq.'

'The wretch!'

If a capture of great importance was announced at the Prefecture, if I had seized some great criminal whose tracks the shrewdest among the agents had lost a hundred times, all at once the bees began to hum, 'Again it's that cursed Vidocq who's taken him.' The length of the rue de Jerusalem and rue Sainte-Anne, from pub to pub, the echo repeated with an accent of spite, 'Vidocq again; always Vidocq.' That name resounded in the ears of the cabal more disagreeably than that of the Just in the ears of the Athenians.

How happy that clique of thieves, crooks, and informers would have been, if, expressly to provide a means of getting rid of me, they could have revived the law of ostracism! But except for the sort of conspiracies of which M. Coco and his accomplices promised so fortunate a dénouement, what could they do? In the hive silence was imposed on the drones by a 'Watch Vidocq!' The leaders said, 'Take him for an example; what activity he displays! He's always about night and day; he never sleeps; with four men like him, one could answer for the safety of the capital.' This praise irritated the sleepers, but did not tempt them; if they awoke, it was only glass in hand. Instead of rushing where duty called, they formed a small committee and amused themselves working over my carcass.

Thieves often fell to me when I least expected it; one might say that their evil genius urged them to come and find me. It must be agreed that those who threw themselves into the wolf's throat were terribly chancy or devilish stupid. As I saw the ease with which most of them gave themselves up, I was always astonished that they had chosen a profession in which so many precautions are necessary to avert perils. Some were so simple that I considered almost miraculous the impunity which they had enjoyed until the moment they met me for their sins. It is unbelievable that individuals who were created expressly to fall into all snares had waited my coming into the police to let themselves be taken. Before my time the police must have operated without common sense, or else I was favoured by singular luck. In any case luck is worth a good deal, as one may judge from the following incident.

One day toward dusk, dressed as a wharf labourer, I was sitting on the parapet of the Quai de Grèves, when I saw coming toward me an individual whom I recognized as one of the habitués of the Petite Chaise and Bon Puits, two pubs famous among the thieves.

'Good evening, Jean Louis,' this individual accosted me.

'Good evening, my boy.'

'What the devil are you doing there? You look sad enough to scare the life out of anyone.'

'What do you expect, my man? When one is hungry, one doesn't laugh.'

'Hungry! That's a little strong for one who passes for a thief.'

'Nevertheless, that's it.'

'Well, come on and take a drink at Niguénac's. I still have twenty sous, and one must eat.'

He took me to the wine merchant's, ordered a half-litre, left me alone a moment, and came back with two pounds of potatoes. 'Come,' he said, placing them smoking hot on the table, 'here are some gudgeons fished up with pickaxes.'

Although I had had an excellent dinner an hour before, I fell on the potatoes and devoured them as if I had not eaten for two days. Mouthful followed mouthful with prodigious speed. I gave only a twist and down it went; I did not see why I was not choked; my stomach had never been more complaisant. Finally, I came to the end of my ration; the meal was over; my comrade offered me a drink, and spoke in the following terms.

'On the faith of a friend, and as sure as my name's Masson, which was my father's name and his father's before him, I've always looked on you as a good fellow. I know that you've had great troubles; I've been told that; but the Devil isn't always at a poor man's door, and, if you want, I can make you earn something.'

'That wouldn't be without need, for I'm seedy.'

'I see it, I see it [looking at my clothes which were fairly ragged]; it looks as though you were out of luck for the moment.'

'Oh, yes, I sure need to get a fresh rig.'

'In that case, come with me; I can open a room which I'll rifle this evening.'

'Tell me where; if I'm to go into the affair, I must know.'

'It's simple; all you have to do is to stay on watch.'

'Oh, if that's so, I'm your man. But you could tell me in two words.'

'Don't worry, I tell you. My plan is made; it's certain money; the fence is only two steps away. As soon as we've stolen, we've sold; it's rich; I'll do well for you.'

'Rich, eh? Well, let's go.'

Masson led me along the boulevard Saint-Denis until we came to a large pile of stones. He stopped there, looked around to see whether anyone was noticing him, and then approached the pile, removed some rubble, plunged his arm into a cavity, and brought forth a bunch of keys. He then led me to the neighbourhood of the place, nearly opposite a police station, and pointed out a house into which he was going to enter.

'At present, my friend,' he said, 'don't go far, and keep your eyes open. I'm going to see whether the woman is out.'

Masson opened the door on the alley, but it had hardly closed on him before I ran to the station, where the chief recognized me. I warned him hastily that a robbery was being committed at that very moment, and that there was no time to lose if he wanted to seize the thief in possession of the things he was carrying off. When I had given warning, I withdrew and went back to the place where Masson had left me. I was hardly there when someone came toward me.

'Is that you, Jean Louis?'

'Yes, it's me,' I answered, expressing my astonishment that he came back with empty hands.

'Don't talk about it! A devil of a neighbour came to the landing and bothered me; but what's postponed isn't lost. You'll see presently.'

He left me again, and soon reappeared with an enormous package, under the weight of which he seemed to sink. He passed in front of me without saying a word; I followed, and walking in close file two men of the guard, armed only with bayonets, watched him, making as little noise as possible.

It was important to know where he was going to deposit his burden; he entered a merchant's, rue du Four, where he stayed only a short time. 'That was heavy,' he said, when he came out, 'and I have yet another trip to make.'

I let him operate. He again went up into the room from which he was moving the furniture, and ten minutes had hardly passed when he came down carrying on his head a whole bed, mattress, cushions, sheets, and coverlet. He had not had time to unmake it. As he was about to cross the threshold, bothered by the narrow door, he nearly fell over backwards; but he presently regained his equilibrium and walked off, signing me to go with him.

At the turn of the street, he came near me and said in a low voice, 'I think I'll go back a third time, if you'll go with me and help me take down the curtains from the bed and the window.'

'That's understood,' I answered. 'When one sleeps on straw, curtains are a luxury.'

'Yes, it's grand,' he answered, smiling. 'We've talked enough; don't come farther; I'll pick you up on the way back.'

Masson went on his way, but within two steps we were both arrested. We were taken to the station, then before the commissioner and questioned.

'There are two of you,' said the officer to Masson, and, pointing to me, 'What's that man? Doubtless a thief like you are.'

'What's that man? Do I know? Ask him what he is. When I've seen him again, with this time, it will make twice.'

'Do you tell me that you're not in connivance and weren't together?'

'There was no connivance, my respectable commissioner. He went one way; I came another; suddenly, as he brushed by me, I felt something slip; it was a pillow. I told him, and he picked it up; then the guard arrived and pinched us both.'

The story was good, and I was careful not to refute Masson. On the contrary, I supported him; finally, the commissioner appeared convinced. 'Have you papers?' he asked me. I exhibited my permit, which he judged in order, and my dismissal was pronounced. Marked satisfaction showed on Masson's features when he heard addressed to me the words, 'Go to bed.' This was the formula for setting me at liberty, and he was so joyous that one would have had to be blind not to see it.

He was held as a thief, but it was necessary to take the fence before she had time to get rid of the things deposited with her. The search took place immediately, and surprised, surrounded by material witnesses which were overwhelming, the shop was closed to commerce at the time when she least expected it.

Masson was taken to the Prefecture. The next day, according to the custom established among thieves from time immemorial, I sent him a small four-pound loaf, a ham, and a half-crown. They reported that he was moved by this attention, but he did not suspect that the one who paid for the fraternity was the cause of his misadventure. It was only at La Force that he learned that Jean Louis and Vidocq were one and the same.

One night, half of which I had spent in the evil resorts in the Halle, hoping to meet some thieves who, in that good humour which two or three glasses produce, would talk about their affairs, past, present, and to come, I was withdrawing rather displeased at having swallowed to the detriment of my stomach and to no purpose a goodly number of small glasses of that mitigated spirit, to which vitriol gives a flavour, when, near the corner of the rue des Coutures Saint-Gervais, I saw several persons huddled in the doorways. By the light of the street-lamps I soon made out near them some packages, the size of which they tried to conceal, but their indiscreet whiteness could not fail to attract attention.

Packages at this hour and men who sought the shelter of a door-way when not a drop of water was falling! It did not take a large dose of perspicacity to discover in such a combination of circumstances all that characterizes a suspicious occurrence. I concluded that the men were thieves, and that the packages were the booty they had just stolen. 'Good,' I said to myself; 'seem to do nothing, follow the cortège when it starts, and if it passes a station, lock them up! In the contrary case, I'll follow them where they sleep, take the number, and send for the police.'

So I was weaving my knot, without seeming to be uneasy about what I left behind me; I had hardly taken ten steps when someone called: 'Jean Louis!' It was the voice of a man named Richelot whom I had often met at meetings of thieves. I stopped.

'Oh, good evening, Richelot,' I said. 'What the devil are you doing at this hour in this quarter? Are you alone? How seared you look!'

'At least one ought to be; I've just been bothered on the boulevard du Temple.'

'Bothered, and how?'

'Come nearer; do you see those friends and the bales? You would say as much if you were loaded with stolen goods!'

I approached; suddenly the whole band arose, and when they were standing I recognized Lapierre, Comméry, Lenoir, and Dubuisson. All four were eager to give me a good reception and extend the hand of friendship.

'Well,' said Comméry, 'we've had a fine escape; my heart's still beating the alarm; put your hand there and feel how it goes ticktack.'

'That's nothing,' I answered. 'You're stupid. You ought to have a cab around to take the bundles. You're poor thieves.'

'Poor thieves if you wish, but we had no cab, and we had to get away. That's the reason we went into the little streets.'

'Where are you going now? If I can be useful to you...'

'If you want to scout ahead and come with us to the rue Saint-Sébastien, where we're going to put the stuff, you shall have your part.'

'With pleasure, friends.'

'In that case go ahead, and look and see whether there's anyone, or a patrol.'

Richelot and his companions at once seized their packages, and I went forward. Our journey was lucky, and we arrived without trouble at the door of the house. Each of us took off our shoes to make less noise in going upstairs. We were on the third-floor landing; we were expected; a door opened gently, and we entered a large room dimly lighted, whose tenant I recognized as a journeyman in a lumber yard, who had already been in the hands of justice. Although he did not know me, my presence seemed to disturb him, and while he helped to hide the packages under the bed, I thought I noticed that he asked a question in a low tone, the answer to which spoken aloud revealed its tenor.

'It's Jean Louis, a good fellow, don't worry,' said Richelot. 'I'd answer for him as for myself.'

'If that's the case, let's drink a drop.' He climbed on a sort of stool, and passing his arm along the cornice of an old cupboard brought down a full jar. The glass and the jar passed from hand to hand, and when each had drunk enough, we threw ourselves crosswise on the beds until morning. At daybreak we heard the cry of a chimney-sweep in the streets.

Richelot shook his neighbour, 'Oh, Lapierre, come on to the fence.'

'Let me sleep,' was the answer.

'Come, move.'

'Go alone, or take Lenoir.'

'Oh, God,' I said, 'you're afraid. I'll go, if you'll point out the place.'

'You're right, Jean Louis,' said Richelot. 'But the fence doesn't know you, and she only wants to receive us. Since you propose it, we'll go together.'

We went. The fence lived in rue de Bretagne, No. 14, in the house of a pork butcher who was really the proprietor. Richelot entered the shop and enquired whether Madame Bras was at home. The answer was yes, and after entering an alley we climbed to the third floor. Madame Bras had not gone out, but she esteemed it an honour not to receive anyone during the day.

'At least,' said Richelot, 'if you can't take the merchandise now, give us something on account. Come, it's good stuff, and you know we're honest.'

'That's true, but I can't compromise myself for your beautiful eyes. Come back this evening; all cats are grey at night.'

Richelot took every way to get some money out of her, but she was inexorable, and we retired without having obtained anything. My companion swore, cursed, raged; one should have heard him.

'Well,' I said, 'don't think that all is lost. Why worry? He who refuses may lose; if she won't, another will. Come with me to my fence; I'm sure that she'll lend me five bullets.'

We went to rue Neuve Saint-François, where I had my domicile. I whistled and made Annette hear; she came down in a hurry, and joined us at the comer.

'Bonjour, madame.'

'Bonjour, Jean Louis.'

'Come, if you're good, you'd lend us twenty francs, and I'll return them this evening.'

'Yes, this evening! If you win something, you'll go to La Courtille.'

'No, I assure you that I'll be prompt.'

'Is that so? I don't want to refuse. Come with me, while your comrade waits for you at the pub on the corner of rue de l'Oseille.'

When I was alone with Annette, I gave her my instructions, and when I was sure that she understood, I went to rejoin Richelot at the pub.

'There they are,' I said , showing him twenty francs. 'That's what I call a good one.'

After we had emptied a glass, we went to regain our lodgings, which we entered with a Norman goose of the largest size. At the same time I put the money in evidence, and, as it was destined to revictual us, our host went to get a dozen litres of wine and three loaves of bread. We had such good appetites that all the provisions had no sooner appeared than they disappeared. The jar was emptied to the last drop.

When our meal was over, they talked of opening the packages; they contained magnificent linen, sheets, extremely fine chemises, dresses ornamented with superb embroidery, cravats, stockings, etc.; all these objects were still uncreased. The thieves told me that they had made this haul in one of the finest houses in rue de l'Échiquier, where they had got in through a window after breaking the iron bars.

When the inventory was ended, I offered the opinion that they should make the stuff up in different lots so as not to sell it all in one place. I suggested that they would give as much for half as for the whole, and it was better to get twice as much. The comrades ranged themselves for my opinion and made up the booty in two parts. Now the placing had to be arranged; they were already sure of the sale of one lot, but it was necessary to get a buyer for the surplus. A clothing merchant, named Pomme Rouge who lived in the rue de la Juiverie, was the individual I indicated. He had been described to me for a long time as a buyer from the first comer. Here was an occasion to test him. I did not want to let it escape, for if he succumbed, the result of my combinations would be fine, for instead of one fence, I should arrest two.

It was agreed that the first offer was to be made my man, but they could attempt nothing before night, and until then it would be deadly dull. Thieves haven't sufficient mental resource to keep company more than a quarter of an hour. However, it was necessary to kill time; we still had some money, and it was voted by acclamation to have wine. But they could not drink forever, so that insensibly they stopped using their mouths as funnels and opened them to chatter. The conversation turned on their comrades who were in prison, or who were awaiting trial, and they also talked about the police spies.

'Apropos of police spies,' said one of them, 'doubtless you've heard of a famous rascal who became one, Vidocq, do you know him?'

'Yes, yes, only by name,' echoed the rest.

'They say that when he came from prison where he was sentenced to twenty-four years, he was due for more than life on account of his escape.' And so on and so on.

At last Richelot brought this discussion to an end. 'But the sun's setting. It's time to sell; we'll finish in the cab on the way to the receiver's. I'll go and get one.'

We got into the cab and ordered the driver to stop at the corner of the rue de Bretagne and de Touraine. One of the receivers lived four steps away. Dubuisson, Comméry, and Lenoir got out, taking with them the part of the merchandise they had agreed to sell there. While they were concluding the bargain, by putting my head out of the cab door I saw that Annette had perfectly fulfilled my intentions. I saw inspectors, walking with their heads in the air as if they were looking for a number; others were walking back and forth, as if they were idle, doubtless roaming about in the neighbourhood because they had been posted there.

After we had waited ten minutes, we were rejoined by our comrades who had gone to Bras's; they had received one hundred and twenty-five francs for things which were worth at least six times as much. No matter, they had kept the core, and were quite satisfied to have realized anything, they were in such a hurry to enjoy themselves. We had remaining the packages reserved for Pomme Rouge.

When we reached rue de la Juiverie, Richelot said to me, 'Ah, you're to make the bargain, you know the fence.'

'That wouldn't be the scheme,' I answered. 'I owe him money, and we're on bad terms.'

I owed Pomme Rouge nothing, but we had seen each other. He was well aware that I was Vidocq, and it would have been imprudent to show myself. I left the thieves to arrange matters, and on their return, as the appearance of Annette in the neighbourhood of the shop made me sure that the police were ready to act, I moved that we pay off the cab and go to supper at the Grand Casuel on the Quai Pelletier.

Since our visit to Pomme Rouge, we were eighty francs the better off, so the sum at our disposal was enough to convince us that we need not fear running short, but we were not to enjoy the leisure to spend it. We had hardly breathed in our glasses when the guard entered, and behind it a string of inspectors. One should have seen the faces lengthen at their appearance. There was but one cry, 'We're done for...'

Thibault, one of the inspectors, invited us to exhibit our papers; some had none – others were not in form. I was among the latter. We were bound two by two and taken before the commissioner. Lapierre was coupled with me. 'Have you got good legs?' I said, very low. 'Yes,' he answered, and when we were at the top of the rue de la Tannerie, drawing a knife which I had up my sleeve, I cut the rope. 'Courage,

Lapierre, courage!' I cried. With a push of the elbow in the chest, I upset the veteran who held me by the arm; I made off, and in two jumps I was in a small alley which led to the Seine. Lapierre followed me, and together we reached the Quai des Ormes.

They had lost our traces. I was delighted to have escaped without being recognized. Lapierre was no less pleased than I, for, as he had had no time for reflection, he was far from supposing that I had mental reservations. However, if I had favoured his escape, it was in the hope of being introduced under his auspices into some other association of thieves. By fleeing with him, I banished the suspicions which his companions and he might conceive about me and I retained the good opinion they had of me. As a result, I hoped to manage new discoveries.

Lapierre was free, but I kept him in sight, and I was ready to give him up the moment he was no longer useful. Still running, we reached Port de l'Hôpital, where we stopped and entered a pub to regain our breath and rest. I ordered a drink to bring back our senses. He had not emptied his glass before he became more and more thoughtful. As I seemed to see in the eyes of my friend that dark point of distrust, which, if one does not take care, increases with such speed, I was very glad to give him some marks of interest, the effect of which was to reassure his troubled spirit. Such was my end in advising him to remove from his toilet some articles of little value, which, during the examination of the booty, he and his associates had immediately applied to their own use.

'What shall I do with them?' Lapierre asked me.

'Throw them into the water.'

'I'm not so foolish. New silk stockings and a neckpiece which isn't even hemmed!'

'You're joking, my man, throw them in.'

I observed that I had nothing compromising on me. 'You're like the hares,' I added. 'You lose your memory when you run. Don't you remember that there was no tie for me, and with calves of this size [I raised my trousers], do you want me to put on women's stockings?'

Thieves are both miserly and prodigal. They feel the necessity of getting rid of incriminating evidence, but their hearts bleed at doing so without a profit to themselves. What has been gained by theft is often so dearly paid for that the sacrifice is always painful.

Lapierre wanted at all costs to sell his stockings and neckpiece. We went together to rue de la Boucherie and offered them to a merchant, who gave us forty-five sous. Lapierre appeared to have made up his mind about the catastrophe at the Grand Casuel; however, he was constrained in his manners, and I judged well what was going on inside. In spite of my efforts to rehabilitate myself in his opinion, I was terribly suspect. Such a disposition was hardly favourable to my projects; persuaded that I had to finish with him as promptly as possible, I said to him, 'If you want to, we'll go to supper at Place Maubert.'

'All right,' he answered.

I took him to the Deux Frères, where I asked for wine, pork cutlets, and cheese. At eleven o'clock we were still at table; everyone had gone; our account was brought which amounted to four francs fifty centimes. I at once searched my pockets.

'My five-franc piece, my five-franc piece, where is it?' I went into all my pockets; I felt of myself from head to foot. 'My God, I must have lost it while I was running! Look, Lapierre, haven't you got it?'

'No, I've only forty-five sous.'

I offered the landlord two francs fifty centimes, promising him to bring the rest the next day, but he would not listen. In fact, he put his fist under my nose. 'Do not strike,' I said, 'do not strike, or...' He advanced, and with a master hand, I gave him a slap.

Immediately there was a row; Lapierre saw that it was going to turn nasty and thought it was time to get out; but at the moment he was getting to his feet, leaving me to get out of it as best I could, the waiter took him by the throat and shouted, 'Thief!'

The post was but two steps away; the soldiers rushed in, and for the second time that day we were placed between two ranks. My comrade tried to demonstrate to the corporal that it was not his fault, but the veteran did not waver, and they shut us up in jail. From that time on Lapierre became as taciturn and sad as a Trappist father; he did not open his lips. Finally, at two o'clock in the morning, the commissioner made his rounds and asked that the persons who had been arrested should be presented to him. Lapierre appeared the first and was told that he could go if he would consent to pay. I was called in my turn; I entered the office; I recognized M. Legoix and he recognized me too; in two words I explained the matter and indicated the place where the stockings and cravat had been sold. While he hastened to seize these objects, which were indispensable in bringing Lapierre to sentence, I went back to the latter.

He was no longer silent. 'The veil has fallen,' he said to me; 'I see now how it is.'

'Good, you play your part, but I'll speak more frankly. If you want me to tell you, I think that it was you who got us locked up.'

'No, my friend, it's not I; I don't know who it was, but I suspect you more than anyone else.'

At these words I got angry; he flew into a passion; threats were succeeded by deeds; we fought, and were separated. When we were no longer together, I found my hundred sous, and as the publican had not added to the account the slap he had received, it was sufficient not only to satisfy all his demands, but to offer the gentlemen of the guard – I will not say the stirrup cup, but that small drop which the civilian willingly pays for deliverance.

When this tribute was paid, there was no further reason to hold me. I left without paying my adieux to Lapierre, who was well charged, and the next day I knew that success had crowned my work. Bras and Pomme Rouge had been surprised surrounded by the material proofs of the infamous traffic they conducted. The thieves were seized with the effects which they had immediately put to their own use and they had been compelled to confess. Lapierre alone had attempted a denial, but, confronted by the merchant of the rue de la Boucherie, he ended by recognizing the man, and the accusing stockings and scarf. The whole band, thieves and receivers, were locked up in La Force to await judgment. There they soon learned that their comrade was Vidocq. Their sentence was confirmed and all were sent to prison. The evening of their departure I was present when the fatal collar was put on. When they saw me, they could not help laughing.

'Look at your work,' Lapierre said to me. 'Are you satisfied, scoundrel?'

'I haven't the slightest thing to reproach myself. I didn't advise you to steal. Didn't you call me? Why were you so confident? When one plies a trade like yours, one should be better on one's guard.'

'That's all right,' said Comméry. 'You'll be denounced and sent back to the galleys.'

'While I'm waiting, bon voyage! Keep my place, and if you ever come back to Paris, don't get caught in a trap.'

XXIII
THE CLUE OF THE TWO FOOTPRINTS

DURING THE SUMMER of 1812 a professional thief named Hotot, who for a long time had had aspirations to be restored to employment as a secret agent which he had practised before my admission to the police, offered his services for the fête at Saint-Cloud. This is one of the most brilliant around Paris, and in view of the crowd, pick-pockets are always there in large numbers.

Hotot was brought to me by a comrade on a Friday. His proceedings appeared to me the more extraordinary as previously I had given information about him which resulted in his being brought before the assizes. My first thought was that perhaps he wanted to get near me to play me a bad turn. I gave him a good reception, however, and so showed my satisfaction that he did not doubt my wish to be useful to him. I put so much sincerity into my protestations of kindness in his regard that it was impossible for him to penetrate my intentions.

A sudden change in his countenance at once convinced me that by accepting his proposition I favoured projects which he did not want to confide to me. I saw that he was congratulating himself on having duped me. However that might be, I pretended to have the greatest confidence in him, and it was arranged that on the Sunday, at two o'clock, he would take his post near the main pond to point out to us the thieves of his acquaintance, who, he said, would come to work at that place.

On the day appointed, I went to Saint-Cloud with the only two agents who were then under my orders. When we reached the appointed spot, I sought Hotot; I walked up and down; I looked in all directions, but there was no Hotot. At last, after waiting for an hour and a half, I lost patience and detached one of my agents to explore the crowd and try to find our auxiliary whose lack of punctuality was as suspicious as his zeal.

The agent searched for a whole hour, and, tired of scouring the garden and the park in all directions, he came back and announced that he could not run across Hotot. A moment after I saw the latter running toward me, dripping with perspiration.

'Do you know,' he told me, 'I just raised six thieves, but they saw me and decamped; it's too bad, for they were biting, but what's deferred isn't lost; I'll meet them again another time.'

I appeared to accept this story as it was spoken, and Hotot was soon persuaded that I did not question his veracity. We passed the greater part of the day together, and we separated only toward evening. Then I entered a post of the gendarmes, where the officers told me that several watches had been stolen in a direction entirely opposite to that where, following Hotot's advice, we had been watching. From this it was demonstrated to me that he had drawn us to one point in order to manœuvre more at his ease at another. It is an old ruse which enters into the tactics of diversions and false advice which thieves give so that they need have no fear of the police.

I was careful not to make the slightest reproach to Hotot, and he imagined that I was completely duped; but if I said nothing, I did not think the less, and becoming more and more friendly with him, while he meditated repeating the Saint-Cloud trick, I planned to outwit him on the first occasion. Our intimacy was in a fair way, and it offered me more than I should have dared to hope.

One morning as I was returning with Gaffré from the Fauborg Saint-Marceau, where we had passed the night, I took a notion to make an unexpected call on friend Hotot. We were not far from the street where he lived. I proposed to my comrade of the evening that he come with me; he consented to accompany me; we went up to Hotot's; I knocked; he opened and seemed surprised to see us.

'What a miracle at this hour!'

'You're astonished,' I said. 'We've come to buy you a drink.'

'If that's it, be welcome.' At the same time he went back to bed. 'Where's this drink?'

'Gaffré will do us the pleasure of going to get it.'

I felt in my pocket, and as Gaffré was less miserly with his steps than his money, he willingly undertook the commission and went out. During his absence I noted that Hotot had that tired air of a man who has gone to bed later or earlier in the morning than usual. In addition, the room was in that state of disorder which indicates some extraordinary circumstance. His clothes were thrown about rather than laid, and they seemed to have received a shower of rain; his shoes were covered with a whitish mud and were still damp. Not to conclude that Hotot had just come in, one would not be Vidocq. For the moment I did not draw any other deduction, but my mind soon moved from conjecture to conjecture, and I conceived suspicions which I was careful not to express. I did not want to be curious, that is to say, indiscreet, and for fear of disturbing our friend, I did not ask the slightest question. We talked of the rain and fine weather, but more about fine weather than the rain, and when there was nothing left to drink, we withdrew.

Once outside, I could not help communicating to Gaffré the observations I had made. 'Either I am entirely wrong, or he slept out. He had some expedition on foot.'

'I think so, for his clothes are still damp, and his shoes are still muddy. He didn't walk in the dust!'

Hotot could have hardly imagined that we would talk of him, but his ears must have tingled. Where had he gone? What had he done? we asked each other. Perhaps he's affiliated with a gang! Gaffré was as much intrigued as I, and his suppositions were hardly favourable to Hotot's probity.

At noon, according to custom, we went to report the observations we had made during the night. Our report was most uninteresting; the word 'nothing' was written there *in extenso*.

'Ah!' said M. Henry. 'They're honest folk in the Faubourg Saint-Marceau! I'd have done better to send you to the boulevard Saint-Martin. It seems that messieurs the lead-stealers have again begun their game. They have taken more than four hundred and fifty pounds from a building under construction. The watchman pursued them without being able to catch them, and he is sure that there were four of them. They pulled the trick during the heavy rain.'

'During the heavy rain?' I exclaimed. 'You know one of the thieves.'

'Who is it?'

'Hotot.'

'The man who served in the police and wants to come back?'

'The same.'

I told M. Henry my observations of the morning, and I remained convinced that I was right. I at once started my campaign promptly to change into evidence what were only presumptions. The commissioner of the quarter where the robbery had been committed took me with him to the place, and we found in the ground the deep imprints of two hobnailed shoes; the ground had been pressed down by a man's weight. These traces might furnish precious indications, so precautions were taken that they should not be effaced. I was nearly certain that they would fit perfectly Hotot's footgear, and in consequence I engaged Gaffré to come with me to his place.

In order to proceed to the verification, unknown to the guilty man, I thought up a mode of procedure. When we reached Hotot's domicile, we made a devil of a racket at the door. 'Get up, get up, we've brought the patty.' He woke up, turned the key in the lock, and we entered staggering like two people who are slightly more than drunk.

'Well,' said Hotot, 'I compliment you. You've started early.'

'That's the reason, my friend,' I replied, 'that we've come to get you. You're so shrewd,' I added, showing under its wrappings a purchase we had made en route: 'guess what's inside.'

'How can I guess?'

Then I tore one of the corners of the paper and showed the feet of a fowl.

'Oh, damn it,' he cried, 'it's a turkey!'

'Yes, it's your own brother; and as one tells animals by their feet, do you now understand the analogy?'

'What are you talking about?'

'I said it is roasted.'

'Oh, bah, you're cheating me with venison!'

'Venison, come, smell it.' I passed him the fowl, and while he smelled it and turned it in all directions, Gaffré bent down, took the shoes, and crammed them into his hat.

'How much did that beast cost?'

'Seven livres, ten sous.'

'Seven livres, ten sous! Why, that's the price of a pair of shoes. However, as you say, my man,' the pick-pocket went on, rubbing his hands.

'Well, let's serve it. Is there a knife in this joint?'

'Yes, look in the commode drawer.'

In fact, I found a knife. Now the question was to find a pretext for

Gaffré to go out.

'Oh,' I said to him, while I was laying the cover, 'you'd please me if you'd go to my place and tell them not to wait dinner for me.'

'So that's it, and then you'd stuff yourselves. Oh, no, not that; I don't leave the place until I've swallowed my food.'

'We'll not swallow it without drinking.'

'I'll get up some liquor.'

He opened the window and called a wine merchant. Gaffré was like most of the agents, a good fellow, but as greedy as an owl. His appetite came first and his trade next, so, although he had the shoes which were the important part of the affair, I saw that it would be impossible to get him to abandon the terrain as long as he had not had his part of the lunch. I hurried to carve the bird, and, when the wine arrived, I said to him, 'Come, get to the table, drink, and get out.'

The table was Hotot's bed. We ate like ogres, and the meal was finished promptly.

'Now,' said Gaffré, 'I can go; I don't know how it is with you, but when my stomach's empty, I'm good for nothing. When it's full, it's different.'

'In that case, get out.'

'That's what I'm doing.' He took his hat at once and went.

'Ah, he's gone,' said Hotot, in the tone of a man who was not displeased to be alone with me for a moment. 'Well, my dear Jules,' he went on, 'will there never be a place for Hotot?'

'What do you want? You must be patient; that will come.'

'Yes, but it would help if you gave me a shove. M. Henry listens to you, and if you said two words...'

'That won't be today, for I expect a proper reprimand. Gaffré won't escape either, for we haven't reported for two days.'

This lie was not without intention. It was necessary that Hotot believe that I was not informed about the robbery in which I presumed he had participated. He was not distrustful; I wanted to keep him in this sense of security, and for fear that he would think of getting up, I led the conversation to subjects which interested him most. He talked to me about several matters in succession.

'Oh!' he said, with a sigh, 'if I was only sure of going back into the police with a salary of twelve to fifteen hundred bullets, I could furnish some information ... With what I know at the moment about a small burglary, wouldn't that be a real gift to make M. Henry?'

'Oh, yes.'

'Yes, say. There are three thieves, Berchier, alias Bicêtre, Caffin, and Linois, whom I'll answer to pinch, as sure as you and I make two.'

'If you can, why don't you talk? That would be a fine entrance in the game.'

'I know it, but...'

'Are you afraid of pushing yourself forward? If you render a service, you needn't worry. I'll do a lot to get you admitted.'

'Oh, my friend, you put balm in my soul. You'll get me admitted?'

'Go on, that's not hard.'

'Take a drink on that,' cried Hotot, as if carried away with joy.

'Yes, let's drink to your near reception.'

'Rather today than tomorrow.'

Hotot was delighted; he was already drawing up plans; he dreamt of happiness. I was afraid that he would want to get out of bed. Finally, someone knocked; it was Gaffré, holding in his hand a half-bottle of brandy which Annette had given him. While I poured for the neophyte, Gaffré put the shoes back in place. We continued to talk and drink, and before we withdrew I knew they were the lead thieves whom Hotot proposed to point out. Père Bellemont, a dealer in old iron, rue de la Tannerie, was the receiver he named.

These details were interesting. I told Hotot that I was going immediately to bring them to M. Henry's attention, and advised him to tell me where the three thieves had slept. He promised to indicate their hiding-place, and we separated.

Gaffré had not left me. 'Well,' he said, 'it was he. The shoes fitted perfectly, the imprint is so deep.'

I already understood Hotot's conduct and the role he wanted to play. First, it was clear that he had committed the robbery with the intention of getting some of the products, but he was chasing two hares at the same time. By denouncing his accomplices he gained the end of making himself interesting to the police in order to obtain re-employment. I shuddered at the thought of such a combination. The scoundrel, I said to myself, I'll fix it so that he's paid for his crime, and if the poor devils who helped him in this expedition are sentenced, it's only just that he share their lot.

I did not hesitate to believe that he was the guiltiest of all. According to what I knew of his character, it seemed most probable that he had drawn them in only to manage an occasion to concoct what is termed an affair. I even went so far as to think that if he had been able to do the robbery himself, he would have found it convenient to accuse of the crime individuals whose immorality made them suspect. In either case Hotot was still a great rascal. I resolved to deliver society of him.

I knew that he had two mistresses, one Émilie Simonet, who had had several children by him, and with whom he lived as her husband; the other was Félicité Renaud, a prostitute, who loved him to adoration. I thought I would take advantage of the rivalry of these two women. Hotot was already under observation. In the afternoon I was warned that he was with Félicité, and I went to join him. I took him aside and confided to him that I needed him for an affair of the highest importance.

'You see,' I told him, 'you'll be the bait for a fish we're going to lock up this evening. As you'll be in jail before he is, he won't suspect that you're a decoy, and when he's brought in, it will be easier for you to get close to him.'

Hotot accepted the proposition with enthusiasm. 'Ah,' he sighed, 'here I am again a detective! But first I must say good-bye to Félicité.' He returned to her, and she did not growl at him for leaving her so early.

'Now that you're rid of that person,' I said, 'I'll give you your instructions. You know the small smoke-shop on boulevard Montmartre, opposite the Variétés?'

'Yes, Brunet's.'

'Exactly. Go there and take a place in the back of the shop, with a bottle of beer. When you see two inspectors come in ... You will know them?'

'Will I know them? You should ask an old trooper that!'

'Since you'll recognize them, that's all right. When they come in, you will signal that it's you, so that they won't mistake you for somebody else.'

'Don't worry, they'll not mistake me.'

'They are ordered to arrest you as soon as they see you, and to take you to the station, where you'll stay two or three hours. That's so that the man whom you are to get to confess shall have seen you already in jail.'

'Don't worry. I'll fight so well that I defy the shrewdest to suspect that I'm not really locked up.'

He agreed with such good faith that I really regretted that I was obliged to deceive him in this way; but when I recalled his conduct in regard to his comrades, this slight pity fled never to reappear. He gave me his hand and went. He walked with the speed of satisfaction; the earth no longer bore him. On my part I went no less rapidly to the Prefecture where I found the inspectors. They went to the tobacco-shop. They had hardly crossed the threshold when Hotot, faithful to the recommendation I had given him, pointed with his finger, like a man saying 'It is I.' At this signal the inspectors went straight to him and invited him to show his papers. Hotot proudly answered that he had none. 'In that case,' they said, 'come with us.' And to prevent his fleeing if the notion struck him, they tied him with ropes. During this operation a sort of inner content showed itself on Hotot's features; he was happy to feel himself bound; he blessed his bonds; he looked at them almost lovingly, for, according to his ideas, this apparatus of precaution was merely a form.

Hotot was put in jail about eight o'clock in the evening; at eleven o'clock the individual he was to get to confess had not been brought in; this delay seemed extraordinary. Perhaps this person had escaped pursuit, or had confessed. If that was the case, the aid of the decoy would be useless. I do not know what conjectures the prisoner made; all I do know is that in the end, tired because no one came and imagining that he had been forgotten, he had the chief of the station warned that he was still there. 'That doesn't concern me,' was the response. This aroused no idea on Hotot's part except that the inspectors were negligent. 'If I only had some supper,' he repeated. 'If I only had some of this morning's turkey! If my friend Jules was here ... he does not know, for if he knew...'

While he deplored my ignorance and was far from foreseeing the results of his arrest, which he supposed fictitious, I was exploring the little streets in the vicinity of Place du Châtelet, where I had joined

Émilie Simonet in one of those miserable dives where, to accommodate small purses, the mistress of the house provides girls and drinks. This dive was run by Mother Bariole, a good woman if there ever was one and as honest as it was possible to be in her profession. She had all the regard for me to which a detective can pretend. When I came in, she was in the clouds because I asked for Émilie Simonet, her favourite. Madame Bariole thought I had come to throw the handkerchief in her harem. She called to Émilie, who soon appeared.

'Oh, it's you, Jules! What are you doing in this quarter?'

'I knew you were here, and I said to myself, I must see Hotot's wife and buy her a drink.'

'Agatha,' ordered La Bariole, 'serve a drink.'

Agatha at once, according to custom, pretended to go into the cellar, but in reality she went through the back to the wine-seller's and brought a litre, of which she reserved three quarters, diluting the rest to make up the quantity.

'It's not drugged,' said Émilie, while I poured her a glass. 'Look, it bubbles; that's a good sign.'

Imperceptibly I brought the conversation around to her complaints against Hotot. Émilie had already swallowed a good deal during the day and she was not slow to voice her griefs against her rival and the infidelities of Hotot. During our interview our drinks were renewed several times, and the more she drank, the more this Penelope of Hotot's protested her discretion.

'Well,' I said at last, 'this evening I went to the Champs-Élysées. I saw your man with Féicité, and at first they had a dispute. She said that he had put you in a room in rue Saint-Pierre-aux-Boeufs. He swore that he had not, and that he no longer kept company with you. They made up, and after their conversation, I said that last night he slept at Place du Palais Royal.'

'Oh, that's not true, for he was with friends.'

'With Caffin, Bicêtre, and Linois? Hotot told me that.'

'What, he told you? He's forbidden me to speak of it. That's how it is, and afterward he beats me.'

'Don't be afraid. Even if I am a detective, I have some feelings.'

'I know it, my poor Jules. You had to enter the shop rather than go back to prison.'

'All the same, shop or no shop, I'm a good fellow; and if I had to trouble anyone, it would not be Hotot.'

'You're right, my poor rabbit, one must never betray his comrades. Tell me where my man went with that—' (Molière used the word; the reader can find it.)

'Do you want to know? They went to Bicêtre's place. I won't give you the address, for I didn't ask it.'

'Oh, if they're at Bicêtre's, that's good. I'll give them a fine awakening.'

We arrived in rue du Bon-Puits, and I went in. After I had made sure that Bicêtre was in his quarters, I rejoined Émilie, whose head was unsettled by wine and jealousy.

'Listen,' I said, 'isn't that a pretty trick? They've just gone to supper at Linois's; they couldn't tell me where that is.'

'Perhaps they didn't want to, but that's nothing. I know where Linois lives. Come along with me.'

I allowed myself to be dragged to the rue Jacquelet. I climbed to the sixth floor, where I saw Linois, who knew me only by name.

'I was looking for Hotot,' I said. 'Have you seen him?'

'No,' he answered.

As he was in bed, I withdrew after wishing him good night.

'I must be unlucky,' I told Émilie. 'More drudgery. They came, but they've gone to Caffin's who's to pay for the wine. Where does Caffin live?'

'I can't tell you, but if I know him he's with some woman in the Place-aux-Veaux. Come, I beg you.'

'Do you want to drag me to the four corners of Paris? It's late, and I haven't time.'

'I beg you, Jules, don't leave me. The inspectors would lock me up.'

As complaisance was useful, I listened to her. I started with Émilie toward the Place-aux-Veaux, and gaining courage in each cabaret we flew toward the place where I hoped to complete the information I needed. We flew – my expression is bold, for in spite of the support of my arm, Émilie, who had had too much to drink, had infinite difficulty in putting one foot before another. But the more unsteady her walk became, the more communicative she was, so that she laid bare the most secret thoughts of her unfaithful husband. I learned from her all that it was important for me to know about Hotot, and I had the satisfaction of being convinced that I was not wrong in judging him capable of himself directing the thieves whom he proposed to give up to the police. At one o'clock in the morning I was still exploring with my guide, Émilie to find Hotot, and I to discover Caffin, when a woman we met told us that the latter was at Bariole's or Blondin's.

We entered Mother Bariole's and learned that in fact Caffin was there, but that Hotot had not appeared. At this news Madame Hotot imagined that they wanted to hide something from her. For a quarter of an hour there was a rolling fire of epithets.

'Will you soon finish?' La Bariole at last interrupted. 'Your man, your man! If you think he's with Caffin, go and see.'

Émilie did not have to be told twice; indeed, she proceeded to verify the fact, and returned.

'Are you satisfied?' La Bariole asked.

'There's only Caffin.'

'That's what I told you.'

'Where is the monster, oh, where is he?'

'If you want, I'll take you where he is,' I said.

'Oh, take me! Do that for me, Jules.'

'It's a long way from here to the Hôtel d'Angleterre.'

'You think he's there?'

'I'll answer for it.'

Émilie did not doubt that I had guessed perfectly, and left me no peace until I consented to undertake the trip. The way seemed long, for I was the cavalier of a lady whose centre of gravity wavered excessively, and gave me something to do to retain my own equilibrium. Half-dragging, half-carrying the belle, I got her to the door of the place where she counted on meeting her objective. We went through the rooms; Hotot was not there. Félicité's rival was in a state; her eyes stood out of their sockets; her lips were covered with foam; she wept; she swore – the terrible effects of love and brandy, jealousy and wine. I went out, but instead of acquitting myself of my mission to find Félicité, I went to the station where I asked the chief to arrest Émilie and hold her rigorously in secret confinement.

I had had Hotot arrested so that he should not have time to disimplicate himself by getting rid of the traces of his participation in the robbery, or by gaining impunity from the police. I arrested Émilie for fear that she might return to Bariole's, where in her drunken loquacity she might repeat things which would benefit Caffin. After all my precautions, as Hotot was already in my hands, all I had left to do was to assure myself of his three accomplices. I knew where to take each one of them. I took two agents from the Prefecture, and soon, in the name of the law, I presented myself at Bariole's.

'I'll bet you're searching for Caffin,' she said. 'Good riddance. The second door,' she told us. 'The key's above.'

I could not go wrong; I entered, and signified to Caffin that he was my prisoner.

'Well, well, who's here?' said Caffin, waking up. 'What, is it you, Jules, who's pinching me?'

'What do you want, my friend? I'm not a sorcerer; if someone hadn't denounced you, I shouldn't have come to interrupt your sleep.'

'You're wrong, my son; that's old stuff, and doesn't take.'

'As you wish. That's your affair, but if what they say is true, you're going to clink.'

'Yes, believe that and drink water, and you'll never be drunk.'

'Listen. I've no interest in doing you in. I repeat; I could not guess, and if I hadn't been told that you pinched some lead on the boulevard Saint-Martin, where you were nearly arrested by the watchman, you wouldn't have my visit now. Is that clear? Of the four of you, one's squealed. Guess who it is; if you name him, I'll tell you whether it's he.'

Caffin reflected a moment; then throwing up his head, like a horse arching its neck, he said: 'Come, Jules, I see there's been a scum among us who's squealed. Take me to the commissioner and I'll squeal too. One must be a blackguard to sell his comrades, especially when he's a thief. With you it's different; you were compelled to become a detective.'

'As you say, my friend; if I knew what I know now, I shouldn't be here.'

'Where are you going to take me?'

'To the station, Place du Châtelet, and if you've decided to confess, I'll warn the commissioner.'

'Yes, have him come; I want to sink that scoundrel of a Hotot, for no one else could have squealed.'

The commissioner arrived; Caffin confessed his crime, but at the same time, he did not neglect to charge Hotot whom he designated as his only accomplice. Obviously he was not a renegade. His two friends showed no less loyalty; surprised in the same way in their warm beds and questioned separately, they could not do otherwise than acknowledge their guilt. Hotot, whom they accused of their misfortune, was the only one whom each of them inculpated. This generous trio was sent to the galleys, and the perfidious Hotot was sentenced to keep them company.

XXIV
I ESCAPE BEING SWALLOWED UP

FROM THE TIME I became a secret agent, I had only one thought, and all my efforts were directed to cramping as much as possible the wretches who, wishing to ignore the resources of work, sought their subsistence only in more or less criminal attempts against the rights of property. I had no illusion as to the sort of success I sought, and I was not so mad as to believe that I could extirpate thefts; but in making war with a vengeance on the thieves, I hoped to make them less frequent. I dare to say that my first successes surpassed my expectations and those of M. Henry. My reputation grew with too great rapidity for my liking, for the reputation betrayed the mystery of my employment, and from the moment I was known, it was necessary for me to renounce the service or serve the police openly.

From that time on my task became more and more difficult. However, I was not alarmed by the difficulties, and, as I was wanting neither in zeal nor in devotion, I believed that it would still be possible for me not to forfeit the good opinion authority had conceived of me. Hereafter there was no way for me to pretend with the malefactors. The mask had fallen. In their eyes I was a police spy and nothing more. However, I was a police spy in a better situation than most of my confrères, and when I could not do otherwise than put myself in evidence, the period of my secret mission was still profitable to me, on account of the relations I had preserved, or from the ample store of descriptions and information of all sorts I had classified in my memory. My method was excellent; it is sufficient to say that in less than seven years, I brought to the hands of justice more than four thousand malefactors. Whole classes of thieves were brought to bay, including the rouletiers – they steal the loads on wagons. I had a secret desire to reduce them utterly; I attempted the enterprise, but it was almost fatal to me.

Two of the boldest *rouletiers* were Gosnet and Doré; they were alarmed at my efforts to abolish their industry and suddenly decided to devote themselves to the police. In a short time they brought about the arrest of a goodly number of their comrades, who were all sentenced.

They seemed zealous; I owed to them information of the greatest importance, notably about certain receivers who were so much the more dangerous that in commercial circles they enjoyed a great reputation for integrity. After some services of this nature, it seemed to me that I could count on them; I solicited their admission as secret agents, with a salary of a hundred and fifty francs a month. They wanted no more; they said that a hundred and fifty francs was the height of their ambition. At least I believed it; and as I saw in them my future colleagues, I showed them a confidence which was almost without limits. We shall see how they justified it.

Several months before, two or three of the most adroit of this class of thieves had arrived in Paris, and they did not sleep. Declarations rained on the Prefecture; they executed coups of the most inconceivable boldness, and it was the more difficult to take them in the act in that they went out only at night, and that in their expeditions on the roads near the capital they were always armed to the teeth. The capture of such brigands could only do me honour. To effect it I was ready to dare all perils.

One day Gosnet, with whom I had often talked on the subject, said to me, 'Listen, Jules, if you want to get Mayer, Victor Marquet, and his brother, there's only one way; that's to come and sleep at our place; then we can go out at more convenient hours.' I believed that Gosnet was acting in good faith.

I consented to install myself in the lodgings he occupied with Doré, and we soon began together nocturnal explorations on the roads which Mayer and the two Marquets frequented rather habitually. We met them several times, but as we wanted to take them in action, or at least carrying the booty they had just gained, we were obliged to let them pass. We had already made several of these fruitless promenades when I happened to notice something about my companions that made me uneasy. There was something of constraint in their manner toward me; perhaps they were promising themselves that they would play me a bad turn. I could not read their thoughts, but as a precaution I never went out with them without having on me the pistols with which I had furnished myself on their account.

One night, when we were to go out at two o'clock in the morning, Doré suddenly complained of colic which made him suffer horribly; the pains became more and more acute; he twisted and bent double; it was evident that he could not walk in that state. In consequence the party was postponed until the next day, and since there was nothing to do, I threw myself down and slept. A few minutes later I awoke suddenly; I thought I had heard knocking at the door; heavier blows proved that I was not mistaken. What did the knockers want? Were they asking for us? It was not probable, since no one knew our retreat. One of my companions, however, was getting up; I signed to him to stay quiet; nevertheless, he sprang from bed; then in a low voice, I recommended him to listen, but not to open. He took a place near the door; Gosnet, in bed in the next room, did not move.

The knocking continued, and, as a measure of precaution, I hurried into my coat and trousers. After he had done as much, Doré returned to his watch; but while he was listening, his mistress gave me such an expressive glance that I had no difficulty in interpreting it. I raised my mattress at the foot and saw an enormous parcel of false keys and a jimmy. All was clear; I had guessed the plot, and in order to frustrate it, without saying a word I hastened to place the keys in my hat and the jimmy in my trousers. Then I approached the door and listened in my turn. The visitors were talking very low, and I could not understand what they said. However, I presumed that such an early visit had some purpose. I drew Doré into the second room, and there I warned him that I was going to try to find out what the purpose was.

'As you wish,' he told me.

The knocking began again. I asked who was there.

'Isn't M. Gosnet here?' someone enquired in a mawkish voice.

'M. Gosnet's on the floor below; the same door.'

'Thanks. Excuse our waking you up.'

'There's no harm done.'

They went downstairs, and in two leaps I was in the lavatory, where I threw the jimmy; I was preparing to throw the keys, but someone came in behind me. I recognized an inspector named Spiquette, attached to the magistrate's office; he recognized me too.

'Ah!' he said, 'they're searching for you.'

'For me? Why?'

'Oh, for nothing. M. Vigny, the magistrate, wants to see you and talk to you.'

'If that's all, I'm with you.'

We went downstairs together. The room was full of gendarmes and police spies; M. Vigny was among them. At once he read a writ of arrest against me, as against my hosts and their women. Then to fulfil the wish of the judicial commission, he ordered the most thorough search. It was not difficult for me to see where the blow came from, especially when Spiquette raised the mattress, and, doubtless surprised at finding nothing, looked at Gosnet in a certain way; the latter seemed stupefied. His disappointment did not escape me; I saw that he was fairly baffled. I was completely reassured, and I said to the magistrate: 'Monsieur, I see with sorrow that in the hope of being interesting, they've caused you to make a blunder. You have been deceived. There's nothing suspect here. Besides, M. Gosnet would not allow it; isn't that so, M. Gosnet? You would not allow it? Answer the judge.'

He could not do otherwise than confirm what I had said, but he did not speak heartily, and one did not have to be a sorcerer to penetrate to the depths of his soul.

When the search was over, we were placed in two cabs after we had been bound, and taken to the Palais. Shut up with Gosnet and Doré, I was careful not to express the suspicions I had formed about them. At noon we were questioned, and toward evening we were transferred, my two companions to La Force and I to Saint-Pélagie. I do not know how it happened, but the bunch of keys, which I had kept in my hat, remained unseen to all the observers who ordinarily encumber a prison gate. Although they had neglected nothing in their search, they did not find them and I was not annoyed.

I immediately wrote to M. Henry to announce the plot which had been hatched against me, and I had no trouble in convincing him that I was innocent. Two days later I recovered my liberty and reappeared at the Prefecture with the keys which so luckily had escaped all investigations. I considered myself fortunate in escaping the peril, for I had been within an inch of ruin. Except for Doré's mistress and my presence of mind, no doubt I should again have fallen under the jurisdiction of the prison warders. Carrying burglars' tools, I should have been sentenced again; my condition as an escaped convict would have furnished the reason, and in the end I should have been taken back to prison.

M. Henry reprimanded me on the subject of an imprudence which had been nearly fatal to me. 'Look,' he said, 'where would you be if Gosnet and Doré had conducted that intrigue with a little more skill? Vidocq,' he added, 'take care of yourself. Don't press your devotion too far. Above all, don't put yourself at the discretion of thieves. You have many enemies. Undertake nothing without reflecting deeply. Before you risk a step in the future, come and consult me.'

I profited by his advice and found it good.

Gosnet and Doré did not stay long in La Force. When they came out, I went to see them, but I did not let them see that I suspected their perfidy. However, as I wanted revenge in a game where I had not lost, I set a decoy for them, and not long after I learned that they had committed a robbery, the proofs of which were easy to produce. Arrested and sentenced, they had during the four years time to think of me. When the sentence that fixed their fate had been delivered, I did not fail to pay them a visit; when I told them how I had known and frustrated their projects, they wept with rage.

Gosnet returned to the prisons of Auray from which he had escaped and thought up a means of vengeance which did not succeed. He pretended to repent and summoned a priest. Under the pretence of making a general confession, he confessed to a number of robberies in which he was careful to implicate me. The confessor, to whom my pretended participation had not been entrusted under the seal of secrecy, addressed to the Prefecture a note in which I was violently incriminated; but Gosnet's revelations did not have the result he had promised himself.

The arbitrary treatment which was displayed against the thieves spread among them a mania for denouncing each other. They were driven, if it is permissible to say so, to the height of demoralization. Previously they had formed in the bosom of society a caste apart, which numbered neither traitors nor turncoats; but when they were proscribed *en masse,* instead of drawing their ranks closer together, in their fright they uttered a cry of alarm which made legitimate every expedient of salvation, to the detriment of their ancient loyalty. Once the bond that united the members of the great family of thieves was broken, each one of them, in his own private interests, made no scruple of giving up his comrades. Often when there was a dearth of thefts to point out to me, the denouncers revealed crimes which they imputed to others and

which would have given reasons for their own condemnation. I cite
some examples.

A woman named Bailly, an old thief, imprisoned at Saint-Lazare,
summoned me to give me some information. I went to see her, and she
declared that if I would undertake to set her at liberty, she would indicate to me the authors of five robberies, of which two were burglaries. I
accepted the offer, and the details she gave me were so precise that I
already believed that all I had to do was to keep my promise. However,
on reflecting about the different circumstances she had reported to me,
I was astonished that she could be so perfectly informed. She had designated the names of the persons who had been robbed.

One was a M. Frédéric in rue Saint-Honoré. I went to him first,
and in the course of the information I received, I acquired the certainty
that the informer was the author of the crime. I pursued my enquiry,
and everywhere they gave me her description. It was necessary to proceed to the verification. The complainants were taken to Saint-Lazare,
and there, without being seen by Bailly, whom I showed to them
among her companions, they recognized her perfectly. A legal confrontation followed, and Bailly, overwhelmed by the evidence, made a
confession which was worth eight years' confinement. She had sufficient time to say her *mea culpa*.

A man named Ouasse, whose father was later implicated in the
trial of the grocer Poulain, pointed out to me three individuals as the
authors of a burglary committed at a tobacco-shop. I went to the place
and made enquiries, and I soon acquired incontestable proof that
Ouasse, who had been recently released from prison, was not foreign to
the crime. I concealed my knowledge, but by using him I did so well
that he was arrested as an accomplice and sentenced to imprisonment.
This misadventure should have corrected his mania for denouncing, but
wishing at any price to be a police spy, he made to the King's prosecutor at Versailles different false declarations which cost him two or three
years in prison.

I have already said that thieves do not hold rancour. Ouasse had
hardly been released when he hurried to me about a robbery of which
he advised me. I verified the fact according to his indications and the
robbery was real. But would one believe it? The thief was Ouasse;
arrested and convicted, he was sentenced again. During his detention

this wretch learned of the arrest of his father, and hastened to send me revelations to support the accusations against the latter. It was my duty to transmit them to the authorities, and I did so, but not without feeling all the indignation which the conduct of such an unnatural son should excite.

When the path toward an important discovery bristled with difficulties, the women thieves were perhaps of greater help to me than the men. In general the women have ways of insinuating themselves which in police investigations make them superior to men; combining tact and finesse, they are endowed besides with a perseverance which always leads them to their end. They inspire less distrust, and can get in anywhere without arousing suspicion. M. Henry was a skilful man and he used them in the most difficult affairs.

Following the example of my chief, on many occasions I had recourse to the women police spies; nearly always I was satisfied with their services. However, I needed to be constantly on my guard not to be taken in by them. The following will show how unnecessary it is always to believe in the zeal of those who make the greatest parade of it.

I had obtained the freedom of two famous women thieves on the condition that they serve the police faithfully. They had previously given proof of their skill, but employed without salary, they were obliged to steal to live, and were taken in the act. The penalty which they suffered for these new crimes was the one which I shortened. Sophie Lambert and the girl Domer, nicknamed La Belle Lise, were from then on in direct relations with me.

One morning they came to tell me that they were certain that they could procure the arrest of one Tominot, a dangerous man, who had been sought for a long time. They had, they assured me, just had breakfast with him, and he was to join them that evening at a wine merchant's in rue Saint-Antoine. In any other circumstances I should have been the dupe of the deceit of these two women, but I had arrested Tominot the evening before, and it was rather difficult for them to have had breakfast with him. However, I wanted to know how far they would push the imposture, and I promised to accompany them to the rendezvous. In fact, I went; but, as one can imagine, Tominot did not come. We waited until ten o'clock; finally, Sophie, growing impatient, asked the waiter if a gentleman had not come to ask for them.

'The one with whom you had breakfast?' answered the waiter. 'He came a little before dusk, and asked me to tell you that he would not be able to see you this evening, but he would tomorrow.'

I did not doubt that the waiter was a confederate whom they had coached, but I pretended that I had no suspicion and resigned myself to see how long these ladies would pull my leg. For a whole week they led me from place to place; we were always to find Tominot, but we never met him.

Finally, on the sixth of January, they swore they would bring him, and alleged such good reasons that it was impossible for me to be angry; on the contrary, I showed so much satisfaction at the steps they had taken that to show my content with them I offered to regale them with a Twelfth-Night cake. They accepted and we went together to the Petit Broc, rue de la Verrerie. We pulled the string, royalty fell to Sophie, and she was as happy as a queen. We ate, we drank, we laughed, and as the moment of separation approached, we proposed to complete our gaiety by some drinks of brandy. But the brandy of a wine merchant, no! I was too gallant to my queen to drink a beverage unworthy of her. I announced that I was going to my place to find a drop worthy of her. At this news the company leaped in enthusiasm, and advised me to go and come back as quickly as possible. I went, and two minutes later I reappeared with a half-bottle of cognac which was emptied in the twinkling of an eye.

When the bottle was dry, I said to my two friends, 'You see that I'm a good fellow, now do me a service.'

'Two, my dear Jules!' cried Sophie. 'Come, speak.'

'Well, this is it. One of my agents has just arrested two women thieves; it is presumed that they have in their place a large quantity of stolen articles, but to make a search, it is necessary to know their domicile, and they refuse to tell where it is. They're now at the station; if you would go there and try to worm out of them their secret? An hour or two ought to be enough; that should be easy for anyone as shrewd as you are.'

'Don't worry, my dear Jules,' Sophie said. 'We'll perform the commission. You know that you can rely on us; you could send us to the ends of the earth, and we'd go with pleasure, at least I would.'

'And I would too,' said La Belle Lise.

'In that case you'll take a note to the chief of the post so that he'll recognize you.'

I wrote a note which I sealed; I gave it to them and we went out together. At a short distance from the Marché Saint-Jean, we separated, and while I kept them under observation, the queen and her companion went toward the guardhouse. Sophie went in first and presented the note. The sergeant read it. 'That's good,' he said, 'there you both are. Corporal, take four men and conduct these ladies to the Prefecture.' This command was given by virtue of an order I had sent the sergeant while I went out to get the drink. It was expressed as follows:

> Monsieur, chief of the post, will conduct under safe
> and good escort to the Prefecture of Police the said
> Sophie Lambert and Lise Domer, arrested by the orders
> of M. the Prefect.

The ladies must have had singular thoughts; without doubt they guessed that I was tired of being their plaything. However that might be, I went to see them the next morning at the dépôt, and asked them what they thought of the trick.

'Not bad,' answered Sophie, 'not bad. We haven't stolen.' Then, addressing Lise, 'It's your fault. Why did you look for a man who was in jail?'

'Don't I know it? Oh, if I'd known, I promise you...'

'That's fine, if we only knew how long we'd be at Lazare. Tell us, Jules, do you know?'

'Six months at least.'

'Only that?' they exclaimed together.

'Six months, that's nothing at all,' continued Sophie. 'It's soon over.'

They got a month less than I had announced. When they were free, they came to me to give new information. This time they were exact.

It is a remarkable circumstance that women thieves are ordinarily more incorrigible than men. Sophie Lambert never gave up her habitual transgressions. She had entered on her career at the age of ten; she was not twenty-five, but she had spent a third of her life in prison.

A short time after my entrance into the police service, I had her arrested and sentenced to two years' imprisonment. She practised her guilty trade in furnished hotels, and there was no one more skilled in frustrating the vigilance of the porters or more fertile in expedients to escape questions. This creature was bold; twice she ran headlong into my nets, but after she was free, I tried in vain to trap her. There was no surveillance she did not succeed in escaping, she was so much on her guard. That I finally caught her in the act I owed to an altogether chance circumstance.

I was coming out of my house at daybreak and crossing the Place du Châtelet when I met Sophie face to face.

She came up to me willingly. 'Bonjour, Jules, where are you going so early? I'll bet that you're going to lock up some thief.'

'That might be; what's sure is that it's not you. But where are you going?'

'I'm going to Corbeil to see my sister who's going to get me a place. I'm tired of eating in prison; I'm going to reform. Will you take a drink?'

'Gladly, but I'll treat; a dram at Lapêtre's at six sous.'

'All right, I'll let you, but hurry so I won't miss the diligence. You'll go with me, won't you? It's in the rue Dauphine.'

'Impossible! I have business in La Chapelle, and I'm late already. All I can do is take a small drink on the run.'

We entered Lapêtre's, and as we drank we exchanged a few words, and I said good-bye.

'Good-bye, Jules. Good luck!'

While Sophie withdrew, I turned into the rue de la Hammerie and ran and hid myself at the comer of rue Planche Mibray; from there I saw her go along the Pont-du-Change. She walked rapidly and constantly looked around; it was certain that she was afraid of being followed, and I concluded that it would be apropos to trail her.

I gained the Pont Notre Dame, and, crossing it rapidly, I reached the quai rather quickly so as not to lose her trail. When I reached the rue Dauphine, she in fact entered the office of the stage to Corbeil; but convinced that her departure was only a tale made up to deceive me about the object of her early appearance, I crouched in an alley where I could see the exit. While I was thus picketing, a cab passed; I got in, and I promised the driver a good tip if he would cleverly follow a woman I would point out to him. For the moment we remained stationary; the diligence soon left, and Sophie was not in it. I would have bet on that, but some minutes later she presented herself at the carriage entrance, looked carefully in all directions, and, taking flight, went down rue Christine.

She entered several furnished houses one after another, but from her appearance it was easy to see that no chance had offered; however, she persisted in exploring the same quarter .... I drew the natural conclusion that she had operated without success; as I was persuaded that she had not finished her rounds, I was careful not to interrupt her.

At last, in the rue de la Harpe, she entered the alley of a fruiterer, and a moment after she reappeared carrying in her arms an enormous laundry basket. Although she could not travel rapidly, she was soon in the rue des Mathurins Saint-Jacques; then in the Maçons Sorbonne. Unfortunately for Sophie there is a passage which runs between rue de la Harpe and rue des Maçons. I got down there, and ran to lie in wait, and when she reached the top of the exit, I came out and we met face to face. At my appearance she changed colour and tried to talk, but her trouble was so great that she could not express herself. However, she gradually recovered and pretended to be beside herself.

'You see,' she said, 'a wrathy woman. My laundress ought to have brought my linen to the diligence. She didn't keep her word. I've just taken it away from her and am going to carry it to one of my friends. That prevented my going.'

'You're like me. On the way to La Chapelle, I met someone who told me that my man was in this quarter. That's what brought me here.'

'All the better. If you'll wait, I'll take my basket a few steps and we'll eat a cutlet.'

'It's not worth while, I ... Oh, what do I hear?'

Sophie and I looked at each other in stupefaction; piercing cries came from the basket. I raised the linen, and I saw a child of two or three months whose wails would have shattered the ear drums of a dead man.

'Well,' I said to Sophie, 'doubtless the baby's yours. Can you tell me whether it's a boy or a girl?'

'Go on! Here I am in jail again. I'll remember this, and if they ever ask me the reason, I'll answer nothing, or nearly nothing, merely a child. Another time I steal linen, I'll look at it.'

'And is the umbrella yours?'

'Oh, my God, yes ... As you see, I had something to cover.'

I took Sophie to the commissioner of police. She got five years in prison.

XXV
OUR FRIENDS THE ENEMY

A SHORT TIME before the first invasion, M. Sénard, one of the wealthiest jewellers of the Palais Royal, went to see his friend the curé of Livry. He found him in those perplexities which the approach of our good friends the enemy caused generally. He was worried about concealing from the rapacity of Messieurs the Cossacks, first, the sacred vessels, and, next, his small savings. After hesitating for a long time, although from his occupation he should have been used to burials, the curé decided to put in the ground the objects he proposed to save. M. Sénard, who, like most simpletons and misers, imagined that Paris would be pillaged, decided to cover in the same manner all that was valuable in his shop.

It was agreed that the wealth of the pastor and the merchant should be placed in the same hole. But who should dig the hole? There was a man who sang in the choir – the pearl of honest men, Père Moiselet. They could have every confidence in him; he would not keep back a farthing which was not his; in his capacity as a cooper for thirty years he had had the exclusive privilege of bottling the wines for the presbyter. Churchwarden, sacristan, cellarman, bellringer, general factotum of the church, devoted to his curé, even to the point of getting up early if there was need, he had all the qualities of an excellent servant, without counting discretion, intelligence, and piety. At such a grave moment it was evident that they could look only to Moiselet.

So they chose him, and the hiding-place, arranged with much art, was soon ready to receive the treasures which it was to preserve. Six feet of earth were thrown on the curé's specie which kept company with diamonds worth a hundred thousand crowns which M. Sénard had enclosed in a small box. When the hole was filled, the ground was levelled off, and one would have sworn that it had not been moved since the Creation. 'That good Moiselet,' said M. Sénard, rubbing his hands, 'has arranged everything marvellously. Gad, Messieurs the Cossacks, you'll have a good nose if you find that.'

After some days the armies of the Coalition made new progress, and there were clouds of Kirghiz, Kalmuks, and Tartars of all the hordes and all colours, scattered in the country around Paris. These troublesome guests are, as we know, greedy for booty. They made frightful ravages everywhere; there was no habitation which did not pay tribute, and in their ardour for pillage they did not stop at the surface; everything was theirs as far as the centre of the globe.

In order not to be frustrated in their pretentions as daring geologists, they made a number of soundings which, to the great regret of the natives of the country, revealed that in France the gold and silver mines are shallower than those of Peru. Such a discovery gave them a taste for the work, and they dug with an unparalleled activity. The void they produced in many hiding-places was the despair of the Crœsus of more than one canton. The cursed Cossacks! However, the sure instinct which guided them where there was anything to take did not lead them to the curé's hiding-place. It was like the benediction of heaven; every morning the sun rose, and there was nothing new; nor was there anything new when it set.

Certainly the curé could but recognize the hand of God in the impenetrability of the mystery of the burial operated by Moiselet. M. Sénard was so touched that of necessity he had to mix deeds of grace with the prayers he made for the preservation and safety of his diamonds. In the persuasion that his wishes would be granted, in his increasing security, he began to sleep first on one ear and then on the other.

But one fine day – it must have been a Friday – Moiselet, more dead than alive, rushed to the curé and said, 'Oh, monsieur, I can stand no more.'

'What's the matter, Moiselet?'

'I shall never dare to tell you. My poor curé, that was such a blow; I am still shocked all over! If my veins were opened, not a drop of blood would come out.'

'But what is it? You alarm me.'

'The hiding-place...'

'Have pity! I don't need to learn more. Oh, the war is a terrible plague! Jeanneton, Jeanneton, quick, my shoes and my hat.'

'But, monsieur, you've not had breakfast.'

'Oh, never mind breakfast.'

'You know when you go out hungry, you have pains...'

'My shoes, I say.'

'And then you complain of your stomach.'

'I no longer need a stomach. No, I don't need one any longer. We're ruined.'

'We're ruined ... Jesus Mary! My gentle Saviour! Is it possible? Oh, monsieur, run then ... run!'

While the curé dressed in haste, impatient at the difficulty of latching his buckles – he could never get on his shoes fast enough – Moiselet in the most lamentable tones told him what he had seen.

'Are you sure?' the curé asked him. 'Perhaps they haven't taken everything.'

'Oh, monsieur, God will it. But I had not the heart to look.'

Together they went to the old barn, where they recognized that the removal was complete. As he contemplated the extent of his misfortune, the curé nearly fell over backwards. For his part Moiselet was in a pitiable state; the dear man was more afflicted by the loss than if it had been his own. One should have heard his sighs and groans. That was the effect of love for his neighbour.

M. Sénard hardly expected that the desolation was so great at Livry. What was his despair when he heard of the event! In Paris the police is the Providence of people who have lost anything. M. Sénard's first idea, and the most natural one, was that the robbery of which he complained was the work of the Cossacks. In such an hypothesis the police could not do much, but M. Sénard took it into his head to suspect that the Cossacks were innocent.

A certain Monday, when I was in M. Henry's office, I saw enter one of those small, dry, keen men, who at first sight one would judge selfish and distrustful. It was M. Sénard. He explained briefly his misfortune, and ended with a conclusion which was not too favourable to Moiselet. M. Henry thought as he did that the latter might be the author of the subtraction, and I agreed with M. Henry.

'That's all very well,' the latter observed, 'but our opinion is based only on conjectures. If Moiselet commits no imprudence, it will be impossible to convict him.'

'Impossible?' cried M. Sénard. 'What will become of me? Oh, no, I have not implored your help in vain! Don't you know all, can't you do

all, when you wish? My diamonds, my poor diamonds! Right now I
would give a hundred thousand francs to recover them.'

'You might give double, but if the thief has taken every precaution,
we shall learn nothing.'

'Oh, monsieur, you make me desperate,' answered the jeweller,
weeping, and throwing himself at the knees of the chief of the division.
'One hundred thousand crowns' worth of diamonds! If I must lose
them, I shall die of sorrow. I implore you, have pity on me.'

'Pity! That's easy to say. However, if your man isn't too crafty, by
watching him and by using a skilful agent, perhaps in the end we shall
surprise his secret.'

'How grateful I should be! Oh, I don't mind the money; fifty thousand francs will be the reward of success.'

'Well, Vidocq, what do you think of it?'

'The business is intricate,' I answered M. Henry. 'But if I am given
charge of it, I should not be surprised if I came out of it with honour.'

'Oh,' M. Sénard said to me, pressing my hand affectionately, 'you
give me back my life. Spare nothing, I beg of you, Monsieur Vidocq;
spend all that's necessary to attain a happy result; my purse is open to
you; no sacrifice will be too much. Well, do you think you will succeed?'

'Yes, monsieur, I think so.'

'Come, get back my box, and there are ten thousand francs in it
for you. I have spoken, I don't deny it.'

In spite of the successive reductions M. Sénard made as the discovery seemed more probable, I promised to do everything in my power to
effect it. But before anything could be undertaken, a complaint had to
be entered. In consequence, M. Sénard and the curé went to Pontoise,
and as a result of their declaration, the offence having been stated,
Moiselet was arrested and questioned. The authorities tried in every
way to get him to confess that he was guilty, but he persisted in saying
that he was innocent.

Lacking proofs to the contrary, the commitment was about to
lapse, when, to consolidate it if possible, I enlisted one of my agents in
the campaign. Wearing a uniform and his left arm in a sling, he introduced himself to Moiselet's wife with a billet for lodgings. He was supposed to have come out of a hospital and was to stay in Livry only

forty-eight hours. But shortly after his arrival, he fell, and a convenient sprain made him unable to continue his journey. So it became indispensable for him to remain, and the mayor decided that he should be the guest of the cooper's wife until further orders.

Madame Moiselet was one of those fine buxom women who was not displeased at living under the same roof with a wounded conscript, so she gaily accepted the accident which kept the young soldier near her. Besides, he could console her for her husband's absence, and, as she was not yet thirty-six, she was still of an age when a woman does not disdain consolation. That was not all; evil tongues reproached Madame Moiselet with liking a drink; that was her local reputation. The pretended soldier did not neglect to flatter all the weaknesses to which she was susceptible; first, he made himself useful, and in order to finish winning the good graces of the lady, from time to time he paid for a bottle by taking out a roll from a fairly well-filled money belt.

The cooper's wife was charmed by such kindness. The soldier became her secretary, but the letters she addressed to her dear husband were of such a nature as not to compromise him. They contained not the slightest expression with a double meaning; it was innocence conversing with innocence. The secretary sympathized with Madame Moiselet; he pitied her on account of the one under arrest; and to provoke an opening, he made a parade of that broad morality which admits of all ways of enriching oneself; but madame was too foxy to be the dupe of such language. She was constantly on the alert, and was not less circumspect in her words than in her procedure. In the end, after a few days' experience, it was demonstrated that in spite of my agent's skill he would gain nothing from his mission.

So I proposed to manœuvre myself, and, disguised as a pedlar, I began to go about the vicinity of Livry. I was one of those Jews who keep everything, cloth, jewellery, cotton, etc., etc., and I accepted in exchange gold, silver, precious stones, indeed everything that was offered me. A woman, a former thief, who knew the locality, accompanied me on my tour. She was the widow of a famous thief, Germain Boudier, alias Père Latuile, who died at Saint-Pélagie after serving a half-dozen sentences. She herself had been in prison for six years, where her appearance of modesty and devotion had gained her the nickname 'The Nun.' No one was more skilful in spying on women, or in tempting them by their taste for knicknacks and apparel; she had what they call 'the trick' to the supreme degree.

I flattered myself that Madame Moiselet, carried away by our eloquence and our merchandise, would show us some of the curé's crowns, or some gem of the first water, or even the chalice or paten, in case the bargain was to her taste. My calculations were at fault; she did not succumb. I admired her, and since there was no test which she did not resist, I was convinced that I was losing my time trying new stratagems on her and that I had better experiment on her husband.

Soon the Jew pedlar was changed into a German servant, and in this disguise I began to roam about Pontoise, with the design of getting arrested. I sought the gendarmes by appearing to avoid them, so that on the first encounter, not suspecting that I was seeking them, they summoned me to show my papers. One cannot doubt that I had none; consequently, they ordered me to march with them and led me before a magistrate who understood nothing of the jargon in which I answered his questions. He wanted to know what was in my pockets, and a thorough search was immediately made in his presence. They contained a fair amount of silver and some objects which it was not astonishing that I possessed. The magistrate, as curious as a commissioner, insisted on knowing where the money and objects came from. I sent him about his business with two or three of the best Teutonic oaths, and he sent me to prison to teach me to be more polite in the future.

There I was locked up. At the time of my arrival the prisoners were at recreation in the courtyard. The jailer introduced me among them and presented me in these terms, 'I bring you a chaff-cutter; try to understand him if you can.'

They at once crowded around me, and I was received by a salvo of 'Landsman' and 'Mein Herr' which never seemed to end. During this reception I looked for the cooper of Livry, and it appeared to me that he must be a sort of half-peasant, half-bourgeois, who, in taking part in the concert of salutations addressed to me, had pronounced 'Landsman' in that mealy-mouthed tone which church mice who live on crumbs from the altar nearly always contract. His dress and figure seemed to prove that I had guessed correctly.

I wanted to be sure, so I addressed him in a jargon, 'Mossie, Mossie.' He took this for 'Moiselet.' 'Listen!' I made a song about taking a drink, and I was perfectly intelligible to him. All the buttons on my overcoats were twenty-franc pieces; I gave one to a man, and asked him to bring us some wine. Soon after I heard a turnkey shout, 'Père Moiselet, I've sent up two bottles.' So it was Moiselet! I followed him to his room and we began to drink like two bellringers. Two more bottles arrived; we proceeded only in pairs. The jailer came to drink with us, and Moiselet asked him to place a bed for me beside his own.

The drinks went on at a good rate, and after two or three hours of it, I pretended to be dizzy. Moiselet gave me a glass of straight coffee, and the coffee was followed by water; one can have no idea of the care my new friend lavished on me. I was overcome by drunkenness, and I went to bed and to sleep; at least, that was what Moiselet believed. However, I saw him distinctly fill both his glass and mine and swallow the two.

When I awoke the next day he paid me for the drink, and to regulate the account, he gave me back three francs fifty centimes, which, according to him, was what was left out of my twenty francs. I was an excellent companion; Moiselet had perceived it, and he could not leave me. I finished the twenty-franc piece with him, and I broke into a forty-franc one which went with the same rapidity. When he saw that come to an end, he feared that it was the last. 'Have you another button?' he asked, in a most comical tone of anxiety. I showed him another piece, and he leapt for joy.

The large button had the same destination as its predecessors, and by drinking together there came a moment when Moiselet understood and spoke my jargon nearly as well as I did. We were then able to tell each other our troubles. Moiselet was very curious to know my story. The one I told him was appropriate to gain the sort of confidence with which I wanted to inspire him.

Although my narration was not clear, Moiselet translated it without mistaking the facts. He saw that during the battle of Montereau I had fled with my master's portmanteau and had hidden it in the forest of Bondy. This confidence did not astonish him; it even won his affection the more. This increase in friendship after a confession which made me out a thief proved to me that he had a broad conscience. From then on I was convinced that he knew better than anyone where M. Sénard's diamonds had gone, and that it depended only on him to give me good news.

One evening after we had dined, I boasted of the delights beyond the Rhine. He drew a long sigh, and asked if there was good wine in that charming country.

'Ja, ja!' I answered, 'and charming mademoiselles.'

'Charming mademoiselles too?'

'Ja, ja!'

'Landsman, would you be pleased if I went with you?'

'Ja, ja, very pleased.'

'Oh, you're pleased? Well, I'll leave France and the old woman, and I'll take a little girl in your country.'

Moiselet returned more than once to this project of emigration; he thought of it very seriously, but to emigrate, it was necessary to be free, and no one was hastening to give us the key to the fields. I suggested to him the thought of escaping with me on the first occasion. When he had promised me that we should never leave each other, not even to whisper a last adieu to madame his wife, I was certain that it would not be long before he fell into my nets.

This certainty was the result of simple reasoning. Moiselet wanted to follow me to Germany; one does not travel on nothing; he counted on living there. For this, Père Moiselet must have found the little black hen; here he is without money, so his little black hen is not here, but where is she? We shall soon know, as it is agreed that hereafter we are inseparable.

As soon as my fellow guest had made all his reflections and had decided to become an expatriate, his head was full of castles in Germany. Then I addressed a letter to the King's attorney telling him that I was an agent of the Sûreté, and asked him to order me taken out with Moiselet, he to be taken to Livry and I to Paris.

I did not have to wait long for the order. The jailer came to announce it the evening it was executed. I had all night before me to fortify Moiselet in his resolutions. He persisted in them more than ever, and received with delight my proposition to escape from the hands of our escort as soon as possible. He was so anxious to be on the way that he did not sleep. At daylight I gave him to understand that I thought he was a thief too. He did not answer, but he could not restrain a smile with that expression of modesty which means yes, although he did not dare pronounce the word.

At last came the desired moment of our transfer which was to enable us to accomplish our designs. Moiselet had been ready for three hours. To give him courage I had not neglected to urge on him wine and brandy, and he left the jail after he had received all the sacraments.

We were fastened only by a small cord. On the way he signed to me that it would not be hard to break it. He did not suspect that it would break the charm which so far had preserved him. The farther we went, the more he showed that I was his hope of safety. Every minute he reiterated his prayer that I should not abandon him. At last we reached the decisive moment; the cord was broken; I crossed the ditch which separated us from a thicket. Moiselet had found the legs he had when he was fifteen and dashed after me. One of the gendarmes got down to pursue us, but he was handicapped in running and especially in jumping by his riding-boots and a large sabre. While he made a circuit to get to us, we had disappeared in the woods and were soon out of reach.

We took a path which led us to the woods of Vaujours. There Moiselet stopped, looked around, and went toward some bushes. I saw him bend over and plunge his arm into one of the thickest spots and bring out a spade. He got up abruptly, took some steps without uttering a word, and when he was near a birch on which I noticed several broken branches, he quickly removed his hat and coat and started to dig. He went at it so heartily that his task advanced rapidly.

Suddenly he bent down, and the prolonged 'Ah' of satisfaction which escaped him told me, without my needing a divining rod, that he had discovered his treasure. One would have thought that the cooper was going to fall in a faint, but he came to promptly; further use of the spade and the dear box was bare and he took possession of it.

At the same time I seized the instrument of exploration, and suddenly changing my language, I declared in very good French that he was my prisoner. 'No resistance,' I said, 'or I'll break your head.' At this threat he thought he was dreaming, but when he felt himself grasped by my iron hands, he was convinced that it was not a dream. Moiselet was as gentle as a lamb; I had sworn not to leave him, and I kept my word. On the way to the post of the gendarmes he exclaimed several times: 'I am lost. Who would have thought it? He seemed so simple!' Taken to the assizes at Versailles, Moiselet was sentenced to six months' imprisonment.

M. Sénard was at the height of joy at having discovered his hundred thousand crowns' worth of diamonds. Faithful to his system of reduction, he reduced the reward by half, and they had difficulty in getting the five thousand francs out of him, out of which I had had to spend more than two thousand. For a moment I saw myself out of pocket.

XXVI
IMPORTANT CAPTURES

A SHORT TIME after the difficult exploration which was so fatal to the cooper, some thieves introduced themselves at night, rue de Richelieu, No. 17, where they rifled the apartment of Brigadier-General Bouchu. The effects were valued at thirty thousand francs. Everything worth taking had been taken, from a modest cotton handkerchief to the general's stars on his epaulets. These gentlemen, accustomed to leaving nothing behind, had even taken the linen intended for the washer-woman. The system which consists in not leaving a rag to the person robbed is at times most dangerous to the thieves, for its application necessitates a search and takes so long that it may become disastrous to them.

But on this occasion they had operated in all security; the presence of the general in his apartment had been a guaranty that they would not be disturbed in their enterprise, and they had emptied the closets and trunks with the same security that exists at an inventory after a death. How then can one say that the general was present? Alas, he was; but when one participates in an excellent dinner one hardly knows what will happen! Without hate or fear, and above all without fore-knowledge, they pass gaily from Beaune to Chambertin, from Chambertin to Clos-Vougéot, from Clos-Vougéot to Romanée; then, having run through all the burgundies, mounting the scale of fame, they take champagne, and then happy the guest who, full of memories of that joyous pilgrimage, does not become so confused that he cannot find his lodgings.

As a result of a banquet of this kind, the general had retained his reason to the full, at least I am pleased to think so, but he had returned home overwhelmed by sleep, and as in that situation one is more in a hurry to get into bed than to close a window, he left his open for the convenience of all comers and goers. He did not have to be rocked to sleep; I do not know whether he had agreeable dreams, but what remained lasting to me, at the reading of the complaint which he had lodged, was that when he awoke, he was as naked as a little saint.

Who were the individuals who had stripped him in this way? It was not easy to discover them, and all one could say at the moment with certainty was that they had cheek; for they had carried their irreverence so far as to prove that they considered the general the first sleeper in France.

I was very curious to know the insolent fellows to whom should be imputed a robbery accompanied by such aggravating circumstances. In default of indications from which I could try to trace a course, I turned to that inspiration which rarely deceives me. Suddenly the idea came to me that the thieves who had got into the general's might well be part of the clientele of a man named Perrin, a dealer in old iron, who had long been pointed out to me as one of the boldest fences.

I began by having the approaches to Perrin's domicile watched. This surveillance had no result, but I was still persuaded that to reach the end I proposed, it was necessary to make use of a ruse. I could not interview Perrin myself, because he knew who I was, but I instructed one of my agents who would not be suspect to him. The agent went to see him; they talked of this and that, and they came to speak about business.

'My word,' said Perrin, 'it's not too good.'

'What do you want?' the agent answered. 'I think the ones who were at the general's don't have to complain. When I think that in his full-dress uniform there were hidden twenty-five thousand in bank-notes!'

Perrin had such a quantity of cupidity and avarice that if he had the coat in his possession, this tale would reveal to him a wealth on which he had not counted, and should necessarily make such an impression of joy on him that he would be unable to dissimulate it. If the coat had passed through his hands and he had already disposed of it, he should show a contrary impression. I had foreseen the alternative.

Perrin's eyes did not shine suddenly, no smile came to his lips, but in an instant his face became all colours. Vainly he tried to disguise his trouble; the sense of loss came to him with such violence that he began to stamp his foot and pull his hair.

'Oh, my God! – My God!' he exclaimed. 'Such things always happen to me. Why am I so unfortunate?'

'Well, what's the matter? Did you buy... ?

'Eh, yes, I bought it, but I sold it again.'

'Do you know to whom?'

'Surely I know to whom; to the smelter in the Feydrau Archway. He burns the embroideries.'

'Come, don't give up hope. Perhaps there's a remedy if the smelter is an honest man.'

Perrin gave a jump. 'Twenty-five thousand francs, twenty-five thousand francs! That isn't found under the horses' feet. Why was I in such a hurry?'

'Oh, well, if I were in your place, I would simply try to get back the embroideries before they go into the melting pot. Come, if you want, I'll go to the smelter and tell him that you've found a place for the embroideries in some theatrical costumes and that you want them back. I'll offer him a profit, and probably he'll make no difficulty about restoring them.'

Perrin judged the expedient admirable and accepted the proposition with enthusiasm. The agent was eager to render him a service and he hastened to advise me of what had occurred. Furnished with a search warrant, I at once descended on the smelter. The embroideries were intact and I gave them to the agent to return to Perrin. At the moment when the latter, in his impatience to get the bank-notes, gave the first cut with the scissors to the ornaments, I appeared with the commissioner. We found at Perrin's all the proofs of the illicit traffic in which he was engaged; a mass of stolen objects was recognized in his stores. This receiver was taken to the station and questioned immediately, but at first he gave only vague information which there was no way to turn to account.

After his transfer to La Force, I went to see him and solicited him to make revelations. I could obtain only some descriptions and information – he was ignorant, he said, of the names of the persons from whom he bought habitually. Nevertheless, the little he told me helped me to form plausible suspicions and to fashion my suspicions into realities. I made pass before him one after another a crowd of suspects, and on his indication all those who were guilty were tried. Twenty-two were condemned to irons; among them was one of the authors of the robbery committed at General Bouchu's. Perrin was tried and convicted of receiving, but in view of the usefulness of the information he had furnished, he received the minimum penalty.

A short time later, two other receivers, the Perrot brothers, in the hope of disposing the judges to indulgence, imitated Perrin's conduct, not only in making admissions, but in inducing several prisoners to indicate their accomplices. It was after their revelations that I brought to the hands of justice two famous thieves, Valentin and Rigaudi, alias Grindesi.

Never perhaps in Paris were there a greater number of those individuals who combined the professions of thief and knight of industry than during the year of the first Restoration. One of the most adroit and enterprising was one Winter. He was no more than twenty-six years old; one of those beautiful dark men, whom certain women love for their arched eyebrows, their long lashes, prominent noses, and the air of scamps. Winter had, in addition, a slender figure and a graceful appearance which was not at all unsuited to an officer of light cavalry; so he gave his preference to a military costume which showed all the merits of his person to the greatest advantage. Today he was a hussar; tomorrow a lancer; at other times he appeared in the uniform which took his fancy. At need he was a major, or one of the staff, aide-de-camp, colonel, etc.; he did not use the higher ranks.

To attract still more consideration, he did not miss giving himself a respectable parentage: he was in turn the son of the valiant Lasalle; of the brave Winter, colonel of horse grenadiers of the Imperial Guard; the nephew of General Count de Lagrange, and the first cousin of Rapp. To sum up, there was no name he did not borrow; no illustrious family to which he did not boast of belonging. Born of parents in comfortable circumstances, Winter had received a sufficiently brilliant education to be a match for all his metamorphoses; the elegance of his figure and his most distinguished appearance completed the illusion.

Few men had made a better start than Winter. Early entered on the career of arms, he obtained promotion rather rapidly. He became an officer, but he soon lost the esteem of his chiefs, who, to punish his bad conduct, sent him to the Island of Rhé, in one of the colonial battalions. There he conducted himself so well for a time that it was believed that he had reformed. But he was no sooner given rank than he permitted himself some new follies, and he was obliged to desert to escape punishment. He then came to Paris, where his exploits, either as a sharper or as a thief, brought him the sad honour of being signalled to the police as one of the most skilful in that double trade.

Winter was above his station and made a crowd of dupes in the highest classes of society; he associated with princes, dukes, the sons of the old-time senators, and it was on them or on the ladies of their clandestine society that he exercised his deadly talents. The latter especially, no matter how well informed they were, were never sufficiently so as not to yield to the desire to be fleeced by him. For some months the police had been in search of this attractive young man, who, constantly changing his dress and his lodgings, always escaped at the moment when they flattered themselves that they were about to seize him, when I was ordered to take up the chase and attempt his capture.

Winter was one of those Lovelaces of the pillory who never deceives a woman without robbing her. I imagined that among his victims there would be at least one who in a spirit of vengeance would be disposed to put me on the trail of this monster. As a result of searching, I believed I had met this benevolent auxiliary, but as many times this sort of Ariane, abandoned as they are, feel a repugnance to sacrifice a perfidious man, I decided to approach this woman only after I had taken precautions.

Before undertaking anything it was necessary to explore the terrain, so I was careful not to show unfriendly intentions in regard to Winter, and not to startle the remains of interest, which, in spite of unworthy behaviour, still exist in a sensitive heart, it was as the chaplain of a regiment which he was reputed to have commanded that I introduced myself to the former mistress of the pretended colonel. My costume, my language, and the manner in which I was made up were in perfect harmony with the role I had to play. I obtained at once the confidence of the beautiful abandoned person, who unconsciously gave me all the information I needed. She told me that she had a preferred rival who was already badly treated by Winter, but was still weak enough to see him, and could not help making new sacrifices for him.

I got on good terms with this charming person, and to be the better regarded by her, I announced myself as a friend of her lover's family; the relations of this young madcap had charged me to pay his debts, and, if she would consent to manage an interview for me with him, she would be satisfied first. Madame— was not displeased to find an occa-

sion to repair the breaches in her small fortune. One morning she sent
me a note to advise me that she was to dine that evening with her lover
at La Galiote, on the boulevard du Temple.

I went there at four o'clock disguised as a commissionnaire, and
posted myself at the door to the restaurant. I watched for about two
hours, when I saw in the distance a colonel of hussars; it was Winter,
followed by two grooms; I approached and offered to watch the horses;
they accepted; Winter dismounted; he could not escape me. But his
eyes met mine; with a leap he was on his courser, spurred, and disappeared.

I had thought that I had him and I was greatly disappointed.
However, I did not despair of apprehending him. Some time later I was
informed that he was going to the Café Hardi, on the boulevard des
Italiens. I was there before him with some of my agents, and when he
arrived, all was so well arranged that he had only to get into a cab, for
which I had paid.

Taken before the commissioner of police, he tried to sustain that
he was not Winter, but in spite of the insignia of rank which he had
conferred on himself and the long line of decorations affixed to his
breast, he was well and duly proved to be the individual designated in
the warrant I bore. He was condemned to eight years in confinement.

When I arrested Winter, he had many confrères in Paris. The
Tuileries was notably the place where one met the most brilliant thieves
who recommended themselves to the public admiration by wearing
with all effrontery the crosses of all the orders of knighthood. In the
eyes of an observer in the know the château was less a royal residence
than a forest infested with brigands. It was a resort for a crowd of convicts, sharpers, and thieves of all sorts. The day of a review or of a great
reception all these pretended heroes of fidelity pressed to the rendezvous. As a superior agent of the Sûreté, I thought that it was my
duty to watch over these royalists of circumstance. So I posted myself
on their way either in the apartments or outside, and I was soon lucky
enough to send some of them back to prison.

One Sunday, with one of my agents I was in the crowd on the
Place du Carroussel. We saw coming out of the Pavillon de Flore a personage whose costume, no less rich than elegant, drew all eyes. This
personage must be at least a grand seigneur, for was he not loaded with

ribbons? That would have been recognized from the delicacy of his embellishments, the brilliance of his plume, and the sparkling knot on his sword – but to the eyes of a member of the police, all that glitters is not gold. The man who accompanied me pretended, in pointing out the grand seigneur, that there was a striking resemblance between him and a man named Chambreuil, with whom he had been in prison at Toulon. I had had occasion to see Chambreuil. I placed myself in front of him in order to look him in the face, and in spite of his dress I recognized the ex-convict without difficulty.

It was certainly Chambreuil, a famous forger, whose escapes had won him a great renown among the convicts. His first sentence dated from our fine campaigns in Italy. At that time he followed our phalanx to be within range to imitate the signatures of the contractors. He had a real talent for this sort of imitation, but being prodigal in proofs of his skill, he ended by getting a sentence of three years in irons. Three years soon pass, but Chambreuil could not make up his mind to undergo prison; he escaped and hastened to Paris, where to live honourably he put in circulation a considerable number of notes which he made himself. This industry was again regarded as a crime; he was tried before the tribunal, was convicted, and sent to Brest, where, according to his sentence, he was to spend eight years.

Again Chambreuil broke his bench; but as forgery was his ordinary resource, he was taken a third time and made part of a chain which they expedited to Toulon. He had hardly arrived when he attempted to escape the vigilance of his guardians; he was arrested, taken back to the prison, and placed in the too famous Ward No. 3, where he served out his time, increased by three years.

During this detention he sought means of distraction, and he divided his leisure between denunciations and swindling, one of which was as much to his taste as the other. His preferred way was imaginary letters, which, when he left prison, cost him two years at Embrun. Chambreuil had just been taken there when His Royal Highness the Duke of Angoulême passed through that city; he sent to this prince a petition in which he described himself as a former Vendéan, a devoted servitor, on whom his devotion to royalty had brought persecutions. Chambreuil was immediately set free, and soon after he recommenced to use his liberty as he had always done.

When we discovered him, from the show he made, it was easy to judge that his fortune was in. We followed him a moment to assure ourselves that it was he, and when there was no longer any doubt, I approached him from the front and declared to him that he was my prisoner. Chambreuil thought he could impose on me by sputtering in my face a terrific series of ranks and titles which he said were his. He was no less than the director of the police of the château, and chief of the stud of France, and I was a wretch who should be chastised for my insolence. In spite of the threat, I persisted none the less in desiring him to get into my cab; and as he made difficulties about obeying, we took it upon ourselves to constrain him by force.

Monsieur the director of the police of the château was not disconcerted in M. Henry's presence; far from it; he took an arrogant, superior tone, which made the chiefs of the Prefecture tremble; all feared that I had made a mistake.

'One cannot imagine such audacity,' cried Chambreuil. 'It's an insult for which I demand reparation. I'll show you who I am, and we shall see whether you'll be permitted to use toward me an arbitrariness which the Minister would not have dared to permit.'

I saw the moment when they were going to make excuses and reprimand me. They did not doubt that Chainbreuil was an ex-convict, but they feared they had offended a powerful man, heaped with favours by the Court. At last I sustained with such energy that he was only an impostor that they could not dispense with ordering a search of his domicile. I had to assist the Commissioner of Police in this operation at which Chambreuil had to be present.

On the way the latter whispered in my ear, 'My dear Vidocq, in my writing-desk are some papers which it is important should disappear, promise me to take them, and you'll not be sorry.'

'I promise.'

'You'll find them under a double bottom; I'll explain the secret.'

He indicated how I should take them. In fact, I withdrew the papers from the place where they were, only to add them to the papers which made his arrest legitimate. Never had a forger taken more care in erecting a scaffolding of his trickery. There were cards of all kinds, papers proving the high functions which Chambreuil attributed to himself; he pretended to be in relations with the most eminent personages;

princes and princesses wrote him letters, and he even corresponded with the Prefect of Police.

The light that this search furnished corroborated so completely my assertions about Chambreuil that the authorities did not hesitate to send him to La Force to await judgment. It was impossible to get him to confess before the tribunal that he was the convict whom I insisted on recognizing. On the contrary, he produced authentic certificates by which he could prove that he had not left Vendée since the year II. For a moment the judges were embarrassed to pronounce between him and me; but I collected so many and such strong proofs in support of what I said that his identity was recognized and he was condemned to hard labour for life.

He was confined in the prison at Lorient, where he soon resumed his old habits as a denouncer. So at the time of the assassination of the Duke de Berry, in concert with one Gérard Cavette, he wrote to the police that he had revelations to make on the subject of this frightful crime. They knew Chambreuil and did not believe him; but some persons who were absurd enough to think that Cavette had accomplices demanded that he be brought to Paris; Cavette made the journey, and they learned that he knew no more than they did.

The year 1814 was one of the most remarkable in my life, principally on account of the important captures I made one after another. Some of them gave rise to rather bizarre incidents. For three years a man of almost giant stature was mentioned as the author of a large number of thefts committed in Paris. From the portraits that all the complainants made of him, it was impossible not to recognize a man named Sablin, an exceedingly adroit and enterprising thief, who, set at liberty after several successive sentences, two in irons, had resumed the practice of his trade, with all the advantages of prison experience.

Different writs were issued against Sablin; the most skilled bloodhounds of the police were set on his heels; they had a fine task; he escaped all pursuit. If they were warned that he had shown himself somewhere, when they arrived they were not in time to discover even a trace. All the inspectors at the Prefecture in the end were tired of running after this invisible being, so the task devolved on me of searching for him and seizing him if I could. For more than fifteen months I neglected nothing in order to meet him, but his appearances in Paris lasted only a few hours, and as soon as the robbery had been committed, he disappeared without its being possible to know where he had gone. In some way it became known that of all the agents I was the one Sablin feared the most. When he saw me in the distance, he avoided me so well that never once did I even see his shadow.

However, as lack of perseverance is not one of my faults, I ended by learning that Sablin had fixed his residence at Saint-Cloud, where he had hired an apartment. At this news I left Paris so as to arrive there at nightfall; it was November and the weather was frightful. When I entered Saint-Cloud all my clothes were wet through. I did not even take time to dry them, and in my impatience to find out whether I had started on false advice, I got some information about the new inhabitants from which I learned that a woman whose husband was a pedlar and nearly five feet ten inches in height had recently moved into a house in the Town Hall.

A height of five feet ten inches is not common even among the Patagonians; I did not doubt that they had pointed out to me Sablin's real domicile. However, as it was too late to present myself, I postponed my visit till the next day, and to be certain that my man would not escape, in spite of the rain, I decided to pass the night before the door. I was on watch with one of my agents.

At daybreak the door was opened, and I slipped quietly into the house in order to push on my acquaintance; I wanted to assure myself that it was time to act. But as I was putting my foot on the first step of the staircase, I stopped; someone was coming down. It was a woman whose twisted features and painful walk showed that she was suffering. At my appearance she gave a cry and went back upstairs. I followed her, and went into the apartment to which she had the key. I heard her pronounce these words, in frightened tones: 'It's Vidocq!' The bed was in the second room, and I hurried there. A man was still lying on the bed; he raised his head; it was Sablin. I hurled myself on him, and before he knew what was happening, I had the handcuffs on him.

During this operation madame had fallen on a chair, groaning; she twisted and turned and appeared to be in terrible pain.

'What's the matter with your wife?' I asked Sablin.

'Don't you see that she's in labour? She's been that way all night, and when you met her, she was going to the midwife.'

At that moment the groans redoubled: 'My God, I can stand no more. I'm dying; have pity on me; get help.' One must have had a heart of iron not to be touched by such a situation. But what could I do? It was evident that a midwife was necessary. However, how could we send for her when we were only two to guard a fellow of Sablin's strength? I could not go out; I could not let the woman die; between the calls of duty and humanity I was really the most embarrassed man in the world. Suddenly an historic recollection, well staged by Madame de Genglis, opened my mind; I remembered that the Great Monarch performed the duties of accoucheur for Lavallière. Why should I, I asked myself, be more delicate than he? Suddenly I took off my coat and in less than half an hour Madame Sablin was delivered of a superb boy. When I contemplated my work, I had the satisfaction of seeing that the mother and child were doing well.

Now we had to fulfil the formality of inscribing the newborn in the register. I offered to serve as a witness, and when I had signed, Madame Sablin said to me: 'Monsieur Jules, while you are here, will you do us a service?'

'What?'

'I dare not ask you.'

'Speak, and if it is possible...'

'We have no godfather; would you be so good as to be?'

'As well as another. Where's the godmother?'

Madame Sablin had us call one of the neighbours. We went to the church, accompanied by Sablin, for whom I had made it impossible to escape. The honour of being a godfather cost me not less than fifty francs. In spite of the chagrin he experienced, Sablin was so touched by my behaviour that he could not help showing me his gratitude.

After a good breakfast which we had brought to the room of the new mother, I took her husband to Paris, where he was sentenced to five years in prison. He became a guard at the gate at La Force, where he served his sentence. In this employment Sablin found a way not only to live well, but to lay up something at the expense of the prisoners and the people who came to visit them. He laid by a small fortune which he proposed to share with his wife; but at the time he was set free, my friend Madame Sablin, who also liked to appropriate the property of another, was making atonement at Saint-Lazare. In the isolation in which the detention of his wife threw him, Sablin did as many others do – he turned to evil ways. That is to say, one evening, having taken the fruit of his savings which he had converted into gold, he gambled and lost his all. Two days later he was found hanged in the Bois de Boulogne.

As we have seen, it was not without much trouble that I had brought Sablin to trial. Certainly if all my explorations had necessitated so many steps and measures, I should not have been equal to them, but nearly always success came in a shorter time, and sometimes it was so prompt that I was astonished myself.

A few days after my adventures at Saint-Cloud, one Sébillotte, wine merchant, rue de Charenton, No. 145, complained of having been robbed. According to his declaration, the thieves had got into his place by aid of a ladder, between seven and eight in the evening, and had taken twelve thousand francs, two gold watches, and six silver covers. There had been as much breaking inside as outside. Finally, all the circumstances of the crime were so extraordinary that there were some doubts about M. Sébillotte's veracity, and I was commissioned to clear it up. An interview with him more than convinced me that his complaint gave only real facts.

M. Sébillotte was a man of independent means and was comfortably well off and owed nothing; in consequence I saw in his situation not the shadow of a motive for the robbery, of which he complained, to be faked. Nevertheless, the robbery was of such a nature that to commit it the ins and outs of the house had to be known perfectly. I asked M. Sébillotte what persons frequented his pub most habitually.

When he had named some of them, he said: 'That's nearly all except transients, and then those foreigners who cured my wife. My word we were lucky to meet them. The poor devil had been ill for three years, and they gave her a remedy which did her good.'

'Do you see these strangers often?'

'They came in here to take their meals, but since my wife is better, we see them only once in a while.'

'Do you know what these people are? Perhaps they've been observed.'

'Oh, monsieur,' exclaimed Madame Sébillotte, who took part in the conversation, 'don't suspect them. They are honest; I have proof of it.'

'Oh, yes,' her husband went on, 'she has the proof. Let her tell it; you'll see. Tell monsieur about it.'

Madame Sébillotte began her story as follows:

'Yes, monsieur, they are honest. I would stake my life on it. Then, would you believe it, not a fortnight ago, I was busy counting the money of my lodgers when one of the women with them came in. She was the one who gave me the remedy which gave me such relief; and one can't say that she took a sou for that; on the contrary. You can realize that I could not but be pleased to see her. I made her sit down beside me, and while I put the money into piles of a hundred francs, she noticed a coin. "Oh!" she said, "have you many like that?"

'"Why?" I asked.

'"That's worth a hundred and four sous. My husband will take as many as you have at that price, if you'll put them aside."

'I thought she was joking, but that evening I was never more surprised in my life than to see her come back with her husband. We verified the money together, and as we found three hundred pieces they wanted, I let them have them, and he counted out sixty francs profit. So you can judge from that whether they are honest people, for it depended only on them to have exchanged them.'

The worker is known by his work. Madame Sébillotte's last phrase told me enough about the honest folk she was praising. Nothing more was necessary for me to be certain that the robbery had been committed by the Bohemians. The matter of the exchange was in their manner, and Madame Sébillotte in describing them only confirmed me the more in the opinion I had formed.

I left the two rather quickly, and from that moment all swarthy complexions were suspect to me. I was thinking where I could find the most of that shade, when, passing along the boulevard du Temple, I saw at a table in a sort of pub, La Maison Rustique, two individuals whose copper tint and foreign dress awakened in my mind reminiscences of my stay at Malines. I entered and whom did I see? Christian and one of his confederates whom I also knew. I went straight to them, and offered my hand to Christian, greeting him under the name of Caron. He looked at me a moment; then my features came back to his memory. 'Ah!' he exclaimed, falling on my neck in delight, 'here's my friend.'

It was a long time since we had seen each other, so that necessarily, after the first compliments, we had many questions to ask each other. He wanted to know the reason for my departure from Malines, when I had left him without warning. I made up a yarn which he appeared to believe.

'Good, good,' he said, 'whether it's true or not, I agree. Besides, I've found you again; that's the essential point. Oh, the others will be glad to see you. They're all in Paris: Caron, Langarin, Buffler, Martin, Sisque, Mich, Litle; finally, Mother Lavois is with us – and Betche, the little Betche.'

'Oh, yes, your wife?'

'She has that pleasure. If you're here at six o'clock, the reunion will be complete. We're to meet here to go to the play together. I hope you'll be one of the party; first, since you're here, we must never leave each other. Have you dined?'

'No.'

'Neither have I; we'll go to the Capucin.'

'To the Capucin then; it's very near.'

'Yes, two steps, at the corner of the rue d'Angoulême.'

The landlord of the pub whose establishment bears the grotesque image of a disciple of Saint Francis then enjoyed the favour of a public to whom quantity is more than quality. Here was a place where, without too bad fare and without anyone's taking offence, one could present himself in all possible kinds of dress, any length of beard, and in all degrees of drunkenness. Such were the advantages of the Capucin, without counting the immense common snuffbox, always open on the counter for the pleasure of whoever wanted to regale himself with a pinch as he passed. It was four o'clock when we established ourselves in this place of liberty and enjoyment. It was a long interval until six o'clock; I was impatient to return to La Maison Rustique, where Christian's companions were to assemble. After the meal we went to join them; there they were to the number of six. When we met them, Christian spoke to them in his own tongue. They surrounded me at once, greeted me, embraced me, and vied with each other in fêting me. Satisfaction showed on every face.

'No play, no play!' cried the nomads in a unanimous voice.

'You're right,' said Christian. 'No play; we'll go another time;

drink, my children, drink.'

'Drink,' repeated the Bohemians.

Wine and punch flowed in torrents. I drank, I laughed, I talked, and I plied my trade. I observed the faces, habits, gestures, etc.; nothing escaped me; I recapitulated some information Monsieur and Madame Sébillotte had furnished me, and the story of the hundred-sou pieces; what had been only a conjecture became the basis of complete conviction. I did not doubt that Christian or his confederates were the authors of the robbery denounced to the police. So I applauded the fortuitous glance I had given so apropos into the interior of La Maison Rustique. But it was not enough to have discovered the culprits. I waited until their heads were reasonably exalted by the alcoholic sublimations, and when everyone was in a state where it needed only one candle for him to see two, I went out and ran in haste to the Théâtre de la Gaîté, where I called a police officer, warned him that I was with thieves, and arranged with him that in an hour or two at the most, he should arrest us all, both men and women.

When I had given my advice, I promptly returned. My absence had not been noticed. At ten o'clock the house was surrounded; the officer presented himself with a formidable cortège of gendarmes and police spies. They bound each of us separately and took us to the station. The commissioner had preceded us; he ordered a general search. Christian, who pretended his name was Hirsch, tried in vain to conceal the six silver covers of Monsieur Sébillotte, and his companion, Madame Villemain – that is what she pretended her name was – could not screen from a most rigorous investigation the two gold watches mentioned in the complaint. The others were also obliged to put in evidence the silver and jewels and they were relieved of them.

I was extremely curious to know what reflections this event would suggest to my old comrades. I thought that I read in their eyes that I did not inspire the slightest distrust. I was not wrong, for we were hardly in the lock-up when they began to make excuses for their being the involuntary cause of my arrest.

'You will not believe it,' said Christian, 'but who the devil would have expected that to happen? You did well to say that you did not know us. Don't worry, we'll be careful not to say to the contrary, and as they've discovered nothing compromising on you, you're sure not to be held.' Christian then advised me to be discreet about his real name and those of his companions. 'However,' he added, 'the advice is superfluous, since you're no less interested than we are in keeping silent in this regard.'

I offered the Bohemians to dedicate my first moments of freedom to them; and in the hope that I should soon be set free, they indicated their domiciles, in order that when I went out, I could warn their accomplices. Toward midnight the commissioner had me withdrawn under the pretext of questioning me, and we went at once to the Marché Lenoir. The famous duchess lived there, as well as three other of Christian's confederates, whom we arrested as the result of a search which put in our hands all proofs necessary to prove them guilty.

This band was composed of twelve individuals, six men and six women; they were all sentenced, some to irons, others to confinement. The wine merchant recovered his jewels, his covers, and the greater part of his money. Madame Sébillotte was joyful. The specific the Bohemians had given her had made her health less unsettled; the news of the discovery of the twelve thousand francs healed her radically, and without doubt her experience was not lost on her.

XXVII
THE CLUE OF A SCRAP OF PAPER

FOR ABOUT FOUR MONTHS a large number of murders and robberies with violence had been committed on the roads near the capital without its being possible to discover the authors of the crimes. It was in vain that the police kept watch over certain individuals of bad repute. All their moves were useless, until a new crime, attended by horrible circumstances, furnished some indications from which it was at last permitted to hope that the guilty parties would be reached. A man named Fontaine, a butcher, who lived at Courtille, was going home from a fair in the arrondissement at Corbeil, carrying a money-bag in which he had the sum of fifteen hundred francs. He had passed Cour-de-France and was walking in the direction of Essonne, when, a short distance from an inn where he had stopped to take some refreshments, he met two men rather neatly dressed. The sun was setting, and Fontaine was not averse to travelling in company; he accosted the two unknowns, and at once got into conversation with them.

'Good evening, messieurs,' he said.

'Good evening, friend,' they answered.

The colloquy continued. 'Do you know,' said the butcher, 'that it's almost night?'

'What do you expect at this season?'

'All right, but I still have a good bit of road to make.'

'Where are you going, if we're not too curious?'

'Where am I going? To Milly to buy sheep.'

'In that case, if you'll permit us, we'll go along with you. Since we're going to Corbeil, it couldn't have happened better.'

'That's true,' the butcher answered; 'it couldn't have happened better. So I'll take advantage of your company. When one has money on one, you see, it's better not to be alone.'

'Oh, you have money!'

'I should say so, and a rather large sum.'

'We have some too, but we don't think there's any danger in this canton.'

'Do you think so? Besides, I have something to defend myself with,' he added, showing his stick, 'and with you two along, robbers would look twice, wouldn't they?'

'They'd not meddle with us.'

'No, by God, they'd not meddle with us.'

Talking away in this manner, the three arrived at the door of a small house which a branch of juniper marked as a pub. Fontaine proposed to his companions to empty a bottle with him. They went in; they took Beaugency, eight sous a litre, and sat down at a table. In honour of the occasion they had more than one bottle; when there was no further reason to prolong their stay, each one wanted to pay the score. Three-quarters of an hour went by, and when they decided to go, Fontaine, who had crooked his elbow a little too much, was a little more than gay. In such a situation what man could nurse distrust?

Fontaine congratulated himself on having found such *bon vivants*. Believing that there was nothing better to do than to take them for guides, he put himself in their hands and the three were soon in a cross-road. He walked in front with one of the unknowns; the other followed closely. The darkness was complete; one could scarcely see four yards; but crime has the eyes of a lynx; it pierces the thickest darkness. When Fontaine expected nothing, the *bon vivant* in the rear struck him a heavy blow with his club which made Fontaine reel. He was surprised and tried to turn around, but a second blow sent him down. At the same moment the other brigand, armed with a dagger, hurled himself on him and stabbed him until they thought he was dead. Fontaine had fought a long time, but in the end he succumbed.

The bandits then took his money-bag, rifled it, and went, leaving him bathed in blood. Soon a traveller passed and heard groans. The fresh air had brought Fontaine back to life. The traveller approached him, promptly lavished first aid on him, and hurried to ask for help from the nearest houses. The magistrates at Corbeil were warned immediately; the King's prosecutor arrived on the scene of the attack, questioned the people present, and enquired into the slightest circumstances. Twenty-eight wounds, more or less serious, attested to what extent the thieves had feared that their victim would escape. However, Fontaine could still pronounce some words; but he was too weak to give all the information justice needed. They took him to the hospital, and two days afterwards a notable improvement in his situation gave hope that they would save him.

The removal of the body had been made with the most minute exactness; nothing had been neglected which might lead to the discovery of the assassins. Footprints had been traced; buttons and bits of paper covered with blood had been collected. On one of these fragments which was found not far away and which seemed to have served to wipe the blade of the knife, there were some characters traced by hand, but they had no connection and consequently could furnish no indication from which it was easy to deduce anything. However, the King's prosecutor attached a high importance to the explanation of these signs. They again explored the approaches to the place where Fontaine had been found lying, and a second bit of paper, which appeared like a part of an address, was picked up in the grass. By examining it carefully, they managed to make out these words:

> To Monsieur Rao
> Wine Merchant, Bar
>> Roche
>> Cli

This scrap of paper seemed to have formed part of a printed document, but what the nature of the document was it was impossible to explain. However that might be, as on such an occasion even the slightest circumstance should be stated, while certain intelligence is awaited, they took note of all that might contribute to the enquiry.

The magistrates who assembled these first facts deserve praise for the zeal and skill they displayed. As soon as they had fulfilled the first part of their mission, they went in all haste to Paris to advise with the judicial and administrative authorities. On their request I was brought into conference with them, and, furnished with the report they had drawn up, I began my campaign in search of the bandits. The victim had described them, but it was a question whether I should rely on information which came from such a source. Few men in great danger preserve enough presence of mind to see well, and this time I was disposed to suspect the testimony of Fontaine the more in that it was most precise. He related that during the struggle, which had lasted some time, one of his assailants had fallen to his knees and had cried out in pain. A moment after he had told his accomplice that he was suffering keenly. Other remarks which he pretended had been made appeared to me extraordinary in the state he was in. It was difficult for me to believe that he was very sure in his reminiscences. Nevertheless, I proposed to profit by them, but before all it was expedient that I adopt a more positive point of departure for my expedition.

The part of an address was in my opinion an enigma which it was necessary to solve first. I put my mind at work, and without much effort I was shortly convinced that, except for the name, it might be reconstructed as follows: 'To Monsieur— Wine Merchant, Barrier Rochechouart, Chaussée (Road) Clignancourt.' So it was evident that the thieves had been in touch with a wine merchant of that quarter; perhaps the wine merchant himself was one of the authors of the crime.

I aimed my batteries so as to know the truth promptly, and before the end of the day I was persuaded that I should not be wrong if I grouped my suspicions around a man named Raoul. This man was known to me under rather poor auspices; he had the reputation of being one of the most intrepid smugglers in the business, and the publichouse he kept was the meeting-place for a crowd of evildoers who came there to hold their orgies. Besides, Raoul's wife was the sister of a freed convict, and I was instructed that he had acquaintance with all sorts of people of illfame. In a word, his reputation was abominable, and when a crime was committed, if he had not participated in it, one was at least authorized to say, 'If it wasn't you, it was your brother or one of your relatives.'

Raoul was in some way in a perpetual state of suspicion, either on his own account or that of his associates. I resolved to have the approaches to his pub watched, and I ordered my agents to have an eye on everyone who frequented it, in order to find out whether among the number there was one wounded in the knee.

While the observers were at the posts to which I had assigned them, information which I got on my side apprised me that Raoul received habitually at his place one or two good-for-nothing fellows of rather bad appearance with whom he seemed to be intimately connected. The neighbours affirmed that they always saw them go out together, that their absences were frequent, and that they had no doubt that most of his commerce was contraband. A wine merchant who lived near enough to see all that happened in Raoul's domicile told me that he had noticed that his confrère often went out at dusk and did not return until the next day, often worn out with fatigue and covered with mud to his chin. I was also told that Raoul had a target in his garden, and that he practised firing his pistol there. Such was the gossip that came to me from all sides.

At the same time my agents reported that they had seen at Raoul's a man whom they presumed to be one of the bandits; he did not limp, but he walked painfully, and his dress was like that which Fontaine had described. The agents added that this man was constantly accompanied by his wife, and that the two were in close relations with Raoul. They were sure that they lived on the first floor of a house, rue Coquenard. However, in fear of giving them warning of the steps which prudence prescribed should be made as secretly as possible, they had not thought it expedient to push the investigation further.

This report strengthened my conjectures; I had no sooner received it than I placed my agents on watch at the house they had designated to me. It was night; I waited until day, and before it appeared, I was on picket duty, rue Coquenard. I stayed there and danced attendance until four o'clock in the afternoon; I really began to get impatient when the agents showed me a man whose name and features suddenly came to mind. 'That's he,' they said; indeed, I had scarcely seen the said Court, than, recalling his antecedents, I was convinced that he was one of the bandits I was seeking. His morality, which was most suspect, had drawn him into terrible unpleasantness on several occasions; he had just finished several months in jail, and I well recalled that I had arrested him for fraud with violence. He was one of those degraded beings, who, like Cain, bear the sentence of death on their foreheads.

Without being much of a prophet, one could have boldly predicted that he was destined for the scaffold. One of those presentiments which never deceive me warned me that he was reaching the end of his perilous career into which he had been pushed by fate. However, I did not want to act too precipitously, so that I might assure myself whether he had any means of existence. No one knew of any, and it was notorious to the public that he had nothing and did not work. The neighbours whom I questioned all agreed that his conduct was most irregular. To sum up, Court, like Raoul, was regarded as a finished bandit; one would have condemned them on their appearance alone. I had reasons to see them as downright scoundrels and I hastened to get warrants which would authorize me to seize them.

I got the order for their capture, and the following day, before sunrise, I was at Court's door. When I reached the landing, I knocked.

'Who's there?' he asked.

'Open! It's Raoul,' and I counterfeited the latter's voice.

I at once heard him hurrying, and when he opened, supposing he was talking to his friend, Court asked, 'Is there anything new?'

'Yes, yes,' I answered, 'there's something new.'

I had not finished these words, when by the light of dawn, he saw that I had fooled him.

'Oh!' he exclaimed, with a movement of fright, 'it's Monsieur Jules.' (That was the name the girls and thieves gave me.)

'Monsieur Jules!' Court's wife repeated, still more astonished than he was.

'Well, what of it?' I asked the couple alarmed by so early an awakening. 'Are you afraid? I'm not as black as the Devil!'

'That's true,' observed the husband. 'Monsieur Jules is all right; he's arrested me once, but that's all right; I'm not sore.'

'I believe you,' I answered. 'Is it my fault if you smuggle?'

'Smuggle!' Court replied, in the assured accent of a man who feels a great weight off him. 'Smuggle! Oh, Monsieur Jules, you know that if I did, I should not hide it from you. Besides, you can search.'

While he became more and more at ease, I searched the lodging, where I found a pair of loaded pistols, knives, garments which appeared to have been freshly washed, and some other objects which I seized.

Now I had to complete the expedition. If I arrested the husband and left the wife free, there was no doubt that she would warn Raoul of what had happened. So I took them both to the station, Place Cadet. I bound Court, and he suddenly became sombre and thoughtful. The precautions I had taken caused him uneasiness; his wife also seemed to be making terrible reflections. They were struck dumb when, once at the station, they heard me recommend that they be separated and watched. I ordered that their needs should be provided for, but they were neither hungry nor thirsty. When Court was questioned about it, he responded merely by a shake of his head; he was eighteen hours without touching a mouthful; his eyes were fixed in a stare and his features were without movement. This impassibility indicated only too well that he was guilty. In such circumstances I have always remarked the two extremes, a dreary silence or an unendurable volubility.

Court and his wife were in a place of safety; it remained to take Raoul. I went to his place; he was not there. The waiter who looked after the shop told me that he had slept in Paris where he had lodgings, but that, as it was Sunday, he would not fail to arrive early.

Raoul's absence was a contretemps I had not foreseen. I trembled at the thought that he might take a notion to see his friend. In that case he would certainly be told of his arrest, and it was probable that he would take measures to escape. I was also afraid that he might have seen us on our expedition to rue Coquenard, and my apprehensions doubled when the waiter told me that his master had his lodgings in the Faubourg Montmartre. He had never gone there, and could not tell me about the place, but he presumed that it was around Place Cadet. Each bit of information he gave me confirmed my fears, for perhaps Raoul was late because he suspected something.

At nine o'clock he had not returned; I questioned the waiter again, but without saying anything which would inspire distrust. He could not understand why Raoul was not installed behind his counter; he was really uneasy. The maid who prepared breakfast for my agents and myself expressed astonishment that her master, and especially her mistress, were not so prompt as usual; she was afraid that they had been held by some accident.

'If I knew their address,' she said, 'I'd go and see whether they were dead.'

I was sure that they were not; but what had become of them? At noon we were without news, and I definitely believed that the secret was out when the waiter, who had been on watch at the door for a moment, ran in and said, 'There he is!'

'Who wants me?' asked Raoul.

But he had hardly crossed the threshold when he recognized me.

'Ah, bonjour, Monsieur Jules,' he said, coming toward me, 'what brings you to our quarter today?'

He was far from thinking that I had business with him. In order not to frighten him, I tried to put him off the scent of the visit.

'Oh, as to that,' I said, 'so you've decided to be a liberal?'

'A liberal?'

'Yes, yes, liberal, and what's more, they say you ... but we can't explain matters here. I must speak to you privately.'

'Certainly, go up to the first floor, and I'll follow.'

I went up, signalling to my agents to watch Raoul, and to seize him if he even seemed to want to go out. The wretch did not even think of it, and I soon had the proof, for he came at once as he had promised. He came up to me with an almost jovial air; I was delighted to see him with such an air of security.

'Now we're alone,' I said, 'we can talk at our ease, and I'll tell you why I came. Don't you guess?'

'Really I don't.'

'You've already had trouble about some song parties, which you insist on holding in your pub, in spite of your being forbidden to do so. The police are informed that every Sunday there are meetings here at which they sing songs against the government. Not only do they know that you receive a crowd of suspects, but they are advised that this very day you expect a rather large number from noon to four o'clock in the afternoon; you see, when the police want to know they are ignorant of nothing. That's not all; they pretend that you have in your hands a mass of seditious and immoral songs which are so carefully hidden that to find them we are recommended to come only in disguise, and not to act until the gentlemen of the party have opened their meeting. I am disturbed that I have been charged with such a disagreeable mission. I did not know that I was being sent to someone of my acquaintance, otherwise I should have excused myself, because, as far as you are concerned, a disguise would not serve me.'

'That's right,' Raoul answered, 'and that can't...'

'No matter,' I went on, 'it's better that it should be I instead of someone else. You know that I don't wish you harm, so the best thing you can do is to give me all the songs in your possession ... then, to avoid trouble, if I were to advise you, it would be not to receive men whose opinions might compromise you.'

'I did not know,' Raoul observed, 'that politics was your department.'

'When one's in the shop, he has to do a little of everything.'

'In other words, you do what you're told. That's all one to me; as true as my name's Clair Raoul, I can swear to you that I have been denounced falsely. Is everyone scum? I'm only trying to make a poor living. They're right when they say that someone's always envious. But, listen, Monsieur Jules, I have no rear door. Stay here all day and you'll see whether I'm imposing on you.'

'I consent, but no spree at least; and have someone to get rid of the songs; and nothing of this outside. If you warn the singers...'

'What do you take me for?' Raoul replied with vivacity. 'If I give my word, I don't fail; one either has honour or he hasn't. Besides, to prove that my intentions aren't bad, you needn't leave me; I promise not to whisper a word, not even to my wife when she comes back; so that you can be sure. Say, you must let me cut up the meats.'

'With pleasure; I don't know that the service must stop. I am even ready to give you a hand.'

'You're too good, Monsieur Jules, but I don't refuse.'

'Come on,' I said, 'to work!'

We went down together. Raoul armed himself with a large cleaver, and soon, my sleeves rolled up to my elbow, an apron in front, I helped to cut up the veal destined that day with the salad *de rigueur* to delight the Luculluses of the public-house. From the veal I turned to lamb, and cut off dozens of cutlets. When there was nothing more to be done in the kitchen, I went into the cellar and helped make wine at six sous a litre.

During this operation, I was face to face with Raoul and I stuck to him like his shadow or his cleaver. I confess that several times I trembled lest he might suspect the reason why I watched him so closely. If he had, he would have certainly cut my throat, and I should have fallen without a chance of being rescued. But in me he saw only a familiar face which belonged to the political inquisition, and he was perfectly at ease in regard to the imputations directed against him.

I had performed the duties of a second chef for four hours when the commissioner of police, whom I had warned, arrived at last. I was on the ground floor. As soon as I saw him, I hurried to him, and, after asking him to present himself only after some minutes, I went back to Raoul.

'The devil take them,' I said. 'Now they pretend that we shouldn't be here, but at your place in Paris.'

'If that's so, let's go there.'

'Come on, and when we get there, we'll have to come back here. Look, if I were in your place, while we are here, I'd ask the commissioner to search the pub; that will be a way to make him think you've been wrongly suspected.'

Raoul regarded my advice as excellent and took the step I suggested. The commissioner granted his request, and the search was made with the greatest care. It produced nothing.

'Well,' said Raoul, with that tone of satisfaction which seems to announce the man above reproach, 'will you give me a helping hand, for that trash – to make so much trouble? If I'd committed murder, it would be no worse!'

The assurance with which he uttered the last phrase disconcerted me. I almost had some scruples about believing him guilty, yet he was, and the favourable impression was promptly erased from my mind. It was sad to think that a scoundrel, with his hands still reeking with his victim's blood, could without a shudder proffer words which recalled the crime. Raoul was calm and triumphant. When we got into the cab to go to his place in Paris, one would have thought he was going to a wedding.

'My wife,' he said, 'will be surprised to see me in such good company.'

She came to open to us. At our appearance her face showed not the slightest change; she offered us seats; but we had no time to lose, so without regard to politeness, the commissioner and I proceeded to another search. Raoul was present; he guided us with extreme complaisance.

In order to make the story I had made up believable, we attached the greatest importance to the papers. Raoul gave me the key to his writing-desk. I took up a bundle of papers, and the first one on which I cast my eye was a summons, part of which had been torn off. Suddenly I retraced the form of the scrap on which was written the address annexed to the report of the magistrates at Corbeil ... This scrap fitted exactly in the tear. The commissioner to whom I told my observations agreed with me. At first Raoul watched us with indifference as we examined the summons; perhaps he didn't mind; but suddenly his muscles contracted; he grew pale, and, jumping toward a drawer of his commode where his loaded pistols were, he was about to seize them, when, by a movement no less rapid, my agents hurled themselves on him and put it out of his power to resist.

It was midnight when Raoul and his wife were taken to the Prefecture; Court arrived a quarter of an hour later. The two accomplices were locked up separately. Until now we had only presumptions and half-proofs against them. I proposed to get them to confess while they were still in a stupor. I tried my eloquence first on Court; I used every sort of argument to convince him that it was in his own interest to confess.

'Believe me,' I said, 'tell the truth. Why do you persist in hiding what we know? At the first examination you undergo, you will find that we know more than you think. All the people you attacked aren't dead; they'll produce testimony against you which is crushing; you may keep silent, but you'll be condemned none the less. The scaffold isn't what's the most terrible; it is the torment, the rigour with which they'll punish your obstinacy. justly irritated at you, the magistrates will leave you neither peace nor truce until the hour of execution. If you remain silent, prison will be a hell for you; if, on the contrary, you speak, show repentance and resignation, and, since you can't escape your fate, try at least, then the judges may pity you and want to treat you with humanity.'

During this exhortation, which was really much longer, Court was much disturbed. When I said that all the people he had attacked were not dead, he changed colour and turned his head away. I noted that imperceptibly he lost countenance; his breast inflated visibly, and he breathed with difficulty. Finally, at half-past four in the morning, he fell on my neck; tears flowed in abundance.

'Oh, Monsieur Jules,' he exclaimed between his sobs, 'I am a great sinner. I'll tell you all.'

I was careful not to tell Court of what crime he was accused. As probably he had committed more than one murder, I did not want to be specific. I hoped that by stopping on vague terms, and in the absence of too precise information, he would perhaps put me on the track of some crime other than that for which we were after him. Court reflected a moment.

'Well, yes, I murdered the poultry dealer. He must have had nine lives. The poor devil, to recover from such an assault! This is how it was done, Monsieur Jules; may I die if I lie. There were several Normans who were returning after selling their merchandise in Paris. I thought they were loaded with money, consequently I lay in wait. I stopped the first two who presented themselves, but I found almost nothing on them. At the time I was most frightfully hard up; misery pushed me to it; I felt that my wife lacked everything, which made my heart bleed. Finally, when I was giving up in despair, I heard the noise of a carriage; I ran; it was the poultry dealer. I surprised him half-asleep; I summoned him to give me his purse. He searched and I searched myself; he had in all eighty francs. Eighty francs! What is that when one owes everyone? I had the rent to pay; the owner had threatened to put me out. And to add to my misfortune, I was harassed by other creditors. What could I do with eighty francs? I was carried away by rage; I took my pistols and fired them both into the breast of that gentleman. A fortnight later I got the news that he was still alive. judge my surprise. Since that moment I haven't had an instant's rest. I suspected that he would play me some bad turn.'

'Your fears are well founded,' I said; 'but the poultry dealer was not the only one you murdered; there is that butcher whom you riddled with blows of your knife, after you'd taken his money-bag.'

'As for that,' the scoundrel answered, 'may God have his soul! I'll answer that if he deposes against me, it will be at the Last judgment.'

'You're mistaken, the butcher didn't die.'

'Oh, so much the better!' Court cried.

'No, he will not die, and I must warn you that he has described you and your accomplice so that there can be no mistake.'

Court tried to sustain that he had no accomplice, but he hadn't strength to persist in the lie for long, and he ended by indicating Clair Raoul. I insisted that he name the others, but it was in vain. Provisionally I had to be content with the confessions he had made, and for fear that he would take the idea of retracting them, I immediately called the commissioner, and in his presence, Court reiterated them in the greatest detail.

Doubtless it was a first victory to have induced Court to confess his guilt and sign his declaration, but a second remained to be won. Raoul must be brought to follow the example of his friend. In the end I succeeded. I brought the two together; they embraced, and improvising a ruse which I had not suggested, but which succeeded marvellously, Court said to Raoul, 'Well, so you've done as I did, and confessed? You've done well.'

For an instant Raoul was as if annihilated, but soon recovered his spirits. 'By Jove, Monsieur Jules,' he said, 'that's well played; you've done me in beautifully. As I am a man of my word, I'll do what I told you and hide nothing.'

Immediately he began to make a recital which fully confirmed that of his accomplice. When the commissioner had received the new revelations in the form demanded by law, I stayed to talk with the two murderers; they supped well and drank reasonably. Their faces had become calm; there was no trace of the catastrophe of the evening; they saw that the matter was arranged; when they confessed, they had agreed to pay their debt to justice.

XXVIII
A HERCULES AND A BRIGAND

THE NEWS of our arrival at Corbeil spread instantly. The inhabitants hastened to see these murderers. I too was an object of curiosity. On this occasion I had no trouble in learning what they thought of me six leagues from the capital. I insinuated myself into the crowd assembled in front of the prison gate, and there I had only to lend an ear to hear the most singular remarks. 'That's he, that's he,' the spectators repeated, standing on tiptoe every time the grill opened to let one of my agents come in or go out.

A gendarme saw me among the spectators and came to me, and, touching me lightly on the shoulder, said, 'Monsieur Vidocq, the King's prosecutor is asking for you.' Suddenly all around me I saw the faces lengthen in a strange fashion. 'What, is that Vidocq?' Then, 'It's Vidocq! It's Vidocq!' they repeated, and the most enthusiastic used their elbows to make their way toward me. Some climbed up on others to see me. This whole mass of curiosity-seekers really imagined that I was a more than human figure. The expressions of surprise I caught gave me proof of that.

The crowd was such that it was only with difficulty that I was able to get near the King's prosecutor. This magistrate directed me to take the men under arrest before the judge. Court, whom I took first, seemed intimidated when he found himself in the presence of so many persons. I exhorted him to renew his confessions; he did without too much difficulty as far as the attack on the butcher was concerned, but when he was questioned about the poultry dealer, he retracted what he had told me, and it was impossible to bring him to declare that he had other accomplices besides Raoul.

When the latter was brought in, he did not hesitate to confirm all the facts in the report of the examination he had undergone after his arrest. He related at length and with an imperturbable coolness all that had passed between him and the unfortunate Fontaine up to the moment when he had struck him. 'The man,' he said, 'was only dazed by the two blows of the club; I approached him as if to hold him up. I had in my hand the knife here on the table.'

At the same time he rushed toward the desk, abruptly seized the instrument of the crime, took two steps back, rolling his eyes which shone with madness, and assumed a threatening attitude. This unexpected movement froze in fright all present; the sub-prefect was almost ill; I myself was not without fear.

However, in the persuasion that it was prudent to attribute this movement of Raoul's only to a good motive, I said, with a smile: 'Well, gentlemen, what are you afraid of? Raoul is incapable of committing a base action and abusing the confidence we show him. He took the knife only so that we may the better judge the gesture.'

'Thanks, Monsieur Jules,' said Raoul, charmed by the explanation, and placing the knife on the table. 'I only wanted to show you how I used it.'

The confrontation of the prisoners with Fontaine was indispensable to complete the preliminary examination. The doctor was consulted as to whether the condition of the invalid would permit him to undergo such a hard ordeal, and on his reply in the affirmative Court and Raoul were taken to the hospital. When they were brought into the ward where the butcher was, they looked for their victim. Fontaine had his head wrapped up, his face was covered with linen bandages, and he was unrecognizable. But near him were exposed the garments and shirt which he had worn when he was so cruelly assailed.

'Oh, poor Fontaine!' exclaimed Court, falling on his knees at the foot of the bed decorated with these bloody trophies, 'forgive the miserable creatures who have put you in such a state. Since you have escaped it is by the will of God; He wished to preserve you so that we might pay the penalty for our misdeeds. Forgive us, forgive us!' Court repeated, hiding his face in his hands. While he was thus expressing himself, Raoul, kneeling too, kept silent, and seemed plunged in deep affliction.

'Come, get up, and look the sick man in the face,' said the judge whom I accompanied. They arose.

'Take those assassins out of my sight!' cried Fontaine. 'I know them only too well by their faces and the sound of their voices.'

This recognition and the sight of the guilty were more than sufficient to establish that Court and Raoul had attacked the butcher. But I was further convinced that they had a goodly number of other crimes with which to reproach themselves, and that to commit them there must have been more than the two. This was the secret which it was important for me to draw from them; I determined not to leave them until they had revealed everything.

On our return from the confrontation I had supper served in the jail for the two prisoners and myself. The jailer asked whether he should put knives on the table. 'Yes, yes,' I said, 'put on the knives.' My two guests ate with as much appetite as if they had been the most honest men in the world. When they began to feel the wine, I skilfully brought them back to the thought of their crimes.

'You're not so bad at heart,' I told them. 'I'll wager that you were drawn into this; some scoundrel has ruined you. Why don't you agree? Since you felt a movement of compassion and repentance when you saw Fontaine, it is demonstrated to me that you wish, at the price of your blood, you had not shed that which you spilt. Well, if you keep silent about your accomplices, you'll be responsible for all the evil they may do. Several persons whom you attacked have deposed that there were at least four of you on your expeditions.'

'They're wrong,' Raoul replied, 'on my word of honour, Monsieur Jules. We've never been more than three; the other was a former lieutenant in the customs called Pons Gérard. He lives near the frontier, in a small village between La Capelle and Hirson, Department of the Aisne. But if you want to arrest him, I warn you that he's no funk.'

'No,' said Court, 'he's not easy to bridle, and if you don't take precautions, you'll have your work cut out for you.'

'Oh, he's a hard customer,' Raoul went on. 'You're not a fool, Monsieur Jules, but ten like you would not scare him. In any case you're warned. First, if he gets wind that you're searching for him, it's not far from his place to Belgium, and he'll take himself off. If you surprise him, he'll resist. So find some way to take him asleep.'

'Yes, but he rarely sleeps,' observed Court.

I informed myself about Pons Gérard's habits and made them give me his description. When I had obtained all the information I thought I needed to assure myself of this person, with the idea of establishing the revelations I had just heard, I proposed to the two prisoners to write immediately to the magistrate who had the right to receive confessions. Raoul took his pen in hand, and when he had finished, although it was nearly one o'clock in the morning, I myself took the letter to the King's prosecutor. It was conceived in these terms:

> Monsieur, having returned to feelings more suitable to our position, and profiting by the advice you have given us, we have decided to tell you of all the crimes of which we have been guilty, and to describe our third accomplice. We pray you, in consequence, to come to us to receive our declarations.

The magistrate hurried to the jail, and Court, as well as Raoul, repeated before him all that they had told me of Pons Gérard. Now I had to occupy myself with the last. As it was necessary not to leave him time to learn of the misadventure of his comrades, I at once obtained an order to go and arrest him.

Disguised as a horse-trader, I went with my agents Goury and Clément who passed for my grooms. We were so diligent that, in spite of the rigour of the season and the difficulty of the roads (it was winter), we arrived at La Capelle the next evening, the night before the fair. I knew the country, for I had travelled over it as a soldier, so I needed only an instant to orient myself and make enquiries. All the inhabitants with whom I talked about Pons Gérard painted him as a ruffian who lived only by fraud and robbery; his mere name gave rise to fright; everyone trembled before him; the local authorities to whom he was denounced daily did not dare to repress him. Finally, he was one of those terrible beings who lay down the law to all around him.

However that might be, I was little accustomed to recoil before a perilous enterprise, and I persisted none the less in attempting the adventure. All that I heard of Pons Gérard piqued my *amour-propre*, but how should I come out of it with honour? I did not yet know, but waiting for an inspiration I breakfasted with my agents, and when we had sufficiently filled our stomachs, we set out in search of the accomplice of Raoul and Court. An isolated inn had been pointed out to me as the meeting-place of smugglers. Pons went there frequently; he was well known to the woman who kept the inn, who regarded him as one of her best customers and was much interested in him. This inn had been so perfectly described to me that I needed no other information to find it.

Escorted by my two companions I arrived, entered, and without any ceremony sat down, assuming the manners of a man familiar with the customs of the house.

'Bonjour, Mère Bardou. How goes it?'

'Bonjour, welcome. As you see, everything's quiet. What can I serve you?'

'Dinner. We're dying of hunger.'

'It'll be ready soon. Go into the dining-room and get warm.'

'I'm sure you don't recognize me.'

'Wait.'

'You saw me twenty times last winter, with Pons, when we came during the night.'

'What, it's you?'

'I'm sure of it.'

'I remember you perfectly.'

'And good Gérard, how is he? Always very well?'

'Oh, as for that, yes; he took a drop here this morning on his way to work at Lamarre's.'

I was completely ignorant where this place was situated, but as I pretended to know the locality, I was careful not to enquire. Besides, I hoped that, without asking direct questions, I should get her to indicate it to me.

We had hardly swallowed our first mouthfuls, when Mère Bardou came and told me, 'You were just speaking of Gérard; his daughter's here.'

'Which one?'

'The smallest.'

I got up at once, hurried to the little one, embraced her before she had time to look at me, and questioned her, asking for news of each member of the family one after another. When she had answered, I said, 'Come, that's good. You're a fine little girl; here's an apple to eat, and afterwards we'll go together to see your mother.'

Our meal was promptly ended, and I went out with the little girl and followed her. At first she started toward her mother's house, but once I was sure that the inn-keeper could not see us, I said to my guide, 'Listen, little one, do you know where Lamarre's place is?'

'It's down there,' she answered, pointing in the direction of Hirson.

'Now tell your mother that you have seen three of your father's friends, and that she should prepare supper for them. We'll come back with him. Au revoir, my child.'

Gérard's daughter went her way, and we were soon opposite Lamarre's house, but there were no workers there. I questioned a peasant who told me that they were a little farther on. We continued our way, and when we reached a slight rise, in fact I saw thirty men busy in repairing the main road. As the marker, Gérard should be in this group. We advanced. When we were fifty yards away from the labourers, I pointed out to my agents an individual who from his figure and dress agreed with the description which had been given me. I did not doubt that it was Gérard, and my agents shared my opinion. But Gérard was too well surrounded for me to go alone and seize him. His recklessness made him formidable, and if his comrades came to his defence, it was unbelievable that we should not fail to execute our warrant. This juncture was embarrassing. On the least demonstration on our part, Gérard could either give us a bad time or escape over the frontier. I had never felt a greater necessity for prudence. In this circumstance I consulted my two agents; they were brave men.

'Do what you want,' they answered. 'We're ready to second you in everything, even if we kick the bucket.'

'Well,' I answered, 'follow me, and act only when the time comes. If we aren't the strongest, perhaps we'll be the shrewdest.'

I went straight to the individual whom I supposed was Gérard, my two agents keeping some steps behind me. The nearer I got, the more convinced I was that I was not mistaken. At last I reached my man, and without any other preamble, I took his head in my hands and embraced him.

'Bonjours, Pons, how are you? Are your wife and children in good health?'

Pons was as if dazed by such an abrupt salutation; he appeared astonished and looked me over.

'Gad,' he said, 'the devil take me if I know you. Who are you?'
'What, don't you recognize me? I must have changed.'

'No, I don't recall you at all; tell me your name. I've seen your face somewhere, but I can't remember where or when.'

Then I bent to his ear, and said, 'I'm a friend of Court and Raoul.

They sent me to you.'

'Oh,' he said, pressing my hand affectionately, and turning away from the workers, 'I must have a short memory. Not to know you, and you a friend! Well, come, I'll embrace you.' And he grasped me in his arms as if to smother me.

During this scene the agents did not lose me from sight. Pons noticed them, and asked me if they were with me. 'They're my grooms,' I answered.

'I did not doubt it. Ah, that's not all; you must need refreshments, and these two gentlemen too; we must have a drink.'

'All right. It'll do us no harm.'

'What a nuisance! In this damned country one can't find anything. We can get wine only in Hirson, a long league from here. You must have passed through it.'

'Oh, well, let's go to Hirson.'

Pons said good-bye to his comrades and we went together. On the way I observed him, and it was easy to conclude that this man's strength had not been exaggerated. He was not tall, about five feet four, but he was thickly built. His brown face, tanned by the sun, was distinguished by the strength of his powerfully cut features. He had thick shoulders, neck, and thighs, and enormous arms; add to that a dark, exceedingly thick beard and short hands covered with hair to the fingertips. His stern and pitiless look belonged to one of those physiognomies which can laugh only because they are mobile, but which never show a smile.

While we marched on side by side, I saw that Pons was considering me from head to foot. 'Gad,' he said, stopping an instant to consider me, 'what a fellow! You can boast that you fill your trousers. I'm not thin, and seeing you, they might say that we make a pair. I'm not like that bantam,' he added, pointing to Clément, who was the smallest agent in the brigade. 'I could swallow him for breakfast.'

'Don't you believe it!'

'Possibly, sometimes those little chaps are all nerves.'

After such talk of people who have nothing better to say, Pons asked me for news of his friends. I told him that they were in good health, but as they had not seen him since the Avesnes affair (this was a murder, and when I spoke of it he did not blink), I had left them uneasy as to what had become of him.

'Well, what's brought you into this country?' Pons asked me. 'Will you smuggle by any chance?'

'As you say, my good man. I came here to pass some horses. They gave me to understand that you could give me a lift.'

'Oh, you can count on me,' Pons protested.

Talking along in this way we reached Hirson, where he took us into a shop which sold wine. The four of us were there at a table; we were served, and as we drank, I turned the conversation on Court and Raoul.

'Right now,' I said, 'they are perhaps in difficulties.'

'How's that?'

'I did not want to tell you at once, but a misfortune has come to them. They have been arrested, and I'm afraid that they're still in jail.'

'What's the reason?'

'I don't know the reason. All I know is that I was lunching with Court at Raoul's when the police came. They questioned all three of us; I was released at once. The others were held and are in solitary confinement. You would not have been warned of what's happened to them if Raoul, as he was coming back from his examination, had not been able to tell me a few words in private. It was to warn you to be on your guard, because they've mentioned you. I won't tell you any more.'

'Who arrested you?' asked Pons, who appeared to be disturbed by the event.

'Vidocq.'

'Oh, that blackguard! But what's this Vidocq who causes so much talk? I've never seen him face to face; once I saw the back of someone who was going into Causette's, and they said it was he. But I don't know him, and I would willingly pay some bottles of good wine to anyone who will show him to me.'

'It's not hard to meet him, for he's always rambling about.'

'He'd better not fall in with me. If he were here, I'd give him a bad quarter of an hour.'

'Oh, you're like the rest. If he were here, you'd be quiet and the first to offer him a drink.' (As I said this, I extended my glass and he poured.)

'I? I'd offer him something else.'

'You'd offer him a drink, I tell you.'

'Go on, I'd rather die.'

'In that case, you can die when you want to. I'm he, and I arrest you.'

'What! What! How?'

'Yes, I arrest you,' and, putting my face close to his, 'and I tell you, you coward, that if you flinch, I'll eat your nose. Clément, put the handcuffs on the gentleman.'

Pons's astonishment can easily be imagined. All his features were convulsed; his eyes seemed starting from their sockets; his cheeks trembled; his teeth chattered; his hair stood on end. Gradually these symptoms of an irritation at the top of his body were effaced and took another form. When his arms had been tied, he remained motionless for twenty-five minutes, as if petrified. His mouth hung open; his tongue stuck to his palate, and it was only after repeated efforts that he could get it loose; in vain he tried to moisten his lips with saliva. In less than half an hour this scoundrel's face was successively pale, yellow, livid, offering all the changes that a corpse shows in decomposition.

Finally, Pons came out of his lethargy and articulated these words: 'What, you're Vidocq? If I'd known that when you accosted me, I'd have purged the world of an infamous blackguard.'

'All right,' I said. 'I thank you. Meanwhile, you have fallen into the snare and you owe me some bottles of wine. What's more, I hold you to it. You wanted to see Vidocq; I showed him to you. Another time that will teach you not to tempt the devil.'

The gendarmes whom I called after Pons's arrest could not believe their eyes. During the search which we had been ordered to make at his domicile, the mayor of the commune confounded us with thanks.

'What an eminent service you've rendered the country!' he said. 'He was the general bugbear. You have delivered us from a real plague.'

All the inhabitants were pleased to see Pons in our hands, and there was not one of them who did not marvel that we had effected the capture of this rascal without firing a shot.

I went directly back to Paris. I took Pons to Versailles where Court and Raoul were detained.

On my arrival I went to see them. 'Well,' I said, 'our man is arrested.'

'You have him?' said Court. 'Well, so much the better.'

'He didn't fly?' cried Raoul. 'I'm sure he led you a merry life.'

'He!' I replied. 'He's been gentle as a lamb.'

'What, didn't he defend himself? Hey, look, Raoul, he didn't defend himself.'

'Those terrible fellows have large mouths, but they only swallow little bits.'

'The information you gave me,' I told them, 'wasn't lost.'

Before I left Versailles I wanted to show my gratitude by giving the prisoners a distraction in having them dine with me. They accepted with marked satisfaction, and all the time we passed together, I saw not the slightest sign of distress on their brows. I should not have been surprised if they had become honest men, at least their language seemed to indicate it.

'We must agree, my poor Raoul,' said Court, 'that we practised a devil of a trade.'

'Oh, don't talk about it; any trade that gets its master hanged...'

'And that's not all: to be in constant apprehension; not to have an instant's peace; to tremble at the appearance of every new face!'

'That's very true. I seemed to see police spies and gendarmes in disguise everywhere. The least noise or a shadow seemed to upset all my senses.'

'And when anyone unknown looked at me, I imagined that he was taking my description, and I felt feverish. I felt that in spite of myself I was blushing to the whites of my eyes.'

'One hardly knows how it is when one begins to go wrong. If I had it to do over again, I would rather a thousand times blow out my brains.'

'I have two children, but if they are to turn out badly, I would rather recommend their mother to smother them.'

'If we had taken as much trouble to do well as we did to do wrong, we should not be here. We should be happier.'

'Since we've confessed,' said Raoul, 'I feel as though I were in Paradise in comparison with what I was before. I know that we have a bad moment to pass, but those whom we killed weren't enjoying themselves; at least we serve as an example.'

As we separated, Raoul and Court asked me the favour of coming to see them as soon as they were sentenced; I promised and kept my word. Two days after the sentence was pronounced which condemned them to death, I went to them. When I entered their cell, they gave a cry of joy. My name rang under the sombre vaults like that of a liberator; they showed that my visit gave them the greatest pleasure and they asked to embrace me. I had not the strength to refuse. They were attached to a camp bed, with irons on their hands and feet. They pressed me to their bosoms with the same effusion of heart as real friends who meet after a long and painful separation. A person of my acquaintance, who was present at the interview, was greatly alarmed at seeing me in some way at the discretion of two murderers.

'Don't be afraid,' I told him.

'No, no, don't be afraid of anything,' said Raoul with vivacity. 'There's no risk of our doing harm to Monsieur Jules.'

'Monsieur Jules!' proffered Court, 'there's a man. He's our only friend, and what pleases me is that he hasn't abandoned us.'

As I was about to withdraw, I saw near them two small books, one half-open (it was 'Christian Thoughts').

'It appears,' I said to them, 'that you're reading. Are you by any chance giving yourselves to devotion?'

'What would you?' Raoul answered. 'A preacher came here to confess us; he left that. All the same there are some things in it which, if they were followed, the world would be better than it is.'

'Oh, yes ... better!'

I congratulated the new converts on the happy change in them.

'Who would have said two months ago,' Court answered, 'that I would let myself be bored by a parson?'

'And I,' observed Raoul. 'But when one is in our state, one looks twice. It's not that death terrifies me; I'll take it like drinking a glass of water. You'll see how I'll go there, Monsieur Jules?'

'Oh, yes,' said Court, 'you must come.'

'I promise.'

'Word of honour?'

'Word of honour.'

The day fixed for the execution I went to Versailles; it was ten o'clock in the morning when I entered the prison.

The two culprits were with their confessors. They no sooner saw me than they rose hurriedly and came to me.

'I don't bother you?' I asked.

'You, Monsieur Jules, bother us! You're joking,' said Court. 'There aren't many like Monsieur Jules. He took us, but that's nothing.'

'If it hadn't been he,' said Raoul, 'it would have been another.'

'Who wouldn't have treated us so well,' said Court.

They knelt before the confessors, and stayed in that position for fifteen minutes. Then I saw that they wanted to talk to me.

'Monsieur Jules,' said Court, 'as a result of your goodness, we have a last sevice to ask of you.'

'What is it? I'm ready to do anything to oblige you.'

'Our wives are in Paris. I have a wife ... that breaks my heart ... it is too much for me!' His eyes filled with tears, his voice broke, and he could not finish.

'Well, Court,' said Raoul, 'what's the matter? Are you going to be a child? I don't recognize you, my boy. Are you a man or aren't you? Because you have a wife; haven't I one too? Come, a little courage.'

'That's over now,' Court went on. 'What I have to tell you, Monsieur Jules, is that we have wives, and without commanding you, we want to charge you with some small commissions for them.'

I promised to do all they gave me, and when they had explained their intentions, I renewed my assurance that they would be religiously fulfilled.

'I was sure that you would not refuse,' said Raoul.

'Oh, Monsieur Jules,' said Court, 'how can we thank you for all that?'

'If what the confessor says is not humbug,' said Raoul, 'we'll meet some day, down below.'

'It's a voyage one makes as late as possible,' said Court. 'We are nearly starting.'

'Monsieur Jules, is your watch right?' asked Raoul.

'I think it's a little fast.'

'Look, it's noon.'

'Death gallops. God, how It gallops!' said Court.

'The minute-hand touches the small one,' said Raoul. 'We're not tired of you, Monsieur Jules, but you must leave.'

The executioner arrived. just as they were being placed in the cart, the guilty men made their adieux. 'However, you've just embraced two death's heads,' said Raoul.

The cortège advanced to the place of execution; Raoul and Court were attentive to the exhortations of their confessor. I saw them suddenly shudder; a voice had reached their ears. It was Fontaine who, healed of his wounds, had come to mix with the crowd of spectators. He was animated by a spirit of vengeance; he abandoned himself to transports of atrocious joy. Raoul recognized him; by a glance, accompanied by a silent expression of contemptuous pity, he seemed to tell me that the presence of this man was painful to him. Fontaine was near me; I ordered him to go, and by a sign of the head Raoul and his comrade showed that they were pleased by this attention.

Court was executed first. As he mounted the scaffold, he looked at me as if to ask whether I was pleased with him. Raoul showed no less firmness. He was in the prime of life; his head bounded twice on the fatal plank, and the blood gushed out with such strength that the spectators twenty feet away were covered.

Such was the end of these two men, whose rascality was less the result of an evil nature than of contact with perverted persons, who, in the bosom of society in general, form a distinct caste with its own principles, virtues, and vices. The commissions which the two murderers had entrusted to me were of such a nature as to prove that their hearts were still accessible to good sentiments. I acquitted myself of them promptly, and I preserved the two 'Christian Thoughts' and the two crucifixes they had given me.

Pons Gérard could not be convicted of murder and was condemned to hard labour for life.

XXIX
THIEVES AND ROBBERS

IF THE MULTITUDE had a little more confidence in me than in my
successor, it was really because many times I seemed to it incomprehen-
sible. How many times did I not astonish persons who came to complain
of some larceny? They had hardly told me two or three of the circumstances when I was already on the track. Either I finished the story, or,
without waiting for fuller details, I gave this oracular response, 'So-and-so
is guilty.' They marvelled, but were they grateful? I do not think so, for
ordinarily the complainant was persuaded either that I had committed
the robbery myself or that I had a pact with the Devil. Such was the belief
of my clientèle who could not imagine that otherwise I could be so well
instructed.

The opinion that I was the mainspring, or rather the instigator, of
a great number of robberies was the most popular and the most widely
spread. It was pretended that I was in direct relations with all the
thieves in Paris; that they informed me in advance of the coups they
meditated, and that, if they had been prevented from warning me in
advance for fear of missing a good opportunity, after their success they
never failed to come and share with me. These people added that I was
associated in the profits of the thieves' industry, and that I never had
them arrested except when their activities were no longer profitable to
me. The thieves were, it must be agreed, good-natured to sacrifice
themselves so for the man who sooner or later would deliver them to
justice! A greater absurdity it is difficult to imagine. But as behind every
absurdity there is often a leaven of truth, here is the point of departure.

From my duties I was interested in knowing as much as possible all
the professional thieves, both men and women; I tried to be informed
to the last sou and farthing of the state of their finances, and if I saw a
change for the better in their position, I naturally concluded that they
had procured a windfall. If the improvement agreed with an affidavit,
the conclusion became probable; however, it was still only a conjecture.
But I called to account the slightest particulars proper to reveal the
means of execution employed to consummate the crime; I went to the

places, and often before I had even started the search, I said to the declarant, 'Don't worry. I'm certain to discover the thieves as well as the things stolen.' The following case, the only one of this kind that I want to report, affords the proof.

M. Prunaud, a dealer in novelties, rue Saint-Denis, had been robbed during the night. Force had been used to get into the shop and fifty pieces of calico and several valuable shawls had been taken. In the morning M. Prunaud hurried to my office, and he had not finished telling me about his mishap, before I had named the authors of the robbery. 'It can only have been committed,' I said, 'by Berthe, Mongodart, and their confederates.'

I at once put my agents on their heels and I ordered them to make sure whether they were spending money. A few hours afterwards they announced to me that the two individuals on whom my suspicions rested had been met in a resort, in company with Toulouse and Reverand, alias Morosini; that they were newly dressed, and that according to all appearances their pockets were well filled, for they had been seen with some girls. I knew their fence. I asked that a search be made of his domicile and the merchandise was discovered. The receiver could not avoid his fate; he was sent to the galleys. That the thieves could be condemned it was necessary for me to prepare the evidence by a stratagem of my own invention; they were duly tried and convicted.

To be at the top of my employment, it was necessary that I be capable of making conjectures with some accuracy. Often I was so sure of my facts that not only did I state, *ex abrupto,* the names and residences of the thieves, but I traced their description with precision, indicating the manner in which they had effected the robbery. The vulgar, ignorant of the resources of the police, could not conceive how one could be ignorant and have so much perspicacity. For one unaccustomed to reflection, the illusion was such that without the slightest ill-will toward me, he was justified in supposing a connivance which did not exist. But a full half of the inhabitants of Paris imagined that I had the gift of seeing everything, hearing everything, and knowing everything. So they invoked my assistance on everything, and three-quarters of the time for matters which did not concern my department. One can have no idea of the bizarre demands which were made on me.

One should have been present at a public audience at the Bureau de Sûreté. A peasant entered:

'Monsieur, I was walking in the Zoölogical Garden, and while I was looking at the animals, there was a gentleman dressed like a prince who asked me whether I was not from Burgundy. I said I was; then he told me he was from Joigny, a lumber merchant by trade; we talked about our country, and one thing led to another until he offered to show me the Death's Head. Really he was an honest man, I assure you. I suspected nothing and went along with him. We went out of the garden, and at the gate we met some others; one was a linen merchant.'

'There were two, were there not? A young man and an old one?'

'Yes, monsieur.'

'The old man had brought wine to the warehouse?'

'Yes, monsieur.'

'I see what happened. They did you in?'

'You've hit it, my good sir! Three thousand francs they took from me! A thousand crowns in fine twenty-franc pieces.'

'Ah, gold! Did they not make you hide it?'

'I should say they did make me hide it; so well that I never found it again.'

'That's it; I know your men. Say, Goury [I spoke to one of my agents], wasn't it Hermelle, Desplanques, and the "Père de famille"?'

'It looks like it,' said Goury.

'Didn't one of them have a long nose?'

'Oh, yes, very long.'

'I see I'm right.'

'Damn it, you're right. You've put your finger on it the first time. A long nose! Oh, Monsieur Vidocq, you're a good fellow! I'm not so worried now.'

'Why?'

'Since the fellows that robbed me are your friends, it will be easy for you to find my money. Only try to do it soon; today if possible.'

'We don't go at the job so fast.'

'You see, I absolutely must go back to the country; I'm needed at home; my wife's all alone, and in four days there's the fair at Auxerre.'

'Oh, so you're in a hurry, my good man?'

'Yes, I am; but listen. We can arrange it; simply give me fifteen hundred francs at once and you can have the rest. One can't be more accommodating.'

'That's true, but I don't make bargains of that sort.'

'That only depends on you.'

Another visitor was one of those good shopkeepers in the rue Saint-Denis.

'Monsieur, I've come to ask you to go at once in search of my wife who decamped yesterday evening with my clerk. I don't know the direction they took, but they can't be far, because they took a lot of loot, money and merchandise; they took everything, and if they aren't caught I'll be in a fix. If you get after them promptly, we'll have them.'

'I must call your attention to the fact that we can't act like that; first we must have an order. Begin by getting a complaint against your wife and the ravisher for adultery, in which you will accuse the latter of having taken your effects and merchandise.'

'Oh, yes, I'll enter a complaint, and while I amuse myself in such trifles, the traitors will get away.'

'Probably.'

'Such slowness when there's danger! Anyhow, my wife is my wife; every day and every night the wrong will be worse. I'm a husband; I'm outraged; I'm in my rights. She'll have children, and who will the father be? Since there's no divorce, the law should have foreseen...'

'Well, monsieur, the law has forgotten nothing; there is a prescribed form, and one cannot get away from it.'

'That's pretty form! If that's the case, one might say that the form outweighs the essence. Poor husbands!'

'I know that you have reason to complain, but I can do nothing. Besides, you aren't the only one.'

'Oh, Monsieur Jules, you are so obliging; do me the service of arresting them this very day; take that on yourself, I beseech you. Don't refuse; you won't be sorry.'

'I repeat, monsieur, that to do what you want, I must have a warrant from the judicial authorities.'

'Come, I see only too well that my wife and my fortune have been ravished. What is protected? Vice! That's worthy of the police! If it was a question of arresting a Bonapartist, you'd all be upside down, but as it is about a deceived husband, you do not budge. It's a pleasure to see how the police work; when you see me again, it'll be – it will be never. My wife can come back when she pleases; if she's carried off again, I won't come to you.'

The husband retired very discontented.

The wisdom of the nations has long proclaimed as a truth that wolves do not eat each other, and thieves have the same regard for others of their fraternity. They all consider each other as members of one large family, and although the thieves from the provinces and the Parisian thieves are in general little disposed to help each other, their antipathy or prejudice does not go so far as to injure each other directly. There is always a pact which is respected in some of its generalities; so the thieves have signs of recognition and a special language. To possess this language or to be initiated in these signs, even when one is not one of the craft, is already a title to their benevolence; it is a proof or at least a presumption that one is with thieves. But this knowledge, more invaluable in some circumstances than that of Freemasonry, is not an infallible guaranty of security. Here is a slight adventure which will, I believe, show that I am not wrong.

Père Bailly, former turnkey at Saint-Pélagie, had exchanged that employment for that of keeper at Saint-Denis. He was an old man, rather fond of the juice of the grape. Besides, what jailer is there who does not enjoy a drink, especially when one is invited and does not have to pay for it? During the twenty-five years that he had been in the prisons, Père Bailly had seen many thieves. He knew nearly all of them, and nearly all of them liked him, because he showed himself a good fellow; he did not bother them too much. For those with a full purse he had slight attentions, and we know what slight attentions mean with a jailer.

One day the good man came to Paris to get a small interest which he had amassed as a result of his savings. It was the provision of the ant, the reserve for the morning dram and tobacco for all day. The day of maturity had come. Père Bailly received the money, two hundred francs. we took them, but in coming and going he had had some nips, so that when it came time to go back to his post, he was a little gay; that's not bad, for it gives speed. So he went along in good humour, happy that he had finished to his satisfaction, when under the Gate of Saint-Denis two of his old boarders accosted him, tapping him on the shoulder, 'Well, good day, Père Bailly.'

Bailly turned around with a 'Good day, my boys.'

'Have a drink with us, on the run?'

'On the run, gladly, for I haven't time.'

They went into the Aux Deux Boules.

'A drink for three, quick and good.'

'Well, my boys, what are you doing? Are things going well? It seems so, for you look comfortable.'

'We have no complaint since we've got out. Business is good enough.'

'I'm delighted; I like to see you pleased; but be careful not to return to jail; it's a damned hotel.' He emptied his glass and offered his hand in parting.

'What, already? We don't see you so often; since you're here, we'll repeat the dose. Come, another drink.'

'No, no, another time. I'm in a hurry, and I'm here on foot. I've run about so much since morning and I've a long way to go before I get to Saint-Denis.'

'A minute more or less won't make any difference. Come on, we'll sit down, Père Bailly.'

'I can't refuse. But get them to serve promptly; one glass, and no more, and I'll go.'

The glass was drunk, a third, a fourth, a fifth, a sixth went, and Bailly did not notice that he had not kept his word. Finally, he was drunk, completely drunk.

'That's not to say,' he repeated every moment, 'that I must not go; it's night. That's not all; I have two hundred francs in my bundle, and supposing I should be robbed on the way?'

'What are you afraid of? There's no thief who would be so foolish. They know you're too good for that. Père Bailly, he can go anywhere. There's no danger. To your health, Père Bailly.'

'To yours. I'm not tired, but this time I must go. No more putting it off. Good-night. Take care of yourselves.'

'Since you want to, we'll not keep you longer.'

They helped him place on his shoulder a stick on the end of which was tied the package which contained the cash. As soon as Père Bailly had charge of it, he took flight.

There he was in the Faubourg, fluttering about, stumbling, fumbling, rolling, gravitating, making way slowly, advancing nevertheless by zigzags. At times he described the letter S, at others the letter Z, and all the crooked letters of the alphabet.

The two pensioners consulted what they should do.

'If you are of my opinion,' said one of them, 'we'll take his two hundred bullets, the old niggard.'

'Damn, you're right. His money's as good as another's.'

'Yes, let's follow him.'

'Follow on.'

In spite of his twists and turns, Père Bailly had already passed the Barrier. Still in the grip of the wine, he marched against wind and tide; he pitched, he pitched heavily; he tottered, went back and sideways, so that all the cab-drivers, seeing him in this state, out of humanity offered him a place in their coaches.

'Go your way, you old dummy,' the gracious turnkey replied to this offer. 'Père Bailly – has a good foot and a good eye.'

It would have been well for him if he had been less proud, for when he reached the Plain des Vertus, he was in great embarrassment. Imagine this dean of the jail in the claws of the two thieves! To seize him by the throat and take his parcel was the work of an instant. In vain he tried to give the sign which would have saved him. He shouted the password at the top of his lungs. He called, 'It's Père Bailly.' But neither sign nor words nor his name helped. The thieves took the parcel and disappeared. 'That's rude,' the victim murmured, 'they'll never go to Paradise!'

One large class of thieves is made up of the *cambrioleurs* or house-breakers who rob rooms either by burglary or false keys. For the most part they are young men under thirty. From eighteen to thirty is their best time. I could tell a thousand facts about them, but I will limit myself to the following.

M. Tardiff, a notary at the corner of the rue de la Vielle Draperie, had been the target of a band of thieves, two of whom were Baudry and Robé, famous *cambrioleurs*. One morning, as they were passing the house where the notary lived, they saw a notice; they read it; a room was to let; it suited them; but it was not neat enough. New paper was indispensable, and the woodwork needed repainting. To whom should this necessary work of restoration be entrusted? A young painter had worked in the notary's apartment; they went in search of him and made him talk. Unfortunately, he had an excellent memory for places; there was no lay-out at M. Tardiff's that he did not remember, a nook or corner whose use escaped him; a piece of furniture whose place or use he did not note. Without looking ahead, he furnished all the information.

Six weeks later M. Tardiff was robbed. Who were the guilty? Nothing was known; but one is never betrayed except by one of his own; one of the thieves, after he had his share of the robbery, sold his comrades. All were arrested and sentenced. They deserved their fate, and their sentence would have been just if it had not also included the young painter whose indiscretions at most were only an imprudence. He had fourteen years in irons at Brest.

The mistress of a thief named Charpentier, better known under the two nicknames 'La Tache de Vin' and Trumeaux, had been tried with him on the accusation of robbing with false keys. Although her lover, whose accomplice she was, was condemned to the galleys, she was acquitted for lack of evidence. Henriette – that was her name – was in close relations with Rosalie Dubust. She had no sooner recovered her liberty than she associated with her in robbing rooms. Several declarations made to the police soon called their attention to the two friends.

Henriette lived in the rue du Grand Hurleur. I was ordered to watch her. First, I arranged matters so that I should know her, and one day I took up a position in her passageway and accosted her as she went out.

'Here!' I said to her, 'there you are. I couldn't have met you better, for I was just going to see you.'

'But I don't know you.'

'Don't you remember that I saw you with Charpentier at the Île d'Amour?'

'It's possible.'

'Well, I've come from Brest. Your man sends you his compliments. He would like to come and join you, but the poor devil is on the list of suspects, and it is more difficult than ever for him to escape.'

'Oh, my God, I remember you now. I recall perfectly that we were together at La Chapelle, at Duchesne's, where we were on a bat with some friends.'

After this recognition, in which nothing was lacking, I asked Henriette whether 'she had anything in view.' She promised me marvels, and to prove how much she wanted to be useful to me, she insisted at all cost that I should install myself in her place. The offer to share her domicile was made in such good faith that I could only accept.

Henriette lived in a small room, the furniture of which consisted of a single chair and a truckle-bed, covered by a husk mattress, the appearance of which was far from inviting to rest. She immediately took me into her retreat. 'Sit down,' she said, 'I won't be out long; if anyone knocks, don't open.'

In fact she soon came back with a pint in one hand and in the other two packages of bacon and a pound of bread; it was a poor repast she furnished me. No matter, I pretended to eat with an appetite. When the meal was finished, she announced that she was going to get her man's father and told me to sleep until she came back. As it was necessary to appear to need sleep, I threw myself on the pallet; it was so hard that it seemed to me that I was on a sack of nails.

Two hours later Charpentier's father arrived. He embraced me, wept, and talked to me about his boy. 'When shall I see him again?' he exclaimed, and wept again. But no matter what the sorrow may be, the tears must be wiped away sometime; Père Charpentier made a truce to his grief to propose to me that we take supper with him at Le Sauvage. 'I'll go and get some money, and we'll go there.'

But there isn't always money in hand when one goes to get it. Père Charpentier without doubt was under illusions as to the abundance of his receipts and he reappeared only that evening. He came with the modest sum of three francs fifty centimes and a harlequin, a roll of cat meat, which he had bought in passing the Marché Saint-Jean. He had placed this disgusting mess in a handkerchief full of tobacco. He laid it on the foot of the bed, at the same time saying to Henriette, 'Well, my girl, the waters are low today; we'll not go to the Barrier; but go and get some litres, bread, two sous' worth of oil and two of vinegar to make a *persillade.'* At the same time he looked at the meat with pleasure. 'There are some bits of beef in it,' he observed. 'Run along, my child, and come back soon.'

Henriette was light-footed, and she did not make us wait. The meat with its vinegar dressing was soon ready, and I appeared to lick my chops. When one comes back from prison, one should not be difficult, so, while we ate, the father said, 'Well, my friend, did you have the like of that in quod?'

Among rascals of the same kind they become intimate in a quarter of an hour. Before we had touched the second litre, I was on as good terms with Henriette and her father-in-law as though we had been together for ten years. The latter was an old vagabond who would have done anything if he had still been capable of action.

I arranged with him that he should put me in touch with some thieves, and the next day they brought a man named Martinot. He at once raised the question by speaking of a small affair which might contribute to refitting me.

'Ah,' I said to him, 'I would not expose myself for so little; I want it to be worth the trouble.'

'In that case,' Martinot answered, 'I've what you need, but it won't be for some days. The keys are made; as soon as we have them, you'll be one of us; you can count on it.'

I thanked Martinot, and he brought three other thieves who were to operate with us. I began to have rather a good start. However, for fear of an encounter which might disconcert my projects, I was careful not to go out with my new associates. I stayed with Henriette the greater part of the day, and in the evening we went to a wine merchant's where we spent the thirty sous she had made working on gloves.

Annette might help me in the intrigue in which I was engaged. Resolved to give her a role, if there was need of it, I went secretly to warn her, and that evening, when Henriette and I entered the pub, we saw sitting alone at a table a woman eating supper. It was Annette; I looked at her with a sort of curiosity; she did the same to me.

I asked Henriette whether she knew the person who was examining us so attentively.

'I don't think so,' she answered.

'Then she must be looking at me. I've an idea that I've seen her, I don't know where.'

In order to satisfy myself, I approached the stranger, 'Pardon, madame, I think I have the pleasure of knowing you.'

'Really, monsieur, I've been wondering for an hour ... I said to myself, there's a face I've seen somewhere. Did you live at Rouen?'

'God!' I exclaimed. 'Is it you, Joséphine, and your man, dear Romain?'

'Alas,' she said, sobbing, 'he was arrested at Caën.'

'A long time?'

'Three months. I'm afraid he won't get out soon; he's in bad. But how are you? It seems that you're free.'

'Yes, but who knows whether I won't be back soon.'

'Let's hope not.'

Henriette was delighted with the good ways of the lady; she wanted her to join our company. Finally, we agreed so well that we were as closely united as the fingers of a hand. The pretended Joséphine, as the result of a story so touching that Henriette was moved, told us that she lodged in a furnished house, rue Guerin-Boisseau. After we had exchanged addresses, she said to me, 'Oh, listen, you know that once you obliged my man with a twenty-franc piece; I must give it back to you.' I made some difficulties about taking the twenty francs. However, I yielded, and from that moment Henriette, more touched by this procedure than by the story, entered into a long conversation with the honest better half of my friend. The conversation turned on me.

'Such as you see him, madame,' said Charpentier's so-called wife, pointing to me, 'I would not change him for anyone, even if he were ten times better-looking. He's my poor rabbit. We've been together ten years, and, would you believe it, we've never had the slightest word.'

Annette lent herself admirably to this comedy. Every evening she was promptly at the rendezvous, and we ate supper together.

Finally, the moment came for committing the robbery in which I was to co-operate. All was arranged; Martinot and his friends were ready. We were to rob the room of a money-lender who made short-time loans at high rates. They pointed out the place to me in the rue Montorgueil; I knew the time they were to get in. I gave Annette the necessary instructions to warn the police, and, in order to be sure that they would do nothing without me, I left neither my friends nor my dear Henriette.

We started out on the expedition. Martinot went up, opened the door, and came down. 'We have only to go in,' he said, and while I stayed with him on watch, his companions hurried to collect the booty on our account as well as their own at the expense of the usurer. But my agents followed them closely. I saw them, and at that instant I arranged to distract Martinot so that he would turn his head the other way. The three thieves were surprised while they were breaking into the furniture; they gave a cry and took flight.

As Martinot had carried away the keys, his companions might escape the penalty of the irons, for it was probable that, according to custom, they would allege that they had found the door open. So it was important, not only to arrest Martinot in possession of the keys, but also to establish his relations with the culprits who had been taken. In reaching this result, Annette was of the greatest service. Martinot was arrested with all the things desirable to convict him, without Henriette suspecting anything, only she saw that I was very happy, one title the more to her love.

When the sentiment I inspired was in all its strength, I had a pretended illness. I could recover only by taking certain remedies the cost of which was out of proportion to our pecuniary resources. Henriette insisted on getting them for me, and with this object in view she planned the robbery of a room, in which, as she confided to me, Rosalie Dubust was to help her. The robbery was attempted; its execution was begun. But I had let out the secret. Henriette and her friend were taken in the act. Both were sentenced to ten years at hard labour. At the expiration of her sentence, Henriette came into the surveillance with me. She had a perfect right to reproach me, but she never did.

Henriette, Rosalie Dubust, and Martinot were poor *cambrioleurs.* But there were in the same *genre* thieves of an effrontery which passed all belief. The effrontery of a man named Beaumont was almost marvellous. He had escaped from the prison at Rochefort, where he should have passed twelve years of his life, and had come to Paris. He had hardly returned to this city, where he had already practised his trade, when, to get his hand in, he committed several small robberies. When by these skirmishes he had prepared the way for exploits more worthy of his ancient renown, he conceived the idea of stealing a treasure. One could never imagine what this treasure was. It was the Central Bureau, today the Prefecture of Police!

First, it was fairly difficult to procure impressions of the keys, but he managed to overcome this difficulty, and he soon had in his power all means of opening. But to open was nothing; it was necessary to open without being seen, to get in without fear of being disturbed, to operate without witnesses, and to get out at will. Beaumont had measured the magnitude of this task, and was not deterred.

He had noticed that the office of the chief of the Sûreté, M. Henry, was close to the place which he proposed to enter. He spied for a propitious moment; he wanted some circumstance to remove for some time a neighbour so dangerous; he got his wish.

One morning M. Henry was obliged to go out. Beaumont, sure that he would not return that day, raced to his place, dressed in a black coat, and in this costume which, at that time, announced a magistrate or a public official, he presented himself to the post set on guard at the

Central Bureau. The chief to whom he addressed himself supposed that he was at least a commissioner. On Beaumont's invitation he gave him a soldier whom Beaumont placed as a sentinel at the entrance to the passageway which led to the dépôt and ordered him to let no one pass.

One could not find a better expedient to prevent a surprise. So Beaumont, among a mass of priceless things, could, at his leisure and in complete security, make a choice of what pleased him: watches, jewels, diamonds. He appropriated all that was most valuable and that was easiest to carry off, and when he had finished his venture, he took leave of the functionary and disappeared.

This theft was not long unknown. It was discovered the next day. If a thunderbolt had fallen on the police, they would have been less disturbed than by the news of this event. To penetrate into the holy of holies! The fact appeared so extraordinary that they questioned its possibility. However, it was obvious that a robbery had taken place, but to whom could they attribute it?

Suspicion fell on all the employees, sometimes on one, sometimes on another, when Beaumont was betrayed by one of his comrades, arrested, and sentenced a second time. His stealings might have been estimated at some hundreds of thousands of francs, and most of them were found on him. 'There was enough to make me an honest man,' he said. 'I would have become one; that's easy when one is rich; however, many rich men are scoundrels.' These were the only words he uttered when he was arrested.

This astonishing thief was taken to Brest, where, as the result of a half-dozen escapes which caused him to be more closely guarded, he died in a frightful state of exhaustion.

Beaumont enjoyed a colossal reputation among the thieves, and even today when a braggart boasts of his exploits, they say, 'Shut up, you're not worthy to tie Beaumont's shoestrings.'

One of the most skilful *cambrioleurs* was named Lepetit Godet, alias Marquis, alias Durand, alias Capdeville. I should never end if I wanted to set down here all the names and callings he had taken in the course of his long career. He had been in turn merchant, shipowner, émigré, independent gentleman, etc. After he had played one of the principal roles in the bands which infested so long the south of France, he took refuge in Rouen, when, as the result of a robbery imputed to him, he was recognized and sentenced to life imprisonment. It was the seventh or eighth offence of which he had been convicted.

Capdeville had as confederates three other thieves, Delsouc, Finacette, and Cologne, whose names deserve to be cited in the general history of robbers. He had engaged in the trade when very young, and although he was nearly sixty, he still practised it. Few of the *cambrioleurs* were more enterprising or endowed with more perseverance.

One day the idea struck him to rob a wealthy widow who lived at Saint-Germain-en-Laye. First he explored the approaches to the place and vainly sought to get in. He excelled in making false keys, but false keys are not made by chance, and he could not succeed in making a shadow of an impression. Two months went by in fruitless attempts. Anyone else than Capdeville would have abandoned an enterprise which presented so many difficulties, but he had said that he would succeed and he did not want to be disappointed. A house next to the widow's was occupied by a tenant. Capdeville schemed to get him out, and he manœuvred so well that he was soon installed in his place. M. Fierval was the widow's new neighbour. It was said that he was not like his predecessor. His place was magnificently furnished, and it was easy to see that he was somebody. He had been moved in about three weeks, when the widow, who had not taken the air for a long time, proposed to take a walk. She went to the park accompanied by Marie, her faithful servant. Near the end of this excursion, she was accosted by a stranger who approached her, holding in one hand his hat and in the other a plant.

'You see before you, madame, a lover of Nature, of that beautiful Nature which enchants all noble and tender souls. Botany is my passion, as it was that of the sensitive Jean-Jacques, the virtuous Bernadine de Saint-Pierre. Following the example of those great philosophers, I am seeking simples, and, if I am not mistaken, I shall be fortunate enough to find in this canton precious ones. Oh, madame, it would be for the good of humanity that everyone should know the virtues of this one. Do you know this herb?'

'Really, monsieur, it is not very rare in the neighbourhood; but I will confess my ignorance; I know neither its name nor its properties.'

'You say that it is not very rare? Oh, fortunate country, if it is not rare! Will you be good enough to point out the places where it is most abundant?'

'Willingly, monsieur. But what is this herb good for?'

'What, madame, for everything! It is a real treasure, a universal panacea. With this herb we no longer need doctors. Taken in a decoction, its root purifies the blood, drives out bad humours, aids the circulation, dissipates melancholy, gives suppleness to the limbs, play to the muscles, and heals all maladies up to the age of a hundred. In infusions its stem works marvels. Place a package in a bath and continue its use, and you have discovered the Fountain of Youth. Its leaf on a wound heals it instantly. Furthermore, made into a philtre, it is most powerful in acting against indifference in marriage.'

'You're not joking?'

'No, madame, God help me! As a lotion and a beverage the whole secret is in the method of preparation and the manner of serving...'

'May I be so indiscreet as to ask the receipt?'

'Not at all, madame. Ask and I shall be pleased to tell you.'

'Oh, first tell me the name of this interesting simple.'

'The name, madame, is simply "Good for Everything."'

'Marie, "Good for Everything," do you hear? Remember that. If we took monsieur to the farther end of the park, it seems to me that there's a lot there.'

'If it's not too far, I'll take you where there is more. But perhaps monsieur does not want to go there.'

'I would go to the end of the world, only I fear to abuse your kindness.'

'Don't worry, monsieur. I shall be sufficiently rewarded if you consent.'

Marie guided the seeker for simples, and on the way he explained to madame how he made the infusions, decoctions, applications, and the sublime matrimonial essence. Finally, they arrived. The botanist had never seen in so great quantities the plant whose merits he had just revealed. He was carried away with joy, enthusiasm, and pleasure, and, when he had sufficiently gone into raptures, he started to gather it. Madame also got a store; Marie took it in charge. They botanized eagerly, so that in less than twenty minutes the poor girl bent under her burden. She did not complain; she even proposed to come back again, for Marie had not lost a word of the lesson in pharmaceutics, and was no less eager for experience than her mistress.

The botanizing was finished promptly. Then the botanist and the widow separated after exchanging thanks. The botanist flew toward new discoveries, and the widow regained her manor with her servant, proud for the first time of carrying a bundle of hay, full of beauty, health, wisdom, charms, enchantments, etc.

They went into the house. Such a long walk had given madame an appetite.

'Be quick, Marie, and lay the table; let's have dinner.'

'But, madame, there's nothing ready.'

'All right, we'll eat the left-overs .... Serve yesterday's chicken, and this morning's whiting.'

Marie was not less hungry than her mistress and hurried to execute her orders.

'Oh, God, my God, my God!'

'Marie!' cried the widow, 'you grieve me!'

'Oh, madame!'

'What's the matter with you, Marie? Have you broken your leg?'

'The silver...'

'Well, the silver?'

'We've been robbed.'

'Where is your head?'

'I swear it...'

'Be still, careless; in washing up you've left it lying about.'

'Oh, madame, they're all taken.'

'What do you say?'

'Is it possible there's none left?'

'There's none left! You're a fool, my poor Marie.'

As she pronounced these words, the widow got up impatiently, hurried to the drawer, and pushed Marie aside.

'Go away, blockhead. Good heavens! Oh, what a terrible thing! Oh, the scoundrels, the blackguards, the wretches! Oh, move, Marie, move; you stand there like a mummy. She doesn't move, the miserable creature! Have you milk in your veins?'

'But, madame, what do you want me to do?'

'That's another of your pretty tricks! I told you to close the doors when you went away; they came into the dining-room! That's it. When we came back, the safety catch was not as it was when we went out. Look, if they ever rob me, I'll answer that it won't be my fault. When I go out or come in, my keys never leave me, but you! Six thousand francs' worth of silver ... a fine day's work you've done! I don't know what to do with you! Come, get out of my sight! Get out, I tell you!'

Marie was terrified and went into the next room; but she came back at once, and shouted, 'God! your room has been forced, the writing-desk opened; everything is upside down.'

The widow wanted to assure herself that Marie was not wrong. The catastrophe was only too real. She measured its extent at a glance. 'The monsters!' she said, 'I'm ruined!' And she fainted.

Marie dashed to a window and called for help. 'Thieves! Murder! The guard! Fire!' Such were the words which echoed in the street.

The neighbours, the gendarmes, and the commissioner invaded the house; they made a general search from top to bottom, and found no one. Then one of those present proposed that they go down to the cellar. 'To the cellar, to the cellar,' they repeated unanimously. Candles were lighted, and while Marie lavished care on her mistress, who had at last recovered her senses, the commissioner, preceded by his scouts, made the proposed descent. They visited the first vault, there was nothing; a second, again nothing; a third, next to the neighbour's cellar. On the ground were bits of plaster. They went on, and in the dividing wall they saw – opening large enough to let a man through. From that moment all was explained. Two hours previously they had seen a carriage before the door of the great gentleman from Paris – that is how they designated Capdeville – who, they assured, got into this vehicle, after placing in it a trunk which seemed very heavy.

This trunk contained the gold, silver, jewels, and silverware of the widow; it was worth a considerable sum. Capdeville never reappeared, and it was impossible to reach him.

After he had robbed the widow, Capdeville went to Rouen, but he was soon back in Paris. However, he did not make it his residence for long. A prey to domestic sorrows, disgusted with the world and its perfidies, worried about his health, discontented with himself and everybody else, Capdeville was a misanthrope who wanted at all costs to bury himself in the country. With this end in view he scoured the vicinity of the capital.

At Belleville he noticed a house which from its isolation suited his love of solitude. In the shades of this place hereafter he would air his melancholy and exhale the sighs of his suffering soul. Capdeville hired an apartment in the habitation on which his gaze had rested so affectionately.

But a misanthrope could not bear for long the shelter of the same roof with other human beings. He must have an abode where he could ignore the fact that he was not the only one on earth; so he expressed the desire for such a place, no matter what the cost, if he would see there no vestige of the society of which he complained so much; he would accommodate himself to anything from a château to a cottage.

Capdeville loudly announced his intention of making a voyage of discovery in search of this hermitage where he could pass his old age. He enquired of the people about rural properties which were for sale within a radius of ten leagues. It was soon notorious that he intended to make an acquisition. They knew something that would suit him, but he wanted only a patrimonial property. 'Well,' they said, 'if he's so scrupulous, let him search himself.' In fact, that is what he decided to do. Determined to make a tour to examine what would suit him, he was ostentatious in the preparations for his departure; he would be away only three or four days; but before he left it was easy for him to find out whether there was any danger in leaving in a writing-desk some ten thousand francs which he did not want to take with him. He was reassured on this point, and in full security he did not hesitate to start out on his voyage.

Capdeville did not go far. During his stay in the house he had just left, he had had the leisure to take impressions which he needed to get into the lodgings of the owner. In addition, he had observed that the latter was accustomed to dine in Paris and that he came back only late at night. By returning at dusk, Capdeville was certain of having before him all the time necessary for him to operate. When the sun had set, under cover of darkness he passed unseen into Belleville, entered the house by means of false keys, opened the owner's apartment, and took everything, including the linen.

Toward the end of the fifth day the neighbours began to get uneasy because the misanthrope did not reappear; the next day they became suspicious. Twenty-four hours later, there was only one opinion about him: he was a thief. After such a trick, distrust misanthropes. But whom can one trust? Philanthropists? No more.

One of the boldest of the women house-breakers was named Adèle d'Escars. I have never seen a prettier person. She seemed to have been created as a model for the divine Madonnas which sprang from the imagination of Raphael. Her hair was a magnificent blond; her large eyes were blue and gave expression to all the gentleness of her soul. A heavenly forehead, a ravishing mouth, her features full of candour, a graceful form, and a nearly ethereal elegance – such were the beauties assembled in Adèle. Physically she was an accomplished being; morally, either through fate or the effect of evil dispositions in her nature, she did not shine with such perfection.

Adèle belonged to an honest family, but one which was poorly off. She was hardly fourteen when she was torn from her family by one of those procuresses in which Paris abounds and was placed in a house of debauchery. Once launched in the career into which she had been dragged, Adèle rapidly underwent all its vicissitudes. She was sought by some of the tools of the police who turn by turn imposed on her the obligation of being their mistress. It was in their company that she became familiar with the idea of theft. She still had scruples, but these men insensibly succeeded in removing them. They showed her the advantages of an industry in which they were engaged, and this industry became hers. Her début was brilliant. She did not begin, like so many others, by taking purses and watches, for Adèle aimed higher. Among her lovers were several who excelled in the art of making false keys. She applied herself to acquiring this dangerous skill, and she made such rapid progress that she soon had a voice in the Chapter of *Cambrioleurs,* who took her on their expeditions. Adèle rather promptly gained the reputation of having a good head. Some more or less grave accidents which happened to her most intimate friends gave her an opportunity to prove that she also had a good heart. All recognized in her that virtue which is called probity: she never abandoned anyone among them who was struck by the fatality of thieves. If a sentence separated her from her well-beloved, she always chose to replace him with one of his best comrades. But he became her knight only on condition that he would not prevent her giving assistance to the unfortunate prisoner. Thus Adèle had a series of attachments, who, all equally dear, ended by being cast into prison, or at least into jails ... In order to make their lot the easier, she doubled her courage and cunning.

However, the number of these pensioners increased so much that in order not to be obliged to suppress this extra pay, which would have lost her her reputation for probity, she had to impose a cruel deprivation on herself. She no longer had a lover. Adèle had sufficient experience to dispense with a collaborator. She flew on her own wings, and

worked alone for two years with inconceivable good fortune.
Everything went well for her. Finally, there came a time when the abundance of booty surpassed all her hopes and for the first time she experienced an embarrassment of riches.

Adèle was on the crest of the wave, but she suddenly felt the
weight of the isolation to which she had resigned herself. She felt a void
which she could not define, or rather which defined itself so well that
she promised herself to listen to the first gallant who whispered sweet
nothings to her, provided, however, that he was one to her taste. The
one she pleased and who pleased her, too, was Rigottier, the most amiable of billiard sharps. As the result of a sweepstakes in which he had
been the winner, he whispered a host of expressions inspired by love,
his features covered with blushes, for Rigottier was really in love. Adèle
previously had almost died from fear of having to take the initiative,
and she received his declaration. In the joy of her triumph she took care
not to make him sigh. To have pity on herself, she took pity on him,
and as their sympathy was obvious, the union was made at once without invoking the ministration of any officer of the civil state.

Adèle was not ignorant of the fact that a woman should not hide
anything from her husband, so she had no sooner united her lot with
Rigottier than she pressed him to share her small talents and revealed to
him all the wealth she had taken. He was delighted with the skill with
which she managed the file. He wanted to see whether he had any talent for it. Adèle recognized that he had; she cultivated it, and as no lessons profit better or more rapidly than those given by an adored master,
in a short time Rigottier knew how to fashion a key with as much perfection as the most expert of locksmiths.

Decidedly in following the luck of a cue on the green cloth where
fortune is often unfaithful, Rigottier was separated from his vocation.
Adèle undertook to reclaim him, and her efforts were crowned by the
most complete success. Nevertheless, she did not want him to make the
adventure before he was perfectly trained, she was so afraid that he
would be compromised by a blunder. At first, she took him only to act
as sentry; but after some expeditions, during which to his regret he was
left to fold his arms, it was agreed that he should take an active part.

A lady reputed to be wealthy lived in rue de la Feronnerie. She had
much money, so the maidservant assured, and Adèle made it a fête to
rob her. The keys had already been made; they worked marvellously.

Now the only further question was a propitious moment to use them. The maid had promised to let them know when her mistress would be absent; she kept her word. One day she announced that madame would go out that evening; so they consulted about the means of execution. 'Come,' said Adèle to her pupil, 'there's no drawing back. You'll come in with me. I want to see how you'll take it. The job is grand. We couldn't choose a better for your first attempt.'

Rigottier did not draw back. He went with Adèle, and when they were certain that the lady had gone out, they went up to her apartment and entered without difficulty. Once inside, in order to be at home they bolted the door, and proceeded on the spot to break open all objects they thought might hold money: a secretary, two commodes, a wardrobe, and a chiffonier were broken open, but nowhere did they find the money of which the maid had spoken. Where could the sum be? A note on which they cast their eyes told them that it had gone to the notary the evening before. That was enough to make them pull their hair. But far from giving up to a useless despair, the deceived couple took in at a glance a mass of objects which the search had brought to light, and decided that from this mess there might be reasonable consolation, and in order to procure them they laid violent hands on the jewels, silverware, laces, and linen.

The trick was done in an instant. All that was valuable was carefully put into bundles; the bolt was drawn; they were about to go out, when Adèle, carried away with satisfaction, threw her arms around her lover's neck and embraced him. Rigottier was worthy of her; she admired his coolness; she could not praise enough the aplomb with which he had seconded her. In her enthusiasm she embraced him again. One kiss demanded another; Rigottier gave her ten; the exchange was rapid; they were carried away; they gave themselves to each other; they forgot everything; the pair were no longer on earth where there were gendarmes, informers, laws, tribunals, memory, expectations. Love had removed dangers; thunder might fall, the floors break, the house fall in, the universe be blotted out; the couple neither heard nor saw.

But the streets of Paris have two sides, and it is sometimes prudent to consider the disadvantages of having neighbours. The lady whose absence caused such deep security had not gone far. Opposite her lodgings and on the corresponding floor lived one of her friends. She was playing cards there, when suddenly, as they were dealing, her gaze turned mechanically on one of her windows.

'Oh!' she exclaimed, 'something extraordinary must be happening in my bedroom!'

'What is it?'

'Look, there's a light there!'

'You must be mistaken; it's the reflection.'

'What do you mean, reflection? Perhaps I'm blind; I can see it move.'

'Yes, move; you're always that way.'

'Oh, indeed! This time you won't say it's an illusion. Look, Monsieur Planard, don't you see the curtains move at the window beside the bed?'

'You're right; I think I see some movement. What the devil does that mean unless there are thieves?'

'Thieves! Oh, my dear Monsieur Planard, you give me an idea! My God, it's thieves! Quick, quick, go down!'

'Go down!' the entire company repeated, and each one according to his agility went downstairs two, three, or four at a time, to get down first.

The lady whose apartment had been visited unknown to her was more agitated than her curtains; she rapped abruptly on the porter's shutter.

'My candle, my candle!' she demanded with an impatience mixed with uneasiness. 'But hurry, there are thieves in the house!'

'Thieves?'

'Yes, thieves.'

'Where are they?'

'In my place.'

'In your place, Madame Bourgeois? You're joking.'

'No, I'm not joking. Go at once and warn the chief.'

The porter hastened to fulfil his mission, and he soon reappeared accompanied by M. Desloyers, who at the mere word of thieves had taken his measures for the attack.

'Ah, my friends,' he said, 'let us be prudent; above all, no noise! We'll go up. Hush, I seem to hear something ... it's a carriage. One moment, don't hurry; everyone take off his shoes. Hush, you Monsieur Tripot [he addressed the porter], as they may be in strength, take your cleaver; Madame Merlin, take your broom, and Mademoiselle Tripot, the fire shovel; the ladies will each take a chair to overwhelm the enemy. Now, forward. I'll support the retreat, and if there is any resistance, I shall be everywhere that seems best to me; go on, pass, I follow.'

All staggered up the stairs. When they reached the second floor, they stopped and arranged themselves in battle array on the landing. The porter formed the advance guard. He quietly put the key in the lock, and the door opened. 'Ah!' There was a cry of surprise, astonishment, indignation, scandal. There was a man and a woman, broken furniture, and bundles one upon another – what a picture! Inside and outside all were frozen still, as if petrified. No one spoke or moved, so great was their stupefaction. The porter was silent, too, but that could not last. He broke the silence with 'The commissioner must come.'

The commissioner, the constable, and the guard, summoned by a neighbour, soon came. They seized the two lovers. Adèle was questioned first. She was not disconcerted; she protested that her presence in the room where she had been surprised was due only to chance; she did not know the man; she had never seen him before in her life; but as she was a prostitute, he had accosted her in the street, and they had gone up together; the door was open ... she knew nothing about the bundles, and if a robbery had been committed, it had nothing to do with her.

The lie was well thought out, but Rigottier, with whom Adèle had not been able to consult, did not speak the same language, and from this difference in what they said, it resulted in their being sentenced to six years in irons. Rigottier went with the chain gang in 1802. Ten years later I met him on the Quais; he had escaped; I arrested him. Since then he has died in prison.

At the expiration of her sentence, Adèle came out of Lazare with nine hundred francs. She had completely reformed, and proposed to lead an irreproachable life. Her first care was to procure a small amount of furniture and a decent dress. When she had made these acquisitions, she had a hundred and fifty francs left. It was enough to keep her out of misery for the moment, but that would not last long. She went in search of work, and as she was a skilled seamstress, she found it easy to be busy. Employed in a shop for some months, she was content with her lot; but the existence of an ex-prisoner, man or woman, is precarious. Once they knew that she had been imprisoned in Saint-Lazare, tribulations began which one rarely escapes once one has been in the hands of justice. Without giving any other cause for complaint, Adèle was pitilessly discharged.

She moved to another quarter and succeeded in getting another place. In charge of the linen room in a furnished hotel, to be thereafter sheltered from indiscretions, she resigned herself to having relations only with persons who had given her their confidence. In spite of this precaution, she was not safe against the memories of the past. Pointed out, recognized, she was again discharged. From that day she presented herself nowhere without experiencing the effects of that reprobation which results from an infamy perpetuated by prejudice.

Adèle's only resource was her needle; in vain she sought to make it yield. Three months went by, and she met no charitable soul who by utilizing her skill sympathized with her situation. The time came when to live she had to pawn her clothes, and as a result of small loans all her wardrobe went to the pawnshop, into that abominable gulf dug by hypocritical usury under the guise of necessity. Reduced to absolute nakedness, Adèle decided to put an end to her misery by suicide, and she was going to throw herself into the Seine, when on the Pont-Neuf she met Suzanne Golier, one of her companions in prison.

'Come, come,' said Suzanne, 'you don't drown without the rest of us. Come to the house. My sister and I have opened a workroom where we do embroidery; we have work; you'll help us; we'll live together; if there's only bread – well, we'll eat only bread.' The proposal could not have been more opportune. Adèle accepted.

It was then the beginning of winter. The work went well enough, but the end of the Carnival brought the dead season. At the end of six weeks Adèle and her friends were plunged into the most frightful distress. Frédéric, the husband of one of them, had set up as a locksmith. If he had had customers, he would have come to their aid. Unfortunately, he did not make enough to pay his rent and license. They were in the greatest poverty.

One day Adèle was in the shop with this man; he had not had the slightest nourishment for forty-eight hours. 'Come,' said the locksmith, affecting to joke, although he spoke the words in the most sinister tone, 'we must die, little one, there's no more barley...'

'Yes, we must die,' he repeated, and while he forced himself to smile, his features became distorted and a cold sweat broke out on his forehead.

Silently Adèle, her face covered with a deadly pallor, was bending over the work-bench. Suddenly she straightened up; she shivered, 'We must die ... we must,' she sighed, looking with a feeling difficult to describe at the tools around her. The gleam of a horrible hope had come to her. Adèle was frightened; she was agitated; she was taken with a furious fever. Between the agony of hunger and the terrors of her conscience, she endured the most cruel punishment. During her torture, her hands rested on the bunch of keys; she pushed them away. 'God!' she cried, 'take away these instruments of crime. When I want so much to be good, shall my last resource be in them?' And so that she should not succumb, the unfortunate woman took to flight.

Before the tribunal Adèle confessed all her crimes; but, to lessen her guilt, she combined with her confessions the story of her tribulations. The jurors groaned, but they had to sentence her to life imprisonment; it was the first time such a terrible sentence had been given a woman. When they came to shave her head and to put on the grey smock, Adèle burst into a flood of tears. 'To have done everything to be honest or to die, and to be thrown alive into a tomb ... Never, never, forever, forever!' she repeated constantly in the most harrowing tones; her moans were broken by her sobs; her moans have never ceased.

THE END

TRANSLATOR'S NOTES

(ORIGINALLY APPEARED AS THE FOREWORD IN THE 1935 EDITION)

VIDOCQ has two valid claims for inclusion on the rolls of fame - as the Legendary Detective and as Father of the Detective Story. François Eugene Vidocq, to give him his full name, was, as the *Memoirs* tell us, born in Arras in 1775. After a somewhat adventurous and riotous career, which included an army career that at times brings a smile, he fell into the company of criminals, with the result that, although he always insisted that he was innocent of the charge, Vidocq was sentenced to the galleys or convict prisons. He escaped, was recaptured, escaped again, and after many vicissitudes was finally incarcerated in the great prison of La Force. Then (1809) he offered his services as a police spy. From that he rose in the force, from being practically the first paid secret agent or detective in the Sûreté, to head of the detective branch upon which the protection of Paris depended. The account of these years from his birth until he resigned from the service in 1827 forms the body of the *Memoirs*.

Upon his resignation Vidocq opened a paper mill, all of the employees of which were ex-convicts who had found it impossible to earn an honest livelihood on account of the prejudices against them. Naturally enough this venture failed and Vidocq lost his life's savings. Later, he served in the political police, but, according to one account, anxious to get back into his old work, he foolishly organized a daring theft, was discovered, and dismissed from the service. In view of the emphasis of his remarks about *agents provocateurs,* written some years previously, it seems difficult to believe that he would have fallen into such an error. According to another account - and nearly every fact about Vidocq, as with all legendary characters, is in dispute - he was 'framed' by some of his enemies. His last years were spent in poverty. He died in Brussels in 1857. Such in brief was the career of an extraordinary man, who started the work of detection in anything like the modern sense of the word and whose writings have been the inspiration of all detective, mystery, and crime stories for the past century or more.

Whether the *Memoirs* of Vidocq are genuine or 'spurious' has been a question which has disturbed many critics, who appear to overlook the fact that their value and importance remain exactly the same, whether they are spurious or not. Ever since their publication this charge has been constantly repeated. There are good grounds for believing that such statements were current before the *Memoirs* appeared. The English translation which appeared almost simultaneously with the French version - sufficient proof that Vidocq was already legendary in England as he was in France - notes that doubts have been cast on the truth of the work. It would seem a natural conclusion that Vidocq's enemies - for he had made many and powerful ones during his quarter of a century in the police - were afraid of his revelations, and on learning of his project of writing his memoirs hastened to discredit them in advance for their own protection. As this English edition of over a century ago points out, Vidocq was discussing men then alive and able to retaliate, and it would seem somewhat futile to make charges which it was impossible to substantiate. And whatever Vidocq was or was not, he certainly had intelligence.

In addition, he was writing at a time when his audience would be familiar with the crimes he was describing, whether his fame was as great as he claimed; in fact, most of his meticulous details could be checked at once, and if his account was notoriously 'spurious,' Vidocq would have immediately become a laughing-stock. Now Louis Philippe later offered him the charge of his political police; kings rarely use notorious laughing-stocks for so important a place. Furthermore, competent critics have come to the conclusion that fundamentally Vidocq was an honest man; he lived some thirty years after the publication of his work, and he never withdrew anything in it. He admitted that he had turned the material on his early life over to a 'literary person,' to put into shape, as he himself could not write at the time on account of a broken arm. But when he saw the result - his own character, he said, had been constantly placed in the worst light - he decided to do the rest of the work himself. He added that in spite of the literary touches the 'facts are there.' Curiously enough, this man of action was vain of his style and boasted of how the Prefect had praised it. How many memoirs and autobiographies written in our own day would be labelled 'spurious' if all were included on which the help of a writer had been sought?

To one who has given study to the four volumes and their 350,000 words which form the original edition of the *Memoirs,* the unqualified statement that Vidocq's work is 'spurious' comes as an irritation. If one were to judge merely from the many bizarre incidents in an extremely picturesque career, one might not be tempted to disagree, although, in fact, none of the incidents in themselves are unbelievable, but that all of the extraordinary happenings could have occurred in one man's life may give room for skepticism. If one reads the original with care, and considers, he will reach the conclusion that whoever the author was he was an honest man, interested in the problems of what today is termed criminology, with a glimmering of some of the work of Lombroso, the ardour of an enthusiast to remedy the horrible conditions in the galleys, and to do something to alleviate the lot of the convict in his re-entrance into society. We know that Vidocq lost his savings in an attempt to do the last; we know that in his work he was eager for new methods, and we can well believe that he, intelligent man as he certainly was, reacted to the evil conditions of the prisons of the day and devised ways and means for improvement. Now, while it does not necessarily follow that the writer and the man with the same aims and enthusiasms were identical, there is at least sufficient analogy so that any statement of a lack of genuineness in the *Memoirs* should receive qualification.

But the importance of the book known as *The Memoirs of Vidocq* depends in no degree on who was the actual author. Ever since this material appeared in print, it has been a source of inspiration for some of the greatest works in literature. *Les Misérables* must be regarded as a direct descendant of Vidocq. The problem posed by Jean Valjean is clearly defined and emphasized again and again by Vidocq. In fact, whole chapters, scenes, pages of Hugo's masterpiece are stamped Vidocq. The *Vautrin* of Balzac, as the author freely acknowledged, is Vidocq. Dickens went to Vidocq for *Great Expectations.* Gaboriau's *Lecoq* was Vidocq himself; Vidocq's facial mobility and mimetic faculty, to which he alludes in the first lines of his *Memoirs* were elaborated in *Lecoq.* This feature of *Lecoq* has been criticized as an artificial conception of Gaboriau's, but that Vidocq possessed an extraordinary faculty of this kind is an undisputed fact. Edgar Allan Poe and Conan Doyle were both fascinated by Vidocq, and the result in literature is a permanent contribution. Works of lesser note written in Vidocq's manner are innumerable. The genealogy of the detective or crime mystery story is here.

In offering this edition of *The Memoirs of Vidocq* in modern idiom to readers to whom Vidocq, in spite of his fame, is a mere name, a tradition, the effort has been to give not only all the incidents - the best criminal stories in the world - but also to include sufficient other material from the work to show the man's psychological insight, his own characteristics, his burning flame for the alleviation of the lot of the criminal. Much material of no value to the reader in the present day, much interpolation, was discarded at once, but, further, the somewhat verbose accounts of events have been edited and abridged to fit the modern tempo. The result, it is hoped, is a readable picaresque narrative with the double interest – that of the story itself and that it is to this masterpiece of roguery that the great minds of literature have turned for inspiration.

E. G. R.
BURFORD
November 16, 1934

Ordering Information

AK Press
674-A 23rd Street,
Oakland, CA 94612-1163,
USA

Phone: (510) 208-1700
E-mail: akpress@akpress.org
URL: www.akpress.org

Please send all payments (checks, money orders, or cash at your own risk) in US dollars. Alternatively, we take VISA and MC.

AK Press
PO Box 12766,
Edinburgh, EH8 9YE,
Scotland

Phone: (0131) 555-5165
E-mail: ak@akedin.demon.uk
URL: www.akuk.com

Please send all payments (cheques, money orders, or cash at your own risk) in UK pounds. Alternatively, we take credit cards.

For a dollar, a pound or a few IRCs, the same addresses would be delighted to provide you with the latest complete AK catalog, featuring several thousand books, pamphlets, zines, audio products and stylish apparel published & distributed by AK Press. Alternatively, check out our websites for the complete catalog, latest news and updates, events, and secure ordering.

Title: *You Can't Win*
Author: Jack Black
ISBN: 1 902593 02 2
Price: $16.00

You hold in your hands a true lost classic, one of the most legendary cult books ever published in America. Jack Black's autobiography was a bestseller and went through five printings in the
late 1920's. It has led a mostly subterranean existence since then
– best known as William Burrough's favorite book, one he
admitted lifting big chunks of from memory for his first novel,
Junky.

But it's time we got wise to this book, which is itself a
remarkably wise book – and a ripping true saga. It's an amazing journey into a hobo underworld: freight hopping around the
still wide open West at the turn of the 2oth century, becoming a member of the "yegg" (criminal) brotherhood and a highwayman, learning the outlaw philosophy from Foot-and-a-half
George and the Sanctimonious Kid, getting hooked on opium, passing through hobo jungles,
hop joints and penitentiaries. This is a chunk of the American story entirely left out of the
history books – it's a lot richer and stranger than the official version. This new edition also
includes an Afterword that tells some of what became of Black after he wore out the outlaw
life and washed up in San Francisco, wrote this book and reinvented himself.

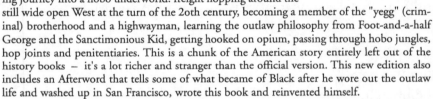

Title: *Sister of the Road*
Author: Dr. Ben Rietman
ISBN: 1 902593 03 3
Price: $15.00

Swapping tales around the campfire in hobo jungles, hanging
out on free love commune farms and in artistic circles in
Greenwich Village, working oin a whorehouse, circulating
among tramps, yeggs, pimps, bohemians, wobblies and other
radicals ... despite the plentiful woes, this is a portrait of an
entrancing world. It's a window onto a wildy under-appreciated
dropout culture that gets left out of history books.

Sister of the Road meant to assault the puritanism and hypocrisy of conventional society
and in this it succeeded. The free-thnking and free-loving ways of Bertha Thompson, the
rowdy and funky world conjured in this book, were all too much for the guardians of pro-
priety when it was first published in 1937.

Reviews like this by sociologist Herbert Blumer were typical: "Students of social pathol-
ogy and those interested in the more undignified undercurrents of modern life should find
this volume to be informative and provocative". But today Boxcar Bertha's nonjudgemental
curiosity and restless hunger for adventure are damned inspiring.

Title: *BAD: The Autobiography of James Carr*
Author: James Carr
ISBN: 1 902593 64 2
Price: $16.00

James Carr started fighting when he was young and never gave up. He was a child prodigy of crime in the streets of L.A. and scourge of half a dozen boys' homes and reform schools. In his teens he rapidly advanced to bookmaking and armed robbery, a career that was quickly cut short by arrest. In prison he fought harder than ever, and became one of the most notorious rebels in the seething California Penal Sysem..

Becoming best friends with George Jackson in Folsom, they led the notorious Wolf Pack, which first fought its way to a position of strength in the prison race war, then, caught up in the radical currents of the 60's, worked to stop the war entirely in order to work solely against the system.

Carr was an extreme example of nietzsche's dictum about what doesn't kill you makes you stronger. He describes in unflinching detail the horrors of prison life – the race riots, murder, rape, and corruption – from the standpoint of one who has overcome them. Carr transformed himself from an openly rebellious con whose actions were self-defeating into a shrewd, thoughtful and impressive person who ultimately engineered his own release.

Title: *Beggars of Life: A Hobo Autobiography*
Author: Jim Tully
ISBN: 1 902593 78 2
Price: $16.00

A bestseller in 1924, this vivid piece of outlaw history has inexplicably faded from the public consciousness. Jim Tully takes us across the seamy underbelly of pre-WWI America on freight trains, and inside hobo jungles and brothels while narrowly averting railroad bulls (cops) and wardens of order. Written with unflinching honesty and insight, *Beggars of Life* follows Tully from his first ride at age 13, choosing life on the road over a deadening job, through his teenage years of learning the ropes of the rails and living one meal to the next.

Jim Tully (1891-1947) was a best-selling novelist and popular Hollywood journalist in the 1920s and 30s. Known as "Cincinnati Red" during his years as a road-kid, he counted prizefighter and publicist of Charlie Chaplin among his many jobs.